Textiles

Textiles

Andrea Wynne

Advisors: **J.N.F.K. Afenyo**   **P. Nkulenu**   **B.C. Adahjie**

MACMILLAN

First published 1997 by
MACMILLAN EDUCATION LTD
London and Basingstoke
Companies and representatives throughout the world

ISBN 0-333-61658-8

10	9	8	7	6	5	4	3	2	1
06	05	04	03	02	01	00	99	98	97

This book is printed on paper suitable for recycling and
made from fully managed and sustained forest sources.

Printed in Hong Kong

A catalogue record for this book is available from the
British Library.

The author and publishers wish to acknowledge, with thanks, the following
photographic sources:
African Textiles fig 1.1
Courtesy of Allied Signal Inc. of Petersburg V.A. figs 6.1; 6.2
Allertex fig 6.11
University of Arizona, Electron Microscopy Facility, Division of Biotechnology figs 6.4; 6.7
Ardea fig 1.3 (photography Wardene Weisser)
Bolton Institute figs 3.4; 3.5
ICI fig 5.3
International Institute for Cotton figs 5.8; 5.9; 5.10; 5.11; 5.12; 5.16
The Textile Institute, Manchester figs 2.1; 2.2; 2.3; 2.4; 2.5; 2.6; 2.7; 2.8; 2.9; 5.14; 5.15;
5.18; 5.19; 5.20; 5.21; 5.22
American Savio Corporation fig 6.5
Murata of America Inc. of Charlotte NC fig 6.7
By courtesy of Savio Macchine Tessili s.p.a. Italy fig 12.9
Alan Thomas figs 1.4; 1.5
TRIP fig 1.2 (photograph H. Rogers)
WIRA fig 3.6

The cover photograph is courtesy of Savio Macchine Tessili s.p.a. Italy
Illustrations by 1-11 Line Art

The publishers have made every effort to trace the copyright holders, but if they
have inadvertently overlooked any, they will be pleased to make the necessary
arrangement at the first opportunity.

Contents

Acknowledgements

The author would like to thank The School of Textile Studies at Bolton for use of their material. In particular, thanks to Professor Anand, Paul Greenwood and Akbar Zarei for their encouragement and help.

Thank you to Elizabeth Hartley for all her patience.

Introduction

This textbook has been designed to give a basic grounding – a taste of the textile industry – for both students and workers alike. Of the wide subject area that is Textiles, this book covers from fibre through to finished fabric.

Designed especially for Secondary and Technical schools, Colleges and Training Institutions, this book covers a wide range of the necessary syllabus and course material for a number of countries.

Each topic is introduced, then explained with the help of photographs and colour diagrams. A summary with revision questions appears at the end of each chapter, with answers and general hints on answering questions at the end of the book. A glossary finally covers the key points of the book.

It is wise for any person connected to the textile industry in any way to remember safety at all times – most of the machinery used in textile processing is potentially hazardous. Students and textile workers must have a healthy respect for such machinery.

I wish you enjoyment and success in your Textile career.

What is a fibre?

Introduction

The role of textile fibres for clothing, bedding and furnishing is so central to our lives that the history of fibres is almost as old as the history of our civilisation. The design of fabrics and clothes has long been regarded as an art form. Some fibres such as wool, silk, cotton and linen have been known and used for thousands of years.

Man-made fibres on the other hand have a history only as long as the 20th century and most of the fibres that we are familiar with today have only been produced in the last 40 years, but man-made fibres have made a great difference to present-day society, in the types of clothes that we wear as well as the comfort and convenience of living.

While reading this book, you are probably enclosed in several layers of fibres, and probably have your feet on yet another layer. Each of these products whether a garment, upholstery or a carpet is so common that they are taken for granted, but each is the product of a long chain of operations.

Many products that use fibres are less obvious. Travelling by car, contact with the road is through tyres in which the rubber is reinforced by textile fibres. The road itself may have been laid on a **geotextile** foundation in which fibres are used to give the road a firmer base. Travelling by aircraft, train, bus or ship, parts of the vehicle will also certainly be made from fibre reinforced plastics.

General fibre characteristics

Fibre – A unit of matter characterised by flexibility, fineness and a high length to width ratio.
Fibre, **staple** – A fibre of definite length (usually 10–500 millimetres).
Filament – A fibre of indefinite length.

The above definition for textile fibres is very broad, but what are the general characteristics of fibres? There is no such thing as a perfect fibre. So many things are demanded of fibres in the many different uses, ranging from cars to carpets, from satellites to socks, or from tyres to tights. A variety of fibres is needed to satisfy all of the many uses and the likes and tastes of individuals. However, some characteristics can be identified which all fibres must have if they are to be commercially successful: a high length to diameter ratio; strength; extensibility and elasticity; resistance to chemicals, heat and sunlight; and ability to take colour.

Length to width ratio

Fibres generally have a small cross-sectional area and a length which greatly exceeds the width. For cotton and wool, the length to diameter ratio is in the region of 2000:1 to 5000:1. These fibres are produced naturally in short lengths, known as staple fibre. The fibre lengths vary from 10 to 50 millimetres for cotton and from 50 to 200 millimetres for wool. Many man-made fibres are also produced as staple, so that they can be processed on the same machinery as the natural fibres.

Man-made fibres can be produced with many kilometres of yarn on a single package. The length to diameter ratio of the fibres is then infinite. This type of yarn is termed continuous filament. Silk is the only natural continuous filament fibre. Some man-made fibres intended for processing into staple are produced as a continuous length but with hundreds of thousands of fibres together. This rope of fibres or filaments is termed a **tow**.

Strength

The strength of a textile material ultimately depends on the strength of the individual fibres from which it is made. Consequently, fibres must have a certain level of strength if they are to be useful. A high strength is clearly more important in fibres used for reinforcement of the rubber in a tyre than for the fibres used in a knitted jumper.

Extension and elasticity

In use, stresses will frequently be applied to textile materials. The materials need to extend under the stress and be flexible. The fibres in a pair of tights need to extend every time the wearer bends her legs. But having extended, the fibres need to be elastic and return to their original length. If they do not, the tights will quickly become wrinkled at the knees and ankles. Tights are just one particular application; all fibres need to be extensible and elastic in use, but to differing degrees.

Reaction to chemicals, heat and sunlight

In normal use and during care procedures, fibres will be exposed to conditions which may damage them. These conditions may include chemicals such as acids, alkalis, bleaches, detergents, or organic solvents including dry cleaning fluids, and physical effects such as heat or sunlight. The extent to which fibres are exposed depends on the particular use.

Resistance to sunlight is more important in curtains than it is in underwear, but almost all fibres are exposed to harmful conditions to some extent. Domestic washing powders are mildly alkali and contain a bleach. The temperature during normal ironing can easily reach 200°C. The effect on the fibres will in most cases be slow and involve some weakening, with perhaps yellowing of white fibres and loss of brightness of coloured products. It can be more drastic; **cellulose acetate** fibres are dissolved by nail varnish remover.

Reaction to dyestuffs

Most fibres are naturally an off-white colour. Life would be very dull if all textile products were off-white. Consequently, fibres need to be coloured and ideally, they should be coloured by dyeing at a late stage of processing; this enables a quick response to customer demands for the latest shade. Polypropylene fibres can only be coloured by injecting pigment as the fibres are made. This is a less flexible process than dyeing and reduces the number of uses for these fibres.

Classification of fibres

Classification involves organising objects into groups for convenience. For fibres, the most convenient grouping divides them initially into natural and man made. These

Figure 1.1   Cotton is easily dyed.

basic categories can then be further subdivided. The natural fibres are divided according to their origin. The cellulosic fibres come from plant materials, the protein fibres from animal sources and there are a few mineral fibres. The man-made fibres include some from naturally occurring polymers, some from regenerated and modified regenerated fibres, some from fully synthetic polymers and some from minerals. These categories are shown in Table 1.1 and will be discussed in more detail below.

Table 1.1   General fibre classification

Natural fibres		
Cellulosic	Protein	Mineral
Cotton (seed hair)	Wool	Asbestos
Flax (bast)	Silk	
Jute (bast)	Mohair	
Sisal (leaf)	Cashmere	
Ramie (bast)	Other animal hairs	

Man-made fibres			
Regenerated	Modified	Synthetic	Mineral
Viscose rayon	Cellulose diacetate	Polyamide	Glass
	Cellulose triacetate	Polyester	Steel
		Polyacrylic	Carbon
		Polyolefin	
		Polyvinyl	
		Elastane	

Natural fibres

CELLULOSIC FIBRES

This category includes by far the most important textile fibre, cotton, which makes up nearly 50 per cent of the total weight of fibres used in the world. Growing cotton is very important economically to many countries which export the fibre in return for foreign currency. In addition, they can use the seed oil for cooking and the remainder of the plant for animal feeds. The cotton fibre is the seed hair of the cotton plant. Other cellulosic fibres are extracted from alternative parts of plants.

The bast fibres, flax, jute and ramie, are extracted from the stems of particular plants by a controlled rotting process known as retting. Jute is used mainly for packaging materials and flax, which becomes known as linen, is used for speciality fashion fabrics. Sisal comes from the leaves of the plant.

Figure 1.2 Harvesting cotton.

MINERAL FIBRES

Asbestos is the only naturally-occurring mineral fibre. It has been used in heat-resistant materials, thermal insulation, brake blocks and reinforcement in sheet materials for buildings. The use of asbestos is now rapidly declining following the discovery of health risks from asbestos dust.

PROTEIN FIBRES

These fibres make up a small proportion of the market by weight but a much higher proportion by value. The major fibre in this category is wool with its crimp and excellent elasticity giving woollen fabrics valued properties. Silk is only available on a small scale but is prized as the only natural continuous filament fibre. Other animal hair fibres such as

Figure 1.3 A silk worm.

mohair, cashmere and vicuna are only produced on a small scale but are sold at very high prices.

Man-made fibres

REGENERATED FIBRES

Regenerated fibres are manufactured from a natural polymer, cellulose, which is obtained from wood. Cellulose is also the starting product for the manufacture of paper. The cellulose is reacted chemically so that it will dissolve in sodium hydroxide solution, then reformed by extruding the viscous solution called viscose into dilute sulphuric acid solution. The viscose fibres are chemically similar to cotton and share the desirable property of moisture absorbency.

By adapting the basic production process, a range of viscose fibres with different characteristics, including high tenacity, high wet modulus, crimped and inflated fibres, can be produced for different uses. At one time, viscose continuous filament for tyre cord and for textile applications was produced but this has declined and now staple fibre and tow are mainly produced.

The viscose process is long and complicated and the by-products give rise to environmental problems. There is much interest at present in producing man-made cellulosic fibres by an alternative process using a solvent for the cellulose.

MODIFIED REGENERATED FIBRES

These fibres include cellulose diacetate and triacetate. The raw material is again cellulose, but in these fibres it is modified chemically so that the polymer can be dissolved in an organic solvent. The polymer solution can then be extruded into hot air which evaporates the solvent leaving the fibres. The polymer remains in the chemically modified form and is not converted back into cellulose.

Cellulose fibres are produced almost entirely as continuous filament yarns and are used in soft silk-like dress fabrics. Most cigarette filter tips are made from cellulose diacetate fibres.

SYNTHETIC FIBRES

This group includes three major classes and several minor ones. The term synthetic means that the polymer is entirely man made.

The first synthetic fibre was a polyamide (nylon). The first polyamides were produced in the United States in 1938 and were used initially for stockings. The application rapidly expanded into parachute fabrics and later to many other textile products including shirts, bedsheets, underwear, carpets and reinforcement of rubber in tyres and belts. In the last 15 years, polyamides have been displaced in some uses such as shirts, bedding and underwear by polyester/cotton blends. The properties of polyamides, particularly the excellent elasticity, make them very suitable for carpet piles, rubber reinforcement and tights and stockings.

Polyester was first produced commercially in 1953 and, having expanded rapidly, is now the largest man-made fibre in terms of volume of production. Polyester staple fibre is very commonly used blended with cotton or other cellulosics in shirts, blouses, dresses, trousers and sheeting. Blends of polyester with wool are used in suitings and trousers. Polyester continuous yarn is often used for seat belts, sewing threads and yacht sails, as well as apparel items such as blouses. An interesting development is polyester microfibres, extremely fine filaments, which give fabrics a soft silky handle.

Acrylic fibres were first produced in 1948. The fibres have a soft, warm handle and are well suited to the production of high-bulk yarns. These find many applications in knitwear, carpets and pile fabrics. A variant of acrylics called modacrylic has greatly reduced flammability and is used for children's nightwear as well as upholstery fabrics for aircraft, trains and public rooms.

The polyolefin fibres, polythene and polypropylene, are of increasing importance and their production now totals about eight per cent of all synthetic fibres. Polypropylene in particular is used for carpets, upholstery fabrics, geotextiles (fabrics for ground and soil reinforcement) and is now becoming more widely used for clothing. The textile uses of polythene are limited due to the low melting point (120°C).

The other synthetic fibres are produced on a much smaller scale. The polyvinyl fibres are mainly polyvinyl chloride or polyvinyl alcohol. The polyvinyl chloride fibres are used in thermal wear but do not have a wide range of applications. Polyvinyl alcohol fibres are rare on the European market but are manufactured by a number of Japanese producers.

Elastane fibres can be extended from three to five times their original length before they break. Small proportions are used where fabrics with stretch properties are needed. Elastane fibres are found in swimwear, stretch trousers and lingerie.

The aramids are the newest class of fibres. Chemically, they are modified polyamides. One type of aramid fibre has exceptionally high tenacity, up to three times that of other fibres. The other type has excellent resistance to heat and flame although normal tensile properties. The best known brand names are Kevlar for the first type and Nomex for the second; both are products of the DuPont Company of the USA.

MINERAL FIBRES

These fibres are glass, steel and carbon, all of which are found in industrial end-uses. Glass is used for low-cost reinforced plastics for ships, car and vehicle parts and many other applications such as thermal and electrical insulation products. Steel fibres are used for reinforcing rubber in tyres and belts and for filters where chemical resistance is important.

Carbon fibres are manufactured from acrylic fibres and are also used for reinforcement of plastics. Carbon fibres are very expensive and consequently go into high-cost, high-performance reinforced plastics such as aircraft parts and some leisure goods like squash and tennis rackets, where the user is prepared to pay for the superior performance.

Figure 1.4 Polyamides are used in rubber tyres.

Fibre usage

The selection of a fibre for a particular end-product involves choice from each natural and man-made generic type. Within each fibre generic type there will also be a range of different fibres available. For the natural fibres, these can include varieties with different staple length and **linear density**. Man-made fibres are also available in different staple lengths and linear densities; they are produced as both continuous filament and staple usually. Most fibre types are also available in a whole spectrum of other modifications to give specific properties, for instance differing **lustre**, varying **tensile** properties, anti-static, anti-soiling, dye variation etc.

The type of fibre chosen for a particular end-product will be determined by the best balance of the following major quantifiable properties: tensile properties including tenacity, extension at break, modulus and elasticity; moisture absorbency; optical character including light reflectance and fibre shape; chemical resistance to damaging environments likely to be found in the application; and electrical and thermal character, including ability of the fibre to dissipate a static charge or to give a fabric the required warmth or coolness.

Not all of the above characteristics depend solely on the fibre. The appearance of a product will be influenced by whether it is made from staple fibre or continuous filament yarns. If continuous filament yarns are used then the appearance will depend on whether they are textured. Similarly, the warmth of a fabric will depend on the construction of the yarns and the fabric as well as the characteristics of the fibre.

The consumer will also have a set of requirements from textile products and may well use different terms. Typical terms used by the consumer are hard-wearing, easy care, comfort, appearance, value for money and safety of the product. These attributes can not be objectively measured, but each depends on a number of textile properties which can be measured. See Table 1.2.

Easy care means that a textile product can be washed by machine and that, after drying, the article will be wearable without pressing.

Certain fibre generic types may be recognised as having well-defined advantages. Cotton is known for its comfort (moisture and thermal character) and pleasing appearance (low lustre and surface irregularity); wool is considered comfortable (warmth due to the natural crimp); regenerated cellulose – viscose – has advantages of low cost and comfort (high moisture absorbency); synthetic fibres such as polyester, polyamide, acrylics and polypropylene have a relatively low cost, durability (strength and toughness) and easy-care properties (low moisture absorbency and thermoplasticity).

The ultimate marketability of a textile product depends on a balance of the above subjective properties and on the cost.

Table 1.2 Testing for textile properties

Customer term	Textile property	Test for property
Comfort	moisture character	(absorbency/transport)
	flexibility	(softness/resilience)
	elasticity	
	thermal character	(warmth/coolness)
Appearance	optical character	appearance, lustre,
	elasticity	crease resistance,
		shape retention
Durability	tensile strength	
	toughness	abrasion resistance
	flexibility	
	elasticity	
Easy care	moisture character	low absorbency
	elasticity	
	dimensional	**thermoplasticity**
	stability	
Safety	flammability	
	chemical resistance	

Figure 1.5 Cotton is known for its comfort.

Fibre blends

For some products the ideal set of properties will not be obtainable from just one generic type of fibre. Instead, a blend of two more fibres will be used.

There are a number of reasons for blending fibres: to produce a better balance of technical properties for a particular textile product; to produce a cheaper product by blending a low-cost fibre with a more expensive one; and to produce special colour effects by blending fibres with different dyeing characteristics. However, there are costs as well as benefits in blending fibres. It adds an extra process to the many involved in manufacturing. Blending is also a process that has to be carefully controlled to avoid variability in the product. The wet processing sequence has to be selected to avoid chemical conditions that will damage either fibre. Dyeing may well have to be carried out in two stages, one to colour each fibre.

The most common blend is polyester/cotton, usually in the proportions 50/50 or 67/33 although other proportions are now used in some products. Blends with more than 50 per cent cotton are often termed 'cotton rich'. These blends combine the softness and moisture absorption of cotton with the dimensional stability, hard-wearing and easy-care qualities of polyester. The convoluted shape of the cotton fibres gives products greater bulk and cover compared with 100 per cent polyester. Fabrics are still rather lean compared with 100 per cent cotton, however. The effects of blending are not entirely beneficial though. Cotton burns readily while polyester tends to melt back from a flame and consequently does not burn. In polyester/cotton blends, the cotton prevents the polyester from shrinking away from a flame and the mixture burns very fiercely.

Fibres for products

Consider the requirements of the following end-products.

BED SHEETS

The consumer expects a soft and warm handle with easy-care properties. Sheets are expected to be hard wearing and dimensionally stable. The majority of bed sheets are manufactured from polyester/cotton blends.

SHIRTING

Shirts are expected to absorb perspiration as well as being non-creasing and retaining their shape in wear. Easy-care properties are essential and shirts must be hard wearing to give a long service life. Like bed sheets, most shirts are made from polyester/cotton blends.

KNITTED JUMPERS

Jumpers are worn for warmth and need to be elastic so that they do not lose their shape in wear. Easy-care properties are useful. Wool is often used, but its high cost is a disadvantage. It also requires hand washing, although finishes that enable woollen garments to be machine washed are now available. Acrylic fibres are cheaper and have better easy-care characteristics. Increasingly, cotton is used for jumpers and polyester/cotton for sweatshirts.

SWIMWEAR

Swimwear needs to fit the body closely but also allow freedom of movement. The fibres must be resistant to salt water, as well as to chlorinated water in swimming baths. Almost exclusively, polyamides are used as the main fibre, with about ten per cent of **elastane** to give stretch properties. This combination dries quickly since neither is water absorbent. The resistance of either fibre to chlorinated water is limited, however.

TOWELS

The most important characteristic of fibre for towels is the ability to absorb water. It is useful that the towel will retain its shape in use and be soft to the touch. Cotton is the major fibre used although viscose could also be used.

TIGHTS

Tights must fit the legs closely, yet be sufficiently elastic to allow movement. The fibres must be strong and extensible to give resistance to snagging, and highly elastic to prevent wrinkling. Polyamide is used for the main part of the tights while a small quantity of elastane is used for the waistband.

TROUSERS

The fibres used for trousers can vary greatly according to consumer requirements. In all, easy care and dimensional stability for shape retention are important. For warmth, polyester/wool is effective, with the natural crimp of the wool making the fabric bulky so that it will hold a layer of warm air. This blend is less easy care, however. With less warmth in wear, 100 per cent polyester can be used with excellent easy-care properties. Summer trousers are often made from polyester/cotton and denim jeans are 100 per cent cotton. Jeans do not have easy-care properties but are hard-wearing; creasing in use is often a positive advantage to the consumer.

Commercial importance of fibres

Fibre production

The figures in Table 1.3 show the world fibre demand for the principal textile fibres in the years 1980 to 1993.

Table 1.3　World fibre demand 1980–93 (millions of tonnes)

	1980	1981	1982	1983	1984	1985	1986	1987	1988	1989	1990	1991	1992	1993
mmf														
cellulosics	3.24	3.20	2.95	2.93	3.00	2.93	2.86	2.83	2.90	2.94	2.76	2.41	2.29	2.25
synthetics	10.48	10.83	10.15	11.08	11.80	12.44	12.93	13.74	14.42	14.75	14.91	15.96	16.18	16.18
natural														
cotton	13.99	15.30	14.74	15.06	15.27	16.57	18.28	18.24	18.48	18.73	18.71	18.65	18.76	18.97
wool	1.61	1.62	1.62	1.64	1.66	1.72	1.74	1.77	1.81	1.87	1.96	1.93	1.72	1.66
total mmf	13.72	14.03	13.10	14.01	14.80	15.37	15.79	16.57	17.32	17.69	17.67	17.69	18.25	18.43
total natural	15.66	16.98	16.42	16.76	16.99	18.35	20.08	20.07	20.35	20.67	20.74	20.65	20.55	20.70

Table 1.4　World production of cotton (000s tonnes)

	1979/80	1984/85	1990/91	1991/92	1992/93	1993/94	1994/95
Europe	620	786	944	851	879	804	936
Africa	1165	1259	1213	1170	1285	1204	1120
Asia/Oceana	2610	3437	4474	5170	4742	4939	5229
Americas	4816	4830	5153	5415	4413	5179	4824
Socialist*	2717	2569	—	2473	2074	2133	2280
China	2212	6249	4508	5675	4508	4150	4756

*excluding China

The main feature demonstrated by these figures is the dominant position of cotton. Although cotton's share of the total textile market has fallen from approximately 80 per cent in 1959 to 42 per cent in 1989, the actual production has increased and continues to increase due to improved yields of cotton from each hectare of land. Table 1.4 gives figures for cotton production.

The figures for man-made fibres in Table 1.3 show that, while the production of cellulosic man-made fibres is almost constant, the production of synthetic fibres is increasing rapidly. This is most marked for polyester.

The future

What of the future? In 1993 the people of the world used on average 7.5 kilograms of fibres each. This figure was much higher for some countries, for instance in the USA the average fibre consumption per person was 29 kilograms. In developing countries the average consumption was 4.5 kilograms.

In the year 2004, it is estimated that the total world fibre usage will be over 50 million tonnes. This will be an increase of roughly 14 million tonnes on the 1992 figure. It is estimated that 90% of this projected increase will be processed in developing countries, and this raises several questions. Will the land used for producing natural fibres increase, putting pressure on the land available for producing food? Will the production of man-made fibres increase? Will the yield of cotton fibre per hectare increase? We will all have to wait for the turn of the century to find answers to these questions.

CHECK YOUR UNDERSTANDING

● Textile fibres are used in every aspect of modern society in products as diverse as garments and geotextiles.

● Fibres can be defined as being flexible and having a high length to width ratio. They can be in staple or definite length form, or be continuous filaments of indefinite length.

● To be of use, fibres must have certain levels of strength, extensibility and elasticity, be resistant to chemicals and sunlight, and be capable of coloration.

● Fibres are classified firstly as being of either man made or natural origin. These categories can be further split into cellulosic, protein or mineral for natural fibres, and regenerated, modified regenerated, synthetic and mineral for man-made fibres.

● The fibre type chosen for a particular end-product depends on the best balance for that end-product of: tensile properties (strength); moisture absorbency; optical character; chemical resistance; electrical and thermal character.

● Terms used by consumers such as hard wearing, easy care, comfort, appearance and safety of the product cannot be determined by objective measurement – each depends on a number of textile properties.

● Different fibre types are blended mainly to produce a better balance of textile properties for a particular end-product. Other reasons include reducing costs and creating special effects.

● The most common blend is polyester/cotton. Polyester has dimensional stability, is hard wearing and easy care: cotton has a soft handle and good moisture absorbency.

● Cotton fibre still has the largest share of the world fibre market. Its market share has fallen since the 1950s, but its production has risen.

● Synthetic fibres have increased their share of the fibre market, mainly due to polyester fibre production.

● If the demand for fibres continues to increase at a similar rate, there could be competition for land between food producers and fibre producers in the natural sector by the year 2000. The solution could be for man-made fibres to step in and fill the gap by increasing their production.

REVISION EXERCISES AND QUESTIONS

1 What is the difference between continuous filaments and staple fibres?
2 What natural fibres occur in continuous filament form?
3 Why is it desirable to be able to dye fibres at a late stage in the end-product processing route?
4 What are the major subdivisions of natural fibres?
5 What are the major subdivisions of man-made fibres?
6 What other factors, apart from fibre type, influence the properties of the end-product?
7 What fibre characteristics influence comfort?
8 Name a disadvantage of blending polyester with cotton.
9 Which natural fibre has the largest world production?
10 Which man-made fibre has the largest world production?

Fibre Properties 2

Introduction

When choosing clothing (or other textile products such as carpets and curtains), we match the product to our requirements. If we live in a hot climate, for instance, we want cool, absorbent, loose clothing for maximum comfort.

The necessary performance of each end-product must be carefully considered before choosing suitable materials for manufacture. There is no 'wonder fibre' because different products require vastly different (and sometimes conflicting) properties in the raw material. A swimsuit needs to hold little water and drain quickly; a towel must absorb and hold as much water as possible.

It is clear that we need to know the individual fibre properties in detail before we can hope to choose the best fibre for the end-product. This chapter will cover the appearance, dimensions, behaviour under stress and moisture properties of textile fibres.

Fibre morphology

Morphology is 'the science of form', and so fibre morphology relates to the shape and appearance of fibres. The ideas are applied to both man made and natural, staple fibres and continuous filaments. This chapter will deal with the gross morphology – the things we can see with the naked eye, or low magnification (less than 500 times), rather than at a molecular level.

Appearance

VISUAL INSPECTION

Fibres and filaments are essentially cylinders but there are certain features obvious from visual observation that can,

with experience, be used to identify them or at least classify them by the broad categories introduced in Chapter 1.

COLOUR

Many fibres appear to be white to the naked eye although, as we will see later, they are in fact transparent. These will almost certainly be man-made fibres. Some man-made fibres may be supplied with a fugitive tint (a temporary identification stain) of green, blue or pink water soluble dye, in order to prevent accidental mixing of fibre types, which would otherwise look to be similar 'white' fibres, for example triacetate and diacetate.

Natural fibres generally have some colour, at least in their unprocessed form. Wool and mohair tend to be creamy coloured. Some sheep and goats have darker coloured fleeces of black, brown or grey which are normally processed separately. Unprocessed cotton looks from off-white, through creamy to yellow tinged. Flax and other vegetable fibres, in their unprocessed form, are generally brown in colour.

OBVIOUS DIMENSIONS

Different types of natural fibres have characteristic ranges of length, for example:

		Length (mm)
Cotton	Egyptian	35–45
	USA	25–35
Wool	Coarse	> 150
	Medium	100–150
	Fine Merino	50–80

Cotton and other fibres processed in a similar way are described as short staple. Wool and other fibres processed in a similar way are described as long staple.

If man-made fibres are cut into staple fibres rather than used as continuous filament, their lengths will be similar to one of the natural fibres above, for example:

Man made		Length (mm)
	Long staple for carpets	100
	Long staple for outer apparel and upholstery	50–80
	Short staple for light apparel	32–45

The cross-section dimension is referred to as fineness or coarseness. With cotton, longer fibres are normally finer fibres but, with wool, longer fibres are coarser. In Table 2.1, the fineness is expressed in decitex. This is the number of grams for 10 000 metres of the material; the finer the fibre, the lower the decitex value.

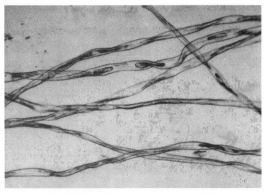

(a)

Table 2.1 Fibre length/fineness relationship

	Length (mm)	Fineness (decitex)
Cotton		
USA	25–35	1.5–2
Egyptian	35–45	1–1.5
Wool		
Fine Merino	50–80	3–4
Medium	100–150	4–6
Coarse	> 150	> 10
Man made		
Short staple	32–45	1–2
Long staple	50–80	3–6
Carpet	100	10–20

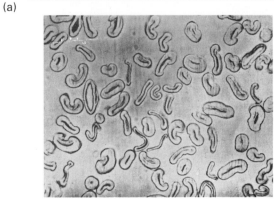

(b)

Figure 2.1 Raw cotton.

INSPECTION UNDER LOW MAGNIFICATION

Using an eyeglass or low-power microscope, it is possible to recognise fibres in terms of their cross-sectional and longitudinal appearance.

In Figure 2.1, cotton is recognised by a kidney bean-shaped cross section and convolutions along the length. The fibre is essentially a collapsed tube.

Mercerised cotton, which has been treated with a concentrated sodium hydroxide solution, has a more circular cross section due to a swelling of the fibre during treatment.

Wool, shown in Figure 2.3, has an oval cross section and scales on the longitudinal surface.

Silk is extruded by different varieties of silk worm with different cross section, but the fibres are essentially triangular with a smooth longitudinal appearance.

Flax being extracted vegetable matter has an angular cross section with an irregular longitudinal surface.

Man-made fibres produced by different manufacturing methods can have different cross-sectional shapes but many are circular.

(a)

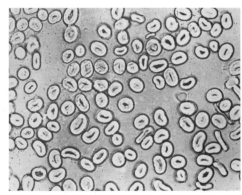

(b)

Figure 2.2 Mercerised cotton.

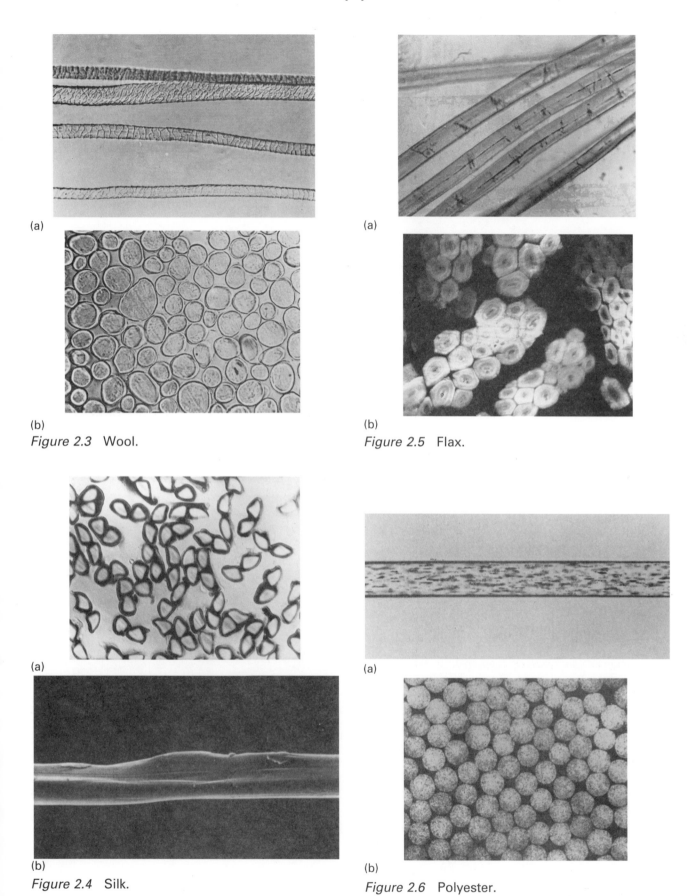

(a)

(b)

Figure 2.3 Wool.

(a)

(b)

Figure 2.5 Flax.

(a)

(b)

Figure 2.4 Silk.

(a)

(b)

Figure 2.6 Polyester.

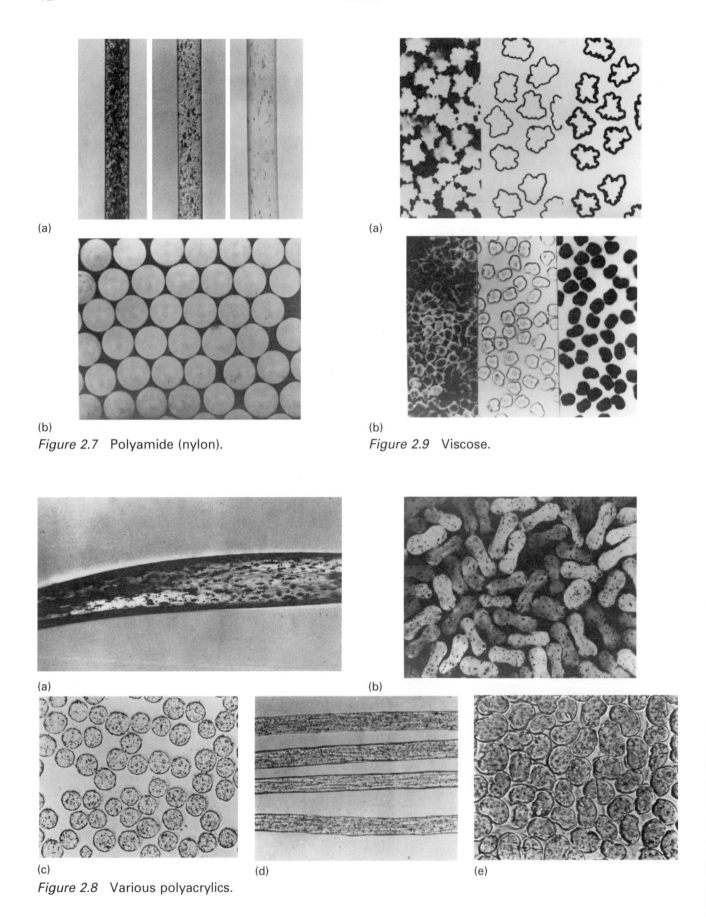

(a)

(b)

Figure 2.7 Polyamide (nylon).

(a)

(b)

Figure 2.9 Viscose.

(a)

(b)

(c)

(d)

(e)

Figure 2.8 Various polyacrylics.

Optical properties of fibres

The optical properties of fibres relate to how the fibres refract or bend light and how they reflect light internally or externally. Refraction depends on the basic characteristics of the **polymer** matter from which the fibre is built. Reflection depends essentially on the shape of the fibre cross section and the nature of the longitudinal surface.

FIBRE LUSTRE

Looking at an object, it is the reflected light from it that can be seen. On a mirror surface, we get a specular reflection in which the reflected rays of light are parallel to each other.

Other surfaces may give a diffuse reflection where the incident light rays are reflected in different directions.

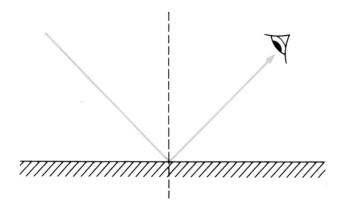

Figure 2.10   Specular reflection.

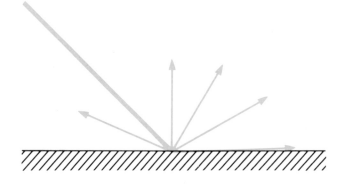

Figure 2.11   Diffuse reflection.

Fibres appear lustrous when there are specular reflections from the outer surface and/or the internal surface.

Thus, fibres with circular cross section generally appear more lustrous than those with irregular cross sections. Fibres with smooth longitudinal surfaces appear more lustrous. Fibres with optical cross section, such as silk or trilobal

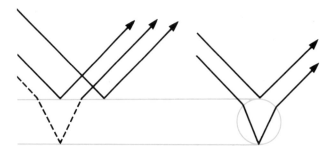

Figure 2.12   Lustrous fibres.

nylon, also appear more lustrous, for example mercerised cotton appears more lustrous than the raw cotton as a result of the more circular cross section.

RELATIONSHIP BETWEEN FIBRE FINENESS AND LUSTRE

If all other parameters are the same, then finer fibres produce a more lustrous effect because they have a greater surface area, for reflection, for the same mass of fibre. This can be significant in dyeing because the surface reflection is 'white' light and tends to dilute the colour from the dye.

Not all the fibres in yarns will be visible on the surface. Perhaps 25 per cent of the fibres will be visible but the argument will still hold true. If finer fibres are used for a particular yarn there will be more fibres in the cross section and so more fibres on the surface to give points of reflection. Hence, the same amount of dye may give a different shade if finer rather than coarser fibres are used. Another consequence of the greater surface area with finer fibres is that the rate of the dyeing process itself will be increased.

DELUSTRANTS

A lustrous fibre may not always be required, particularly if it is to be dyed. Little can be done to change the character of natural fibres but man-made fibres can be delustred (or produced with less lustre).

The principle involves the introduction, during the **extrusion** process, of small inert particles which reduce the amount of specular reflection and increase the amount of diffuse reflection. These particles are usually titanium dioxide, with a particle size of about 0.8 μm added at the rate of one or two per cent. The particles become distributed through the interior and on the surface of the fibres. Other consequences of the delustrant are that fibres tend to be more abrasive and suffer about a five per cent reduction in strength.

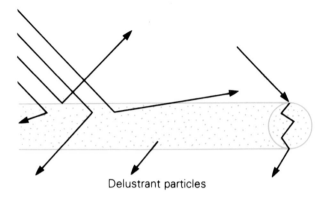

Figure 2.13 Effect of delustrant.

Lustrous man-made fibres are termed bright fibres; delustred man-made fibres are termed matt fibres if they contain relatively large amounts of delustrant, or semi-dull if they contain less.

FIBRE REFRACTIVE INDEX

Although fibres have been described as transparent, their optical and other properties are not uniform in all directions. In comparison, glass is homogeneous and has uniform characteristics in all directions.

Refractive index is a measure of how light is bent as it passes through the surface of a material. Because the internal structure of a material, such as a fibre, is three dimensional, it is normal to consider the refractive index parallel and perpendicular to the fibre axis.

Glass has the same values of the refractive index in both directions. Some fibres have different values. This difference is a measure of birefringence. The higher the birefringence, the greater the difference between bending of light along the fibre main axis compared with bending of light across fibre width.

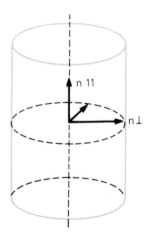

Figure 2.14 Refractive indices in fibres.

Table 2.2 Typical values for birefringence

	$n_{||}$	$n_{\perp}$	$n_{||} - n_{\perp}$
Cotton	1.578	1.532	0.046
Wool	1.553	1.542	0.010
Silk	1.591	1.538	0.053
Flax	1.596	1.528	0.068
Nylon	1.582	1.519	0.063
Polyester	1.725	1.527	0.188
Acrylic	1.520	1.524	−0.004
Triacetate	1.474	1.479	−0.005
Viscose	1.539	1.519	0.020

Key where: $n_{||}$ is the refractive index parallel to the main fibre axis; $n_{\perp}$ is the refractive index perpendicular to the main fibre axis; $n_{||} - n_{\perp}$ is the birefringence.

Fibres such as polyester, which have a large value for birefringence, behave almost as a prism and split white light into the colours of the spectrum. The practical significance of this becomes more obvious if a bright fibre is dyed to a dark colour (blue or green). At certain viewing angles, a different coloured sheen can be seen on the surface of the fabric: a green sheen on blue or a blue sheen on green. The effect is often inaccurately described as a dyeing fault but it is not detected by colour measurement. The two-colour effect is normally referred to as dichroism. The simplest way to minimise the effect is to use matt fibre rather than bright fibre so that the reflections and refractions are diffuse rather than specular.

Fibre dimensions

The dimensions are among the most important characteristics of fibres. The length, which is only meaningful for staple fibres, is normally expressed in millimetres. The fineness is expressed as a diameter in micrometres or as a linear density in decitex.

The fineness of fibres affects the means of processing, in that fine fibres are extremely delicate, but they do enable the finest yarns and so the sheerest fabrics to be produced. Coloration and efficiency of the finishing process are also affected; the larger surface area of finer fibres will affect the rate of dyeing and the colour or shade of the product using the same amount of dye. Fibre fineness is a major factor in product comfort, handle and drape; finer fibres require less force to twist and/or bend them. Finer fibres individually require less force to break them and so fabrics containing them have lower resistance to abrasion, giving a lower product-wear life. For reasons of wear and pile rigidity, carpet fibres are extremely coarse.

The fibre length determines the means of processing – short staple or long staple. Yarn properties are also affected and, in general, longer (and finer) fibres produce finer and stronger yarns. Hence, fibre length is a convenient (though subjective) indicator of fibre fineness and so quality and/or price. Properties of the textile product, such as yarn hairiness, strength, **fabric handle** (feel), drape and **pilling** tendency are all influenced by fibre length. (Pills are fibres which have tangled to form a ball shape which stands proud of the fabric surface.)

Fibre fineness

The transverse dimensions of fibres can be expressed in several ways.

1. Fibre diameter, which is measured in micrometres or μm (10^{-6} m), can only really apply to fibres which are circular or nearly circular, such as some man-made fibres and wool.
2. Mass-per-unit length (linear density) can easily be applied to irregular cross sections, which make up the majority of fibres. Effectively, this quantity is a measure of cross-sectional area since:

$$\text{cross-section area} \times \text{length} \times \text{ fibre density} = \text{mass}$$

$$\frac{\text{mass}}{\text{length}} = \text{cross-section area} \times \text{fibre density}$$

If the fibre density is a constant for a given fibre then the mass-per-unit length is just a constant multiple of the cross section area.

3. Air flow measurement. Neither of the above measurements may be very accurate if there is variation along the length of a fibre or large variation between fibres. With cotton in particular, the **Micronaire** test value, or similar, is used to assess fineness. The basic principle is that the air flow through a fixed mass of fibre in a standard chamber will be determined by the average fineness (and length) of the fibres.

LINEAR DENSITY – TEX

The measurement of fineness in terms of linear density (expressed in terms of the quantity tex) can be used for fibres and also rovings, slivers, webs and yarns.

The linear density, in tex, is the mass in grams of 1000 metres of the material. For example, if 5000 metres of a fibre has a mass of 0.6 grams then the linear density is:

$$\frac{0.6}{5000} \times 1000 = 0.12 \text{ tex}$$

If one metre of sliver has a mass of 1.4 grams then the linear density is:

$$\frac{1.4}{1} \times 1000 = 1400 \text{ tex}$$

If 100 metres of yarn has a mass of 2.25 grams then the linear density is:

$$\frac{2.25}{100} \times 1000 = 22.5 \text{ tex}$$

Because the numbers obtained in the first two examples are either small or large, derived units as multiples of tex are often used. A linear density of 0.12 tex may be expressed as 1.2 decitex (dtex) or 120 millitex (mtex). A linear density of 1400 tex may be expressed as 1.4 kilotex (ktex).

Tex is defined as the mass in grams (g) of 1000 metres (m) of material:

$$\text{tex} = \frac{\text{mass (g)}}{\text{length (m)}} \times 1000$$

Decitex is the mass in grams of 10 000 metres of material:

$$\text{dtex} = \frac{\text{mass (g)}}{\text{length (m)}} \times 10\ 000$$

Kilotex is the mass in grams per metre:

$$\text{ktex} = \frac{\text{mass (g)}}{\text{length (m)}}$$

RELATION BETWEEN CROSS-SECTIONAL AREA OR FIBRE (EFFECTIVE) DIAMETER AND TEX

For a 1.2 dtex fibre of density 1.35 g cm^{-3} (1350 kg m^{-3}):

$$\text{area} \times \text{length} \times \text{density} = \text{mass (kg)}$$

$$A \times 1000 \times 1350 = \frac{1.2 \times 10^{-1}}{10 \times 1000}$$

$$\text{therefore, } A = \frac{1.2}{10 \times 1000 \times 1000 \times 1350}$$

$$= 88.8 \times 10^{-12} \text{ m}^2$$

If the effective diameter is δ then,

$$A = \frac{\pi \times \delta^2}{4} \quad \text{and} \quad \delta^2 = \frac{A \times 4}{\pi}$$

$$\delta = 10.64 \times 10^{-6} \text{ m} \quad \text{or} \quad 10.64\ \mu\text{m}$$

Fibre length

With staple fibres, the individual fibre length is less important than the distribution of fibre lengths in a sample of fibres.

Staple fibre diagrams vary for different varieties of natural fibres.

Man-made fibres can be cut to any length but are normally cut to a length appropriate for the processing system. They are not all cut to the same length but with some variation to avoid certain problems in spinning.

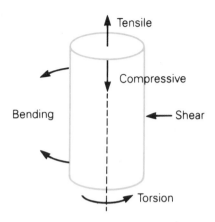

Figure 2.16 Fibre stress/strain.

Fibre tensile properties

> **Tensile stress** is the pull along the direction of the major axis of the fibre.

In engineering terms:

$$\text{stress} = \frac{\text{load}}{\text{area of cross section}}$$

As a result, the units are N m^{-2} (Newtons per square metre) or N mm^{-2} (Newtons per square millimetre) or mN mm^{-2} (milliNewtons per square millimetre).

In textiles, when we use tensile stress, we are generally comparing the tensile stress in two (or more) samples rather than being interested in an absolute measure of stress. It is relatively difficult to measure or define the cross-section area of a fibre because of the shape and the possibility of air spaces down the centre of fibres (cotton and wool). Also, strength for the same mass of material is a normal reference between samples of yarn or fabric.

Therefore, in textiles we use specific tensile stress, defined as:

$$\text{specific tensile stress} = \frac{\text{load}}{\text{mass per unit length}}$$

The units of specific tensile stress are therefore N tex^{-1} or mN tex^{-1}.

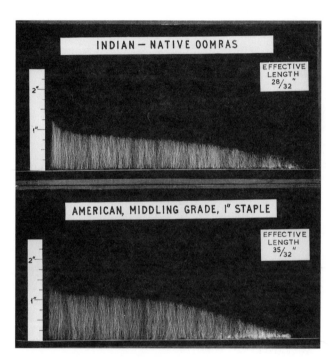

Figure 2.15 Typical staple diagrams for cotton.

Fibre load/extension properties

One of the important properties of materials is their 'strength'. There is no single scientific definition of the term 'strength' although we use it, and related words, in everyday language. 'Strength' essentially relates to the load-bearing property (stress) and the consequential change in dimensions (strain).

In real terms, a fibre is a three-dimensional structure and the stress and strain can be associated with any direction. The different directions are qualified by particular terms.

TENSILE STRAIN

When a load is applied to a fibre, there will also be a deformation which will result in some change in length, called strain.

The elongation is the change in length (final length minus original length); so that the tensile strain is given by:

$$\text{tensile strain} = \frac{\text{elongation}}{\text{original length}}$$

This is a dimensionless quantity. It is just a number, because a length term is divided by another length term.

The tensile strain is more often expressed as percentage extension:

$$\text{extension } \% = \text{tensile strain} \times 100\%$$

STRESS/STRAIN CURVES

A stress/strain curve is a graphical representation of the relationship between stress and strain in a specimen (fibre) as either the load or the extension is increased up to the break point.

The values associated with the curve for a particular textile material may depend on: the type of specimen (single fibre, fibre bundle, yarn or fabric); the dimensions of the sample; the atmospheric conditions in the testing laboratory; the mechanical details and the speed of the testing machine – in particular whether the machine uses the principle of **constant rate of loading** or **constant rate of extension**.

As a consequence, it is important to know something about the above factors before comparing curves for different materials. Remembering this, the general principles of stress/strain can be considered.

Although the stress/strain curves for a range of fibres at first sight appear quite different, the general shapes of the curves have many similarities.

By careful adjustment of the scales on the axes for the curves for different fibres, a typical shape can be identified (Figure 2.18).

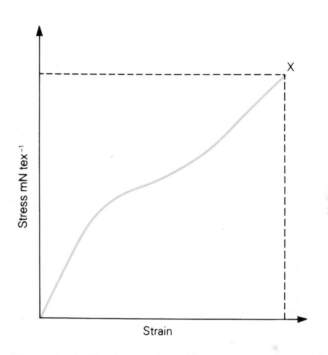

Figure 2.18 Typical stress/strain curve for a fibre.

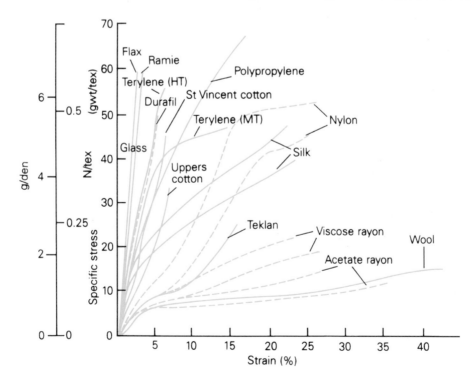

Figure 2.17 Typical stress/strain curves.

MODULUS

A stress/strain curve starts from zero stress and zero strain. The slope of the first part of the curve gives the **initial modulus**. The slope usually remains constant over this initial part of the curve. Effects in this region are normally described as elastic, in that stress is proportional to strain and if the fibre is only deformed by a small extension, or load, it should recover to the original dimension.

$$\text{Initial modulus} = \tan \alpha = \frac{\text{change in stress}}{\text{change in strain}}$$

The units for initial modulus are the same as for stress or specific stress (because strain has no units).

The significance of this quantity is particularly important when different fibres are blended together. It indicates that, at a particular strain, each of the blend components will make different contributions to the total stress in a yarn. Ideally, fibres in a blend should have very similar initial moduli.[v]

YIELD POINT

After the initial straight part, the curve bends down towards the strain axis. In this area, small changes in load produce large changes in length. The change in direction in fibre stress/strain curves is not as sharp as that for metals. As a result, values for yield stress and yield strain cannot be read directly but have to be obtained by construction (or computation).

Coplan's construction for obtaining yield stress and yield strain is shown below in Figure 2.20.

The significance of yield stress and yield strain is that if a fibre is deformed beyond these values, it will not recover to the original dimensions.

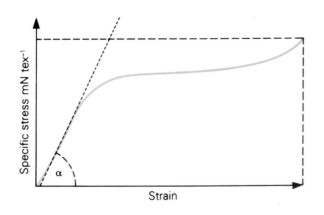

Figure 2.19   Initial modulus.

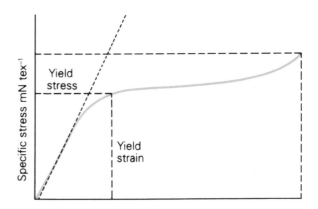

Figure 2.20   Yield point.

Table 2.3   Typical values from fibre stress/strain curves

	Breaking stress tenacity mN tex^{-1}	Breaking strain %	Initial modulus mN tex^{-1}	Yield stress mN tex^{-1}	Yield strain %
Cotton –					
Sea Island[1]	450	6.8	730	N/A	N/A*
USA[2]	320	7.1	500	N/A	N/A*
Wool (typical)	110	42.5	230	57	5.0
Silk	380	23.4	730	156	3.3
Flax	540	3.0	1800	N/A	N/A*
Nylon	470	26.0	260	407	16.0
Polyester	470	15.0	1060	300	10.0
Acrylic	270	25.0	620	115	5.0
Tricetate	125	26.0	320	75	3.2
Viscose	210	15.7	650	68	1.9
Glass	260	8.0	2850	N/A	N/A*

*No marked yield point.
[1]A very long and fine variety of cotton.
[2]A cotton of medium length and fineness.

Elasticity

When a tensile load or extension has been applied to a structure, there is some change in dimensions. When the load is removed, forces from inside the structure attempt to pull it back to its original shape.

A material is said to be perfectly elastic if it recovers all the change in dimensions after the applied load or extension is removed. Unfortunately, few materials are perfectly elastic and some deformation is left in the structure.

The practical consequences of this can be seen in the elbows and knees of garments which go baggy after use or in the cuffs and neckbands of sweaters.

The effect is measured in terms of **elastic recovery**.

$$\text{Elastic recovery} = \frac{\text{recovered extension}}{\text{total extension}}$$
$$= \frac{\text{extended length} - \text{recovered length}}{\text{extended length} - \text{original length}}$$

Elastic recovery is often expressed as a percentage.

Bending and twisting

When a fibre is assembled into a yarn with twist, it lies in a helical path. In this three-dimensional arrangement, the fibre is subject to both bending (flexing) and twisting (torsion). The handle and drape of fabrics depends on the bending of the yarn (and other factors).

BENDING AND FLEXURAL RIGIDITY

In order to bend a ruler gripped between both hands, two twisting forces in opposite directions have to be applied at the ends. The twist force is called a couple.

In a more scientific way, the effect is measured in terms of **flexural rigidity**.

> Flexural rigidity is defined as the couple required to bend the structure (a fibre) to unit curvature.

This gives the following relationship for a fibre:

$$\text{flexural rigidity} = \frac{1}{4\pi} \times \frac{\text{shape factor} \times \text{modulus} \times \text{tex}^2}{\text{density}}$$

Some values for the specific flexural rigidity of fibres are shown in Table 2.4. Shape factor is a measure of the shape, specifically in relation to bending. A solid circular cross section gives a higher shape factor than an irregular cross section.

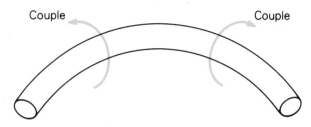

Figure 2.21 Bending or flexing.

Hollow sections give higher shape factors and hence greater flexural rigidity than solid cross sections. A particular example of this are the 'white' kempy wool fibres, associated with Harris Tweed, which have an airspace (medulla) down their centre and so act like a tube. (For rigidity and lightness, metal tables and chairs are made from tubular frameworks.)

Modulus is a measure of the intrinsic stress/strain behaviour of the material. Tex is the linear density of the fibres. The term is squared and a change in fineness has a more significant effect on the flexural rigidity than the other factors. If the fineness is reduced by a factor of two then the flexural rigidity is reduced by $2^2 = 4$. A practical example of this factor is that, in order to produce glass fibre which is sufficiently flexible for conventional processing, it is extruded with much finer filaments to compensate for the higher modulus value.

Density is on the bottom line of the equation, as high density will give a smaller cross-section area for the same shape factor.

Table 2.4 Typical values for specific flexural rigidity

	Specific flexural rigidity (mN mm^2 tex^{-2})	Flexural shape factor
Cotton	0.53	—
Wool	0.24	0.80
Silk	0.60	0.59
Triacetate	0.25	0.70
Nylon	0.20	0.90
Viscose	0.35	0.75
Polyester	0.30	0.90
Acrylic	0.40	0.75
Glass	0.89	1.00

TWISTING AND TORSIONAL RIGIDITY

> The resistance to twisting of a fibre is called its **torsional rigidity**. It is defined as the couple (turning force) required to put unit twist between the ends of a specimen of unit length.

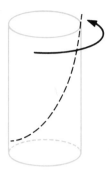

Figure 2.22 Twisting or torsion.

Some values for the torsional rigidity of fibres are shown in Table 2.5.

Table 2.5 Typical values for specific torsional rigidity

	Specific torsional rigidity (mN mm² tex⁻²)	Torsional shape factor
Cotton	0.16	0.71
Wool	0.12	0.98
Silk Tussah*	0.16	0.35
Bombyx	0.16	0.84
Triacetate	0.06	0.70
Nylon	0.05	1.00
Viscose	0.06	0.95
Polyester	0.07	1.00
Acrylic	0.15	0.07
Glass	0.02	1.00

*Wild silk with a flat cross section.

If the twist (angular deflection) is expressed in radians, the following relationship applies to a fibre:

$$\text{torsional rigidity} = \frac{1}{2\pi} \times \frac{\text{shape factor} \times \dfrac{\text{specific}}{\text{shear modulus}} \times \text{tex}^2}{\text{density}}$$

If the twist is expressed in terms of one turn per unit length then the equation becomes:

$$\text{torsional rigidity} = \frac{\text{shape factor} \times \dfrac{\text{specific}}{\text{shear modulus}} \times \text{tex}^2}{\text{density}}$$

Shape factor is equivalent to the quantity used in flexural rigidity but is a different value because it applies to a different three-dimensional direction. Specific shear modulus is a measure of the intrinsic stress/strain behaviour of the material in the shear direction. As with flexural rigidity, tex is the most important factor because it is squared. Finer fibres are more easily twisted. In a similar way to flexural rigidity, a higher density will give a smaller cross-section area for the same shape factor.

OTHER FACTORS AFFECTING BENDING AND TWISTING

In addition to the factors (shape, modulus, tex² and density) discussed in the previous section, torsional and flexural rigidity are affected by the presence of moisture. Fibres are more easily twisted and bent as their absorbed moisture increases.

Temperature has a limited effect in the normal room temperature range but at higher temperature, particularly with **thermoplastic** polymers (deforms in heat without changing chemically), fibres are more easily deformed. Obviously, if the temperature is too high, the fibre will melt and so has no flexural or torsional rigidity.

Fibres and moisture

A fibre, yarn fabric or finished textile product is surrounded by air. The air contains oxygen, the other gases, various pollutants and moisture vapour. The amount of moisture varies from day to day and is normally expressed in terms of relative humidity.

Relative humidity is the amount of water vapour in air expressed as a percentage of the maximum amount that the air can hold at the particular temperature – the higher the temperature, the more moisture the air can hold.

On a wet day, the relative humidity will be high so that wet laundry will not dry in the open air because the air will not hold any more vapour.

Since the properties of fibres vary with the moisture condition, testing should be done under controlled conditions. A standard atmosphere is defined as one of 65 per cent relative humidity at a temperature of 20°C. Processing of textiles, particularly in yarn and fabric production, will normally be carried out at higher temperatures and, in particular, at higher relative humidities because the materials are easier to process.

A textile material placed in a given atmosphere takes up or loses moisture until it reaches equilibrium, when no further change takes place. As a consequence, the amount of moisture within a fibre can, and does, vary.

Regain and moisture content

The amount of moisture in a textile material could be expressed in either of two ways.

$$\text{Moisture content (\%)} = \frac{\text{mass of moisture in the sample}}{\text{mass of the undried sample}} \times 100$$

$$\text{Moisture regain (\%)} = \frac{\text{mass of moisture in the sample}}{\text{mass of the dry sample}} \times 100$$

Regain is normally used because it refers to the dried sample, that is the amount of actual fibre. Moisture content is less useful because, if the amount of moisture changes, both the top and bottom lines of the relationship change.

The regain of a textile material depends on the relative humidity of the air around it, so a set of agreed recommended allowances for regain are used. The recommended allowances are the regain of the materials in the standard temperature atmosphere. This is extremely important from a commercial point, as a bale of fibre, for example, will be heavier if it is left in a higher temperature and humidity than the standard atmosphere. Fibre is bought by weight, so it is very important to ensure that the correct allowance for water in the fibre is taken into account. A typical procedure would involve measuring the average regain of a consignment of textile material and then calculating the correct invoice mass, applying the recommended allowance. Some typical regain values are shown in Table 2.6.

Table 2.6 Recommended allowance for regain

Fibre type	Allowance (%)
Cotton	8.5
Wool	14–19
Mercerised cotton	up to 12
Silk	11
Flax	12
Viscose	13
Nylon	6
Polyester	1.5 or 3
Acrylic	1.5
Triacetate	4.0
Polypropylene	0
Glass	0

CALCULATION USING MOISTURE REGAIN

A sample of cotton fibre, mass 2.5 grams, taken from a consignment of mass 5000 kilograms, had an oven dry mass of 2.35 grams.

$$\text{Sample regain} = \frac{2.5 - 2.35}{2.35} \times 100\% = 6.38\%$$

If the recommended allowance for the textile material is 8.5 per cent then:

$$\text{correct invoice mass} = 5000 \times \frac{(100 + 8.5)}{(100 + 6.38)} = 5099.6 \text{ kg}$$

EFFECT OF REGAIN ON LINEAR DENSITY

A sample of 20 tex yarn from a spinning room, of mass 2.15 grams, was found to have an oven dry mass of 1.95 grams.

$$\text{Yarn sample regain} = \frac{2.15 - 1.95}{1.95} = 10.25\%$$

If the regain in a standard temperature atmosphere should be nine per cent, then under these conditions:

$$\text{linear density} = 20 \times \frac{(100 + 9)}{(100 + 10.25)} = 19.77 \text{ tex}$$

So, linear density will effectively change with atmospheric conditions, which confirms the recognised fact that all measurement of properties of textile materials (fibres, yarns and fabrics) should be carried out in a standard atmosphere.

Effect of moisture on fibre properties

In general, most of the properties of fibres are dependent to some extent on the presence of moisture from the atmosphere on the temperature.

SWELLING

If the amount of moisture absorbed within a fibre alters, there will be changes in dimensions. This can occur both in the cross section and along the length of a fibre.

One direct effect is that the density of the dry fibre will be different from that of the fibre that has absorbed moisture.

The practical consequence of fibre swelling is more evident in fabrics. Fibre swelling will result in shrinkage of twisted structures such as yarns and ropes, and shrinkage of woven fabrics. An example of this effect is associated with the use of canvas tents. If it rains, it is recommended that the ropes are slackened, otherwise the fabric may tear as the shrinkage results in tension.

In **ventile fabrics** used in showerproof garments, the initial swelling of the fibres will close the pores in the closely woven structure so that it becomes impermeable to water.

EFFECT OF MOISTURE ON STRESS/STRAIN PROPERTIES

For most fibres, when the amount of absorbed moisture increases, the fibres become weaker. The specific breaking stress is reduced and the per centage breaking extension increases.

The exceptions are cotton and the natural cellulosic fibres, which get stronger as the amount of absorbed moisture increases. The specific breaking stress increases and the per centage extension at break reduces.

This again underlines the need for evaluation of these properties under standard atmospheric conditions.

CHECK YOUR UNDERSTANDING

- Natural fibres such as cotton and wool have some colour naturally. Cotton fibres are short staple, wool fibres are long staple. Longer cotton fibres are also finer, but longer wool fibres are coarser.
- Man-made fibres are white and can be manufactured to the required fineness and length to suit the processing system to be used.
- Some fibres can be classified by their appearance under low magnification: wool and hair fibres have surface scales; cotton has convolutions. Other fibres such as polyester, polyamide and polypropylene have almost identical regular-sized circular cross sections.
- Fibres with circular cross sections or smooth longitudinal sections appear to be more lustrous. Finer fibres also appear to be more lustrous and tend to look a paler shade when dyed.
- Particles (usually titanium dioxide) can be added to man-made fibres to make them more appear to be less lustrous. These are known as delustrant particles.
- If a fibre has a large difference between its refractive indices (a large birefringence) it may appear to be dichromatic. To minimise this effect matt fibres may be used.
- Fibre fineness affects: processing means; coloration and finishing efficiency; rate of dye uptake and shade; fabric comfort, handle and drape; resistance to abrasion.
- Fibre length affects: processing system choice; yarn tenacity and fineness; yarn hairiness; fabric drape; handle and pilling tendency.
- Specific stress and strain are used to measure the tensile properties of textile fibres. The initial modulus is used as a measure of the elasticity of the fibre, but once the fibre is stressed beyond the yield point, it will not recover to its original dimensions.
- Finer fibres are more easily twisted or bent. Small changes in the tex value will give larger changes in the bending or twisting behaviour of fibres than any other factor.
- There are standard allowances for moisture uptake of fibres; the amount of moisture in the fibre mass will obviously affect the weight and so the price.
- Fibre swelling causes yarns and woven fabrics to shrink.
- Natural cellulosics are the only fibres that increase in tensile strength when wet; all other fibres become weaker when wet.

REVISION EXERCISES AND QUESTIONS

1 Which fibres can be classified or identified by their appearance alone?
2 Why do finer fibres appear to be more lustrous in a yarn?
3 How does mercerisation of cotton fibres increase lustre?
4 How is lustre in man-made fibres modified?
5 How do fibres with a high birefringence cause problems in coloration?
6 Calculate the decitex value of the man-made fibre below:
    100 metres of fibre weighs 0.035 grams.
7 What are tensile properties?
8 When is the initial modulus considered to be particularly important?
9 Why are the flexural and torsional rigidities of fibres important?
10 Why is a standard testing atmosphere necessary?
11 Calculate the moisture regain and content of the following sample:
    sample weight = 5.55 grams
    dry sample weight = 5.0 grams.
    What fibre is this?
12 Why do fabrics shrink when wet?

Fibre testing and identification

The textile processor needs to know the characteristics of the fibres they are dealing with. Fibres, especially natural fibres, are often variable and many techniques are available to test fibre properties. Some rely on personal opinion (known as subjective tests), while others give reproducible results, usually in numerical form (known as objective tests). Some tests are used purely to distinguish one fibre type from another and others are used to determine the exact properties of fibres. Cotton fibres may vary from type to type, but they also vary within each type – from fibre grown in one field to another. It can be essential for successful processing that fibre properties are known beforehand. This chapter will cover the following topics: fibre fineness; fibre length; fibre tensile properties; moisture regain; and fibre identification.

Fibre fineness

Fibre fineness can be expressed in a number of different ways. For some fibres, the diameter is often used, for others the linear density, while for cotton the air flow or micronaire value is common.

Measurement of fibre diameter can only be carried out on fibres with a circular cross-sectional shape. Linear density is most commonly used with any fibre as it is independent of cross-sectional shape. However, it is not easy to measure for staple fibres. As a consequence, several indirect methods of determining fibre fineness have been developed.

Methods of measuring fibre fineness

Four principles used to measure fibre fineness will be discussed: gravimetric; optical; pneumatic; and sonic.

Gravimetric means measurement by weighing, and this is the obvious way of determining the linear density or the mass per unit length of fibres. Two measurements are necessary, one of mass and the other of length.

If the material is in the form of continuous filament, it is only necessary to wind a sample of convenient length (usually 100 metres) and weigh it on a balance.

$$\text{Linear density}(\text{tex}) = \frac{\text{mass (g)}}{\text{length (m)}} \times 1000$$

If the material is in the form of staple fibre then it is necessary to measure the lengths of a large number of fibres and weigh them on a very sensitive balance.

$$\text{Linear density}(\text{tex}) = \frac{\text{total mass (g)}}{\text{total length (m)}} \times 1000$$

For routine purposes, it is more convenient to cut the sample of fibres to the same length (usually ten millimetres) using two razor blades separated by a space. Count out a convenient number (usually 100) and weigh them on a microbalance.

$$\text{Linear density} = \frac{\text{mass (g)} \times 1000}{[nl]} \times 1000$$

where n = number of fibres counted out

l = length cut (in mm)

This method was, at one time, the only reliable method of estimating cotton linear density. It is very slow for routine purposes and has been superseded by instrumental methods.

OPTICAL METHODS

Microscopy is the commonest optical method. It is the standard method for measuring the fineness of wool.

A thick section is cut from a sample of parallel fibres to produce a large number of short lengths. These are mounted on a microscope slide in a suitable mounting medium and viewed longitudinally using a projection microscope. This method is only suitable for fibres with a circular cross section.

$$\text{Fibre diameter} = \frac{\text{image width}}{\text{magnification}}$$

Using the standard magnification of 500×:

Fibre diameter in micrometres (μm) = 2 × image width (mm)

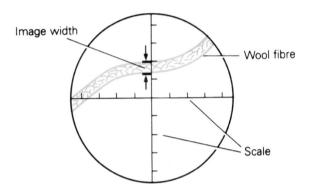

Figure 3.1 Measurement of fibre diameter using a microscope.

PNEUMATIC (AIR-FLOW) METHOD

These methods are the most commonly used for routine purposes because of their speed.

A specimen of fibres is compressed into a cylinder of standard pressure dimensions and air is forced through it at a standard pressure difference. There is a resistance to the flow of air as it passes over the fibre surfaces. The rate of air flow is inversely proportional to the resistance, which in turn is proportional to the square of the ratio of the surface area to the volume of the fibres.

The average fineness of a sample of fibres can be estimated by measuring the volume rate of air flow through a 'plug' of fibres of standard mass under standard conditions. The volume rate of air flow is measured using a flow meter and the pressure difference measured using a manometer. Modern instruments measure the pressure difference, using an electronic pressure transducer, to give a standard rate of air flow.

When dealing with cotton, the results of air-flow methods are influenced by the maturity (development of the secondary wall), making it difficult to obtain an accurate measure of linear density. Modern instruments are available which determine separate values for the linear density and the maturity.

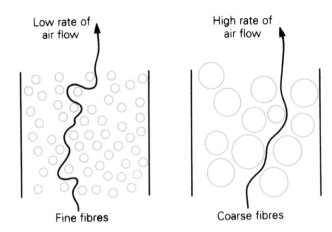

Figure 3.2 Air flow through fine and coarse fibres.

SONIC (VIBRASCOPIC) METHODS

These were developed for use with man-made fibres where variation between fibres is not as great as with natural fibres. These methods use the same principle as a stringed musical instrument. A perfectly elastic string (one that recovers completely after being stressed) has a natural frequency of vibration (resonant frequency) which depends on its tension, length and mass per unit length. The resonant frequency is the frequency at which maximum energy is absorbed and therefore maximum amplitude produced.

A fibre can be considered as a very small string. The fibre is mounted under tension over two knife edges – to standardise the length – and vibrated electromechanically. The frequency of vibration is changed until the amplitude of vibration is at maximum, as detected by a displacement transducer. The resonant frequency is then measured electronically. The tension, length of fibre and resonant frequency are known; the instrument gives a direct reading of linear density.

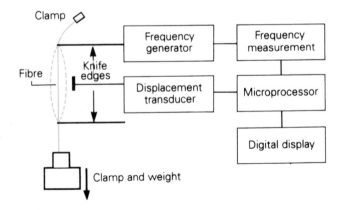

Figure 3.3 Schematic diagram of a sonic fibre fineness instrument.

Fibre length

There is more than one way of expressing what is meant by fibre length. In the simplest terms, the **straightened length** is the distance between the two ends of a fibre when under sufficient tension to hold it straight without stretching it.

However, fibres are never straight in use, so a more realistic method of expression is required. The **extent** of a fibre is the distance it occupies in the direction of the structure's (for example a yarn's) main axis.

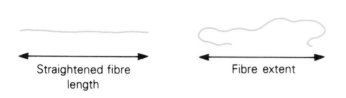

Straightened fibre
length

Fibre extent

Figure 3.4 Straightened fibre length and fibre extent.

Methods of measurement

The principles of measurement can be divided into manual methods and instrumental methods.

MANUAL METHODS

Hand stapling is used by cotton graders and wool classers to assess the staple length of the fibres. A symmetrical tuft of parallel fibres (with the fibres extending an equal distance each side of an imaginary line) is prepared. The staple length, which is approximately equal to the modal length, is determined by subjective visual assessment. In the case of cotton stapling, this length is still quoted in units of 1/32 of an inch.

INSTRUMENTAL METHODS

The simplest instrumental method is the oiled plate method. A glass plate, covered in oil, has a scale engraved on it. A fibre is removed from a sample and pulled along the surface of the plate. The tension created by the oil holds it straight while it is measured.

For the results to be statistically significant when dealing with natural fibres, a large number have to be measured. Instruments have been developed which can rapidly measure a large number of individual fibres and record the results as a frequency table (for example, the WIRA fibre length machine).

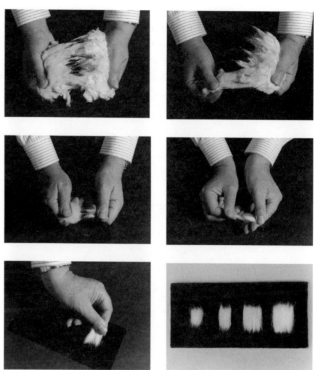

Figure 3.5 The characteristics of raw cotton.

Figure 3.6 The WIRA fibre length machine.

Direct methods which can deal with a large number of fibres at a time have been developed. The oldest of these is the comb sorter. This is illustrated in Figure 3.7.

A representative specimen in the form of a tuft of parallel fibres is prepared and placed in a set of combs. The fibres are removed from the combs a few at a time to straighten them and then replaced in the combs to produce a coterminus edge. The combs are removed successively and the fibres protruding from the remaining combs are extracted and laid down side by side. In this way, the fibres are sorted into length groups.

The outline of the fibres produces a **staple diagram** which is equivalent to a graph of length against cumulative frequency.

Figure 3.7 The comb sorter.

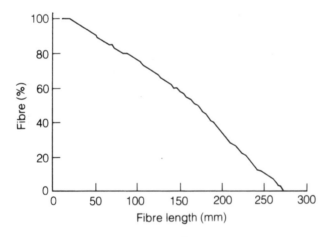

Figure 3.8 Comb-sorter diagram.

INDIRECT INSTRUMENTAL METHODS

These have been designed to overcome the tedious and time-consuming nature of the other methods. Two steps are involved:

1. The preparation of a specimen of parallel fibres with the end of every fibre aligned on a common line.

2. The measurement of some property of the aligned specimen which is proportional to the number of fibres it contains at various points along its length. This stage is carried out by scanning the specimen through a property-measuring system (thickness gauge, photoelectric optical system, or electrical capacitor plates).

Modern instruments only measure the optical density or the electrical capacitance. They are linked to computers for analysis of results.

During processing and use, fibres are not straight and not aligned along a common line. The aligning stage during analysis is very slow compared with the measurement stage. The latest instruments determining the length characteristics of cotton select the specimen by gripping the fibres at random points along their lengths. The specimen is then scanned in a similar manner to the above, using an optical or pneumatic system. Due to the different specimen preparation technique, the graph produced has a different shape to the staple diagram, but can be analysed to yield similar information.

It is claimed that the results obtained are more relevant than those produced by other methods because fibre extent is measured rather than straightened length.

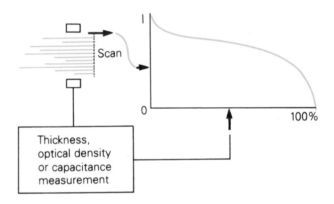

Figure 3.9 Principle of indirect length measurement.

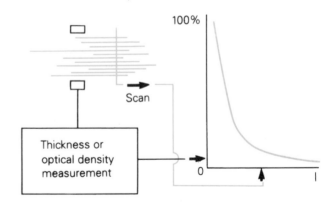

Figure 3.10 Principle of indirect extent measurement.

Fibre tensile properties

The mechanical properties of any material can be measured in various directions. However, the most important mechanical properties of a fibre are its properties under tension in the direction of the structure's main axis.

Principles of measurement

The tensile properties are determined by holding a fibre or filament at both ends, stretching it under controlled conditions, measuring the change in length (elongation) and the tension (load) which develops in it.

Some simple instruments only measure the breaking load of the specimen. Modern sophisticated electronic instruments continuously monitor load and elongation and plot a graph of load against elongation.

The results obtained depend on the dimensions of the specimen (length and thickness). For comparison purposes, the specimen dimensions are taken into account. Modern electronic instruments are often linked to a computer, which converts the load values into stress, corresponding elongation values into strain and plots a stress/strain curve.

$$\text{Stress } (N\,\text{tex}^{-1}) = \frac{\text{load}}{\text{linear density}}$$

$$\text{Strain} = \frac{\text{elongation}}{\text{original length}}$$

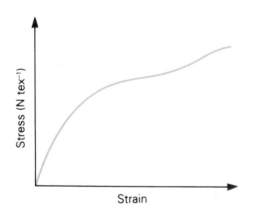

Figure 3.11 Stress/strain curve for a typical fibre.

Mechanical conditions for tensile testing

The conditions under which the test is carried out can influence the results obtained. Three mechanical conditions can be used.

CONSTANT RATE OF LOADING (CRL)

The load on the specimen is increased at a constant rate by varying the speed at which the specimen is increased in length. This is difficult to achieve.

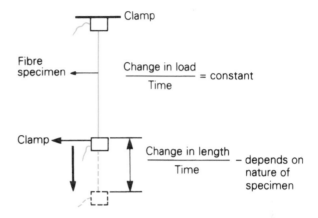

Figure 3.12 Constant rate of loading.

CONSTANT RATE OF EXTENSION (CRE)

The specimen is increased in length by driving the bottom jaw down (or the top jaw up) at a constant speed. The rate at which the load changes is variable.

All modern electronic instruments use constant rate of extension conditions because it is easy to achieve.

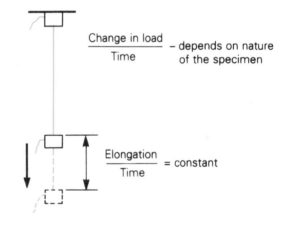

Figure 3.13 Constant rate of extension.

CONSTANT RATE OF TRAVERSE (CRT)

With some simple mechanical instruments, the bottom jaw is driven down at a constant speed to elongate the specimen. The top jaw also has to move down to operate the load-measuring device. The elongation of the specimen is the difference between the two movements. If the rate of movement of the

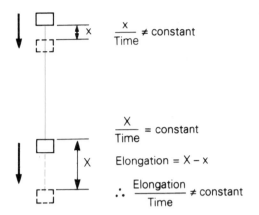

Figure 3.14 Constant rate of traverse.

top jaw is not constant (because the change in load depends on the nature of the specimen), then the rate of elongation of the specimen is not constant. In other words, constant conditions are not achieved. This is shown in Figure 3.15.

Mechanical principles of load measurement

Measurement of elongation is a relatively simple matter. Measurement of load is not. Various principles of measurement can be employed.

BALANCE PRINCIPLE

The basic principle uses the principle of moments. The instrument consists of a horizontal beam with a fulcrum somewhere between the two ends.

A force F, acting at a distance d_1 from the fulcrum, is in equilibrium with the load L on the specimen acting at a distance d_2 from the fulcrum.

Clockwise moment = anticlockwise moment

$$Ld_2 = Fd_1$$
$$\therefore \quad L = \frac{Fd_1}{d_2}$$

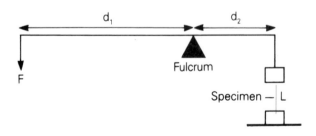

Figure 3.15 Balance method of load measurement.

The load on the specimen is increased by increasing the distance d_1 at which F acts. The force F is usually applied in the form of a weight. If F and d_2 are kept constant then:

$$L \propto d_1$$

The distance d_1 can then be used as a measure of load.

THE PENDULUM LEVER PRINCIPLE

The top jaw of the instrument is attached to a pulley to which is attached a pendulum. As the load on the specimen increases, the top jaw is pulled down rotating the pendulum. The pendulum passes over a scale which is calibrated in load units.

When the system is in equilibrium, the moment exerted by the load L is balanced by the moment exerted by the weight of the pendulum mg.

$$Lr = mgx$$
$$= mgR \sin \theta$$

For a given instrument, mg, lengths R and r are constant. Therefore:

$$L \propto \theta$$

The rotation of the pendulum θ can be used as a measure of load. This principle gives constant rate of traverse conditions.

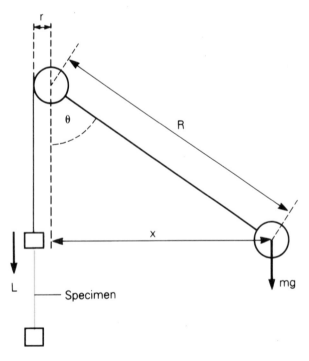

Figure 3.16 Principle of load measurement using the pendulum lever.

THE INCLINED PLANE PRINCIPLE

One end of the specimen is clamped to a plane and the other end to a trolley. One end of the plane is lowered at a constant speed so that the plane rotates. The trolley runs down the plane as the specimen elongates.

Load L = component of weight of trolley,

$\quad mg$ parallel to the plane

$\quad = mg \sin \theta$

$\therefore \quad L = \dfrac{mgx}{d}$

For a given instrument, mg and d are constant. Distance x can be used as a measure of load. If x increases at a constant rate, this principle gives constant rate of loading conditions; the only principle to do so without modification.

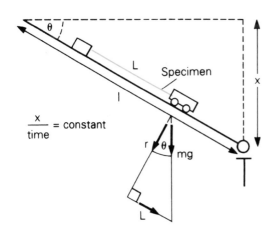

Figure 3.17 The inclined plane principle.

Electronic principles of load measurement

These are rapidly replacing mechanical principles. The simplest of these principles is the **strain gauge principle**. A strain gauge is a long length of resistance wire wound so as to occupy a small area and encased in plastic for protection.

The strain gauge is bonded to the surface of a cantilever spring. The top jaw of the instrument is attached to the spring. As the load on the specimen is increased, the top jaw is pulled down, bending the spring. The top surface of the spring stretches and the bottom surface contracts. This stretches the resistance wire, decreasing its cross-sectional area. The decrease in area increases its resistance, causing an increase in potential difference across its ends when a current is passed through it. The change in potential difference can be used as a measure of load and is measured electronically.

If a very stiff spring is used, its deflection is so small that the elongation of the specimen is equal to the movement of the bottom jaw and constant rate of extension conditions are achieved. Electronic load measurement has several advantages. It is very accurate and very sensitive (single fibre tensile testers are available which can measure loads of less than 0.001 N). The measuring device can be connected to a computer for storage of data, analysis of the results and graph plotting.

FIBRE BUNDLE TENSILE TESTERS

Individual staple fibres are very delicate and difficult to handle. The inherent variation in the properties of natural fibres makes it necessary to measure a very large number for the

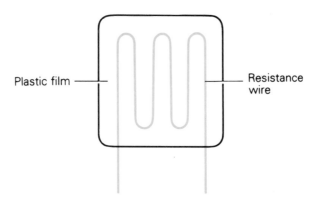

Figure 3.18 Strain gauge.

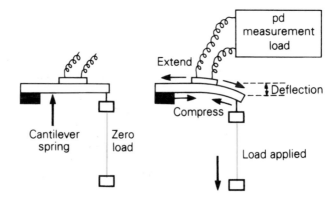

Figure 3.19 Principle of load measurement using a strain gauge.

results to be statistically significant. For these reasons, instruments have been developed which test a large number of fibres at a time in the form of a bundle of parallel fibres. Such instruments can only measure the average properties of the fibre and can provide no measure of variation.

The simplest of these, the **Pressley fibre bundle strength tester**, was developed for use with cotton. This uses the balance principle.

The specimen bundle of fibres is gripped by two clamps. The fibres are reduced to a constant length by trimming the protruding ends.

The clamps are then placed in the instrument so that the bottom clamp is held firm and the top clamp is connected to the beam. The trolley weight is released and rolls down the sloping beam under the influence of gravity, increasing the moment of the force (weight) about the fulcrum. When this exceeds the moment of the load on the specimen, the fibres break and the trolley is arrested. The distance the trolley has moved along the beam indicates the breaking load of the bundle. The broken fibres are then weighed.

An index of strength is calculated:

$$\text{Pressley index} = \frac{\text{breaking load (in lb f)}}{\text{specimen mass (in mg)}}$$

As the specimen is cut to a standard length, its weight is a measure of its linear density. Since:

$$\text{tenacity} = \frac{\text{breaking load}}{\text{linear density}}$$

the Pressley index is an indication of the average tenacity of the fibres (but in unconventional units). No measure of breaking extension is provided.

Modern sophisticated fibre bundle strength testers have been developed which measure load and elongation electronically and are linked to computers for analysis of results, production of load-elongation and stress/strain curves. Despite their sophistication, they only provide a measure of average properties and no measure of variation between fibres.

Moisture regain

There are two principles employed for the measurement of fibre regain in the laboratory: gravimetric and electronic methods. The choice of method depends on the speed and accuracy required.

Gravimetric methods

Since the regain value of a sample of fibres is expressed on a mass basis then it is also the obvious basis for measurement.

STANDARD METHOD

An outline of the procedure is as follows:

1. An empty weighing bottle is weighed accurately.
2. A sample of fibre is placed in the weighing bottle, the stopper replaced and the whole is weighed.
3. The bottle with its contents is repeatedly dried in an oven at $105° \pm 3°C$ (with its stopper removed), cooled (with its stopper in place to prevent re-absorption of moisture) and reweighed until the loss in mass is less than a specified proportion. The final mass is known as the 'oven-dry mass', as the sample cannot be dried completely using an oven.
4. The regain of the sample can then be calculated:

   mass of original sample = mass of weighing bottle with sample − mass of empty weighing bottle

   oven-dry mass of dry sample = mass of weighing bottle with dry sample − mass of empty weighing bottle

$$\text{regain\%} = \frac{\left(\begin{array}{c}\text{mass of} \\ \text{original sample}\end{array} - \begin{array}{c}\text{oven-dry mass} \\ \text{of dry sample}\end{array}\right)}{\text{oven-dry mass of sample}} \times 100$$

MOISTURE TESTING OVEN

Special ovens have been designed which enable regain to be measured without repeatedly removing the sample for weighing. The sample is weighed while in the oven.

Buoyancy effects of the hot-air and convection currents can influence the accuracy of the balance. For this reason, the oven cannot be fitted with a fan.

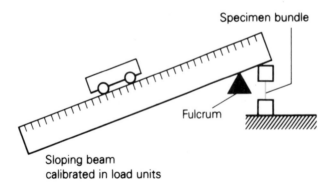

Figure 3.20 Schematic diagram of the Pressley fibre bundle tester.

RAPID DRYING INSTRUMENTS

These use a similar procedure to the standard method. The sample is placed in a pre-weighed container, which has hot air forced through it to give rapid drying. The container can be quickly sealed and re-weighed.

Rapid drying instruments have been developed in which the sample is dried using an infra-red lamp while sitting on the pan of an electronic balance. The balance can be fitted with a microprocessor which calculates regain values from original and dry weights. The sample's regain value is shown on the digital display or printed out.

Electrical regain testing instruments

Textile fibres are classed as insulators, that is, they have a very high electrical resistance. When a fibre absorbs moisture from the atmosphere, its electrical resistance falls to, possibly, a thousandth of its original value, though it still remains very high. The enormous difference in electrical resistance at various regain values provides a method of estimating regain indirectly. Two electrodes are used, separated by an insulating material. When the electrode is pressed onto (or into) a sample, the fibres bridge the gap and a small electric current flows through them. The current flowing depends on the resistance of the fibres, which in turn depends on the regain. The current is measured using a sensitive meter which is calibrated to read the moisture regain directly.

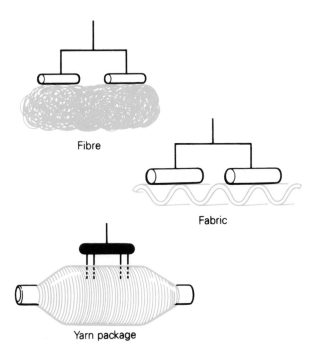

Fibre

Fabric

Yarn package

Figure 3.21 Electrodes used in electrical moisture regain testing.

As different fibres have differing electrical properties, the instrument must be calibrated for the particular fibre under test. Instruments are available with electrodes in the form of flat plates, rollers and sharp probes for testing samples in the form of raw fibre, fabric and yarn packages.

Fibre identification

It is sometimes necessary to know what type of fibre a sample contains. The following tests apply to samples which contain one type of fibre only. For simplicity, only the identification of organic fibres is considered. There is not one single technique which will provide unambiguous identification of a sample and it is usually necessary to carry out a series of tests in a logical order. With common fibres, these tests are relatively simple and take advantage of the differences in structure and properties between the different fibre types. A flow chart summarising the tests for fibre identification is given at the end of this section in Figure 3.24.

Reaction to heat

This test is a preliminary sorting test which places the sample in general categories. The subsequent test applied depends on the results of this test. Heat is provided by a hot non-luminous gas flame. The test is divided into two parts: approach to the flame and behaviour in the flame.

APPROACH TO THE FLAME

This determines whether the fibre is thermoplastic or non-thermoplastic. The sample is pulled out to a fine point and placed near (but not into) the flame. If the fibre shrinks away or melts into a bead, it is thermoplastic. If not, it is non-thermoplastic.

BEHAVIOUR IN THE FLAME

The behaviour of the fibre is noted: whether it burns or not; if so, how and what is the nature of any ash produced; what it smells like. The behaviour enables it to be classified and a decision made as to which test to apply next.

Microscopy

There are two ways of observing specimens of fibres, longitudinally or cross sectionally.

Table 3.1 Burning behaviour of fibres

	Behaviour	Classification	Next test
Non-thermoplastic	Burns rapidly. Fine ash. Smell of burning paper.	Cellulosic	Microscopy
	Burns slowly with irregular flame. Smell of burning hair. Black inflated ash.	Protein	Microscopy
Thermoplastic	Melt with degradation or burning.	Modified cellulosic or synthetic	Elemental analysis

LONGITUDINAL VIEW

A few well-separated fibres are placed on a microscope slide, mounted in a suitable liquid (liquid paraffin) and covered with a cover slip. The appearance of the fibres can be observed using a microscope. The best general purpose magnification to use is 100 times and the appearance of the fibres can be compared with the photographs in Chapter 2.

CROSS-SECTIONAL VIEW

This is not always necessary but may provide useful additional information. The most convenient way to prepare fibre cross sections is to use the plate method. A thin stainless steel plate with a small hole is used. The procedure is outlined below:

1. A doubled length of sewing thread is passed through the hole to form a loop and a tuft of fibres is placed in this loop.
2. The loop is pulled back through the hole to pack the hole with fibres.
3. The tuft is cut flush with each side of the plate using a razor blade.

A drop of mounting medium (decane, for example) is placed on the cross section, which is then observed using a microscope at a magnification of 100 times. The shape of the fibre cross section can be compared with the photographs in Chapter 2.

Microscopy should give enough evidence to identify the sample.

Elemental analysis

Fibres identified as thermoplastic in the test for reaction to heat and flame are tested for the presence of nitrogen and chlorine in their chemical structures.

NITROGEN TEST

A few fibres are placed in an ignition tube and covered with soda lime. The tube is then heated to a high temperature using a gas flame to completely decompose the fibre. The soda lime ensures that any nitrogen is evolved as ammonia and that any acidic compounds are adsorbed. If ammonia is present in the resultant vapour, it will turn wet red litmus paper to a blue colour.

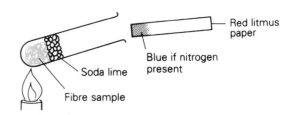

Figure 3.22 Test for nitrogen.

CHLORINE TEST

A clean copper wire with fibres on it is placed in a gas flame. The high temperature decomposes the fibre and ionises the compounds formed. The presence of chlorine is indicated by a green coloration of the flame.

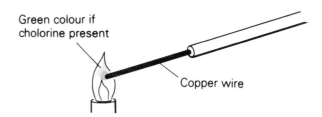

Figure 3.23 Test for chlorine.

Following these two tests, the fibre can be placed in one of four groups:

Table 3.2 Nitrogen and chlorine tests

Group	Nitrogen present	Chlorine present	Fibre
1	Yes	No	Polymide Polyacrylic
2	No	Yes	Chlorofibre
3	Yes	Yes	Modacrylic
4	No	No	Celullose Acetates Polyester polypropylene

Groups two and three provide enough information for a positive identification; groups one and four contain more than one fibre type each, therefore further tests are necessary.

SOLVENT TESTS

Many fibres (but not all) are soluble in specific solvents. A few fibres are placed in a test tube and a few cubic centimetres of the reagent are added. If the fibre does not dissolve, the next reagent in the series is used, with a fresh specimen, until one is found in which the fibre is soluble. It is usually obvious if the fibre sample has dissolved but if it is not clearly visible, a few drops of the reagent from the specimen test tube can be poured into water. If the fibre has dissolved, solid polymer will be precipitated. Safety procedures should be followed as some of the reagents are toxic or corrosive.

Table 3.3 Solvent tests for fibres containing nitrogen only

First reagent in which the specimen dissolves	Fibre
90% formic acid or meta cresol	Polyamide
dimethyl sulphoxide (hot)	Polyacrylic

Table 3.4 Solvent tests for fibres containing no nitrogen and no chlorine

First reagent in which the specimen dissolves	Fibre
70% v/v aqueous acetone	Cellulose diacetate
Glacial acetic acid	Cellulose triacetate
Xylene (boiling)	Polyolefine
Insoluble	Polyester

It is important to use the solvents in the order given as some fibres are soluble in more than one reagent. Reagents are used at room temperature unless stated otherwise.

Fibre identification procedure

The information in Figure 3.24 is a simple scheme suitable for the common organic fibres. When dealing with less common or exotic fibres, some other, possibly more sophisticated, tests are required.

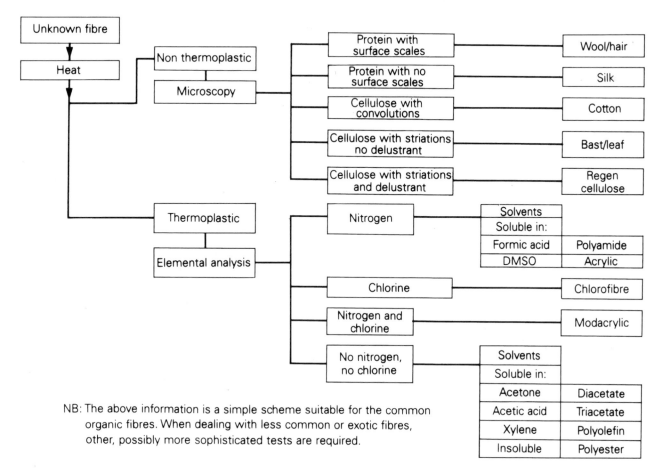

NB: The above information is a simple scheme suitable for the common organic fibres. When dealing with less common or exotic fibres, other, possibly more sophisticated tests are required.

Figure 3.24 Flow chart for fibre identification.

CHECK YOUR UNDERSTANDING

- There are four main methods involved in fibre fineness measurement: gravimetric; optical; pneumatic; and sonic.

- Gravimetric methods of determining fineness can be used for any fibre type; optical methods are only suitable for fibres with a circular cross section; pneumatic methods are usually used for cotton due to ease of operation and speed; man-made fibres can be measured using sonic methods because they are not as variable as natural fibres.

- Traditionally, manual hand stapling was used to assess fibre length. This subjective method is gradually being replaced by objective instrumental methods.

- The fibre extent rather than the straightened length is being used to measure fibres in modern indirect instrumental systems. It is claimed that this technique is more relevant to fibres in processing.

- The most important mechanical fibre property is that of tenacity. There are three mechanical methods used to stress the fibre: constant rate of loading; constant rate of extension; constant rate of traverse. Most modern machines use constant rate of extension.

- There are four principles used to measure the load in tensile testing: balance principle; pendulum lever principle; inclined plane principle; electronic principle.

- Moisture regain can be measured by gravimetric methods or electrical methods: gravimetric methods use changes in sample weight to determine regain; electrical methods use changes in electrical resistance to determine regain.

- There is no single technique to identify a fibre sample.

- The flame or burning test will sort fibres that are identifiable by microscopy from fibres that are identifiable by elemental analysis.

- Longitudinal, and if necessary, cross-sectional views of fibres under low magnification should enable identification of non-thermoplastic fibres.

- Nitrogen and chlorine tests will identify chlorofibres or modacrylics; other fibres need a further solvent test for identification. This should be carried out in the order specified, as some fibres dissolve in more than one solvent.

REVISION EXERCISES AND QUESTIONS

1 Why is linear density not always used to assess fibre fineness?

2 Calculate the linear density of the following:
   100 cotton fibres each cut to a length of 10 mm weighs 0.0017 g.

3 Calculate the fibre diameter in micrometres given the following information:
   image width = 11 mm at standard magnification.

4 What principle do sonic methods use to determine the linear density of a fibre?

5 What are the drawbacks to the following methods used to determine fibre length:
   a) hand stapling;
   b) oiled plate.

6 Why do modern indirect instrumental methods use fibre extent rather than straightened length?

7 Which mechanical tensile testing condition is used on most modern electronic instruments, CRE, CRL or CRT?

8 What mechanical principle does the Pressley fibre bundle tester use? What are the three drawbacks of this apparatus?

9 What is the major drawback of using a gravimetric method to determine the moisture reagin of a fibre sample?

10 What does the approach to the flame part of the burning test tell us about the fibre sample?

11 What can the smell of a sample during the burning test tell us?

12 Why is it necessary to solvent test samples in a certain order?

Fibre chemistry and fine structure

Introduction

Until the introduction of man-made fibres, only a few different fibres from natural sources were available, and until this century there was no clear idea about the nature of the molecules in these fibres.

During the early years of this century, scientists began to acquire the basic knowledge which allowed them to investigate the molecular structures of the plastics that were known at the time. This, together with the investigation of natural materials such as rubber, cellulose, wool and other proteins, established that molecules of these materials are made up of thousands of atoms joined together by chemical bonds.

It was also recognised that within these large molecules, basic sub-units existed consisting of perhaps 10 to 20 atoms. The large molecules were made up from many of the sub-units joined end to end. Hence, the term 'polymer' (many units) was coined.

A few years ago, most polymers that are used today were not known. Nowadays life without them can scarcely be imagined. Telephones, buckets, squeezy bottles, drainpipes, shoes, floor tiles and fibres are just some examples of the many objects made from polymers which are used in everyday life.

The varied properties of the items listed above is amazing, and they are all made from polymers. Equally surprising are the many and varied properties of fibres, yarns and fabrics that have been produced, particularly since the advent of man-made fibres. To understand the structure of fibres, the idea of polymers needs to be looked at in more detail.

Polymers

Polymers are formed when many small molecules join together end to end. The small molecules are termed **monomers** and the process of joining together is called **polymerisation**. The number of the monomer molecules which are connected to each other in a polymer molecule is called the '**degree of polymerisation**' (DP).

In Figure 4.1, the group in the brackets is called the repeat unit of the polymer and n is the degree of polymerisation. The DP of natural fibres is determined by nature during the growth of the plant. A cotton fibre has a DP of 5000–10 000; this means that on average there are 5000–10 000 units joined together in a molecule of cotton polymer. The polymer molecule is on average about 5000 nanometres (nm) long but only 0.8 nm thick. This can be understood by imagining that if the polymer was as thick as a normal pencil, its length would be around 50 metres; that is, half the length of a football field.

In man-made polymers, including fibres, the DP is controlled during the production process. It is very important in determining the properties of the fibre, particularly the tenacity or the dyeability. Some polymers are formed from two or more different monomers reacted together. Such polymers are called **co-polymers**. There is normally no regularity in the order of monomers which make up the co-polymer. Co-polymers are formed to try to produce polymers which have properties suitable for certain uses. A **homopolymer**, produced from one monomer, and a co-polymer produced from two monomers, may be represented as shown in Figure 4.2.

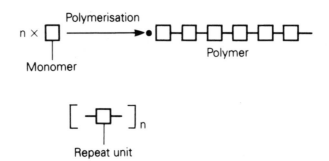

Figure 4.1 Polymerisation.

When some polymers are heated, they soften and in some cases they can melt. The molten polymer can be forced into a mould or, in the case of fibres, through the fine holes in a spinneret. On cooling, the polymer will solidify again in the shape of the mould, or as a fibre. Polymers which melt in this way are called **thermoplastic**. Examples of thermoplastics are polythene, polypropylene, polystyrene, polyamides and polyesters. Thermoplastic fibres can be heat-set; this is a permanent deformation caused by deforming the fibre and heating it to a certain temperature for a certain time. One example of the use of heat-setting is to give permanent creases in trousers, or pleats in skirts.

Other polymers do not melt or soften on heating. They can only be shaped by injecting the monomers into a mould and then heating to cause polymerisation. These polymers are called **thermosetting**. Examples are polyurethane, phenolic resins including Bakelite, and melamine. Thermosetting polymers are used for articles which must not soften when heated, such as electric fittings, saucepan handles and tabletops. They are not used for fibres.

There are differences in molecular structure between thermoplastic and thermosetting polymers. The two types of structure are shown in Figure 4.3.

There are two types of polymerisation process: **addition polymerisation** and **condensation polymerisation**. In addition polymerisation, all the atoms present in the monomer are also present in the polymer. The monomer units simply add to each other to form the polymer. In condensation polymerisation, small molecules, usually water, are eliminated during the reaction.

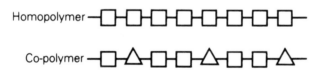

Figure 4.2   Homopolymers and co-polymers.

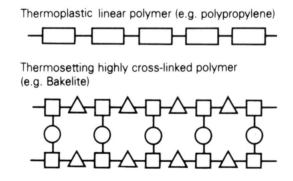

Figure 4.3 Thermoplastic and thermosetting polymers.

Addition polymerisation

The first synthetic polymerisation was carried out in 1933 by heating ethene under very high pressure (1000 atmospheres) with a trace of oxygen as a catalyst. The polythene formed by this process is now a very familiar pliable material used for polythene bags and other packaging materials. This is low-density polythene, so called because the polymer chains branch and consequently cannot pack together efficiently.

More recently, improved catalysts have been developed which enable the polymerisation to take place at atmospheric pressure. This is a tougher product with no polymer chain branching and is called high-density polythene. Two major fiber-forming polymers, (polypropylene and acrylic) and two minor ones (polythene and polyvinyl chloride) are formed by addition polymerisation. These are shown Table 4.1.

Other important materials like polystyrene, polymethyl methacrylate polytetrafluoroethylene (PTFE) and polyvinyl acetate are also produced by this process. The uses of these polymers and the non-textile uses of the ones in Table 4.1 are shown in Table 4.2.

Condensation polymerisation

The fibre-forming condensation polymers are the polyesters and the polyamides (nylons). In both cases in the polymerisation, water is eliminated. The term 'ester' in organic chemistry is given to compounds formed from the reaction between an alcohol and a carboxylic acid. Alcohols have an $-OH$ hydroxyl group and carboxylic acids have a $-COOH$ group.

Table 4.1   Fibre-forming addition polymers

Name	Monomer	Polymer
Poly(ethene)	$CH_2 = CH_2$ $\vert$ CH_3	$- CH_2 - CH_2 -$ $\vert$ CH_{3n}
Poly(propene) (Polypropylene)	$CH_2 = CH$ $\vert$ CH_3	$- CH_2 - CH -$ $\vert$ CH_{3n}
Poly(cyanoethene) (Acrylic)	$CH_2 = CH$ $\vert$ CN	$- CH_2 - CH -$ $\vert$ CN_n
Polyvinyl chloride	$CH_2 = CH$ $\vert$ Cl	$- CH_2 - CH -$ $\vert$ Cl_n

Table 4.2 Some uses of addition polymers

Polymer	Application
Polythene	Packaging, plastic bags, squeezy bottles, food boxes, bowls, buckets.
Polypropylene	Ropes, packaging, carpet backing, gutters and drain pipes.
Polyvinyl chloride	Shoes and wellingtons, window frames and doors, floor coverings, electrical insulation.
Polystyrene	Expanded foam for packaging, moulded components.
Polymethyl methacrylate	Transparent substitute for glass, car rear light fittings ('Perspex').
Polytetrafluoroe- thylene	Low friction coatings (frying pans), slide bearings.

POLYESTER

Polyester means 'many esters' and for the reaction to occur many times to form a long molecule, the monomer molecules must have two groups like the hydroxyl or the carboxylic acid. The fibre-forming polyester is formed from two compounds, and to carry out the reaction, the compounds are heated together at 250 to 270°C. The water formed is removed under vacuum.

POLYAMIDES

Polyamides are formed in a similar way except that one of the monomers is an amine. Amines are organic compounds with an $-NH_2$ group. This time a compound with two amine groups (1,6-diaminohexane) is reacted with a different dicarboxylic acid (hexandioic acid, sometimes called adipic acid). Water is again given off during the reaction.

The numbers in the name Nylon 6.6 refer to the numbers of carbon atoms in the sequences in the repeat unit; six between the two nitrogen atoms and six in the group from the hexandioic acid.

The other type of polyamide used in fibres is Nylon 6. Instead of being formed from two monomers, Nylon 6 is formed from one monomer which contains both an acid and an amine group.

The number 6 is again used to represent the sequence of carbon atoms in the repeat unit. On standing, 6-aminohexanoic acid loses water internally, forming a compound usually known as caprolactam. Caprolactam is the starting product for the polymerisation and a trace of water is added to convert it to the acid, which in turn loses water between molecules to polymerise.

PROTEIN FIBRES

Wool, silk and the other animal hairs are the protein fibres. The polymers can be regarded as condensation polymers, although the process producing the polymer takes place inside the follicle in the skin of the animal or in the silk worm. The exact chemical process involved in the formation of the polymer is not understood. The repeat unit in proteins is an amino acid, which as with the monomer for Nylon 6 contains both an acid, $-COOH$ group and an amino, $-NH_2$ group.

Amino acids are linked to each other by the peptide bond ($-CO-NH-$) to form the protein polymer. The peptide group is identical with the amide link in the polyamide polymer. The wool polymer, keratin, is composed of approximately 20 amino acids. In the fibre, the **keratin** molecule has a helical configuration.

CELLULOSIC FIBRES

The polymer in cotton, flax, jute and viscose fibres is cellulose. The structure of cellulose may be seen as a series of glucose molecules joined together through oxygen atoms to give molecules containing up to 10 000 glucose groups. Regenerated cellulosic fibres like viscose have much lower degrees of polymerisation, several hundred being a typical figure. The source of the cellulose for viscose is woodpulp and the same material is used for papermaking, though in a less refined state. Paper, viscose fibres and cotton are chemically identical.

Cellulose can be considered to be a condensation polymer formed from the glucose units. Initially, two glucose units combine to form a cellobiose molecule with the elimination of water and these polymerise further.

Cellulose does not normally dissolve in solvents. In the viscose process, a solution is prepared by chemically modifying the cellulose. The solution is then extruded into a suitable bath to regenerate the cellulose.

Cellulose is also the raw material for cellulose acetate fibres. The cellulose needs to be refined by scouring and bleaching. It is then reacted with acetic anhydride in acetic acid. This substitutes an acetate group for each of the hydroxyl groups in the repeat unit, giving cellulose triacetate. This polymer is soluble in dichloromethane and the solution can be extruded through fine spinneret holes into hot air using the solvent dry extrusion process. The solvent evaporates leaving the polymer in the fibrous form.

For cellulose diacetate, this polymer is allowed to react with water, reducing the average number of acetate groups in each repeat unit from 3.0 to 2.3. To achieve this, some units must remain fully acetylated while others have at least one hydroxyl group. This polymer is soluble in a different solvent, propanone (acetone), but fibres can be produced as described above.

Characteristics of fibre-forming polymers

There are many polymers available, some are fibre forming, others are not. The properties of polymers for good fibre formation are as follows: a high degree of polymerisation; good **inter-molecular forces**; linear and regular arrangement of monomers; high orientation of molecules; an inflexible repeat unit.

DEGREE OF POLYMERISATION

It is difficult to produce a good-strength staple fibre yarn from very short fibres. In the same way, a good-strength fibre cannot be produced from very short molecules. To produce a fibre with adequate properties, an average length of polymer molecules of at least 0.1 micrometres is needed. For some polymers, notably cellulose in cotton, the molecules are as long as 5 micrometres.

Polymers are often thought of as long molecules; they are certainly long and thin but they are much shorter than fibres. It would take 25 000 molecules, each 0.1 micrometres long, placed end to end to stretch the length of a short staple fibre only 25 millimetres long. Since the molecules are short relative to the fibres, a 'glue' is needed to hold the molecules together and give the fibre strength.

INTER-MOLECULAR FORCES

The 'glue' is the inter-molecular forces. These are forces of attraction between the molecules within a fibre. There are three main types: hydrogen bonds, polar bonds, and Van der Waal's forces.

Individually, all of these inter-molecular forces are weak in comparison to the covalent bonds within the fibre molecules, but the strength of all fibres depends on the number of these forces and the close packing of the polymer molecules.

Hydrogen bonds occur between positively charged hydrogen atoms in one polymer molecule and slightly negatively charged oxygen or nitrogen atoms in adjacent molecules. Hydrogen bonds exist in cellulose and polyamides.

Polar bonds are similar in origin, but occur between slightly charged atoms other than hydrogen in adjacent molecules. Polar bonds are much weaker than hydrogen bonds and are important in acrylic fibres. The nitrogen in the cyanide group is negatively charged and the carbon in the group is positive. Attraction can therefore occur between groups in different molecules. Polar bonds are important in polyester.

Van der Waal's forces are even weaker than polar bonds but they do occur between all adjacent atoms in all fibres. They are, however, the only inter-molecular forces operating in polypropylene fibres. They are also due to slight charges of opposite character in the polymer chains.

LINEAR AND REGULAR MOLECULES

Fibre-forming molecules must be linear and regular. This means that the chains must not be branched, as shown in Figure 4.4. Only linear polymers will be able to approach each other closely enough to form crystalline regions, as shown in Figures 4.5 and 4.6. Likewise, bulky side groups on the chains will prevent the formation of crystalline regions in

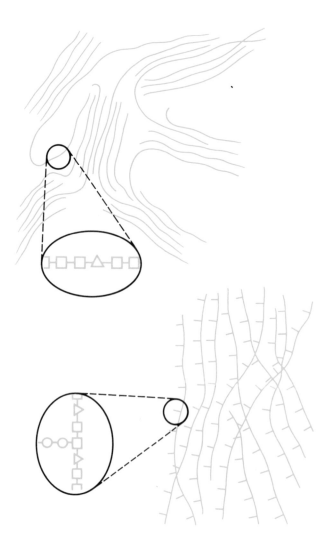

Figure 4.4 **Molecular packing in straight and branched chain polymers.**

the fibre. Polystyrene and polymethyl methacrylate both have large side groups to the polymer chain and do not crystallise. They are good for producing transparent plastic articles, but not good at forming fibres.

MOLECULAR ORIENTATION

The molecules within a fibre must also be lined up or orientated along the fibre axis. This orientation is induced in the fibre structure during extrusion and drawing. These processes will be described more fully in Chapter 5.

INFLEXIBLE MOLECULES

Regions of inflexibility in the fibre-forming molecule help the molecules to pack closely together to form crystalline regions. The inflexibility is due to ring structures in the molecules and these occur in cellulose and in polyester.

Fine structure

Fibre structure can be viewed at three different levels.

1. Gross morphology. This is normally defined as the shape and appearance of a fibre under an optical microscope.
2. Fine structure. This is concerned with the arrangement of the polymer molecules within the fibre.
3. Chemical structure. This is concerned with the characteristics of the molecules which make up the fibre.

The remainder of this chapter will consider fine structure. Fine structure is concerned with the way molecules come together and contribute to the overall structure of a fibre. Unlike microscopic examinations where differences in fibre surface and characteristic shapes can be identified and appropriately labelled, fine structure cannot be observed even by the most powerful of microscopes. The information that exists in this field comes from X-ray studies and other equally elaborate techniques.

The pattern of molecular arrangement within any one fibre varies widely. The molecules may be highly oriented, which means that they run parallel to each other and to the longitudinal axis of the fibre. Alternatively, they may be of low orientation, in which case they mostly lie at an angle to one another, crossing over at various points.

Linear polymer molecules cannot be completely ordered along their entire lengths. They tend to pass through alternating regions of order and disorder. Where several molecules converge and follow the same path for a fraction of their entire length, they give rise to **crystallisation** – parallel arrangements of molecules held together by strong intermolecular forces. Where they fail to come together in the manner described, they form **non-crystalline** or **amorphous regions**.

Many attempts have been made to illustrate this phenomenon by simulation and model making. The fringed micelle is one such model which was first proposed in the 1930s and, to a large extent, still remains fundamentally appropriate.

Fringed micelle model

This model shows how small 'micelles' or crystals are 'fringed' where polymer molecules leave and pass into the non-crystalline regions. A single polymer chain may pass through several crystalline and non-crystalline regions, so enabling many small crystals or crystallites to be formed. Figure 4.5 is a two-dimensional sketch of this model.

The short parallel areas represent regions of order where adjacent polymer segments happen to pack together regularly. The non-parallel regions represent adjacent segments which do not pack together regularly, thereby creating non-crystalline regions.

Fibre properties and fine structure

If a load is applied to a fibre with the structure shown in Figure 4.5, the polymer chains will tend to orientate themselves along the fibre axis. Once the chains are orientated, all of them will be able to resist the load and the fibre will show the resistance to deformation and good tensile strength, which are important characteristics of textile fibres.

During man-made fibre extrusion, the fibre-fine structure formed initially is like that in Figure 4.5. In drawing, the structure is elongated to create an orientated structure. In natural fibres, the molecules are arranged in an orientated manner as the fibre grows. An orientated fringed micelle structure is illustrated in Figure 4.6. Both the ordered and the

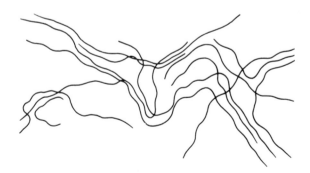

Figure 4.5 Fringed micelle model.

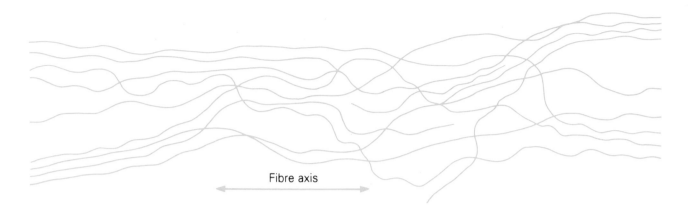

Fibre axis

Figure 4.6 Orientated fringed micelle model.

non-ordered regions are orientated in the direction of the fibre axis.

Fibre properties such as handle, strength, and moisture absorbency are all directly linked to the state of the fine structure.

In the crystalline regions, close packing and efficient intermolecular forces exist, effectively binding the chains together. The ordered regions enhance the fibre tenacity and inflexibility. In the non-crystalline or amorphous regions, where molecules are not closely packed, the intermolecular forces are weak. There is much greater accessibility to moisture and dyes. These regions contribute to the flexibility, extensibility and elasticity of fibres.

In natural fibres, the degree of crystallisation is determined by the growing process and hence can only be altered with difficulty. However, this is not the case in man-made fibres, where the ratio of crystalline to non-crystalline regions can be altered by the choice of drawing (stretching of the fibre which orientates the molecules within) and heat-setting processes to enhance or depress associated properties. In particular, the tenacity and extension at break of fibre are often modified to meet the needs of particular applications.

CHECK YOUR UNDERSTANDING

● All fibres are formed from polymers, but are not the only products containing polymers.

● Polymer means many units. Each individual molecule is known as a monomer and the process of joining all the monomers together to form a long chain molecule (polymer) is known as polymerisation.

● The degree of polymerisation is the number of monomer units in the polymer. These may be all the same type (a homopolymer), or two different randomly arranged monomers (a copolymer).

● There are two types of polymerisation: addition polymerisation, where all the atoms present in the monomer

are also present in the polymer; and condensation polymerisation, where some small molecules are eliminated during polymerisation.

● Polypropylene and acrylic polymers are produced by addition polymerisation.

● Polyester, polyamide, wool, silk, cotton, flax, jute and viscose polymers are produced by condensation polymerisation.

● There are three types of intermolecular forces. In descending order of strength they are hydrogen bonds, polar bonds and Van de Waal's forces.

● The properties of polymers for good fibre formation are: high degree of polymerisation; good intermolecular forces; linear and regular arrangement of monomers; high orientation of molecules; an inflexible repeat unit.

● Crystalline regions are highly ordered areas within the fibre. They give the fibre its tensile and rigidity properties.

● Amorphous regions are where the molecules are not closely packed within the fibre. They give the fibre its flexibility, extensibility and elasticity.

● In natural fibres, crystalline regions develop as the fibre grows. In man-made fibres, the ratio of crystalline to amorphous regions can be altered by drawing and heat setting.

REVISION EXERCISES AND QUESTIONS

1   Why is polythene not used as a textile fibre?

2   What do the numbers of Nylon 6 and Nylon 6.6 refer to?

3   What molecule is cellulose composed of?

4   Why is it not desirable to have a fibre containing mainly crystalline regions?

5   Why do crystalline regions give the fibre strength?

6   How is the ratio of crystalline regions to non-crystalline (amorphous) regions determined in:
      a) natural fibres; and
      b) man-made fibres?

Fibre production

Fibres may be subdivided into natural or man made. With man-made fibres, the producer is able to determine the fibre characteristics and tailor the dimensions to a large extent. Physical and chemical modifications can also be made, for example: matt or bright; strong and less extensible, or weaker and more extensible; and reduced flammability.

Natural fibres, however, are an agricultural crop and the producer has only limited control over the characteristics of the fibres produced; the ground conditions, the weather and the climate are the most important influences. Some chemical modifications are possible, however, such as reduced flammability and creasing.

This chapter will cover the methods of producing the most important fibres, both natural and man made.

Man-made fibre production

Man-made fibres can be modified at any stage during the production process (with additives such as pigments and delustrants) or immediately afterwards (by drawing, crimping or the application of finishes) to suit the end-product. The fibres can be created to match the requirements of the textile. Once engineered to fit a given application, fibre characteristics are identical from batch to batch. Alternatively, if a desired result cannot be achieved by modifying one type of man-made fibre, different types can be blended to give the required performance.

General principles

All man-made fibres are produced from polymers. These substances are solids at normal temperatures. The polymers which are the starting products for man-made fibres may well be in the form of chips, small particles of perhaps one to two millimetres in diameter and two to three millimetres in length.

In order to make filaments from these polymers, their physical shape must be altered, and the polymer chips must be converted to a liquid form. This is necessary as the polymer needs to be forced or extruded through fine holes to form filaments.

The process of producing a man-made fibre is often termed 'spinning'. This leads to confusion with the purely mechanical process of assembling staple fibres into a yarn, which is also called 'spinning'. The process of producing a man-made fibre will therefore be described as 'extrusion'.

There are three methods of extruding fibres: **melt extrusion**; **solvent-dry extrusion**; and **wet extrusion**. The method used for each fibre depends upon the ease of conversion of the polymer from solid to liquid state. If the polymer can be converted to a liquid form easily just by heating, then melt extrusion can be used. If the polymer is chemically damaged by heating but can be dissolved in a suitable solvent which will later evaporate, then dry extrusion is used. If the polymer cannot be heated or dissolved in an evaporative solvent, wet extrusion must be used.

The molecules in the extruded filaments are likely to be randomly orientated within the fibre. For the fibre to have a good tenacity and a reasonably low extension at break, the molecules need to be lined up along the fibre axis. In order to do this, a further process known as stretching or drawing is needed. This increases the tenacity and decreases the extension-at-break. With some fibres, drawing immediately follows the extrusion of the filaments, while in others it is an entirely separate process.

The three processes for man-made fibre production with their advantages and disadvantages will now be described in more detail.

Melt extrusion

This is the simplest of the fibre production processes. It is used for the production of polyester, polyamides and polypropylene. The polymer is melted and extruded through the

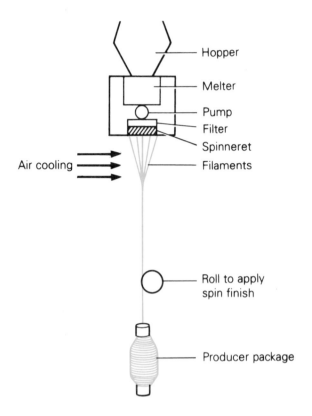

Figure 5.1 Melt extrusion.

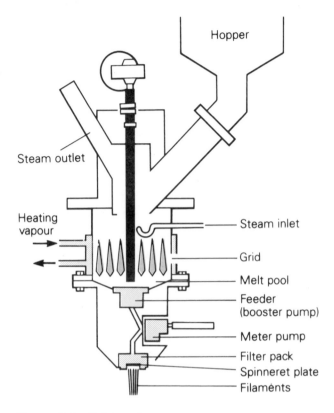

Figure 5.2 Grid melter.

fine holes of a **spinneret**, which is a metal plate with small holes of around 0.5 millimetres diameter drilled through it. The molten polymer passes through the holes in the spinneret plate and emerges into a stream of cool air which causes it to solidify. The solidified bundle of filaments is passed around a rotating roller and then forwarded to a collecting device.

The melt extrusion process can therefore be split into three stages, heating, extrusion and cooling.

HEATING

The polymer is in chip form to make it easy to store and transport. The chips are fed from a hopper into a melter heated to the correct extrusion temperature, dependent on the melting point of the polymer. The atmosphere in the melter must be oxygen free to prevent the oxygen attacking the molten polymer. Nitrogen is used in the melter for most polymers.

Polymer chips can only pass through the grid when they are in molten form. The polymer collects in the melt pool before being pumped through pipes in a steel extrusion block which contains the spinneret. At this stage the molten polymer is filtered to stop the small holes in the spinneret plate becoming blocked, interrupting the polymer flow and so causing broken filaments.

EXTRUSION

The stream of polymer melt is fed to the spinning head assembly. This assembly contains a meter pump which feeds the correct amount of polymer at high pressure to the spinneret plate.

The spinneret is a metal plate, roughly 50 millimetres in diameter, containing fine holes. It may contain from 1 to 50 holes if extruding continuous filament yarns, or over 100 holes if extruding tows for staple yarn production.

A tow is like a thick rope made of thousands of filaments which is later crimped if necessary, then cut into staple

Figure 5.3 Spinneret plate.

lengths, or stretched until the filaments break. Extrusion rates are approximately 1000 metres per minute.

COOLING

The molten filaments pass from the spinneret into a cooling air current which solidifies them. A conditioning tube containing steam allows further cooling and moisture absorption by hydrophilic fibres.

Oil to lubricate and create non-electrostatic properties is added at this stage. This oil is referred to as **spin finish** and is modified slightly to suit different customer types.

FIBRES PRODUCED USING THE MELT EXTRUSION METHOD

For a fibre to melt when heated, it must be thermoplastic. In order to use this extrusion method, the fibre polymer must melt without decomposition and be stable to at least 30° higher than its melting point so that the molten polymer viscosities are low enough for extrusion. The **viscosity** of a liquid is a measure of how thick it is. The longer the molecular chains, the more viscous or thick the liquid is. Mobility in the molten polymer is necessary for it to be extruded through small holes.

The following synthetic fibres are produced using melt extrusion: polyamide (Nylon 6 and Nylon 6.6); polyester; and polypropylene.

Due to high-speed wind up equipment after the cooling operation, extrusion rates of over 4000 metres per minute are possible. Due to air drag on the filaments at such high speeds and tension put on the filaments by the take-up roller, some drawing takes place at this stage. Yarn produced at these high speeds is known as **partially orientated yarn** (POY). This is often used for production of textured filament yarns. To fully orientate the yarn, it must undergo a further drawing operation.

No solvents are used for the polymer, and so the expensive and difficult solvent recovery processes are not needed with this method. If all polymers could meet the conditions necessary for successful melt extrusion, this would be the only method used.

DRAWING

The fibre is not yet suitable for use because the polymer molecules are not highly orientated along the fibre axis. To orientate them, the fibre is drawn, forming areas of crystalline order. In this process the fibre is in a plastic rather than a molten state. Figure 5.4 illustrates one of many arrangements for drawing fibres.

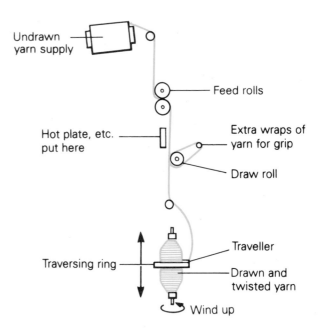

Figure 5.4 Drawing.

Drawing is achieved by passing the filaments over two sets of rollers which operate at progressively higher speeds. Typically, the second set of rollers or **godets** will run at least four times the speed of the first set, so stretching out the filaments. Sometimes the godets are heated to aid the drawing process and this is known as 'hot drawing', as opposed to 'cold drawing'. The draw ratio is the relative difference in the speed of these godets:

$$\text{draw ratio} = \frac{\text{surface speed of take-up rollers}}{\text{surface speed of feed rollers}}$$

END-PRODUCTS

If continuous filament yarns are required, they can be sold directly in **cake** form. The other option is to twist the yarn slightly to prevent filamentation, that is the separation of the individual filaments in the yarn body during processing. During twisting, the yarn is wound on to a **producer package**.

If staple fibre is required, there are again two options. The filaments are collected together in one rope, or tow, containing thousands of filaments. Some yarn spinners will buy the tow directly from the fibre producer. There are methods which convert the tow of continuous filaments to staple fibre lengths while retaining the continuity of the material – a process known as **tow-to-top conversion**. This is popular with worsted yarn spinners. The other option is to firstly crimp the filaments then cut them into exact staple lengths, which are then collected in a highly compressed bale form, in the same way that natural staple fibres are packaged.

Solvent-dry extrusion

If a polymer will not meet the conditions for melt extrusion, an alternative method of converting the solid polymer to a liquid state must be used. Dissolving in solvents is the next choice. If it is possible to use a volatile solvent, that is a solvent which is highly reactive, then the polymer can be extruded into warm air to evaporate the solvent away. This is known as solvent-dry extrusion and is the least used of the major fibre production techniques.

The polymer solution is extruded through a spinneret into a heated gas so that the solvent is rapidly evaporated from the filaments. The filaments drop through the hot gas stream for five to six metres to a rotating roller and are then fed to the wind-up device.

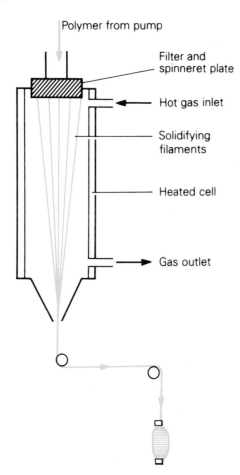

Polymer from pump

Filter and
spinneret plate

Hot gas inlet

Solidifying
filaments

Heated cell

Gas outlet

Figure 5.5   Solvent-dry extrusion.

DISSOLUTION

The obvious limitation of this production method is that it depends on the existence of a volatile solvent for the polymer. Cellulose diacetate fibres are produced using propanone (acetone) as the solvent, while cellulose triacetate fibres are produced from a solution in dichloromethane. Both of these solvents have low boiling points and are easily evaporated.

Some acrylic fibres are made by solvent-dry extrusion. The only suitable solvent, dimethyl formamide, is not particularly volatile. It boils at 153°C, so the air into which the fibres are extruded has to be heated to 130–200°C.

The polymer is dissolved in the solvent, until approximately 25 per cent of the solution is polymer. Due to the high viscosity of the solution, it usually needs to be heated so it will flow sufficiently to be extruded through tiny holes. At this stage, additives may be introduced. If the fibre is to be spun dyed, pigments are added to the solution; if it is to be dull or matt or semi-dull, then different levels of a delustrant can be added. As the name suggests, delustrant reduces the shine of the fibre.

Filtration and deaeration of the solution under a vacuum are necessary steps before the extrusion stage. Filtration will prevent the tiny spinneret holes from blocking, while deaeration removes any air bubbles. These two processes ensure that the flow of polymer during extrusion is not interrupted by broken filaments.

EXTRUSION

The solution is pumped to heated extrusion heads in which one or more spinnerets are located. These heads are often within the spinning cell or chimney so that the evaporating gas passes down around them. The pressures on the spinneret plate are great, due to the high speed of extrusion (500–1000 metres per minute) and the high viscosities of the polymer solution. A thicker spinneret plate is therefore used, with a hole of roughly 0.5 millimetres in diameter.

Hot nitrogen or air is circulated around the cell as the fluid filaments are extruded downwards. The solvent evaporates in the warm gas and is removed as vapour with the gas at the base of the cell.

Recovery and recycling of the solvent is necessary for both economical and environmental reasons. This should be possible, with less than ten per cent loss of solvent. Some of this 'lost' solvent will remain in the filaments.

FILAMENT FORMATION

The filament cross section bears little resemblance to the shape of the spinneret holes, unlike in melt extrusion. This is because solvent loss from the outer filament surface is so rapid that a skin forms. Solvent from the inner regions must diffuse through this skin and as the central region shrinks so the skin collapses about it. The skin rigidity and solvent evaporation rate determines the actual filament cross-section shape.

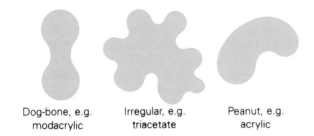

Dog-bone, e.g.   Irregular, e.g.   Peanut, e.g.
modacrylic   triacetate   acrylic

Figure 5.6 Filament cross sections.

AFTER-TREATMENTS

Filaments must be washed to remove any remaining solvent from the extrusion stage. Drawing can also be carried out at this stage, in either air or liquid. The cellulose acetate fibres have sufficient orientation of the molecules after extrusion and are therefore not drawn. The acrylic fibres are drawn as a separate process in the same way as the melt extruded fibres.

FIBRES PRODUCED USING THE SOLVENT-DRY EXTRUSION METHOD

The following fibres are produced using this method: cellulose diacetate; cellulose triacetate; polyacrylonitrile (Orlon, Dralon); and modacrylics.

Due to the mechanics of this extrusion method (the holes in the spinneret must be widely spaced), only a small number of filaments can be produced from a spinning head. The filaments have to be widely spaced to allow evaporation of the solvent without any fibres sticking together. This process is therefore most economic for continuous filament yarn.

The temperatures used are much lower than for melt extrusion, so this process can be used where the polymer would be degraded by high temperatures.

The solvents used are expensive, toxic, flammable and potentially explosive when mixed with air. Approximately three to six kilograms of solvent are extruded per kilogram of fibre and, on both economic and environmental grounds, very efficient solvent recovery is essential.

Wet extrusion

If the polymer does not melt without decomposition and will not dissolve in a volatile solvent, it must be dissolved in a non-volatile solvent to change it from a solid to a liquid state. There are two types of wet extrusion: physical process; chemical regeneration and physical process. In both processes, the filaments are extruded into a chemical bath to solidify them. This is slow (30–80 metres per minute) due to the drag forces on the filaments.

PHYSICAL PROCESS

The polymer solution, or dope, must be deaerated and filtered before being extruded through the spinnerets. The spinnerets are immersed in a **coagulating bath** which contains a dilute solution of the solvent in water.

The spinneret plates need to be resistant to corrosion so they are made from precious metal alloys. The hole size is much smaller than those used in melt and dry extrusion, but large numbers of holes can be used due to the liquid coagulant in the extrusion bath. Spinnerets with 20 000 holes on a 7.5 centimetre diameter face or 167 000 holes on a rectangular face are used. This makes the method economic for staple fibre or tow production.

Continuous washing, drawing and after-treatments are possible due to the low extrusion speed. A hot bath is used during the drawing stage, as the filaments are orientated and reduced to the required thickness. Examples of two fibres produced by this extrusion method are both polyacrylonitrile. They are Courtelle and Acrilan.

The solvents for the acrylic fibres are expensive and efficient purification and recovery are essential.

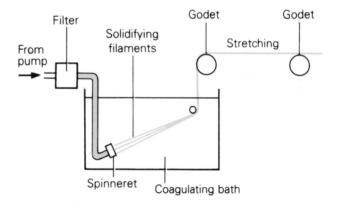

Figure 5.7 Solvent-wet extrusion.

CHEMICAL REGENERATION AND PHYSICAL PROCESS

In the case of viscose fibre, the polymer cannot be dissolved in its original form. The raw material – cellulose – must be chemically modified before it can be dissolved. The solution is then extruded in the same physical way described above, where the extruded fluid filaments are regenerated to cellulose.

The raw material for production of viscose is cellulose. This is usually obtained from wood pulp. The molecular weight of the cellulose molecules in wood pulp is too high for the extrusion process, so it must be chemically changed to soda cellulose. Oxygen is used as a means of reducing the molecular chain length to suitable levels. This oxidisation process must be carefully controlled. The aged, or degraded, soda cellulose is treated with carbon disulphide to form cellulose xanthate. When this xanthate is dissolved in alkali, it forms a brown liquid known as viscose. The viscose liquid is filtered, then left for a few days to allow the xanthate to start to degrade back to cellulose. This makes full regeneration easier during extrusion.

The spinning dope is extruded in the same way as for the physical process, except that the coagulating bath contains acid which neutralises the sodium hydroxide. Full regeneration of the filaments to cellulose does not occur in the coagulating bath, allowing them to be drawn and so orientated while they are still plastic.

In viscose production, the sodium hydroxide and sulphuric acid are relatively cheap and no recovery is attempted.

AFTER-TREATMENTS

As for solvent-dry spinning, the filaments of viscose must be washed to rid them of any chemicals from the coagulating bath. The filaments are dried, then suitable spin finishes are applied.

Natural fibre production

Cotton

Cotton is one of the oldest fibres known to man. Its production and use in various parts of Asia date back to as early as 3000 BC. Its arrival into Europe, however, is much more recent, in places as late as the sixteenth century. Its production and use have increased steadily ever since, so that cotton today is grown in more than 70 countries and accounts for almost half of the world's total production of fibres.

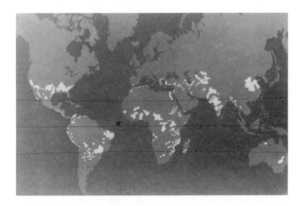

Figure 5.8   Areas where cotton is grown.

THE COTTON PLANT

The cotton plant is a member of the *gossypium* family. The life cycle of the annual variety is about seven months and the plant can grow to a height of two metres. It is cultivated best in warm or hot climates, with plenty of sunshine and an appreciable amount of moisture. Cultivation is restricted to land in a belt from 35° north to 30° south of the equator.

Perennial cotton is wild and grows much taller. Most of the cottons produced today are of the cultivated annual type.

PLANTING AND BOLL DEVELOPMENT

Sowing normally takes place in spring. The seeds take about three months to germinate and develop into young plants before they are ready to flower. The flowering period is very short, lasting two to three days, during which time the flower changes colour from creamy white to pink before finally withering away. A seed pod, or **boll**, is left behind as the fruit of the plant. Inside each boll there may be as many as 30 seeds. Hairs or fibres grow out of the skin of these seeds inside

Figure 5.9   Cotton bolls.

Figure 5.10   Cotton flower.

Figure 5.11 Cotton pod.

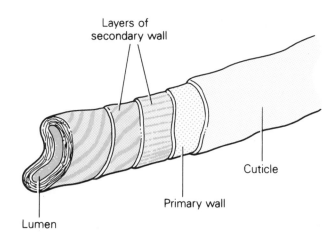

Figure 5.13 Cotton fibre.

Figure 5.12 Burst bolls in a field.

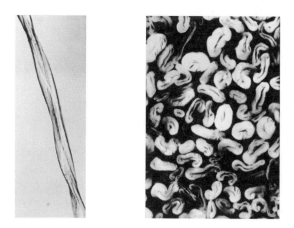

Figure 5.14 Photomicrograph of a cotton fibre.

the enclosed boll. The growth continues for about seven weeks before the boll is finally ready to burst open and reveal the cotton fibres inside. The boll-bursting period may take as long as two to three weeks as different bolls reach maturity at different times.

COTTON FIBRE CHARACTERISTICS

The individual cotton fibre is a seed hair made up from a single cell. It grows to its full length first, then thickens its walls by daily deposits of layers of cellulose, originating from the inner body of the fibre. The fibre has an outer waxy cuticle, a primary wall formed during the first stage of growth, and the secondary wall formed from the layers of cellulose. The fibre is said to be mature if the lumen – the inner canal – forms less than one third of the fibre diameter. Immature or dead fibres have relatively thin secondary walls.

The living fibre is cylindrical in dimension and resembles an elongated balloon, filled with a liquid nutrient. When exposed to sun, the liquid evaporates and the cylinder collapses. It then twists along its axis as it stretches out from its compact state when the boll opens, creating the convoluted ribbon characteristic normally associated with cotton.

COTTON HARVESTING AND GINNING

Hand picking is still common in most developing countries and produces the best quality fibres. A cotton field can be picked selectively as often as necessary and only top-quality mature cotton picked at any one time. This method, however, is slow and involves a lot of labour with considerable costs. It is economically viable only in countries with low labour costs.

Mechanical harvesters are much faster and far more efficient, despite their high initial capital costs. The only drawback with them is their inability to distinguish between open and closed bolls and the large quantity of trash they pick up, which increases the cost of the subsequent processes.

Figure 5.15   Hand picking.

Figure 5.16   Mechanical harvesting.

Harvested cotton is accumulated in large containers, which are sent to a **gin** for cleaning. Here, seeds, twigs, leaves and other foreign objects are separated mechanically from the cotton fibres. **Ginning** may have to be repeated when particularly bad harvests are put through in order to ensure sufficient cleaning. The cleaned cotton is then compressed into standard-weight bales, wrapped and labelled, ready for dispatch.

The cotton seeds are not thrown away or wasted; they are crushed to produce high quality, edible cooking oil and other natural ingredients. The residue, in various forms, is fed to cattle as a food supplement.

EFFECT OF GROWTH CONDITIONS ON COTTON FIBRES

The ultimate quality of cotton depends largely on the conditions under which the plant is grown, and this does not necessarily relate to climate alone. Factors such as seed type, soil variation, geographical location and effective pest control are also important.

Proper irrigation of the plant prior to flowering may be as important as adequate sunshine during fibre growth. Disruption in any part of this sequence influences the fibre quality.

Undernourished and immature fibres are short and thin. These create problems in the subsequent stages of fibre processing, since thin fibres not only break more easily but contribute to yarn irregularity by forming entanglements, or **neps**. These stand proud in yarns and their presence persists right through to the final product. Immature fibres do not dye to the same depth of shade as mature fibres and are therefore visible on the surface of dyed fabrics.

Cotton is prone to attack by pests and diseases whose effects depend on the nature of the menace and the speed at which it is treated. A diseased plant, at its best, may produce stained cotton of low grade or, at its worst, no cotton at all.

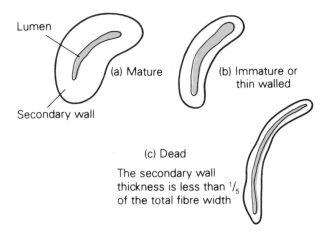

Figure 5.17   Cotton fibre maturity.

COTTON GRADING

Many varieties of cotton are grown in different climates and in all manner of soils and environments. Classification of some sort is necessary to differentiate and evaluate each brand. Grading of this nature has traditionally been carried out by **cotton classers**, who are individuals with considerable experience in handling fibres and who have acquired the skills necessary to categorise fibre types. They assess fibres based on three main criteria: fibre length, colour and trash content.

Despite their expertise, cotton classers' assessments are highly subjective and can vary from one assessor to the next, so affecting standards. In fact, most cotton-producing countries have their own cotton classers, whose judgments on a particular brand may not necessarily fall in line with the rest of the textile community.

Table 5.1 Cotton grades and qualities

Staple length (cm)	Lustre	Decitex	Fibre diameter (μ)	Quality	Example
2.5–6.25	High	1–1.5	10–15	High	Sea Island, Egyptian
1.25–2.75	Medium	1.25–1.9	12–17	Medium	American upland, Peruvian
0.9–2.5	Low	1.3–2.6	13–22	Low	Asian

High volume instrumentation (HVI) is a combination of instruments linked to a central computer, which are gradually replacing cotton classers by providing accurate, objective, repeatable data based on at least five measurable parameters: trash content; micronaire value (a measurement of fibre fineness and maturity); colour; fibre length; and strength. These properties can now be measured rapidly for each bale of fibre.

Table 5.1 shows the range of cotton grades available with respect to their length, lustre and fibre diameter.

Wool

Wool and other animal-hair fibres are a form of clothing purposely evolved by nature to keep the animals dry and warm. Prehistoric humans soon discovered they too could keep warm by wrapping the furry skin of a slaughtered animal around their bodies. Ancient Egyptians and Babylonians went much further by exploiting the full potential of these animals to their own advantage. They not only used the carcase and the milk and its by-products as their main source of food but its skin for making clothes and containers.

Spinning of wool fibres into yarn and interlacing them into flexible fabrics gradually followed. Although wool has been around for as long as history can record, it only started as a serious industry around the 11th and 12th centuries. Despite its long history and its accessibility to humans, wool today accounts for just five per cent of the total fibre market by weight, although 15 per cent of the market by value. This relatively low figure of wool production may be attributed to many factors. The number of animals producing the wool determines its availability, which in turn is dependent on the number of sheep that can live on an area of land. Wool is also a rather expensive fibre to produce and is not within the financial capabilities of the majority of the world's population. New man-made fibres have increasingly gained a

substantial market by offering wool-like properties at significantly lower prices.

TYPES OF SHEEP AND WOOL

Sheep are raised in many countries around the world, either for their meat or their wool or both. Countries such as Australia, New Zealand and South Africa are among the leading producers of wool. There are almost as many different types of wool as there are sheep in the world, depending on their breed variety and geographical location. However, they may be divided into two main categories: sheep living in the wild; and domesticated or interbred sheep.

The living habits and characteristics of sheep living in the wild have not changed for centuries; they have simply adapted to adverse climatic conditions by either developing a double coat to survive extreme cold conditions or have accumulated fat in their tail to combat long dry seasons.

Domesticated sheep, however, are effectively engineered by man to produce what is basically demanded of them. Certain varieties are bred for their meat only and their low quality wool is a mere by-product, while others are raised for their wool or cross bred to produce optimum qualities of both meat and wool. Domesticated sheep only produce an undercoat and, unlike the wild variety, have lost the habit of moulting.

The ultimate **wool quality** relating to the fineness, length, physical strength, handle, lustre, absorbency and inevitably price depends on many factors. The type of sheep, for example Merino or Blackface, governs the fineness of the fibres. This is also affected by the climatic conditions under which the animal is raised, for example harsh and coarse wool is often a direct consequence of extreme environments whereas a fine, short-staple wool is often produced in warm, dry climates. The overall health of the animal is the final major factor affecting quality as some diseases can enter the bloodstream of the animal and directly affect wool quality.

Figure 5.18   Photomicrograph of a wool fibre.

WOOL FARMING

In large wool-producing countries, sheep are usually rounded up towards the end of spring in 'sheep stations' and prepared for shearing. Animals may be washed a couple of days before shearing to reduce the dirt and grease present on the wool. They are then segregated according to their age, sex and type, as each class would produce a different quality of wool, and crowded into small pens where they are effectively forced to sweat, which will soften the wax on their skin, making it easier to remove the fibres by shearing. They are pulled out of the pen one by one and sheared using mechanical or, more usually, electrical shears. A skilled shearer will take about two and a half minutes to shear a sheep. Once the shearing is complete, the animal is allowed to return to the open.

The wool is removed in one piece because grease and entanglement holds it together. This is now referred to as a **fleece**. The fleece is tidied up and visible bits of dirt and extra-short fibres are removed ready to be sold. The sale is carried out either by direct transaction or, more traditionally, by public auction.

The newly shaven animal is then labelled by coloured dyes for identification. A few months after shearing, when the new wool has grown long enough for insects and mites of various kinds to breed on, the animals are once again rounded up and dipped or showered in a strong solution of pesticides.

As in the case of cotton, **wool classing** is also carried out by professional assessors who examine the animals prior to shearing with respect to their health, living condition, age and breed. The shorn-off wool or fleece is then appropriately classed according to fibre length, fineness, fibre character – e.g. lustre and overall condition – dirt and grease content.

Worsted yarns are spun from better-quality, longer fibres and are used to make high-quality clothing or suiting materials. **Woollen yarns** are spun from inferior wool of short staple length and are normally used in the knitting sector.

Jute

Jute is one of the world's most important natural fibres, being exceeded in quantity of production only by cotton. It is a **bast fibre** obtained from stalks of dicotyledonous plants, needing a fertile soil and damp climate for its growth. The plant grows from seed in approximately six months to a height of about five metres and is harvested after flowering by cutting near the ground. The open network of fibre strands from the stem of each plant is extracted by **retting**, where the plant is exposed to microbiological action in clean, slow-moving water, which causes the fibre bundle to separate from the woody stem. They are then washed and dried.

Natural jute has a yellow-to-brownish colour and a silky lustre. It is a low-cost fibre but rather labour intensive. The world's main jute-growing countries are Bangladesh, India and Thailand. It has been used traditionally for clothes, carpet backing and, more recently, for packaging.

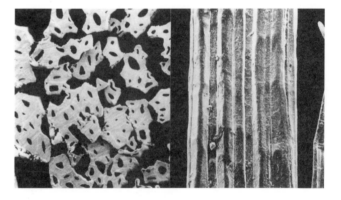

Figure 5.19   Photomicrograph of a jute fibre.

Flax

Flax, or **linen** as it is more commonly known in yarn and fabric form, has also been used for a long time. Like jute, flax fibre occurs in the stem of the flax plant (*linum usitatissimum*), which grows to a height of one metre or so. Flax is a cellulosic fibre, with natural colouring matters and impurities which are removed during bleaching.

The seeds are sown in the opening months of spring and the plants are ready for harvesting towards the end of summer. Fibre extraction from the plant and subsequent retting and

Figure 5.20 Photomicrograph of a flax fibre.

washing are similar to the technique adopted for jute. Eastern Europe and Russia are the main producers of the fibre, followed by France and Belgium. Prior to the advent of man-made fibres, flax or linen fabrics were popular for their ease of use and durability, but now it accounts for little more than one per cent of total fibre production.

Ramie

Ramie is also a bast fibre which has been grown in China for centuries. After retting, ribbons of fibre are stripped from the stem and are then known as **china grass**. Due to the presence of a large quantity of gum, the ribbons must be boiled to separate them into fibres for spinning. Although the fibres are coarser than flax and do not have the same softness, they are more lustrous and pure white in colour.

Ramie is often blended with cotton for use in clothing such as shirts, suitings, sweaters and blouses. It also has industrial uses such as ropes, twine and nets.

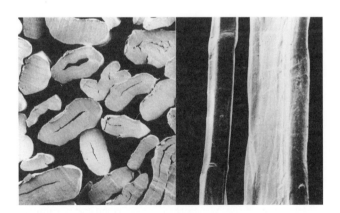

Figure 5.21 Photomicrograph of a ramie fibre.

Silk

Silk fibre is produced by the larvae of a moth known as *Bombyx mori*. These larvae or **silkworms** breed on mulberry leaves, growing to as much as 10 000 times their newly hatched weight.

When the silkworm is ready to begin its transformation into a moth, it extrudes liquid silk from two tiny holes in its head. The filaments harden as they come into contact with air, before being wound into a ball around the silkworm forming its cocoon. Silk fibres are retrieved by treating the cocoons in hot water baths before the moth eats its way out. The hot water kills the moth and removes the wax inherent in the fibre assembly allowing smooth unwinding of the cocoon. The filament produced may be as long as three kilometres.

Silk is a protein fibre with a lustrous appearance. In fact, the fibres appear as transparent rods under the microscope and have a distinctive triangular cross-sectional dimension. High tenacity and relatively good moisture regain make silk suitable for exotic dyeing and printing. Silk fabrics and garments are really luxury articles, usually associated with high fashion. Japan, Thailand and China have traditionally produced silk and to a large extent they still remain as the main producers of this unique fibre.

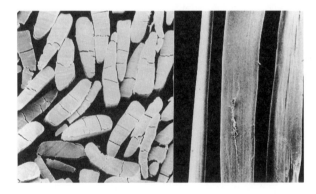

Figure 5.22 Photomicrograph of a silk fibre.

Fibre modifications

Most generic types of fibres can be modified so that they are better suited for particular uses. These modifications can be either physical or chemical.

Physical modifications

The drawing process during fibre production can be used to alter the tensile properties of a fibre. A high draw ratio increases the tenacity and the initial modulus of the fibre while decreasing the extension at break. Polyamides for reinforcing rubber in tyres need a high tenacity and a high modulus. Polyamides for blending with wool in carpets need a lower tenacity to be compatible with the wool.

The appearance of fibres can be altered in a number of ways. Normally, man-made fibres are lustrous and translucent. A small proportion of titanium dioxide (one per cent or less) in a fibre gives a matt appearance.

Melt-extruded fibres usually have a circular cross section and are cylindrical in shape. Non-circular spinneret holes are used to produce fibres with different shapes. A Y-shaped spinneret hole gives trilobal fibres with a glittery appearance. In a carpet, trilobal fibres do not show soiling to the same extent as circular fibres.

An annular-shaped spinneret will give circular fibres with a hollow centre. Polyester fibres with this shape have greater bulk than normal fibres and are used for the waddings in anoraks and duvets. Figure 5.23 shows some spinneret and fibre shapes.

Thermoplastic fibres such as polyester, polyamide and polypropylene can be textured. In normal continuous filament yarns, the individual fibres are straight and closely parallel. The result is that the yarns have low bulk and poor warmth-retaining properties. In textured yarns, the individual fibres are set into a wavy (crimped) pattern. This increases the bulk of the yarns and, consequently, the warmth of garments made from them. Textured polyamide fabrics can have stretch properties and are used, for example, in ski wear.

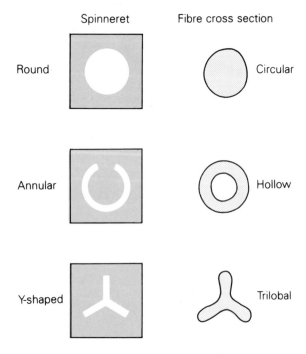

Figure 5.23 Spinneret hole shapes and fibre cross-sectional shapes.

Chemical modifications

Fibres are often modified chemically to give them particular characteristics. The polymers in man-made fibres can be altered by including other monomers to form co-polymers. Almost all acrylic fibres are co-polymers and include an additional monomer which gives affinity to either acid or basic dyes. Some acrylics, usually termed modacrylics, include extra monomers to reduce the flammability of the fibres. Polyamides can be modified to dye deeper.

Natural fibres can also be modified to improve their properties. The modifications are often applied as finishing treatments on yarns or fabrics. Cellulosic fibres can be treated to reduce the creasing of fabrics in use and during washing; they can also be treated to reduce their flammability. Cotton fibres can be mercerised – a swelling treatment to increase the fibre lustre (it also increases the tensile strength and dyeability). Wool can be treated so that fabrics do not felt and shrink when they are washed by machine.

CHECK YOUR UNDERSTANDING

- Man-made fibres can be tailored to suit the requirements of the end-product.
- All man-made fibres are produced from polymers, which are converted to a liquid form prior to being extruded through a spinneret. The filaments produced are solidified then drawn to develop the desired tensile properties.
- There are three main methods used to produce man-made fibres: melt extrusion (the simplest method), solvent-dry extrusion and wet extrusion. The polymer chemical properties determine which method is used.
- The end products of the man-made fibre producer are: cake (directly from the filament production line); producer package (the filaments in the yarn are given a slight twist to prevent filamentation); tow (a continuous rope of thousands of filaments for converting to top used in the worsted industry); and bale (highly compressed and crimped cut staple lengths).
- Filaments and staple fibres are usually given a spin finish, which is an oil after-treatment with non-electrostatic properties.
- Cotton is the seed hair of a plant, with a two-stage growth. First, the fibre grows to its full length, then the hollow tube is strengthened daily by layers of liquid cellulose. When mature, the fibre has a central lumen, or canal, of less than one third of the fibre diameter. The remainder is composed of layers of cellulose with an outer waxy cuticle.
- Cotton seeds are planted in spring. The plants develop flowers some three months later. The pod, or boll, remaining after flowering contains roughly 30 seeds from which the cotton fibres grow. The fibres dry out when the boll finally bursts, and are harvested by hand or machine.

- There are many different varieties of cotton, and within any one variety there will be variations in length, fineness and lustre. Grading of cotton was traditionally done by trained experienced individuals, but new instrumentation which assesses every bale of cotton is gradually replacing the subjective grading system.

- Wool is the hair from sheep. It may be the by-product from animals bred for meat alone, or a major product of animals bred for both wool and meat. Australia, New Zealand and South Africa are the main producing countries of this relatively expensive fibre.

- Sheep are rounded up in spring and sorted according to sex and age. After sweating the animals to soften the protective grease which coats the fibre, the sheep are sheared. The fleece is tidied by removing the damaged fibres from the legs and belly, then auctioned off. The sheep is given an identification mark and later in the year it is dipped in pesticide.

- There are many varieties of wool. The quality – fineness, length, strength, handle, lustre, and absorbency – is determined by climatic conditions, health of the individual animal and breed type.

- Jute has the second largest production of natural fibres. It is a bast fibre obtained from the stem of a plant and is grown mainly in Bangladesh, India and Thailand.

- Flax is another bast fibre grown mainly in Eastern Europe, Russia, France and Belgium. It is more commonly known as linen when spun into yarn.

- Ramie is also a bast fibre originally grown in China.

- Silk is the only natural filament, produced by a moth larvae. The cocoon of the larvae is unwound to give as much as 3000 metres of a twin filament.

- Physical modifications of fibres include: tenacity and extension for man-made fibres (increasing the draw ratio increases the tenacity and reduces the extension at break); appearance in man-made fibres by altering the amount of delustrant added to give a more lustrous or matt fibre; cross-sectional shape of melt-extruded man-made fibres, so altering the lustre; bulk in man-made fibres by altering the cross-sectional shape (hollow polyester); and texturing, which gives man-made continuous filaments more stretch, bulk and warmth.

- Chemical modifications include co-polymer production, for example acrylic fibres given extra monomers to reduce flammability (known as modacrylics). Natural fibres can be altered to reduce creasing and flammability or to stop felting.

REVISION EXERCISES AND QUESTIONS

1 Why is the simplest form of extrusion – melt extrusion – not used for all polymers?

2 Why is wet extrusion sometimes necessary?

3 What does drawing do to man-made fibres?

4 What fibres are produced on each of the three extrusion processes?

5 Why are mechanical cotton harvesters used in industrialised countries?

6 What are cotton seeds used for after ginning?

7 What problems do immature cotton fibres create?

8 What cotton fibre properties do modern High Volume Instruments test?

9 Why has wool only got a 15 per cent share of the market value?

10 What is wool quality dependent upon?

11 How are jute, flax and ramie fibres extracted from the plant?

12 Trilobal fibres have a more glittery appearance. What is the other advantage associated with this cross-sectional shape?

13 Acrylic fibres are usually co-polymers. One co-polymer, modacrylics, has the ability to reduce flammability. What other benefits could another co-polymer acrylic give?

Yarn parameters and characteristics

Introduction

Textiles are an essential part of our daily life. We wake up in the morning, throw back the bed covers, dress in a variety of woven or knitted clothes and perhaps climb into vehicles with textile-reinforced tyres. All these textiles are formed from and many are held together by yarns.

The end-product requirements of many of these textiles are very different. Carpet yarns need to be bulky, resilient and wear resistant; underwear has to be made from soft, absorbent, smooth yarns; and seat belts must be composed of optimum-strength yarns. Care must be taken when designing yarns to ensure that the character and properties are correct for the end-product. Often a compromise balance of properties is accepted since optimisation of any one property can usually only be obtained at the expense of another. Strength, elasticity, extension, handle, resistance to abrasion, appearance and aesthetic appeal of the yarn must all be viewed in the light of the end-product requirements.

The properties and character of yarns are obtained partly from those of the constituent fibres, and partly from the way that the fibres are arranged, that is the yarn structure. Differences in the structure of some yarns may be subtle, even under a microscope, but they lead to major differences in the end-product performance.

Yarn types

'A textile yarn is an assembly of substantial length and relatively small cross section of fibres and/or filaments with or without twist.'
Tubbs, M. C. (ed.) *Textile Terms and Definitions*, 9th edn, The Textile Institute, London, 1991.

Looking at the above definition, there is very little restraint on what could be classed as a yarn. This is because the definition must hold true for every single yarn, no matter how obscure. It is more easily understood if we build some sort of classification system for yarns.

To make the first split of this huge class of yarns, we can divide all yarns into either staple-spun yarns or continuous filament yarns. These may be either single yarns or compound (more than one) yarns.

Spun-staple yarns consist of staple fibres assembled and bound together by various means (usually twist) to produce the required characteristics such as strength, handle and appearance.

Continuous filament yarns are produced either by combining the required number of filaments together as in the silk throwing process or, more commonly, by producing the required number of filaments and thickness of filaments simultaneously in one spinning operation, as in the case of man-made fibres. The typical filament yarn is, therefore, a collection of parallel filaments lying close together and virtually straight, running the whole length of the yarn. As the filaments are as long as the yarn itself, there is no need for them to be bound together. Yarns with one filament are referred to as **monofilaments** and those with more than one as **multifilaments**.

Both staple and filament yarns can then be subdivided further.

Filament yarns

The range of filament yarns is not as diverse as that for spun-staple fibre yarns. **Flat continuous filament** yarn is the name given to the standard filament yarn to distinguish it from a **textured continuous filament**. Filaments can be extruded from two different substances forming a bicomponent filament yarn, or sheets of polymer can be cut into strips forming tape yarns.

FLAT CONTINUOUS FILAMENT YARNS

Man-made continuous filament yarns may be produced in either monofilament or multifilament form. In addition, the filaments may be matt (dull) or bright (lustrous), according to requirements. Standard-filament yarns are known as 'flat' filament yarns, in contrast to textured yarns.

Figure 6.1 Flat continuous filament yarn.

TEXTURED YARNS

These are man-made continuous filament yarns that have been modified by subsequent processing to introduce durable crimps, coils, loops or other distortions into the filaments. There are several different texturing methods which introduce deformations into the filaments in a number of different ways.

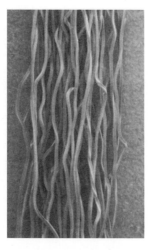

Figure 6.2 Textured continuous filament yarn.

BICOMPONENT YARNS

Yarns can be produced from two different components at the fibre extrusion stage. The components may be designed so that differential shrinkage occurs during later process stages to introduce kinking or spiralling, imitating the natural structure of wool fibres.

TAPE OR SPLIT FILM YARNS

Thin sheets of polymer may be cut into narrow strips or ribbons to produce tape or film yarns. The strips may be fibrillated (split along their length to form a network of interconnected fibres) to give an appearance similar to that of a flat filament yarn.

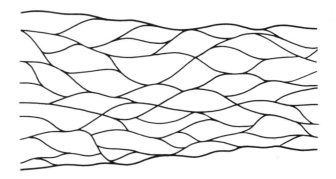

Figure 6.3 Split film yarn.

Staple fibre yarns

There is a vast range of staple fibre yarns that can be classified in a number of ways: by fibre length (short staple being less than 60 millimetres, long staple greater than 60 millimetres); by yarn construction (single, plied, cabled, multiple, fancy); and by spinning method, which is a much more detailed method of classification, as the following shows.

RING SPUN YARNS

These are produced on the ring and traveller system from a wide variety of fibre types. This is the most popular system of staple fibre yarn production, as it utilises a wide range of fibre types, fibre finenesses and fibre lengths. The component fibres are twisted around each other to set up frictional forces between the fibres to impart strength to the yarn.

Figure 6.4 Ring spun yarn.

ROTOR SPUN YARNS

Like ring spun yarns, they consist of fibres bound together by twist. Rotor spun yarns are generally only produced from short staple fibres. There are a number of differences in quality between ring and rotor yarns. In general, rotor yarns are more regular but weaker than comparable ring spun yarns.

Figure 6.5 Rotor spun yarn.

TWISTLESS YARNS

These are yarns produced from staple fibres where the consolidation of the fibres is by means of some form of adhesive.

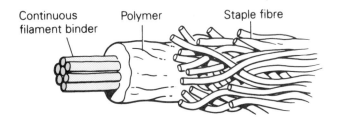

Figure 6.6 Twistless yarn – bobtex.

FASCIATED YARNS

These are yarns consisting of a parallel bundle of fibres bound into a compact structure by surface wrappings at irregular intervals of staple fibres. Air-jet yarns are a typical example.

Figure 6.7 Air-jet spun yarn.

WRAP SPUN YARNS

These yarns consist of a parallel bundle of staple fibres bound into a compact structure by another yarn, usually continuous filament. They can be produced using both long and short staple fibres.

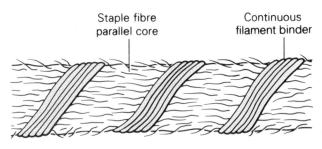

Figure 6.8 Wrap spun yarn.

CORE SPUN YARNS

Core yarns are characterised by having a central core wrapped with staple fibres. These are produced in a single operation by simultaneously feeding a yarn and staple fibres through the delivery rollers of a spinning frame. A wide range of core yarns can be produced, for example: cotton with filament core; hair fibres with cotton core; and various fibres with an elastomeric core.

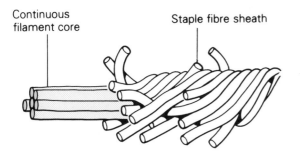

Figure 6.9   Core yarn.

SELF-TWIST YARNS

Self-twist yarns are two-ply yarns produced in a single operation. During manufacture, each component is twisted in alternating directions in short segments. The two components are subsequently put together in such a way that they twist together (self-twist) to form the final yarn. Self-twist yarns are predominantly produced from long staple fibres.

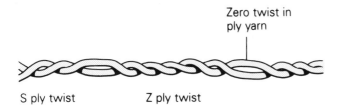

Figure 6.10   Self-twist yarn.

FRICTION SPUN YARNS

These yarns are produced on spinning systems which use two rotating rollers to collect and twist individual fibres into a stable yarn structure.

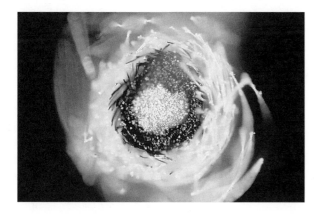

Figure 6.11   Friction spun yarn.

Compound yarns

These are quite simply yarns with more than one strand. Sometimes they are referred to as complex or multiple yarns.

FOLDED OR DOUBLED YARNS

A yarn in which two or more single yarns are twisted together in a single operation, for example two-fold, three-fold, four-fold.

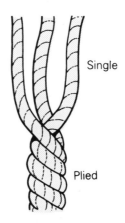

Figure 6.12   Folded or doubled yarn.

CABLED YARNS

A yarn in which two or more folded yarns are twisted together in one or more operations. Folded and cabled yarns can be produced from staple yarns, continuous filament yarns or a combination of both.

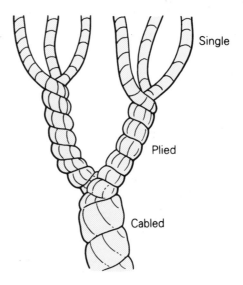

Figure 6.13   Cabled yarn.

Novelty yarns

There are a wide range of yarn types generally produced in small quantities which differ from the normal appearance of staple or continuous filament yarns.

FANCY YARNS

A yarn that differs from normal construction of single and folded yarns by way of having deliberately produced irregularities in its construction. Fancy yarns can be made from any fibre in staple or continuous filament form. Typical effects are knops, loops, snarls and slubs.

METALLISED YARNS

These are generally produced from aluminium sheets which have been laminated with plastic film. This is then cut into thin strips to form a flat yarn.

Yarn parameters

There are numerous ways of describing yarns. The two main parameters are a measure of the thickness of the yarn and the degree and direction of twist.

Grist systems (count or linear density)

Different end-uses require yarns of different thickness. Measuring the diameter of a yarn is not an easy task because not all yarns have a circular cross section, and some are easily deformed during measuring. Even if a suitable system was developed for measuring the yarn diameter, the time involved in taking enough readings to make sure the results were accurate would be too great.

The accepted way to indicate the thickness of a yarn or of material from other stages in yarn processing, is to give the **count** or linear density. A length of the material is measured out, then weighed.

The textile industry has developed different yarn production systems in different localities and each of these has chosen a different way of expressing the count or linear density to suit its own local conditions. The linear density is expressed directly – mass per unit length; the count is expressed indirectly as the length per unit mass. Each system is referred to as being either direct or indirect. For example, the cotton count system is indirect (the lower the number the coarser the material), while the tex system is direct (the lower the number, the finer the material).

Obviously, it would be easier if there was only one system that was used by everyone. In 1956, the textile section of the International Organisation for Standardisation voted that the tex system should be the universal system, but many countries have been very slow in adopting this chosen system.

DIRECT SYSTEMS

The tex system
The tex number is defined as the weight in grams of one thousand metres of the material.

$$\text{tex} = \frac{\text{weight in g}}{\text{length in m}} \times 1000$$

The denier system
People might be familiar with this system as it is used for ladies hosiery, for example 15 denier tights or 10 denier stockings.

Denier is a direct system, defined as the weight in grams of nine thousand metres of the material.

$$\text{denier} = \frac{\text{weight in g}}{\text{length in m}} \times 9000$$

INDIRECT SYSTEMS

The cotton count system
This was developed by the short-staple cotton spinners. The definition of the cotton count is the number of hanks of 840 yards in length that weigh one pound in weight.

For yarn, it is conventional to measure out a lea (a length of 120 yards) and weigh this in grains. The grain is a division of the pound. There are 7000 grains in one pound. Again, approximately 20 yards of roving and 10 yards of sliver are considered to be sufficient, this then being converted to cotton count using the formula:

$$\text{cotton count} = \frac{\text{length in yd}}{\text{weight in grains}} \times \frac{7000}{840}$$

The worsted count system
This is another indirect system, very similar to the cotton count system, but the unit of length used is different. The worsted count is defined as the number of hanks of 560 yards in length that weigh one pound in weight.

The woollen system (Yorkshire)

Again, an indirect system that uses a different unit of length. Woollen count is defined as the number of hanks of 256 yards in length that weigh one pound in weight.

There is more than one system used by the woollen industry. Others include Irish, Galashields, Dewsbury, West of England.

The metric system

This is an indirect system with a major difference. It uses metric rather than imperial units and has been used for export. Most spinners who export their yarn to Europe are requested to quote metric count in their package labels.

The metric count is defined as the number of kilometre metre lengths that weigh one kilogram.

CONVERSION FACTORS

There are a number of conversion factors used to convert between the systems:

$$\text{cotton count } (Ne_c) = 590.5 \div \text{tex}$$
$$\text{metric count } (Nm) = 1000.0 \div \text{tex}$$
$$\text{worsted count } (Ne_w) = 885.8 \div \text{tex}$$
$$\text{woollen count } (Ny) = 1938.0 \div \text{tex}$$
$$\text{denier} = \text{tex} \div 0.1111$$

Yarn twist

A minimal amount of twist is inserted in continuous filament yarns, just sufficient to hold the filaments together during subsequent processing. Twist is needed in the majority of staple spun yarns to bind the individual fibres together to form the yarn.

DIRECTION OF TWIST

Twist can be inserted in either of two directions, clockwise or anticlockwise. The usual designation for twist direction is to use the letters S or Z. A single yarn has **S twist** if, when it is held in a vertical position, the fibre inclination to the axis of the yarn forms the centre of the letter S. Similarly, the yarn has **Z twist** if the fibre direction forms the centre of the letter Z.

The majority of single yarns are spun with the twist in the Z direction, S twisted yarns are often called reverse twisted by the spinner. The twist characteristics, that is the way the yarn behaves, is totally unaffected by the direction of twist in single yarns.

The direction of twist is very important in yarn doubling as the direction and amount of doubling twist in relation to the single yarn twist affects many of the resultant yarn properties.

The twist level is usually denoted as the amount of twist (turns) per unit length, that is turns per metre or turns per centimetre. For most purposes, this simple method of expressing the amount of twist is adequate but the expression has no reference to the angle of twist, for example a coarse yarn with eight turns per centimetre has a totally different angle of twist and character to a fine yarn with eight turns per centimetre.

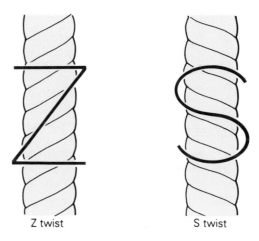

Figure 6.14 Twist directions.

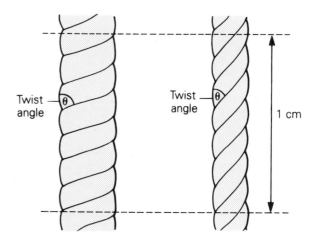

Figure 6.15 Coarse and fine yarns with the same twist level but different twist angles.

TWIST FACTOR

The angle of twist is the factor that determines how the yarn will behave. Yarns with a low twist level will have a lower angle of twist, and will be relatively soft, bulky yarns. Yarns with higher twist angles will be strong, lean and hard yarns, while over-twisted yarns will have very high twist angles; they will be very hard, weaker and twist lively, that is they will snarl easily when not under tension.

In terms of the characteristics of the twisted material, it is the twist angle (θ) which is the important factor, yet all machine calculations use the measure of turns per unit length. It is essential that the relationship between these two measures is understood.

In Figure 6.16, (a) represents a length of yarn ℓ with a diameter d and one complete turn of twist has been inserted. If the surface were peeled from the yarn and laid flat, it would look like the rectangle shown in (b). It is then possible to determine the following relationships:

$$\tan \theta = \frac{\pi d}{\ell}$$

$$\ell = \frac{1}{\text{turns per unit length}}$$

$$d = \sqrt{\text{yarn tex}}$$

$$\therefore \tan \theta = \text{turns per unit length} \times \sqrt{\text{yarn tex}}$$

So to spin a range of yarns with different values of tex but with the same twist characteristics (determined by the helix angle θ), the ratio of turns per unit length to the $\sqrt{}$ yarn tex must be kept constant. This relationship is usually expressed in the following way:

$$\text{turns per unit length} = \frac{K}{\sqrt{\text{tex}}}$$

where K is referred to as the twist factor and the turns per unit length are in turns per metre.

For the tex system,

$$\text{twist factor} = \sqrt{\text{tex}} \times \text{turns per m}$$

but with an indirect system like cotton count,

$$\text{twist factor} = \frac{\text{turns per inch}}{\sqrt{\text{cotton count}}}$$

Some typical tex twist factors are listed in Table 6.1.

Table 6.1 Typical twist factors

Short staple end-use	Tex twist factor
Doubling weft	2900–3200
Ring weft	3200–3500
Ring warp	3800–4300
Voile	4900–5300
Crepe	5700–7700
Rotor	3700–4700

The actual twist factor used depends on the fibre type (in particular, the shape of the cross section and coefficient of friction), the fibre length (longer fibres require lower twist factors) and the end-use.

TWIST/STRENGTH CURVES

The purpose of twist in spun-staple yarns is to bind the fibres together and so give the yarn strength. If the level of twist is low, when a load is applied, the yarn may break due to fibre slippage not fibre breakage. As the level of twist increases, this heightens the level of cohesiveness (binding) between the fibres and the yarn will be stronger and more compact. There is an optimum level of twist beyond which the yarn strength will begin to fall. This can be related to two factors: coherence of the fibres due to twist and fibre obliquity (the fibre angle). These two factors can be seen in Figure 6.17. The curve of a typical staple yarn is also shown, where strength rises to an optimum and, as further twist is inserted, the strength begins to fall.

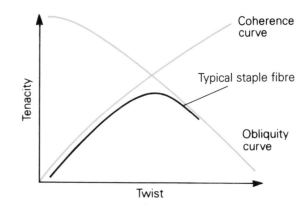

Figure 6.17 Twist/strength curve.

Yarn characteristics

The definition of a textile yarn leaves no doubt of the wide variety of yarns produced in the textile industry. Some of these yarns will have similar characteristics, others will have

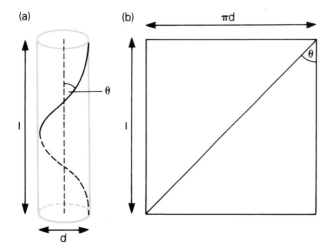

Figure 6.16 **The twist angle.**

quite different characteristics. This is not surprising when the various end-uses of textile yarns are considered, for example clothing, household fabrics, industrial/medical yarns and fabrics are three quite different applications.

VARIABLES IN YARN PRODUCTION

Careful scrutiny of the definition of a yarn shows that, at one extreme, a textile yarn can be a monofilament of synthetic origin while, at the other extreme, it may be a staple yarn produced from natural fibres. Between these two extremes the yarns produced in the industry are endless in variety because there are so many variables. Some of these are listed below.

1. Type of fibre or filament.
2. The dimensional and physical characteristics of the fibre or filament, such as length characteristics, fineness, cross-sectional shape, crimp and density.
3. The mechanical properties of the fibre or filament, for instance tenacity, extensibility, elasticity, torsional rigidity and flexural rigidity.
4. The general properties of the fibre or filament, such as surface properties including frictional properties, resistance to abrasion, dimensional stability, moisture regain, resistance to bacteria, fungi, mildew, moths, static properties, colour, and properties when wet.
5. The yarn production systems, including carded cotton or short-staple system, combed cotton system, woollen system, worsted system and the other systems developed from the above.
6 The method of final yarn formation, for instance ring, rotor, wrap spinning, core spinning, air jet spinning and friction spinning.
7. The components of the yarn: 100 per cent natural fibres, 100 per cent man-made fibres, blend of natural and man-made fibres, blend of fibres with filaments.
8. The linear density of the yarn and the level of twist.
9. Yarn in single, plied or cabled state and the construction if plied or cabled.
10. If the yarn is 100 per cent filament in construction, is it flat or textured? If textured, what is the method of texturing?

Table 6.2 Physical properties and performance characteristics of different yarn types

Yarn type	General yarn properties
Staple yarns: Carded cotton Combed cotton Woollen Worsted Linen	Excellent handle; good covering power; good comfort rating; reasonable strength; reasonable uniformity.
Continuous filament yarns: Natural Non-synthetic Synthetic	Excellent uniformity; excellent strength; can be very fine; fair handle; poor covering power.
High bulk yarns: Staple Continuous filament	Good covering power with light weight; good loftiness or fullness.
Stretch yarns: Continuous filament	High stretchability; good handle and covering power.
Special end-use: Tyre cord Rubber Core yarn Cabled Split film	Purely functional; designed to satisfy a specific set of conditions.
Novelty yarns: Fancy yarns Metallic	Excellent decorative features or characteristics.

NOTES ON THE VARIABLES

Natural fibres have characteristics typical of the group to which they belong – for example cotton, wool, flax and jute have characteristics which identify them as natural cellulosics – and there is little that can be done to change these characteristics. Different varieties are produced within each fibre group, each with slightly different characteristics, for example American upland cotton differs from Egyptian type cotton. In addition, the properties or characteristics of the fibres in a bale of Egyptian type cotton will differ in length, fineness and maturity of the cotton fibres.

Man-made fibres are a different proposition because they can be produced in different staple lengths (and normally all of the same length in a bale), different degrees of fineness, different cross-sectional shapes, with or without crimp, and their mechanical properties can be modified. Consequently, they can be produced on various yarn production systems and the fibre properties can be modified to fit in with end-use requirements of the yarn.

The yarn production system used and the method of final yarn formation are two important factors which affect the structural geometry of the yarn and these, together with the physical properties of the fibres or filaments, combine to give a yarn of certain physical properties and performance characteristics.

Yarns can be classified according to their physical properties and performance characteristics, as shown in Table 6.2.

CHECK YOUR UNDERSTANDING

● A yarn can be defined as an assembly of substantial length and relatively small cross section of fibres and/or filaments with or without twist.

● The basic classification of yarns is by constituents: continuous filament or staple spun. Continuous filament yarns can be further subdivided as flat (multifilament and monofilament) standard yarns, or textured filament yarns.

● Staple yarns are broadly classed as short staple or long staple. There are many ways of subdividing staple yarns, for example by construction – single, plied, cabled, compound, fancy; or by spinning method – ring, rotor, friction, wrap, fasciated, self-twist, core, twistless.

● The thickness of a yarn can be expressed directly: mass per unit length, as in the case of the tex system – or indirectly: length per unit mass, as in the case of the cotton count system. With direct systems, the higher the number, the thicker the yarn; with indirect systems, the higher the number, the finer the yarn.

● The twist direction, S or Z, has no affect on the single yarn characteristics. The angle of twist in the yarn determines its behaviour: low twist angles give soft, full, weak yarns; high twist angles give strong, hard, lively yarns.

● The twist factor describes the relationship between twist level and yarn thickness. With continuous filament yarns, minimal twist is inserted.

● Yarn characteristics are partly determined by those of the constituent fibres and partly by the arrangement of these fibres (yarn structure).

● The yarn structure is affected by: production system; spinning method; linear density; twist angle; simple or complex structure (plied, cabled, single); flat filament or textured; and fibre characteristics such as crimp, surface characteristics, mechanical properties.

REVISION EXERCISES AND QUESTIONS

1. Name the only continuous filament yarn that is composed of natural filaments.
2. Why are the twist levels only minimal in continuous filament yarns?
3. Calculate the tex value for the following yarn:
   100 m weighs 4.2 g
4. Calculate the cotton count for the following yarn:
   120 yd weighs 60 grains
5. Convert the yarn in Question 3 to cotton count.
6. Convert the yarn in Question 4 to tex.
7. Calculate the twist factor of the following short staple ring spun yarn:
   turns per m = 700
   tex value = 30
8. What could the yarn in Question 7 be used for?
9. How could the end-products of yarns be classified?

Staple spinning systems

The basic principles of staple spinning are common to all spun-yarn manufacturing routes. It is in the detailed application of these principles that the differences between the systems become apparent.

The main staple spinning systems are: carded cotton/short staple; combed cotton; worsted; and woollen. The different characters of these yarns are developed through the fibre type used and the spinning system which determines the arrangement of these fibres. What might appear to be small differences in the appearance of these yarns leads to large differences in their performance in the end-product.

General principles

In the case of most yarns spun from staple fibres, it is necessary to carry out of the following operations in order to produce a satisfactory product.

1. Mix and blend the raw material to provide a basic quality and to achieve the required characteristics in the final yarn.
2. Open and clean the raw material to remove unwanted impurities.
3. Separate the fibres to individuals.
4. Improve the regularity of the material (at this stage called sliver) in terms of variations in mass per unit length and blend composition, in order to achieve acceptable processing and end-use requirements.
5. Align the fibres with the sliver axis to reduce resistance to longitudinal fibre movement.
6. Draft and twist the strand in order to produce a product which has the required mass per unit length and twist/strength characteristics in relation to its intended end-use.

Processing objectives

Mixing

The term mixing is applied to the combination of similar raw materials which produce a single product, for example a Russian cotton blended with an American Uplands cotton. The objective of this is to achieve a basic product uniformity that results from the combination of a variety of raw materials, each exhibiting a degree of variability. It is also a safeguard against other potential problems. For instance, continuity of supply may be best ensured by mixing several varieties of the same raw material so that if one component becomes unobtainable owing to shortage or cost, it can be replaced by a similar alternative without seriously affecting the product characteristics.

Blending

Blending usually refers to the combination of fibres from different origins, for example polyester blended with cotton. The basic objective of blending is to give the end-product certain characteristics which are unobtainable from a single component, such as strength, crease resistance, colour, effect, or price.

Opening

The number of fibres in a length of yarn is very low when compared with the mass of fibres from which it was produced, for example a typical cotton bale may contain 3.5 billion fibres whereas a 20 tex ($30\,Ne_c$) yarn has approximately 140 fibres in its cross section. To effect such a dramatic reduction, there is obviously a need for a fine subdivision of the raw material if an acceptable product is to be produced.

The first stage of this subdivision is referred to as opening and consists of mechanically separating the bales into smaller and smaller tufts of fibres. This separation releases many of the impurities present in natural fibres and these can be removed as waste.

Cleaning

This is an intrinsic part of the opening process when dealing with natural fibres, though man-made fibres just require opening. The type and amount of cleaning is dependent upon the size and amount of impurity in the raw material, the end-product requirement and the subsequent processing route which may include further cleaning points. Typically, a cotton bale will contain roughly five per cent impurities and approximately three and a half per cent of this will be removed during opening and cleaning.

Fibre separation

This is achieved by a process known as **carding**, which continues the subdivision of tufts until each fibre is separated. Several other important secondary effects also take place during carding, including: further cleaning (one per cent of extra waste may be removed) which allows the separation and removal of very fine dust; some improvement in fibre alignment; a considerable reduction in mass per unit length (drafting) and the production of a continuous rope of separated fibres called a sliver; removal of a small per centage of short fibres which are unsuitable for spinning; and a high degree of blending caused by fibre movement during separation.

An additional process, referred to as **combing**, may follow carding. This extends these effects by removing short fibres (up to 20 per cent), removing any remaining impurities and greatly improving fibre alignment.

Regularising and fibre alignment

This process follows either carding or combing. It consists of combining a number of slivers and drafting them to produce a single sliver. This relatively simple action has three important effects. It is called **drawing** and it reduces the irregularity present in single slivers by a factor equal to the square root of the number of slivers fed. The drafting action improves fibre alignment, straightening the fibres and aligning them with the sliver axis. The combination of a number of slivers allows blending to take place. In some cases, for example a blend of combed cotton with carded polyester, blending can only take place during this process, as the fibres have followed different processing routes up to this point.

Drafting and twisting

This is the area in which the greatest number of options are available depending upon the count and quality of the yarn being produced. The objectives of this process are simply to draw out the material to the required fineness and insert the required amount of twist.

Depending upon the final count required, the draft imposed on the sliver may be so large that a two-stage operation is required. This is the case in ring spinning where an intermediate product referred to as a roving is produced from the drafted sliver.

These general principles can be applied to all spinning systems, as the examples in Table 7.1 show.

Table 7.1   General principles applied to main yarn production systems

General principles	Carded cotton / Short staple	Combed cotton	Worsted	Woollen
Mix and blend	Opening and cleaning line	Opening and cleaning line	Sorting and blending	Sorting and blending
Open and clean	—	—	Scouring and drying	Scouring and drying
Separate the fibres	Carding	Carding and combing	Carding	Carding
Improve regularity and fibre alignment	Drawing	Drawing	Gilling and combing	—
Draft	Speed frame *	Speed fame	Reducing	Tape condenser
Draft and twist	Ring spinning	Ring spinning	Ring spinning	Ring spinning

*Omitted if rotor spinning.

Drafting

Drafting occurs when the number of fibres in the cross section of an output material is lower than those in the cross section of the input material. Drafting is therefore the reduction in linear density of the material and can be found in a variety of processes during yarn manufacture, for example carding, combing, drawing, reduction at the speedframe and ringframe, and reduction at the rotor-spinning machine.

The mechanisms used to effect a draft on the material vary depending on the process but they all have one thing in common, that is the fibres are required to move relative to one another along the axis of the material.

In the case of the card and the rotor-spinning machine, drafting is effected by fibre separation, transport and reassembly, whereas combing, drawing and reduction at the speedframe and ringframe rely on a technique called roller drafting. It is this last technique, drafting by the use of rollers, that will be dealt with in detail in this chapter.

Roller drafting

The basic idea of roller drafting is a relatively simple one. If a roving or sliver is passed between one pair of rotating rollers (called the input rollers), it will move at their surface speed. If the same sliver or roving is then guided between another pair of rollers (called the output rollers) which are rotating six times as fast as the input rollers, the material emerging from these rollers will be six times as long as the material going into the input rollers and only one sixth of its thickness (the linear density will have been reduced by a factor equal to the draft, in this case six).

Calculation of draft

The draft can be calculated by determining the ratio of input linear density to output linear density, or by determining the relative speeds of the input or output rollers. Both methods are shown schematically below:

$$\overset{\text{input}}{\longrightarrow} \boxed{\text{drafting system}} \overset{\text{output}}{\longrightarrow}$$

3600 tex   600 tex
10 m/min^{-1} 60 m/min^{-1}

$$\text{draft} = \frac{\text{input tex}}{\text{output tex}} = \frac{3600}{600} = 6$$

$$\text{draft} = \frac{\text{output speed}}{\text{input speed}} = \frac{60}{10} = 6$$

Notice that the draft does not have any units. It is a ratio.

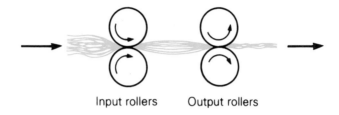

Figure 7.1 A roller drafting system.

The drafts found on spinning and spinning-preparation machines are not fixed but can be changed to give the output linear densities required. Typically, drafts are in the region of:

card	100
drawframe	6–8
speedframe	4–8
ringframe	15–50
rotor machine	80–180

Factors affecting roller drafting

There are five factors which must be taken into consideration when studying roller drafting systems. These are:

1. the total draft;
2. the **roller setting** (the distance between the points where the fibres are gripped by the rollers, often referred to as nip points or nip lines);
3. the fibre length;
4. the evenness of the input material; and
5. the evenness of the output material.

This last factor is very important as it is the evenness of the output material, which is often used as a measure of the effectiveness of the drafting process. Factors 1–4 all affect factor 5 to some extent.

The major problem with roller-drafting systems is the control of the fibres during the drafting process where, in the drafting zone between the **roller nips**, fibres are moving at different speeds and the spacing between the fibres is being increased.

Perfect drafting

As its name implies, this is a theoretical approach to drafting and can only occur when all the fibres are of equal length, when they are free to move independently and are presented to the drafting system in an orderly arrangement.

Drafting occurs when the fibres slide past one another under the influence of the drafting rollers. This effect is represented schematically in Figure 7.2.

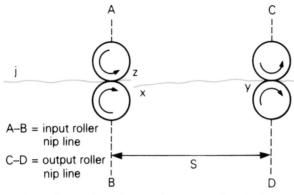

A–B = input roller
        nip line

C–D = output roller
        nip line

S = roller setting (distance between roller nips)

Figure 7.2 Perfect drafting.

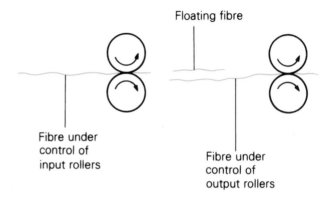

Figure 7.3 Real drafting.

To produce such an orderly progression of fibres through a roller-drafting system, it is important to note that the roller setting (S) is just greater than the fibre length; the fibres, once gripped by the output rollers (C–D) are immediately accelerated to output roller speed.

A brief description of a fibre passing into the system is as follows: a fibre (jz) enters the system and remains under the control of the input roller nip A–B, the fibre moving at input roller speed until it reaches the position xy. At this position the input roller releases its control of the rear of the fibre (x) just as the output roller D–C grips the front of the fibre (y) and the fibre is accelerated to output roller speed, sliding past the other fibres. In this way the spacing between the fibres is increased by the ratio equal to the difference in roller speeds. The draft, and the linear density of the material, is reduced by this ratio.

It can be seen that, to maintain the orderly arrangement of fibres, it is important that the roller setting is just greater than the fibre length. This ensures that a fibre is either under the control of the input rollers or under the control of the output rollers, that is it is controlled at all times as it passes through the system.

Real drafting

It is very unlikely that all the conditions necessary for perfect drafting would ever exist in a textile material.

Fibres are not all the same length. Natural fibres normally exhibit large variations in length. Natural and man-made fibres both take up convoluted shapes during carding, effectively reducing their length, limiting their mobility so they do not have the freedom to move independently and finally produce a disorderly arrangement of fibres with variations in thickness along its length.

Roller settings are based on the need to accommodate the longer fibre lengths to avoid the possibility of fibres being gripped at both ends. However, this has the effect of allowing the majority of fibres to pass into the drafting zone free of control from either pair of drafting rollers. These fibres are referred to as **floating fibres**.

Floating fibres rely on the movement of other fibres sliding past them to propel them through the drafting zone. They tend to move erratically and form periodic variations in the linear density of the output material. These variations, which are typically two to three times the fibre length, are called **drafting waves**.

Doubling

All roller drafting systems introduce drafting waves. Their size can be modified by the effects of doubling (combining two or more intermediate products to produce one final product) and the use of fibre-control techniques such as **pressure bars**, multiple roller configurations and **apron drafting** systems.

Several slivers are fed into the back of the drawframe. Not only does this prevent the delivered material from becoming thin and unmanageable but it also improves the evenness and blend of the final sliver. A doubling of six or eight per drawing process is common in short-staple drawing, but in worsted manufacture the amount of doubling depends on the drawing system being used, and may be as high as 16. Slivers are doubled at each drawing passage, and a typical short-staple system would double six times in the first drawframe passage, then a further six times in the final passage, giving a total number of 6 × 6, which is 36 drawframe doublings.

During drawing, all the fibres should travel at a controlled speed to avoid the introduction of irregularities. All drafting systems introduce some irregularities, but the benefits obtained by doubling should more than offset this.

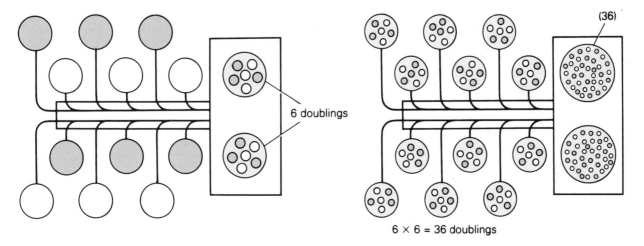

Figure 7.4 Plan view – drawframe doubling.

Spinning methods

The insertion of twist into a strand of fibres is the conventional method used to generate the forces necessary to prevent the fibres slipping past one another. It is this resistance to fibre slippage which gives rovings, slubbings and yarns their axial strength.

Twist is inserted by rotating one end of a strand of fibres relative to the other end; one complete rotation of 360° inserting one turn of twist.

Twisting forces the generally parallel arrangement of fibres into a spiral or helical formation, the angle of the helix (θ) being dependent on the amount of twist inserted. If the angle is small, that is if the twist level is low, then when axial tension is applied the fibres will slip past one another. If the angle is large, then the fibres resist slippage and the effect of increasing the tension is to break individual fibres until the whole structure eventually ruptures. This effect is illustrated in Figure 7.5.

Twist inserted into a length of drafted material does not distribute itself evenly but varies from place to place depending on the thickness of the material. The helix angle (or twist angle) is always constant but the twist level (measured in complete turns per unit length) varies, as can be seen in Figure 7.6.

It can be seen from Figure 7.6 that as the yarn diameter or thickness increases so the level of twist (turns per unit length) decreases. A decrease in twist level means that the fibres can slip past one another more easily. The greater the variation in thickness along the length of a yarn, the greater will be the variation in the distribution of twist. Consequently, less even yarns have a high proportion of weak places in which fibres are free to slip. This causes the yarn to break more frequently in processing.

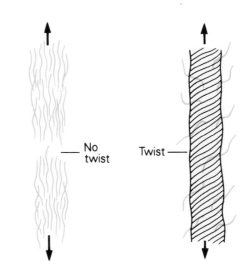

Figure 7.5 The effect of twist.

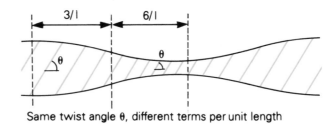

Same twist angle θ, different terms per unit length

Figure 7.6 Effect of yarn diameter on twist distribution.

This effect is used to advantage in woollen spinning where drafting against twist is used. A low level of twist is used to control fibre movement by allowing limited drafting (fibre slippage) of the thicker places in the slubbing prior to final twist insertion.

Bobbin and flyer twisting

This technique is found on speedframes, flyer frames or reducers. It is used in the preparation of rovings and slubbings for the final spinning stage.

The mechanisms used for the insertion of twist and the winding-on of the roving are usually similar to those shown in Figure 7.7. By reference to this figure, it can be seen that the material is delivered from the front rollers of the roller-drafting system, passes into the top of the flyer and down the hollow leg to emerge next to the presser. The presser guides the twisted roving onto the bobbin surface. In this example, both flyer and bobbin are positively driven.

Each revolution of the flyer inserts one turn of twist into the material. In order to maintain a constant twist level, the flyer is driven at a constant speed. Flyer speeds are relatively low when compared to other systems which insert twist, for example ring or rotor spinning. This is due to the delicate nature of the material and to the flyer assembly mounted on the spindle. Spindle speeds are usually in the range 800–1800 revolutions per minute.

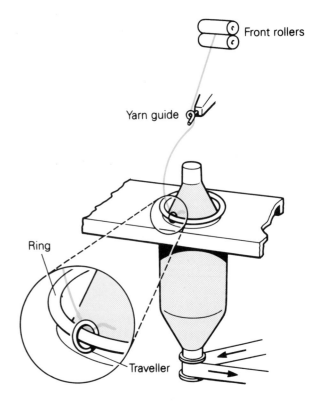

Yarn guide

Ring

Traveller

Figure 7.8 **Ring twisting.**

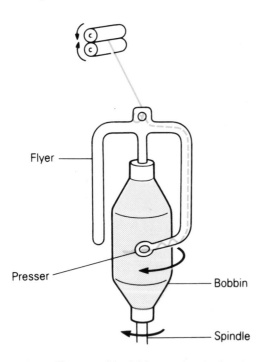

Figure 7.7 **Flyer and bobbin method of twist insertion.**

Ring twisting

The mechanism used for twist insertion in ring spinning and ring doubling is the ring and traveller. The ring, a metal O positioned horizontally over a spindle has a small C-shaped strip of metal clipped to its edge. This C-shaped strip is

called the traveller and is free to rotate around the ring. Directly above the top of the spindle is the yarn guide. Yarn passes from the front rollers of the drafting system or creel, through the yarn guide, under the traveller and on to the package mounted on the spindle.

When the spindle rotates, the length of yarn between it and the traveller drags the traveller around the ring, one turn of twist being inserted for each revolution of the traveller. Twisting and winding on to the package occur simultaneously, because the traveller revolutions are less than those of the spindle (friction between the traveller and ring retard the traveller speed), allowing the yarn to be wound onto the package surface.

Rotor spinning

In rotor spinning, the flow of material is interrupted, making this an open-end spinning method. Fibres are separated and fed into the groove of the twisting element, the rotor.

To begin twisting the fibres assembled in the spinning groove, a length of yarn must be introduced in the reverse direction down the yarn withdrawal tube and into the rotor.

As the yarn enters the rotor, it is acted upon by the air circulating within the rotor and centrifugal force produced by rotation. Consequently, the yarn turns at right angles at the navel while simultaneously rotating with the air in the

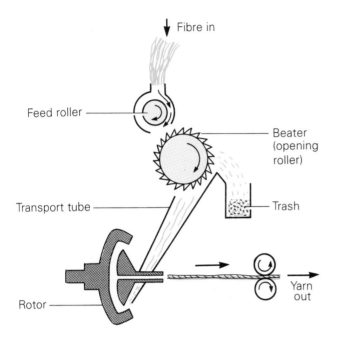

Figure 7.9 Rotor spinning.

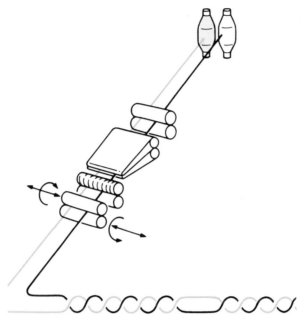

Figure 7.10 Self-twist spinning.

rotor. This combined movement causes the yarn arm to rotate about its own axis. When this rotating open-end yarn touches the fibres assembled in the spinning groove, twist runs from the rotating yarn arm into the fibres. If the yarn is then withdrawn from the centre of the rotor, fibres become attached to the rotating end and are peeled from the spinning groove producing a rotor spun yarn.

To establish a stable continuous spinning system, fibres are fed into the unit from the sliver at the same rate as they are being removed as yarn.

Self-twist spinning

This method of spinning is suitable for long-staple fibres (wool or long-staple man-made fibres) and can be used on the worsted processing system in place of conventional ring spinning.

Two rovings are fed to a roller-drafting system with double aprons for fibre control during drafting. After drafting, the attenuated material passes through a pair of rollers that reciprocate and rotate simultaneously. This has the effect of rolling the material first in one direction, then back in the opposite direction. As the material is passed through the rollers at the same time as it is rolled sideways, the two single yarns delivered have an alternating S then Z twist.

As the twist is in opposite directions, in equal amounts in adjacent parts of the yarn, it is false twist. If the yarn was left in this state, it would simply untwist itself, as all the twist in one part would cancel out with the twist in the adjacent part of yarn.

To prevent this happening, the two single strands are guided through different paths so that when they are allowed to come together, the twist cycles in each strand are out of phase. Due to the torque forces in the strands, they try to untwist. Because they are lying next to each other, they twist together as they attempt to untwist. The resulting yarn is known as a self-twist yarn (ST yarn).

For many applications, self-twist yarn is too weak, so a further twisting operation is used to produce what is known as a self-twist twisted yarn (STT yarn). The production rate for this yarn is 220 metres per minute, which is more than ten times that of the conventional ring-spinning machine.

This yarn is intended mainly for the production of fine two-ply yarns, primarily for knitting. If the yarn is to be used for weaving, it is usually STT yarn rather than ST yarn due to the tensions involved in the weaving process.

Friction spinning

As with rotor spinning, this is an open-end spinning system. There are different manufacturers of friction spinning machines, who have different methods of feeding fibres to the twisting element, one being similar to those used in rotor spinning. The feature common to both is this twisting element itself.

Twist is inserted by a pair of friction rollers. In one case both these rollers are perforated and in the other case only one is perforated. Fibres are sucked on to the surface of the roller(s) and rolled in the nip of two rollers which rotate in

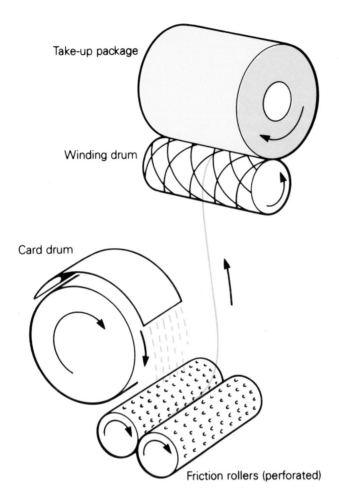

Figure 7.11   Friction spinning.

the same direction. The resulting yarn is taken off from the side and wound on to a package. The delivery rate is 300 metres per minute.

Wrap spinning

Sliver is fed into a conventional roller-drafting system. When drafted, the fibres are guided in a straight line through the centre of the rotating hollow spindle. The wrapping yarn or binder is wound onto this spindle and feeds through the centre of its spindle with the drafted fibres.

The wrapping yarn is wound around the twistless core of drafted fibres due to the rotation of the spindle. This permanent twist is inserted between the delivery rollers and the yarn guide at the bottom of the hollow spindle. The yarn is then wound onto a cone by the driving and traverse drum.

Fancy wrap yarns are also made by this method which can produce in one operation an effect yarn which might otherwise require several separate twisting operations on a conventional system.

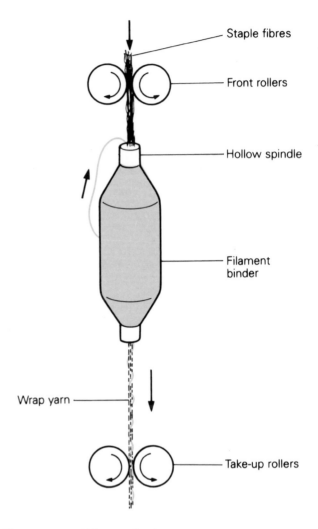

Figure 7.12   Wrap spinning.

■ CHECK YOUR UNDERSTANDING

● The general principles involved in staple-yarn spinning are mixing and blending, opening and cleaning, fibre separation, regularising and alignment, and drafting and twisting.

● The objectives of mixing are to achieve a uniform product and maintain continuity of supply. Blending can also combine the characteristics of different fibre types to produce an end-product that would be unobtainable from only one single fibre type.

● Opening and cleaning begins the reduction in fibre mass, so releasing some impurities. This cleaning action is only necessary for natural fibres.

● Separation of fibres to an individual state is carried out by the carding process. Further cleaning also occurs.

● Many staple-spinning systems use the drawing process to align and blend fibres and to regularise the material prior to the final twisting stage.

● Generally fibres are held together by inter-fibre friction caused by twisting. The final reduction in linear density and twisting occur at the spinning stage.

● Drafting is mainly carried out by pairs of rollers. Any drafting process introduces irregularities in the linear density of the material due to imperfect control of fibres.

● Roller drafting is affected by the total draft, the roller settings, the fibre length, and the evenness of the input material. It can be judged by the regularity of the output material.

● Doubling is combining two or more intermediate products to form a final product which improves the evenness and blend. Irregularities caused by drafting can be offset by doubling.

● Examples of spinning methods are bobbin and flyer, ring twisting, rotor spinning, self-twist spinning, friction spinning and wrap spinning.

REVISION EXERCISES AND QUESTIONS

1 What does the carding process achieve in addition to fibre separation?

2 What does the combing process do?

3 How are fibres aligned?

4 Why is drafting and twisting a two-stage operation in ring spinning?

5 Calculate the draft of the drawframe given the following information:

    output sliver tex   = 3.6
    input sliver tex   = 4.0
    number of slivers fed = 6

6 What conditions would be necessary for perfect drafting?

7 What are the benefits of doubling?

8 Describe how twist is distributed in staple yarns.

Short-staple spinning

Introduction

The staple fibre spinning sector can be split into two divisions – **short-staple spinning** and **long-staple spinning**. Traditionally, cotton was the short-staple fibre, being processed as either a carded quality or, with additional processes, a combed quality. The waste or very short cottons were processed on the **condenser** system.

Since the advent of man-made fibres, short-staple spun yarns may be composed of 100 per cent cotton, a blend of cotton and man-made fibres of suitable length and fineness, or 100 per cent man-made fibres. The processes of opening and cleaning, blending and carding are common to all short-staple spinning systems. Carded yarns are submitted to the further processes of drawing, reducing and spinning while combed yarns follow the same process route as the carded yarn, with the additional processes of comber lap preparation and combing.

Table 8.1 Short-staple spinning systems

Carded yarn	Rotor yarn	Combed cotton
Mixing and blending	Mixing and blending	Mixing and blending
Opening and cleaning	Opening and cleaning	Opening and cleaning
Carding	Carding	Carding
Drawing	Drawing	Comber preparation (2 processes)
Reducing	Rotor spinning	Combing
Spinning	—	Drawing
—	—	Reducing
—	—	Spinning

Opening and cleaning

The term impurity is used to described material other than fibre which is found in raw or processed stock. It is particularly important in the case of the natural fibres as it is often used to determine raw material quality and price. Generally, impurities must be removed during the spinning process, so the type and amount of impurity is also of importance to the yarn manufacturer. Impurities are also found in man-made fibres but the levels are much lower than those found in the natural fibres.

Types of impurities in raw cotton

The types of impurity found in raw cotton following ginning can be classified as follows.

SEED

The largest type of impurity found in raw cotton. It may consist of: unginned seeds, with fibres still attached; ginned seeds; or under-developed seeds and part seeds.

CHAFF

A collection of vegetable fragments, most of them consisting of leaf, bract, shale and stalk. Bract is a form of small leaf growing beneath the cotton boll. Shale is the silvery lining of the interior of the boll.

DIRT

Small fragments of chaff are sometimes referred to as dirt but the term should really only be applied to the sand and soil which originates from the cotton field.

DIRT AND MICRODUST

The finest of impurities consisting of very fine particles of chaff, dirt, small fibre fragments and mildew spores. Microdust particles are very small indeed, often a fraction of the fibre diameter, and are generally embedded in the waxy coating surrounding the cotton fibre.

TRASH

The term **trash** is often applied to the combination of all the above impurities. Trash contents and the type of impurities comprising the total trash vary from cotton growing region to region. Normally, the total trash content lies between one to ten per cent of the raw cotton weight. The amount of trash determines the amount of cleaning required. Recent work by machine manufacturers has attempted to determine not only the amount of trash present but how easy it is to remove, as it is thought that this last factor is of greater importance than just the total amount of impurity present.

Removal of impurities from raw cotton

In the early stages of cotton processing it is necessary to give a preliminary opening and cleaning of raw cotton before it is subjected to the more intense treatment of the carding process.

> The objectives of the opening and cleaning process can be summarised as follows. The density of the raw cotton mass is reduced by an opening process which allows tufts to be torn apart without fibre damage. Reducing the tuft size exposes new fibre surfaces, and this allows impurities to be removed, thereby improving the blend and regularity of the feedstock delivered to the next process. These objectives must be achieved with the minimum amount of fibre damage.

The techniques used to open and clean cotton are basically mechanical and consist of spiked surfaces, beaters and air currents.

SPIKED SURFACES

This action opens up the fibre tufts and some cleaning does occur. The action consists of gripping the cotton between two sets of spiked surfaces moving in opposite directions. Fibre is held by both surfaces and the relative movement subdivides the material into two parts.

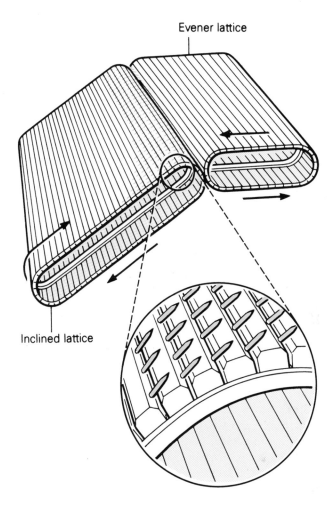

Evener lattice

Inclined lattice

Figure 8.1 Spiked surfaces.

BEATERS

This term is applied to a variety of techniques. A beater is a revolving drum which may have either blades, spikes or pins mounted on its surface. Fibre is fed on to the surface of the drum (it may just be supported by the air current rotating with the drum, in which case an opening action results), and if the fibre is held by a pair of feed rollers while being acted upon by the surface of the drum, an opening and cleaning action occurs. The cleaning results from the liberation of trash which is ejected below the machine.

AIR CURRENTS

Some trash, particularly the dust and microdust, is too light to be ejected in the way described above. In most opening and cleaning lines, a de-dusting process is now included. This consists of passing the fibre over a perforated surface where air currents draw off the dust-laden air.

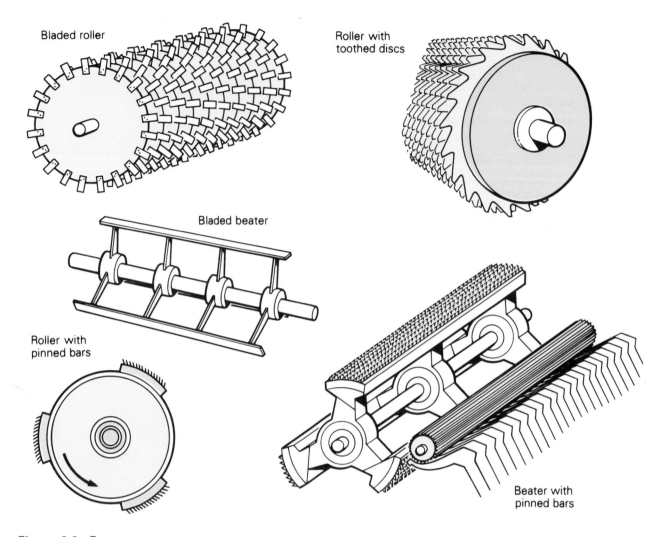

Figure 8.2   Beaters.

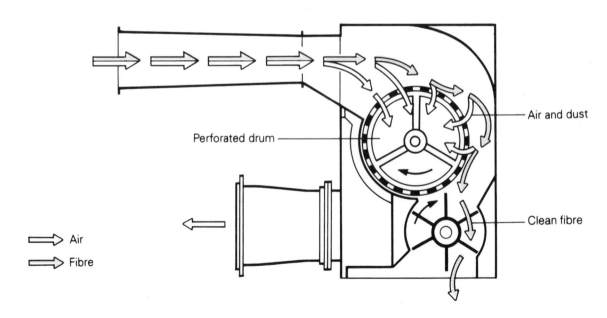

Figure 8.3   Air currents.

Cleaning efficiency

The effectiveness of the opening and cleaning process is often judged by a factor known as cleaning efficiency. This can be calculated as follows:

$$CE\% = \frac{WT_1 - WT_2}{WT_1} \times 100$$

where $CE\%$ = cleaning efficiency,
WT_1 = weight of trash in raw fibre (%),
WT_2 = weight of trash in processed fibre (%).

Generally, cleaning efficiencies vary in inverse proportion with the amount of trash in the raw material for instance.

Trash content (%)	Cleaning efficiency (%)
1	35
5	65
8	80

Blending

Before the introduction of man-made fibres, the divisions of the textile industry were well defined. There was little blending of the different types of natural fibres because they are quite dissimilar in character and generally incompatible. For example, in terms of fibre length, cotton is about 25 millimetres whereas wool is about 70 millimetres.

Nowadays a diverse range of man-made fibres is available and since these fibres can be manufactured in various lengths, to varying degrees of thickness and with a variety of cross-sectional shapes, they can be made compatible with almost all natural fibres.

Reasons for blending

There are a variety of reasons why fibres are blended together: to produce an end-product with characteristics unattainable from one component; to produce special effects; to ensure continuity of supply and avoid batch-to-batch variations; to improve processability and spinning performance; and to exploit advertising/consumer appeal.

The most popular reason for blending is that of combining the properties of different fibres. A typical example is polyester/cotton. A yarn spun from this combination will have the easy-care properties (low moisture regain) of the polyester and the comfort properties (high moisture regain) of the cotton. Wool/nylon is another example, and a good end-use for this blend is in carpets. Nylon is a man-made fibre with high abrasion resistance; wool, a natural fibre, is springy and resilient. With this blend, the nylon improves the abrasion resistance and the wool contributes warmth and resilience. In addition to natural/man-made fibre blends, natural/natural fibre blends can be produced with care (wool/cotton), or man-made/man-made blends (polyester/viscose).

Blends are also used to create aesthetic effects which can only be obtained by blending different fibres, for example cross dyeing effects produced using fibre blends or yarn blends. Viscose rayon and acetate rayon are blended together and woven into fabric in the white state. Then, since the two fibres have different dye affinities, they can be dyed different colours to give a special effect. Irregular yarns can be manufactured by blending two fibres of different staple lengths, whereas blending two fibres with different degrees of fineness produces a hairy or wild yarn (during the spinning process, the coarse, more rigid fibre migrates to the outside of the yarn, producing a hairy appearance).

Bulked staple yarns can be produced by blending relaxed and unrelaxed fibres, usually acrylic. Hot-wet processing in yarn or fabric causes shrinkage in the unrelaxed fibre, so if a blend of unrelaxed and relaxed fibres is produced and then subjected to a hot-wet process, the unrelaxed component will shrink, causing the yarn to increase in bulk. Consequently, the other fibre wrinkles, creating bulk in the yarn or fabric.

The appeal of luxury fibres may be exploited by the inclusion of fibres like linen (flax), silk or cashmere in low proportions. The same may be true of certain brands of man-made fibres.

The economics of yarn production are dependent on a number of factors, including raw material costs, and processing factors such as end breaks and waste loss. Sometimes the low-level introduction of other fibres may improve spinnability, for example a low proportion of polyester fibres added to low quality cottons.

Blending in staple yarn manufacture

Blending can be carried out at various stages in processing using a variety of techniques ranging from fibre production to fabric formation. The following are typical examples:

1. production of bicomponent fibres;
2. blending of fibres in raw fibre form;
3. blending during stages of yarn production;
4. blending during air texturing (combining two or more yarns together);
5. production of folded yarns;

6. core or wrap spinning combining staple and filament; and

7. mixing of yarns during weaving/knitting.

This chapter will consider only points two and three from the list above.

Blending in staple manufacturing systems can be carried out at the process stages shown in Table 8.2, using the blending types shown.

During processing there is controlled blending of some components which are precisely weighed, for example using weigh pan hoppers. In other cases, the blended fibres are brought together at random.

Table 8.2 Blending in staple manufacturing

Blending type	Process stage
Bale mixing	Prior to impurity removal
Tuft blending	During opening and cleaning
Sliver blending	At the drawframe
Ribbon web blending	Ribbon lap/blending drawframe
Roving blending	Ringframe

BLENDING SYSTEMS

Various blending systems have been developed for different fibres and different processing routes. The systems may be classified into the following groups, dependent on the principles involved:

1. stack blending;
2. batch blending;
3. direct continuous blending; and
4. sliver blending.

Blending in short-staple spinning

Of the blending groups listed above, the ones in common use for short-staple spinning are **direct continuous blending**, and **drawframe blending** which will be dealt with under drawing later in this chapter. Direct continuous blending is primarily used on the short-staple (cotton) processing route where a variety of systems have been developed.

HOPPER BLENDERS

These are widely used in conventional processing. The hopper opener consists of the following: feed lattice, apron lattice, inclined spiked lattice, and an evener roller or evener lattice, as shown in Figure 8.4.

Material is manually placed on the feed lattice and fed into the hopper where it comes into contact with the spikes of the inclined lattice. The amount of material allowed to progress is controlled by the settings between the inclined and evener roller or lattice and the speed of the inclined lattice.

The material is then passed on to a further conveyor for subsequent processing. A weigh pan may be used at this point to accurately weigh the components. Figure 8.5 is an example of a hopper blender with weighpan.

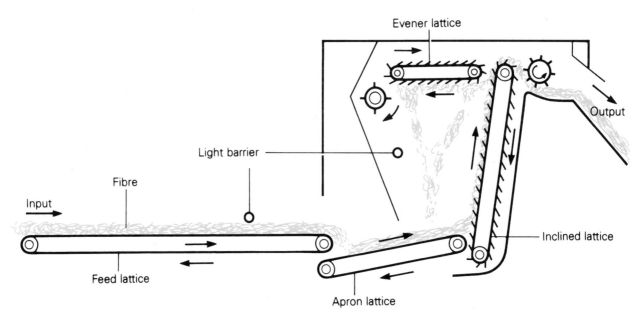

Figure 8.4 Hopper blender.

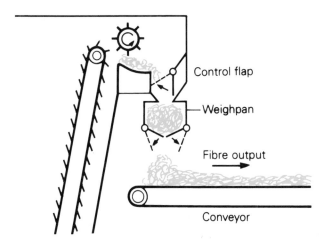

Figure 8.5 Hopper blender with weighpan.

AUTOMATED BALE OPENING

With a group of weighing hoppers, dependable mixing/blending can be guaranteed and human error largely precluded. Nevertheless, the bales have still to be manually fed. In the past ten years, there have been increasing developments and use of automated bale opening systems. These systems improve the blending potential by removing small tufts from a large number of bales of raw material. Weigh pans can be installed in the process sequence to control the blend accurately.

IN-LINE BLENDING MACHINERY

With the advent of automation, machinery manufacturers have produced a number of in-line automatic blending machines. The purpose of these machines is to create a delay in the process.

A typical example of an in-line blender is the Multimixer. In this machine, the blending chamber is usually in six or ten sections. The fibres are fed into the top of the blender and removed at the bottom. Each compartment is filled in sequence and the operation is fully automatic. Each compartment is emptied at the same rate, the fibres having been opened by a plucking roller before being deposited in the blending channel.

Effects of blend variation

One of the main problems in producing blended yarns is blend variation. Blend variation can be considered as being either long-term or short-term. Long-term variations may be caused by changing fibre supplier, using dyed fibre from different dye lots, or a variation in moisture content of fibres

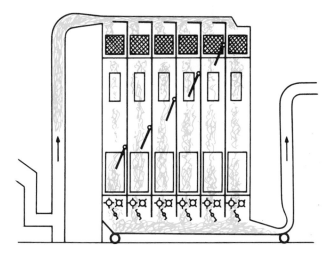

Figure 8.6 Blending chamber or an in-line blending machine.

when the blend proportions are determined by mass. The method of combining and recombining fibres during the manufacture of yarns – a process called doubling – is designed to remove all but the longest of these variations. However, if they persist, they produce **barrenness** in fabrics caused by changes in the hairiness, lustre or surface characteristics (including colour) of the yarn.

Short-term variations in the degree of mixing in the yarn are caused by inadequate fibre separation, an inadequate number of doublings in relation to the draft between the card and the yarn, or too few fibres in the yarn cross section. These factors are outweighed by the relative colours of the blend components when visual assessment of the blend irregularity is made. Short-term variations produce streakiness in fabrics and it has been found that streakiness is most apparent when there is a great contrast between the colours, for example black/white or yellow/purple. The streakiness is most apparent when the darker of the two components reduces in proportion from 50 per cent to 10 per cent, after which it seems to disappear (though this may be due to the way we see the distribution of fibres on a fabric surface).

Carding

This process follows the initial opening of the raw material. It is a particularly important process because it is responsible for separating, still further, the tufts of fibre fed into the machine and reducing them to an individual fibre state.

The separation of fibres allows the removal of much of the remaining impurity and it enables the fibres to move as individuals rather than in groups during the processes which follow carding. It should also be understood that unless the fibres are separated into individuals, they cannot be spun into smooth, uniform yarns, neither can they be blended satisfactorily with other fibres.

Finally, the carding machine reduces the overall thickness of the material into the form of a light web which is then compressed into a continuous thick strand or sliver.

> **Carding** is carried out by passing the entangled fibres between closely spaced surfaces covered with sharp metal teeth. The surfaces are moved relative to each other and the fibres are disentangled.

Figure 8.7 shows the conditions that apply for successful carding. Note the direction of movement of the two surfaces and the direction of inclination of the teeth. These teeth do not touch and the distance between them is known as the setting.

The card is the machine which carries out the carding process and there are two common types of card, the **roller and clearer card** and the **revolving flat card**. Both cards have positions where fibre separation is taking place, and also places where transfer of fibres occurs. This second action known as **stripping** is achieved by using toothed surfaces arranged as shown in Figure 8.8.

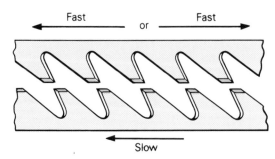

Figure 8.7 Carding action.

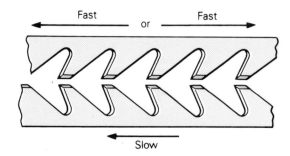

Figure 8.8 Stripping action.

The short-staple card

This machine is used for cotton and man-made fibres of staple length up to about 50 millimetres, though longer man-made fibres can in certain instances be processed with reasonable success.

Figure 8.9 shows a short-staple revolving flat card, so called because of the series of horizontal flats situated above the cylinder. Each flat consists of a T-shaped metal bar with teeth on one surface. The flats are linked together and rotate slowly above the cylinder to achieve the carding action.

Material from the blowroom is presented to the feed roller of the card in the form of either a **lap** or as loose fibre in a vertical chute. The layer of fibre passes between the feed roller and feed plate at the rate of one to two metres per minute.

The taker-in, with a speed of 700 or more revolutions per minute, rapidly reduces the feed material into smaller

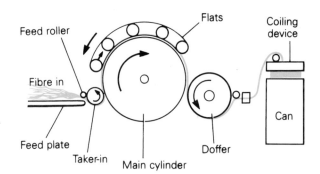

Figure 8.9 Revolving flat card.

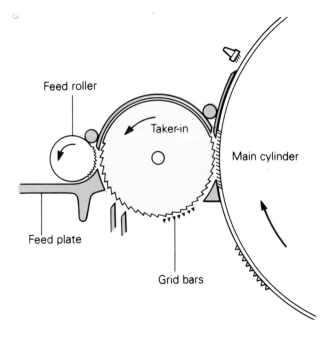

Figure 8.10 The taker-in region.

groups or clusters of fibres. This assists the release of much of the heavier trash and impurities which drop into the compartment below the taker-in. The good material travels towards the cylinder which, because of the direction of rotation and inclination of the teeth, strips the fibre from the taker-in and takes it into the main carding area between the cylinder and flats. This is the region in which the groups of fibres are progressively reduced to an individual state.

From the cylinder/flats region, the fibres pass to the doffer which has teeth opposing the cylinder teeth as shown in Figure 8.11.

The arrangement and speed of the parts at this point result in a condensing action. In other words, the fibres on the cylinder surface are transferred to the doffer and form a layer. This layer is removed from the doffer as a film, or web, and passed through a funnel-shaped guide before being compressed into sliver form by a pair of heavily weighted calender rollers.

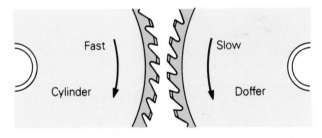

Figure 8.11 Teeth arrangement, cylinder/doffer region.

DRAFT

For every metre of material fed to the machine, approximately 100 metres of sliver are delivered. This is known as the mechanical draft and is expressed simply as a number.

$$\text{Mechanical draft} = \frac{\text{length delivered per unit time}}{\text{length fed per unit time}}$$

The actual draft at a card depends on the thickness of material fed and delivered. To be more precise, the actual draft is calculated as shown below.

$$\text{Actual draft} = \frac{\text{mass per unit length fed}}{\text{mass per unit length delivered}}$$

WASTE REMOVAL

The heavier impurities and dirtier varieties of waste found in raw cotton are removed from below the taker-in as described above. When processing man-made fibres, however, the amount of waste is very much less and of a different type.

A second waste extraction point is found at the front of the card where the revolving flats leave the carding position and begin their upward movement. A residue of light waste, short fibres and neps remains on the flats and this is removed, by various means, in the form of strips. The percentage of flat strips and also the amount of taker-in waste is adjustable depending on the type of raw material being processed and the end-use of the yarn.

To summarise, the objectives of the revolving flat card are to separate the tufts of raw material into individual fibres, remove as much as possible of the remaining impurity and reduce the material fed into the machine to sliver form.

Drawing

> The fibres in card slivers are separate individuals but they are arranged in a disorganised and random way. It is necessary to improve their straightness and alignment if strong, commercially useful yarns are to be produced.

Better alignment is achieved by passing the slivers through one or more processes of drawing. During this process, the slivers travel through a series of pairs of rollers, each successive pair of rollers having a slightly greater surface speed than the previous pair. This causes the fibres to slide past one another and, in so doing, they become straighter and more parallel to each other.

Figure 8.12 shows different drawing arrangements. These are known as drafting systems and are generally used in short-staple processing.

The point of contact between two rollers is known as the nip, and the distance between two successive nips is the roller setting. The roller setting should be just greater than the fibre length. The machine which carries out the drawing process for cotton and short-staple man-made fibre is known as a drawframe. This process is so important that the material is given two or, if different fibre types are blended together, three passages through the drawframe.

Doubling

The sliding of the fibres which occurs during drawing (known as drafting) causes them to become spaced out along the direction of the material flow and this leads to a reduction in thickness of the strand. To compensate for this, drafting is normally accompanied by doubling, during which several slivers are fed into the back of the drawframe. Not only does

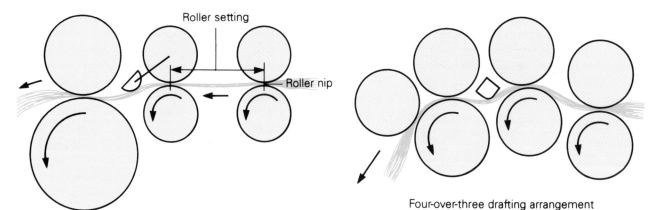

Three-over-three drafting arrangement

Four-over-three drafting arrangement

Three-over-four drafting arrangement

Figure 8.12   Drafting systems.

this prevent the delivered material from becoming thin and unmanageable but it improves the evenness and blend of the final sliver. A doubling of six or eight is common in short-staple drawing.

It is at the first drawframe passage that drawframe blending can occur, when slivers of the different fibres to be blended are fed to the same drafting head of the machine. A common example is that of 50 per cent polyester/50 per cent cotton, where three slivers of cotton are alternated with three slivers of polyester in the creel to produce first-passage sliver. These slivers are doubled at the next passage six times, then a further six times in the final passage. This will give a total number of $6 \times 6 \times 6$, which is 216 drawframe doublings.

During drawing, all the fibres should travel at a controlled speed to avoid the introduction of irregularities.

The drawframe

Figure 8.13 illustrates a typical drawframe. Although the drafting system is the most important part of the machine, the following should be noted: suction cleaning of rollers, which also reduces dust released during drafting; and electrical stop motions which prevent damage to the operator, the machine, and reduce waste.

Current drawframes deliver sliver at more than 650 metres per minute, which may amount to almost 200 kilograms of sliver per hour at each delivery. For example, if we assume five kilotex sliver is delivered at 650 metres per minute at 100 per cent efficiency, the production would be:

$$\frac{650 \text{ m min}^{-1} \times 60 \text{ min} \times 5 \text{ ktex}}{1000} = 195 \text{ kg per hour}$$

Remember: tex = weight in g of 1000 m of material

ktex = weight in g of 1 m of material

$$\text{ktex} = \frac{\text{tex}}{1000}$$

Combing

In staple fibre processing, combing is an optional process in the preparation of high quality yarns. In the processing sequence of cotton, it follows the carding operation and requires preparation of material to feed the comber (two passages) and combing. Combed material is then passed through the drawing process.

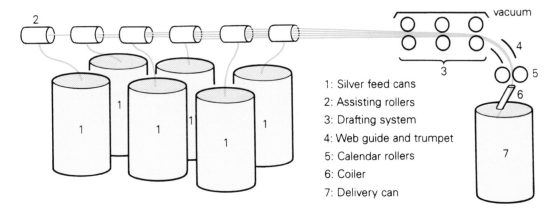

Figure 8.13 Drawframe.

1: Silver feed cans
2: Assisting rollers
3: Drafting system
4: Web guide and trumpet
5: Calendar rollers
6: Coiler
7: Delivery can

Objectives of the combing process

> The objectives of the combing process are to remove a predetermined amount of short fibre, remove nep and impurities remaining in the material after carding and to improve the degree of parallelisation of the fibres. This enables the yarn manufacturer to produce more uniform and consequently stronger yarns, to produce yarns which are more lustrous, compact and less hairy than carded yarns, to produce cleaner yarns and finer yarns.

The combing operation results in an improvement in the yarn's quality and enables a spinner to spin finer yarns than would be possible with the same fibre converted into a carded yarn. In short-staple cotton processing, combing is used in the production of combed cotton yarns.

The introduction of the combing machine revolutionised the textile industry because finer and more uniform yarns could be produced. By the early part of this century, with the aid of the combing machine and fine spinning mules, the spinning of yarns much finer than 100 cotton count was quite common. For various reasons, the demand for these yarns has declined and now it would be difficult to find a spinner who could supply yarn finer than 100 cotton count.

Degrees of combing

Obviously, the quality of the combed yarn and the fineness to which the cotton can be spun will depend upon the type and quality of raw cotton used and the degree of combing. The latter is the amount of short fibre that is extracted during the combing process.

SCRATCH-COMBING (4–7 PER CENT WASTE EXTRACTION)

It may be possible under certain circumstances to buy a cheaper cotton and semi-comb it to compete with a carded yarn produced from a more expensive cotton. In recent years, this type of combing operation has been introduced to rotor spinning plants.

COMBING (12–17 PER CENT WASTE EXTRACTION)

Waste extraction in this range is the most popular and most spinning mills using American Upland type cottons have this range of waste extraction.

SUPER-COMBING (17–20 PER CENT WASTE EXTRACTION)

Used usually for Egyptian type cottons where high quality fine yarns are required.

DOUBLE-COMBING (18 PER CENT FOLLOWED BY 5 PER CENT)

Rarely done nowadays but was necessary when spinners were producing extremely fine yarns from Egyptian and Sea Island cotton.

Preparation for combing

If card slivers were presented directly to the combing machine, the waste extraction would be very high, there would be a high fibre-breakage rate and probably excessive

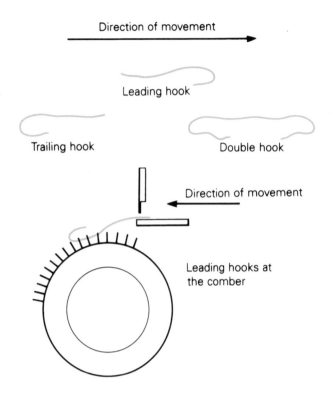

Direction of movement

Leading hook

Trailing hook   Double hook

Direction of movement

Leading hooks at
the comber

Figure 8.14   Fibre hooks.

damage to the needles of the comber. Consequently, there is a need for the card sliver to be prepared for the combing operation. The carding process produces a certain degree of fibre orientation to the axis of the card sliver and the presence of **hooked fibres**, both leading and trailing.

The majority of the hooked fibres are trailing in the card sliver and it has been established that if these fibres are presented as leading hooks to the combing machine, better results are obtained. This is because more hooked fibres are straightened out to their full extent and pass into the combed sliver rather than into the waste.

To present the majority of the hooks in the leading position to the combing machine, an even number of machines must be used in comber lap preparation. As well as ensuring that the hooked fibres are correctly presented, the lap preparation process also has the function of reducing the number of hooked fibres and improving their orientation. Drafting by means of rollers is the method by which this is achieved. The magnitude of the draft will determine the degree to which this is done but care must be taken not to over draft because this could lead to other problems. Doubling is necessary to produce a sheet of material which is wound on to form a lap. Doubling also helps to improve the uniformity of the material fed to the comber and assists in further blending.

Some short-term irregularity is introduced by drafting and under certain conditions irregularity can be introduced by top roller slippage. The latter is more likely to happen if the

card sliver is too bulky. Modern lap preparation machines are better equipped to deal with this problem than earlier machines.

METHODS OF COMBER LAP PREPARATION

Various methods have evolved in the past 130 years and the following three are the main ones in present use:

1. sliver lap machine – ribbon lap machine;
2. drawframe – lap former;
3. drawframe – superlapper.

In each case, the end result is a lap which is fed to the combing machine, the objective being to produce a lap uniform in mass/unit length, across its width and along its length, with the fibres reasonably orientated, the minimum of hooked fibres and the majority of hooks in the leading position.

Combing cycle of operation

In a 360° cycle, a predetermined amount of the lap sheet is combed, short fibres are removed and the long fibres are passed forward into the sliver. In order to explain the full operation in the 360° cycle, it is normal to split it into three distinct phases. The parts of the machine involved in the description are as follows:

1. top and bottom nippers;
2. feed rollers;
3. top comb;
4. cylinder; and
5. detaching rollers.

CYLINDER COMBING

The lap is gripped by the top and bottom nippers and the protruding fringe is combed by the cylinder needles. Any fibres not held by the nippers will be treated as short fibres and removed as waste. The major part of cylinder combing is done during the time that the nippers rock backwards. Only when the last two or three rows of needles are passing through the fringe are the nippers rocking forward.

PREPARATION FOR THE OVERLAP

During the previous phase, the detaching rollers are stationary (not revolving) but the back top detaching roller is rocking backwards.

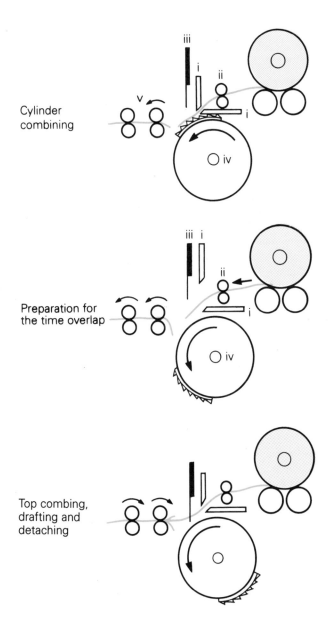

Cylinder combining

Preparation for the time overlap

Top combing, drafting and detaching

Figure 8.15 Combing cycle of a cotton comber.

In this phase, the detaching rollers rotate backwards and the previously combed material is projected backwards and downwards. At the same time, the top nipper is raised and the nipper assembly is rocking forwards.

The feed rollers, which were stationary during the previous phase, feed a previously determined amount of lap, thereby increasing the length of the fringe. As the nippers move forwards, the leading edge of the lap fringe is thrust towards the nip of the detaching rollers. Eventually, the leading edge will reach the nip of the detaching rollers and the back top detaching roller will have rocked forwards to make the entry of the fringe into the nip more accessible. During this phase, the top comb is also descending.

TOP COMBING, DRAFTING AND DETACHING

At the instant when the leading edge of the fringe reaches the nip of the detaching rollers, the rollers change their direction of rotation to a forward movement. Consequently, fibres are removed from the lap fringe and the piecing is made.

Drafting takes place because the surface speed of the detaching rollers is higher than the velocity at which the nippers are moving forwards. After the piecing has been made, the top comb descends into the now continuous length of material. Fibres held by the detaching rollers are pulled through the top comb but other fibres may be held back by the top comb. When the nippers reach their most forward position, detaching commences because the detaching rollers continue to rotate in a forward direction. Detaching is completed when the nippers begin to rock backwards and a complete separation takes place. The top nipper also descends and grips the lap, leaving a fringe projecting ready for the next cycle.

This cycle of operation takes place from three to five times per second on a modern comber.

Reducing

This is the preparation of rovings for the final spinning stage. After the drawing stage in the case of carded yarns, or the combing and drawing stage in the case of combed yarns, the sliver is ready for spinning. The impurity level and fibre arrangement have been improved sufficiently, so all that remains is to draft the sliver to the required thickness and to insert the correct amount of twist for the end-use requirements. Unfortunately, the desired reduction in linear density of the drawframe sliver is too much for one machine to cope with satisfactorily, so the intermediate stage of reducing with the speedframe is used. Due to this reduction in sliver linear density at the speedframe, a weak strand is produced. To process this strand, a small amount of twist must be inserted to give it the strength to wind on a package, and later wind off the package at the final spinning stage. The strand is now known as a roving. The mechanical problems concerned with handling a weak strand of material make the speedframe a complex piece of textile machinery.

The objectives of the reducing stage are to draft the material to the required linear density, to insert the required level of twist and to produce a stable package which will withstand transport, handling and storage.

Drafting

If slivers were fed directly to the ringframe, very high drafts would be required to reduce it to the linear density required. To reduce the draft at the ringframe and produce more regular yarns, a partial reduction in linear density is carried out at the speedframe. The technique is similar to that found on all roller drafting systems, aprons being used in the front zone to control fibre movement. Drafts are in the range of six to fifteen.

Twisting and winding-on

The mechanisms used for the insertion of twist and the winding-on of the roving are usually similar to those shown in Figure 8.16. By reference to this figure, it can be seen that the material is delivered from the front rollers of the roller-drafting system, passes into the top of the flyer and down the hollow leg to emerge next to the presser. The presser guides the twisted roving onto the bobbin surface. In this example, both flyer and bobbin are positively driven.

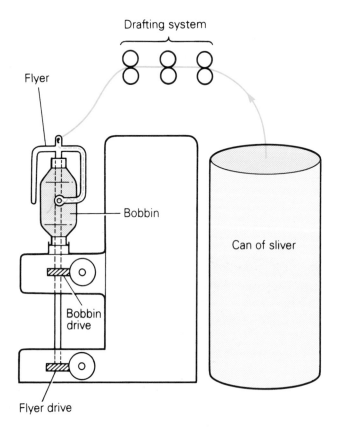

Figure 8.16 Speedframe.

Method of twist insertion

Each revolution of the flyer inserts one turn of twist into the material, and to maintain a constant twist level the flyer is driven at a constant speed. Flyer speeds are relatively low when compared to other systems which insert twist, ring or rotor spinning for instance. This is due both to the delicate nature of the material and to the flyer assembly mounted on the spindle. Spindle speeds are usually in the range of 800–1800 revolutions per minute.

The actual twist level inserted depends upon the fibre type and the linear density of the material. Longer, finer fibres require less twist than shorter, coarser fibres, finer rovings require more twist than coarser rovings (all other factors being the same).

The objective of twist on this machine is to prevent end breakages during package formation at the speedframe and when unwinding at the ringframe. Too much twist increases costs and makes the material difficult to draft.

Package formation

After twisting, the roving is guided onto the package surface by the presser. The roving is positioned in layers along the bobbin surface, this being achieved by a mechanism which moves the bobbin up and down, each movement being known as a lift. At the end of each lift, the distance moved by the bobbin is reduced and in this way, a tapered bobbin like the one illustrated in Figure 8.17 is produced. The tapered ends of the package are designed to resist damage during transport and handling.

In order that winding onto the bobbin surface can occur in a controlled way, there is a difference in speed between the flyer and bobbin. The bobbin speed exceeds the speed of the

Figure 8.17 Roving bobbin.

flyer by sufficient revolutions to wind on the material delivered by the drafting system. When the bobbin diameter is small (at the beginning of package formation), more revolutions are required than when the bobbin diameter is large (at the end of package formation). It can be seen then that the bobbin speed varies as the package is built. The difference in the speed of bobbin and flyer must be very carefully controlled; if it is not and the bobbin revolutions are too high for the package diameter, the roving will be pulled apart.

The bobbin speed is controlled by a mechanism which allows the bobbin revolutions to be reduced for each layer of roving wound onto the surface, so the bobbin slows down during package formation, but it always exceeds the speed of the flyer. This technique is called bobbin lead.

Ring spinning

Yarns produced by the ring spinning method currently account for about 85 per cent of all staple yarns produced. It is, therefore, by far the most popular method and is likely to retain this position because of the following advantages.

1. Ring spinning is a very flexible method of yarn manufacture. It is possible to process most fibres into yarns using ring spinning and the range of linear densities which can be produced is the widest of any spinning system.
2. The yarns produced possess the performance, aesthetic and tactile properties with which consumers are accustomed. Ring-spun yarns have levels of irregularity which provide interest in flat fabrics, have a pleasant handle due to the orderly fibre arrangement and surface hair and have predictable strength and elongation characteristics.
3. The mechanisms used in ring spinning are relatively uncomplicated and tend to require lower levels of capital and personnel investment than alternative systems.

> The three basic objectives of ring spinning are to draft the input material to the linear density required in the final yarn, to insert the required amount of twist, and to wind the yarn onto a package which is suitable for handling, storage and transport and is capable of being unwound at high speed in subsequent processing. In the case of ring spinning, all three objectives are achieved concurrently. Ring spinning is therefore a continuous method of yarn and package formation.

Drafting

The technique used is usually roller drafting. Ringframe roller drafting systems generally consist of three lines of rollers with aprons mounted on the middle rollers.

By reference to Figure 8.18, it can be seen that a single weighting arm holds the top roller assemblies in position above the bottom rollers which are driven. Pressure is applied to the rollers by this arm which is spring loaded. The pressure provides the force to grip the fibres at the roller nips and to rotate the top rollers when the bottom rollers are driven.

The total draft is distributed between the two **drafting zones** in the assembly. The two zones are referred to as the back zone (back to middle rollers) and the front zone (middle to front rollers). The total draft (back to front rollers) may be as high as 50–60 with back zone drafts in the range of 1.2 to 2.0.

The draft distribution may be calculated as follows:

$$\frac{\text{total draft}}{\text{back zone draft}} = \text{front zone draft}$$

In the following example, the total draft = 40 and the back zone draft = 1.25

$$\text{front zone draft} = \frac{40}{1.25} = 32$$

It can be seen from this that by far the largest draft occurs in the front zone. It is for this reason that the aprons are positioned in this zone. Their role is to control fibre movement, particularly the short fibres and so to limit the

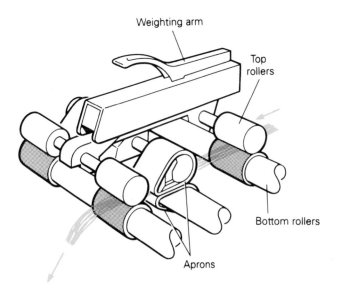

Figure 8.18 Ringframe drafting.

level of added irregularity caused by drafting waves. The aprons have the effect of extending the control point of the middle rollers almost up to the nip of the front rollers, thereby reducing the proportion of 'floating fibres' and minimising uncontrolled fibre movement. Their effect is shown diagrammatically in Figure 8.19.

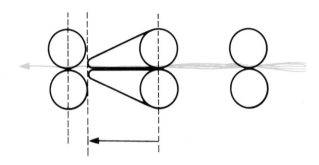

Figure 8.19 Aprons effectively extend the roller nip.

Twisting

The mechanism used for twist insertion in ring spinning is the ring and **traveller**. The ring, a metal O positioned horizontally over a spindle has a small C-shaped strip of metal clipped to its edge. This C-shaped strip is called the traveller and is free to rotate around the ring. Directly above the top of the spindle is the yarn guide. Yarn passes from the front rollers of the drafting system, through the yarn guide, under the traveller and onto the package mounted on the spindle.

When the spindle rotates, the length of yarn between it and the traveller drags the traveller around the ring, one turn of twist being inserted for each revolution of the traveller.

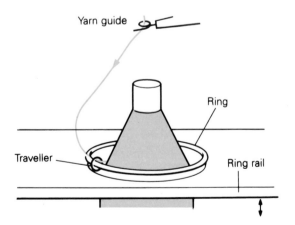

Figure 8.20 Ring spinning.

If the drafting rollers were to remain stationary and the spindle rotated, twist would be inserted in the length of yarn between the package and the front rollers and the twist level would increase for each revolution of the traveller.

However, the front rollers are not stationary; they deliver drafted material which requires twisting and winding on to the package surface. So twisting and winding-on occur at the same time. This is accommodated by the traveller revolutions being less than those of the spindle, due to the friction between the traveller and ring retarding the traveller speed. The difference in the revolutions allows the yarn to be wound on to the package surface. This effect is best illustrated by the following example:

> the drafting rollers are delivering material at 20 metres per minute;
> the spindles are rotating at 15 000 revolutions per minute;
> the ring tube package diameter on the spindle is 40 millimetres;

$$\text{traveller revs} = \text{spindle revs} - \frac{\text{length delivered}}{\pi \times \text{package diameter}}$$

$$\text{traveller revs} = 15\,000 - \frac{20 \text{ m min}^{-1}}{\pi \times 0.040 \text{ m}}$$

$$\text{traveller revs} = 15\,000 - 159 \text{ rev min}^{-1}$$

$$= 14\,841 \text{ rev min}^{-1}$$

It can be seen that the traveller lags behind the spindle speed by 159 revolutions per minute when the package diameter is 40 millimetres. Package diameters do vary and consequently so does traveller lag, increasing when diameters are small and decreasing when diameters are large. However, the difference between spindle speed and traveller speed is relatively small – in this example, 1.06 per cent – and the calculations for twist normally ignore it, abbreviating the calculation for twist insertion to:

$$\text{turns unit length (m}^{-1}) = \frac{\text{spindle rev min}^{-1}}{\text{front roller delivery m min}^{-1}}$$

Rotor spinning

Rotor spinning is the most successful alternative to ring spinning for the production of short-staple yarns. It dominates the coarser end of the yarns market producing acceptable yarns in the 20 to 600 tex range. Finer yarns can be produced but the economics of yarn production and the characteristics of the yarns themselves tend to deteriorate as the yarns become finer.

Long-staple rotor-spinning machines are produced and these are used mainly for the production of coarse yarns from long-staple man-made fibres. The scaly surface, fibre crimp and grease found on wool fibres have made it difficult to spin using this technique.

Like all other spinning methods, the objectives of the rotor spinning process are: to draft the material to the linear density required; to insert the desired level of twist, determined by subsequent processing route and end-use; and to produce a package suitable for subsequent processing that will withstand handling, transport and storage without sustaining damage.

The rotor-spinning technique is different to the other traditional forms of yarn formation. It requires a definite break in the flow of fibres, unlike other systems which increase the distances between fibres but never break the continuity of the strand. Package formation is also an integral part of other systems, whereas in rotor spinning it is quite separate to drafting and twist insertion. The technique is represented schematically in Figure 8.21.

Drafting

Rotor-spinning machines do not use roller drafting to reduce the linear density of the material. They produce yarns directly from sliver and consequently the drafts are too large to be accommodated by roller drafting systems. Drafts are normally in the range of 100 to 200.

A sliver is passed under a feed roller and slowly advanced onto the surface of a revolving opening roller. The surface of the opening roller is covered with small teeth or pins, which pluck individual fibres from the leading edge of the sliver. This is represented in stage 2, Figure 8.21. The fibres continue to rotate with the opening roller until they enter an air-flow passing down the fibre transport tube and into the rotor itself. When the fibres enter the rotor, which may be 40–80 millimetres in diameter and be revolving at 40–100 000 revolutions per minute, they are affected by centrifugal force and slide into a specially designed spinning groove cut into the inner edge of the rotor. The fibres become arranged in a continuous layer all around the

spinning groove and can be thought of as a length of twistless yarn. This is represented in stage 3, Figure 8.21 and is shown in Figure 8.22.

The drafting stage in rotor spinning is, therefore, divided into two parts: drafting to individual fibres and assembly of fibres in the spinning groove to give the linear density of yarn required.

Twist insertion

To begin twisting the fibres assembled in the spinning groove, a length of yarn must be introduced in the reverse direction down the yarn withdrawal tube and into the rotor.

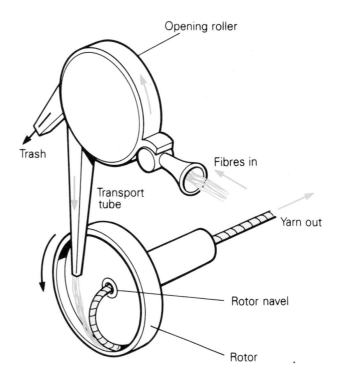

Figure 8.22 Rotor-spinning unit.

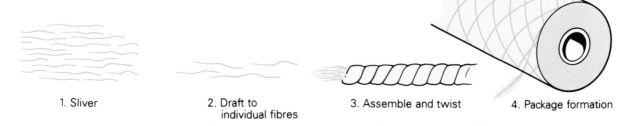

1. Sliver   2. Draft to individual fibres   3. Assemble and twist   4. Package formation

Figure 8.21 Basic principles of rotor spinning.

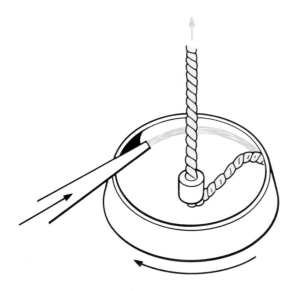

Figure 8.23 Yarn formation in the rotor.

As the yarn enters the rotor, it is acted upon by the air circulating within the rotor and centrifugal force due to rotation. Consequently, the yarn turns at right angles at the navel while at the same time rotating with the air in the rotor. This combined movement causes the yarn arm to rotate about its own axis.

When this rotating open-end yarn touches the fibres assembled in the spinning groove, twist runs from the rotating yarn arm into the fibres. If the yarn is then withdrawn from the rotor, fibres become attached to the rotating end and are peeled from the spinning groove producing a rotor spun yarn.

To establish a stable continuous spinning system, fibres are fed into the unit from the sliver at the same rate as they are being removed as yarn.

Twist is calculated in a similar way to that found in ring twisting:

$$\text{turns unit length } (\text{m}^{-1}) = \frac{\text{rotor rev min}^{-1}}{\text{yarn delivery speed m min}^{-1}}$$

For the same yarn linear density, twist levels are usually higher in rotor spun yarns than in ring spun yarns.

Package formation

As the yarn is already formed when it leaves the rotor-spinning unit, it can be wound into a finished package, unlike ring spinning where the package size is limited by both ring diameter and lift.

Generally, cross-wound packages are produced either as parallel-sided cheeses or cones with small tapers.

The yarn may be waxed on the machine ready for knitting and most modern machines monitor both the length of yarn

produced (so that all the packages are the same size) and the yarn evenness, removing faults at the spinning stage. The end product is, therefore, an endless fault-free package requiring no other processing prior to use.

Yarn structure

The way the fibres are assembled into a yarn in rotor spinning is different to that found in ring spun yarns. A rotor yarn structure can be divided into three zones:

1. The core: This is the most orderly part of the structure and is very similar to that found in ring-spun yarns. The fibres occupy a series of interlocking spirals. It is this zone that is responsible for the tensile properties of the yarn.
2. The sheath: Wrapped around the core is the sheath. It has a disorderly fibre arrangement and is responsible for the bulk and handle of the yarn.
3. **Wrapper fibres**: Some fibres become wrapped tightly around the yarn at right angles to the yarn axis. As these increase in number, the handle of the yarn becomes harsher.

> Generally, rotor spun yarns are bulkier, less hairy, more extensible, weaker, and more even than their ring spun equivalents.

■ CHECK YOUR UNDERSTANDING

● The impurity present in cotton is vegetable matter, dust and dirt. The total trash content can be between one to ten per cent on the weight of raw fibre.

● Cotton impurity is removed by mechanical means: spiked surfaces, beaters and air currents.

● Blending can take place at many stages of textile processing. In short-staple spinning, direct continuous blending prior to carding is commonly used, as is drawframe blending.

● The main purpose of carding is to separate fibres to an individual state. This is achieved by passing them between closely spaced surfaces covered in sharp metal teeth. The main actions are those of carding and stripping; the revolving flat card carries out the carding function for short-staple processing.

● Drawing aligns and straightens fibres; doubling improves the blend and uniformity of the material. The drawframe carries out these tasks in short-staple processing.

● The combing process removes a predetermined amount of short fibres, leading to less surface hairs, better control of the drafting process and so more regular yarns. It removes neps and impurities giving a cleaner yarn and aligns fibres further, giving a more lustrous, compact and subsequently a stronger yarn.

● The speedframe reduces the thickness of the sliver prior to the final spinning operation. A small amount of twist is inserted to enable the roving to be wound on to a package at the speedframe and to subsequently wind off the package without stretching.

● Ring spinning is still the most dominant spinning method; it drafts the fibres to the final yarn thickness required and imparts strength to the yarn by inserting twist.

● Generally, rotor-spun yarns are bulkier, less hairy, more extensible, weaker and more even than their ring spun equivalents.

REVISION EXERCISES AND QUESTIONS

1 Calculate the cleaning efficiency of the opening and cleaning process given the following information:
   weight of trash in processed fibre = 1.8%
   weight of trash in raw fibre = 5.2%

2 Name factors which can cause blend variation.

3 Calculate the actual draft of the carding machine given the following information:
   kilotex of feed = 400
   tex of sliver = 3500

4 If two slivers of 3.9 kilotex polyester fibre and four slivers of 4.0 kilotex cotton fibre were fed to one delivery head of a drawframe, what would be the resulting fibre blend?

5 Why is scratch combing (removal of 4–7 per cent short fibre) carried out?

6 Why must the amount of twist inserted at the drawframe be so carefully controlled?

7 Calculate the twist level for the following ring spun yarn:
   spindle revolutions per minute = 15 000
   front roller delivery rate (metres per minute) = 16

Texturing and tow-to-top conversion

Introduction

> The product of the man-made fibre producer is, in the first stage, a continuous filament yarn or **tow**.

One way of processing man-made filaments to produce a yarn similar in properties to one made from natural fibres is to cut up the filaments into short lengths (staple fibres) and spin them on conventional staple spinning machines. This method is widely used to produce 100 per cent man-made staple yarns and also man-made/natural fibre blends.

This process of cutting up a continuous filament yarn only to reassemble it in another yarn form seems illogical. It is not surprising, therefore, that in the 1950s new methods were developed to add crimp and deformation (texture) to continuous filament yarns in order to confer on them some properties similar to those of yarns made from natural fibres. This process is known as **texturing**.

Sometimes texturing is not suitable. The appearance might not be right, or blends with natural fibres may be desired, in which case tow-to-top conversion is the alternative to conventional staple spinning. A tow is a collection of thousands of parallel continuous filaments of man-made fibres and the rope formation makes it easy to cut or break into staple form to be later processed by conventional spinning machinery into yarn. During the tow-to-top conversion process, the filaments in the tow are cut or broken while preserving the continuity, evenness and parallel arrangements of the fibres. The tow is converted to a sliver, or **top**.

Reasons for texturing

> The general endeavour in texturing continuous filament yarns is to simulate the properties of staple yarns. In comparing flat filament to textured yarn, the following properties may be affected: an increase in bulk of the yarn; better cover when used in fabrics; greater comfort; improved surface characteristics; softness of handle; opacity; improved thermal insulation; and better moisture absorption.

The objectives of texturing have been achieved to a greater or lesser degree with the various types of textured yarns but the yarns have also shown unusual properties, such as very high extensibility and unusual yarn structure. For example, a textured yarn produced by the false twist process could have an extension at break in the region of 400 per cent and consequently be used in a knitted fabric requiring a high degree of stretch. A modified false-twist textured yarn can be produced, which will have a much lower extension at break and a higher bulk.

The moisture absorption of textured yarn is also much higher than that of standard, or flat, continuous filament yarn and staple spun yarn. For intance, a false-twist textured yarn will absorb approximately five times more moisture than the flat continuous filament yarn.

Types of textured yarn

Textured yarns can be classified into three major groups:

Stretch yarns are characterised by having very high extensions and good recovery but possess only moderate bulk. Stretch yarns, used extensively in stretch-to-fit garments, are produced mainly by false twist.

Modified stretch yarns may be defined as those with characteristics intermediate between stretch and bulk yarns. They are produced by modifying the stretch characteristics, usually by a further heat treatment, after which they retain some stretch but have increased bulk.

Bulk yarns have high bulk and moderate stretch and are used where bulk and fullness of handle are of greater importance than extensibility.

Texturing methods

> All texturing processes consist of methods in which the continuous filaments are deformed in some way and this deformation is usually set into the filaments by heating and cooling. In most cases, thermoplastic fibres are required to accomplish the process efficiently.

There are four main methods of producing textured yarns: false twist method; stuffer box; crinkle yarns (knit de knit, gear crimping); and air-jet texturing. A fifth method, knife-edge crimping, is now obsolete.

The texturing method that has dominated the field since the development of the major synthetic fibres is the **false twist** (twist-set-untwist) method which accounts for approximately 85 per cent of total textured yarn production.

Even though the false twist method dominates the market, the other methods are of importance and may in fact claim an increasing share of this market in the future. There are two reasons for this. The first is that there is a considerable consumer demand for the 'natural fibre look' and if this cannot be met by natural fibre yarns, some of the other texturing methods produce yarns nearer to this than does the false twist method. The second reason is an economic one. It is advantageous to combine extrusion, drawing and texturing in one operation and some of the other methods are nearer to the high speed (3000–6000 metres per minute) required for the link with extrusion spinning than is the present false twist method.

False twist texturing

This process, which was originally an intermittent process performed in three steps, consists of inserting a very high twist into a continuous filament yarn, setting this twist by a heat treatment and then completely untwisting the yarn. Because of the stable state of the yarn in its fully twisted heat-set condition, the untwisted yarn behaves like an assembly of springs. When the tension is reduced, each filament tends to buckle causing the yarn to bulk up into a mass of tangled filaments.

This intermittent process was soon replaced by a continuous false twist process in which the yarn is passed through a twisting mechanism, which imparts temporary twist to the yarn travelling towards it and removes it as it passes beyond it. (This happens because a yarn twisted at some point between its ends will receive an equal but opposite twist, thus reducing the twist level to zero.)

A heater is placed in the path of the twisted yarn before the twisting mechanism to set the twist before it is removed at the spindle, thus performing the three texturing steps, twist-heat set-untwist, in one operation. A diagrammatical representation of the process is shown in Figure 9.2.

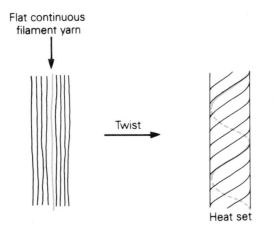
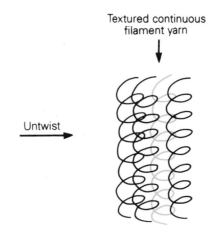

Figure 9.1 False twist texturing principle.

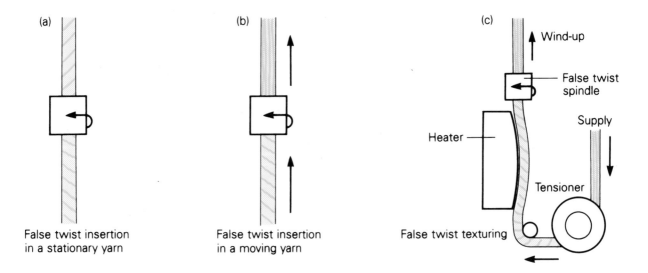

Figure 9.2   Continuous false twist texturing.

Modern devices can insert this false twist into moving yarn at rates up to six million revolutions per minute, producing yarns at a speed exceeding 1200 metres per minute.

Yarn produced by this method is called a stretch yarn because of its large capacity to contract at low tension and stretch under high tension. It also has a high torque. Textured yarns produced by this method are almost entirely nylon or polyester in the range of 22–220 decitex.

Until a few years ago, the starting product for any texturing process was a fully drawn continuous filament yarn. Since texturing machines use feed rollers for transporting yarn in and out of the texturing zone and for stretching to control tensions, it is not surprising that the idea was conceived to eliminate a separate drawing stage and combine it with texturing. This is **draw texturing**. There are two types of draw texturing, sequential and simultaneous.

SEQUENTIAL DRAW TEXTURING

In sequential draw texturing, a separate draw zone is added at the front of the texturing zone. As these two processes are still essentially independent of each other, fully drawn yarn is fed into the texturing zone.

SIMULTANEOUS DRAW TEXTURING

In the alternative simultaneous draw texturing process, the undrawn yarn is fed directly to the texturing zone where, by slowing down the input speed rollers, the yarn is simultaneously drawn, twisted and heat set. Figure 9.3 shows a simplified diagram to illustrate the two types. It also illustrates a post-texturing process.

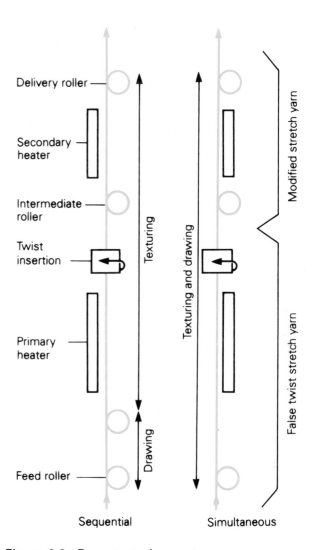

Figure 9.3   Draw texturing systems.

POST-TEXTURING PROCESS

Many items of clothing, especially outer wear, require the bulk and warmth provided by the false twisted yarns but not the excessive stretch and residual torque. Before use in woven or knitted structures, the textured yarn can be stabilised – usually by a second heat treatment – which has the effect of reducing their stretch, suppressing their residual torque and giving increased bulk.

Originally, this **stabilisation** was a discontinuous process, the textured yarn being overfed on to a loose package and then heat set. The process is now continuous and is achieved by adding a second heater in the process line after the twisting unit and allowing the yarn to be overfed into the heater. The principle of post texturing is shown in Figure 9.3.

Stuffer-box texturing

The process of producing a textured yarn by the stuffer-box method is an extremely simple one. It is based on the principle of heat setting filaments which are held in a confined space in a compressed state (deformation) and then withdrawing them in a crimped form.

Yarn is propelled by a pair of feed rollers into a tube where it is restrained at the exit. By compressing the yarn into the stuffer box, the individual filaments are caused to bend or fold into a zig-zag configuration. By simultaneous heat setting during this compression state, the deformation is set into the yarn. This method gives the yarn a high bulk, soft handle and less stretch than false twist yarns. Figure 9.4 shows the basic principle.

This method is widely used to crimp man-made staple fibres.

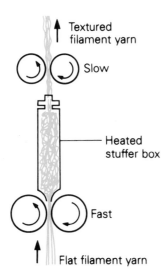

Figure 9.4   **Principle of stuffer-box texturing.**

Crinkle-type textured yarns

This type of yarn can be produced by two different methods, the knit de knit method or gear crimping.

KNIT DE KNIT

In this method, the production of the textured yarn is very simple. A flat yarn is knitted, the knitted fabric is heat set and the fabric is then unravelled (de knit). The crimp frequency and shape can be varied by changing the needle gauge and fabric structure.

Yarns produced by this process are torque-free and therefore do not require post setting. The fabric produced from such yarns has a pronounced sparkle, boucle-type texture, good stretch and recovery and good handle.

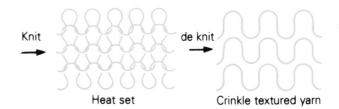

Figure 9.5   **Principle of knit de knit.**

GEAR CRIMPING

If a filament yarn is passed through closely meshed gears, bulk can be generated in the structure. The gear head is heated so that the crinkle produced in the yarn is permanent. Figure 9.6 shows the simplified process.

Air-jet texturing

The air-jet texturing process was originally developed by DuPont. In simple terms, bulk in a continuous filament yarn can be produced by blowing a stream of air into a yarn while it is being delivered at a higher rate than it is being taken up. The air stream causes turbulence, which allows the

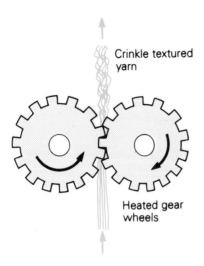

Figure 9.6 Principle of gear crimping.

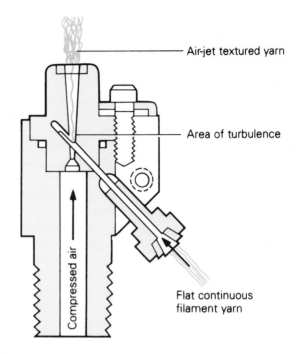

Figure 9.7 Principle of air-jet texturing.

formation of random loops in the overfed yarn. During processing, the yarn contracts in length to the same degree as the overfeed. The yarn produced has an appearance more akin to staple yarns.

The only common feature that air-textured yarns have with false twist yarns is the fact that they are produced from continuous filament. However, they have a completely different appearance, they do not possess the elasticity of false twist yarns and have aesthetic properties similar to staple-fibre yarns. The presence of protruding filament loops give the yarn the handle, bulk and appearance of a spun product.

Polyester, polyamide, polypropylene, viscose, acetate and combinations of these materials may be used to produce a wide range of yarns. The process can also be used to produce blended yarns. Note that this is the only process that can texture non-thermoplastic fibres.

The yarns used generally are partially oriented (POY) or occasionally **low oriented (LOY)**, which are then drawn prior to the texturing jet. After being pre-drawn, the yarn reaches the texturing box and the yarn may well be wetted (this increases the effectiveness of air entangling by 50–100 per cent). The yarn is then fed to the air jet, at a higher speed than it is taken off. The selection of jet is dependent on the machine manufacturer.

An air stream transports the yarn filaments through the jet at high speed. After leaving the jet, the filaments are fed out of the air stream at an angle. Individual filaments of the yarn are separated and vibrate forcefully, resulting in filaments of varying lengths. They form loops which interlace and co-mingle. Figure 9.7 shows the basic principle of air-jet texturing.

The production speed of air-jet texturing is limited by yarn stability and texturing uniformity. Feeder yarns of 100–440 decitex are textured at speeds ranging from 400–600 metres per minute.

The yarn leaves the texturing zone slightly damp. It then passes through a heat-stabilising zone to consolidate the loop structures.

One feature of the air-texturing process is the possibility of mixing several filaments in one jet. This offers the possibility of unlimited variations such as mixtures of different basic materials, colour mixes and structural effects (varying length of overfeed).

The end-uses of air-jet textured yarn are varied. The looped structure gives fabric produced from such yarns a soft and pleasant handle with an appearance similar to spun products but with a high bulk. Air-textured yarns made from fine polyester or polyamide filaments are used in the sports/leisure wear field to produce fashion fabrics with good handle and appearance. The following list gives some of the applications of air-jet textured yarns: outer wear; sportswear; furnishing fabrics; curtaining; wall covering; car seat fabric/interiors; blankets; and luggage.

With more economic and versatile techniques using air-jet technology, the interest for the use and applications of air-textured yarns should increase in the future.

Tow-to-top conversion

A tow is a collection of thousands of parallel continuous filaments of man-made fibres. The rope formation makes it easy to cut or break into staple form to be later processed by conventional spinning machinery into yarn.

Tow-to-top conversion cuts short the processing route for converting man-made staple fibre into yarn form. There are no difficulties in processing cut staple on conventional spinning machinery, but the processing requires sliver formation and fibre parallelisation which seems to be wasted effort when it is considered that the material in its original tow form was a collection of parallel filaments. During this tow-to-top conversion process, the filaments in the tow are cut or broken while preserving the continuity, evenness and parallel arrangements of the fibres – the tow is converted to a sliver, or top.

Application of tow-to-top convertors

In the short-staple processing sector, man-made fibres are crimped, cut to length and delivered in bale form by the fibre producer. A similar situation existed in the long-staple processing sector until tow-to-top conversion was introduced in the 1950s. Attempts to introduce tow-to-top conversion in the short-staple sector have so far failed because the short fibre length required means that two processes would be necessary; a convertor and a reconvertor.

Today a large proportion of man-made fibres supplied to the Worsted processor are in the form of tow, which they then process through a convertor to form top; man-made top can be processed to form 100 per cent man-made fibre yarns, or it can be blended with wool at the **gillbox** for a wool/man-made blended yarn.

> Many advantages come from using the tow-to-top system when compared to the conventional staple processing route. Production costs are lower due to a reduced number of operations and a saving in floor space, the changeover time from one fibre quality to another is greatly reduced, evenness and cleanliness of the resultant sliver is improved, finer yarns can be spun due to better sliver quality, and there is the possibility of producing high bulk yarns – yarns with a modified structure.

Methods of tow-to-top conversion

There are basically two methods used to convert tow to top: **crush cutting**, which cuts the filaments to the required length; and **stretch break**, which ruptures the filaments by stretching them until they break.

CRUSH CUT

This method of conversion shears the filaments in the tow at an angle, hereby ensuring that the continuity and parallel arrangement of the fibres is retained. The fibre ends are then redistributed – the top is 'shuffled' – to give a continuous product. This method has the advantage of not altering the fibre characteristics (other than length).

The disadvantage to the system is its lack of flexibility. As can be seen from Figure 9.9, to alter the staple length of the fibres would require a change of the expensive cutting roller, with the associated down-time of the equipment. A further disadvantage is the inability of the system to cope with filaments of less than 1.2 decitex, and shorter than approximately seven centimetres.

The cutting machine can be split into the following areas: creeling, feeding, cutting, de-bonding, drafting and shuffling, delivery and crimping.

In the creeling and feeding section, the tow is taken from the supply package, its width is controlled by a series of guides and it is tensioned prior to being fed to the cutting section.

The cutting is obviously the most important section, requiring careful monitoring. Cutter blades on the cutting roller are arranged in a helical pattern and held in contact with a smooth steel anvil roller under high pressure. The approximate staple length produced by the cutters can be calculated by dividing the circumference of the cutting roller by the number of cutter blades. These blades must remain sharp to avoid production of multiple-length staple fibres.

As the system uses crushing, the filaments must undergo a separating action to prevent them remaining stuck together during subsequent processing. The two pairs of de-bonding

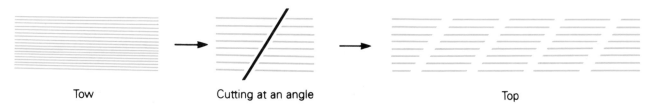

Tow   Cutting at an angle   Top

Figure 9.8 Principle of crush cutting.

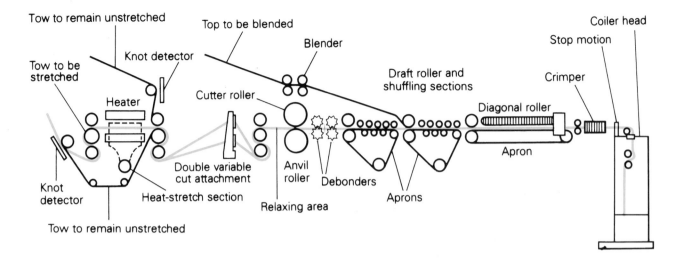

Figure 9.9 Crush cut conveyer.

rollers have intermeshing flutes which separate the sheet of filaments by a flexing action.

Drafting and shuffling affects the depth-wise overlapping of the fibres by use of an apron supporting the sheet of fibres while several top scratch-fluted rollers rotate at a faster speed. The sheet is now reduced in thickness, needing only one more shuffling operation before crimping.

The sheet is formed into a bulky sliver by a scrolling action prior to being crimped (the method used to crimp the fibres is a stuffer box). After it is coiled into a can, the sliver is ready to enter the worsted processing system at the gillbox.

STRETCH BREAK

If a tow is passed between drafting rollers and a draft is applied that is greater than the stretch capacity of the fibres they will be broken, provided that the rollers can hold the filaments securely. Not all filaments will break in the same place, producing a sliver of variable length fibres.

The stress on the fibres during this conversion process will alter the structure of the fibre. This can be a disadvantage, giving a lower breaking extension, an increase in shrinkage on wetting and a modified cross-sectional shape. A further disadvantage is the production of some very short fibres. The advantages to the system when compared to crush cutting are that the staple length can be altered by a simple alteration of machine settings, that fibre fineness and required staple length are not restrictions, and shuffling to redistribute fibre ends is unnecessary.

The machine is fed in a similar way to the crush-cut convertor, controlling the tension and width of the tow. The in-feed rollers pass the filament between heater plates in the heat-stretch zone. Partial cooling of the filaments takes place just prior to the intermediate rollers which, with the aid of the delivery rollers and breaker rollers rupture the filaments.

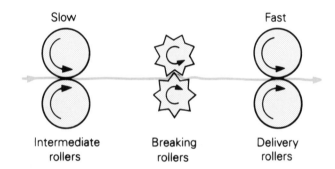

Figure 9.10 Principle of stretch breaking.

These breaker rollers control the breaking of the filaments by giving a localised stretching to the already stretched filaments passing between their sharp intermeshing teeth.

The need for redistribution of the fibres after breaking is removed due to the random fibre length (the necessary inter-fibre cohesion for sliver formation is already there). A slight tensioning draft is given to the top before crimping and coiling of the sliver into a can.

High-bulk yarns

High-bulk yarns are produced by blending relaxed and unrelaxed fibres together. The resulting yarn is then given a heat relaxation treatment to relax or shrink the unrelaxed fibres. Fibres within the yarn are held together by inter-fibre friction, so the pre-relaxed fibres must buckle outwards when the unrelaxed fibres shrink, creating bulkiness and a warm, soft handle to the yarn.

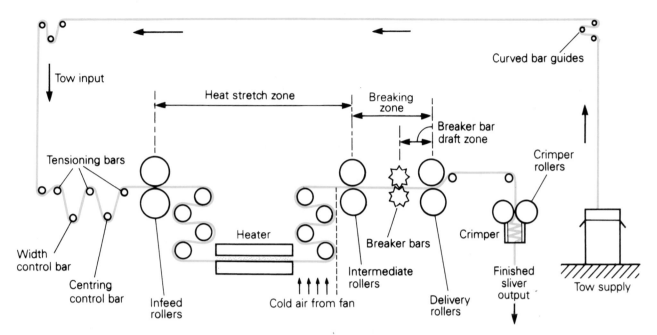

Figure 9.11 Stretch break converter.

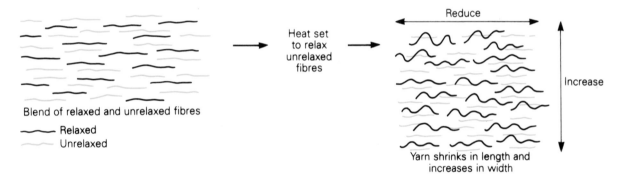

Figure 9.12 Principle of producing high-bulk yarns.

This method of yarn production is particularly popular for acrylic yarns used for knitwear, the most popular blend being 55 per cent relaxed, 45 per cent unrelaxed fibres.

After stretch breaking, it is usual practice to fully relax fibres as the characteristics have been altered by the convertor. Blending of tops that have undergone this relaxing treatment in an autoclave with unrelaxed tops at the gillbox will produce a high-bulk yarn.

■ CHECK YOUR UNDERSTANDING

● Texturing alters the appearance of filament yarns by introducing permanent deformations such as loops, crinkles and spirals to simulate the properties of staple-spun yarns.

● Textured yarns can be divided into three main types: stretch yarns, modified stretch yarns and bulk yarns.

● The four main methods of producing textured yarns are false twist texturing, stuffer-box texturing, crinkle yarns – gear crimping or knit-de-knit – and air-jet texturing.

● False twist texturing was originally a three-stage process of twist-heat-untwist. It is now done in one continuous process.

● Thermoplastic yarns are generally required for texturing. Air-jet texturing can be carried out on a wide range of products, thermoplastic or non-thermoplastic.

● Tow-to-top conversion cuts short the processing route for converting man-made staple fibres to yarns in the long-staple processing sector.

● Crush cut is the simplest form of staple fibre formation in tow-to-top conversion. The fibre properties are not altered by the process, but have to be redistributed. The stuffer-box method is used to crimp the fibres.

● Stretch breaking produces a variable length staple fibre.

The method is more flexible but modifies the fibre characteristics. High-bulk yarns can be produced from stretch-broken top.

REVISION EXERCISES AND QUESTIONS

1   What are the advantages of air-jet texturing when compared to false twist texturing?

2   Which type of textured yarn – stretch, modified stretch or bulk – are yarns produced from the following texturing methods classed as:
    a) false twist textured;
    b) air-jet textured?

3   Name the two types of draw texturing. What is the basic difference between them?

4   To what use, other than the production of textured continuous filament yarns, is the stuffer-box texturing method put to?

5   Why do the other three texturing methods threaten to take a larger share of the market away from false twist texturing in the future?

6   Which staple-spinning system utilises top produced by the tow-to-top conversion system?

7   What are the advantages of using tow-to-top conversion compared to conventional sliver processing?

8   What are the limitations of the crush cut method of tow-to-top conversion?

9   What process is usually carried out after the stretch break conversion method?

Plied, cabled and fancy yarns

Introduction

Doubling is a process in which two or more single yarns are combined together by means of twist. The yarns produced are known as ply yarns or folded yarns. These yarns are necessary for certain end-uses where, for instance, superior strength or regularity are required.

For any given quality of yarn, a folded yarn is more expensive than a single yarn of the same linear density. For example, a single 24 tex yarn is cheaper than a two-fold 12 tex yarn, even though the resulting linear density is the same – 24 tex. Extra processes are needed to produce these yarns and this inevitably increases their cost, for instance the single yarns may have to be rewound from spinners packages to remove faults and then assembly wound. The process of **assembly winding** arranges for the required number of single yarns to be wound side by side without twist on to a cheese. The cheese then forms the supply for the doubling process.

Typical end-uses for ply and cabled yarns include sewing threads, tyre cords, carpet yarns, crochet/embroidery threads, high quality suiting fabrics and conveyor belts. A more detailed list of end-uses will be given later.

Sometimes even a ply yarn does not fulfil the end-use requirements. In this case, a further twisting operation is used to produce a cabled yarn.

> A plied yarn is produced in one twisting operation. Cabled yarns are produced by two or more separate twisting operations – the first operation is known as preparing and, the second as cabling. A plied yarn may be produced during the preparing operation and then two or more of the plied yarns are twisted together in the cabling operation.

Ply yarn properties

It is possible to vary the proportions of single and ply twist in such a way that certain other properties are emphasised.

1. Uniformity. The final yarn will be more uniform.
2. Tenacity. It is possible to produce a stronger yarn.
3. Uniformity of tenacity. The variation in strength is reduced.
4. Snarling tendency. By using the correct amount and direction of twist it is possible to produce a balanced yarn with little or no tendency to **snarl**.
5. Lustre. It is possible to produce yarns with a high degree of lustre if the correct amount and direction of twist is used.
6. Extension at break. The final yarn will have a modified extension a break.
7. Novelty yarns. Using one or more of the following techniques, novelty yarns may be produced:

- combination of different fibre types;
- combination of different colours of yarns;
- combination of different yarn linear densities;
- combination of different yarn lengths; and
- high levels of ply/cabling twist.

General principles

Yarn doubling route

The following is the normal sequence from single yarn to folded yarn.

99

Winding and clearing
↓
Assembly winding
↓
Doubling
↓
Cone winding

This route will vary depending on the method of doubling.

Conventional folded yarns

The following points should be observed when producing conventional folded yarns: the single yarns should have the same linear density, amount of twist, direction of twist and tension.

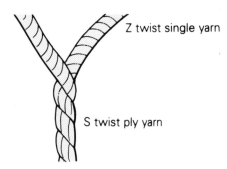

Figure 10.1 Example of a folded yarn construction.

Twist in plied and cabled yarns

It is obvious that in a single yarn the direction of the twist has no effect on the character of the yarn, but if two yarns are going to be plied, the direction of the twist in the single yarn components is important. It is customary to twist the ply yarn in the opposite direction to the twist used in the initial spinning process to produce a conventional folded yarn.

If the twist in the single and plied state is the same, (both Z twist or both S twist) then different characteristics will be obtained than if the twist in the plied state is opposite to the twist in the single state (S singles with Z plied, or Z singles with S plied).

The tendency for yarns to snarl can cause great problems to the customer, especially if the customer is a weft knitter. When a yarn snarls during knitting at least two or three thicknesses of yarn are trying to pass through the needles to form knitted loops. They will of course fail, causing at the very least holes in the fabric. The snarl could break needles or even cause a **press-off**. With some man-made fibre yarns, this can be eliminated by a process called **heat setting**. If

the yarn is composed of thermoplastic fibres, the yarn package can be steamed at the correct temperature to set the twisted shape into the fibres. This will result in the yarn losing its urge to untwist and it will become **torque-free**. As the yarn is not attempting to untwist, it will not snarl. With yarns composed of non-thermoplastic fibres, heat setting will not be possible. The other way of producing a torque-free yarn is to ply the yarn using twist opposite to that used in the single-yarn components. This is obviously independent of the fibre type, so can be used for any staple spun yarn. The S on Z yarn shown in Figure 10.1 would be balanced if the correct ratio of single to doubled twist is used.

D/S RATIO

The doubled to single twist ratio (**D/S ratio**) is the level of twist in the plied yarn relative to the level of twist in the single yarn components. For example, if the single yarn has a twist level of 714 turns per metre, and the doubled yarn has a twist level of 500 turns per metre, the D/S ratio of the plied yarn would be:

$$\frac{500}{700} = 0.7$$

Certain D/S ratios are used to maximise the given doubled-yarn characteristics: for maximum lustre, a D/S ratio of approximately 0.7 is used; for maximum tenacity it is approximately 1.5; for maximum balance it is 0.5; and for maximum extension the ratio is greater than 0.7.

Many other factors affect the yarn characteristics, for example yarn tension during doubling will affect the yarn tenacity, extension and lustre. Obviously it is not possible to have both maximum lustre and maximum balance in the same yarn. A compromise must be made and the yarn characteristics desired must be prioritised for each end-use.

Designation of doubled yarn structures

Some form of notation is needed to describe plied and cabled yarns. This must include the values for linear density, amount and direction of twist, number of component yarns.

There is more than one method of describing a plied or cabled yarn.

TEX SYSTEM

Within the tex system, there are two ways of describing a yarn. It might be a single to doubled designation, or a doubled to single designation. Both these methods use the same symbols, except that in the former, the multiplication sign (×) is used, whereas in the later, the solidus (/) is used.

Single to doubled designation

1 Single yarns. Here only the linear density, direction and amount of twist are necessary, for instance 40 tex Z 660. This is a single yarn with a linear density of 40 tex, Z twist direction and 660 turns of twist per metre.

2. Ply yarns. The information for the single-yarn components is given as above. A multiplication sign separates this information from the ply information, that is from the number of single yarn components, the direction and amount of ply twist, for instance 34 tex Z 660 × 2 S 400; R 69.3 tex. The symbol R indicates the resulting yarn tex after the doubling operation. The resulting yarn tex used in the example is not twice the tex value of the single yarn as might be expected. This is due to twist contraction. The nominal or approximate resulting yarn tex would have been 68 tex. The actual value is found by using the correct test method.

3. Cabled yarns. The designation of the ply yarn components of the cabled yarn would be as above. Again, a second multiplication sign separates this information from the cable information (the number of ply yarn components, direction and amount of cabling twist). For instance, 20 tex Z 700 × 2 S 400 × 3 Z 200; R 132 tex.

Doubled to single designation

1. Ply yarns. The resulting yarn tex is given first, following the symbol R. The direction and amount of ply twist are followed by the solidus (/), the number of single yarn components, the direction and amount of single yarn twist. This system has the single yarn tex to finish. For example, R 69.3 tex S 400 / 2 Z 600; 34 tex.

2. Cabled yarns. The symbol R, cabled yarn-resultant tex, direction and amount of twist are given first, followed by the information for the ply and single yarns as given above, for instance 20 tex Z 700 × 2 S 400 × 3 Z 200; R 132 tex.

COTTON COUNT SYSTEM

In this case, the single yarn count is given first, then the number of single yarn components, again these are separated by a solidus. For example, 30/2 is a two ply cotton count yarn, composed of two single 30s yarns, with a resultant count of 15s cotton count.

WORSTED AND WOOLLEN SYSTEMS

For a simple ply yarn, the number of single-yarn components is given first, then a solidus (/), then the count of the single yarn components. The resulting yarn count is found by dividing the count by the number of single yarn components. For instance, if two single yarns of 30s worsted count are twisted together, they would be designated as 2/30s. The resulting count of the plied yarn would be 15s worsted count.

Methods of twisting

There are three main methods used in the production of folded yarns, conventional ring twisting, **two-for-one twisting** and **stage twisting**.

Ring twisting

This uses the ring and traveller technique and is similar to ring spinning. The single-yarn packages, which may or may not be assembly wound, are supported in a creel and the unwinding yarn is led downwards through a roller delivery system. The delivery system should be capable of controlling the yarn supply rate positively, without slippage.

From the delivery system, the yarn passes down through a hinged lappet guide and to the take-up package via a traveller. The take-up package is situated on a revolving spindle, which

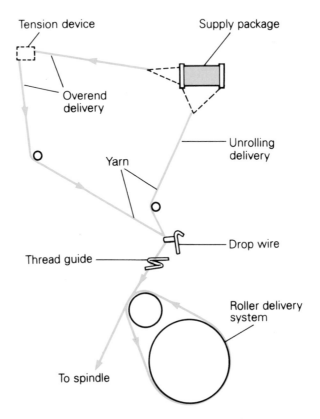

Figure 10.2 **Ring doubler creel showing two methods of delivery.**

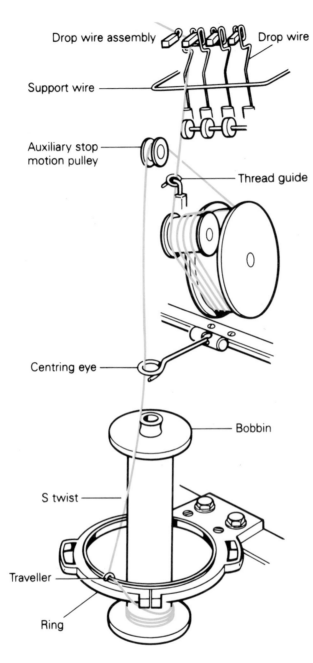

Figure 10.3 Ring doubler.

rotates within a steel ring. The traveller, which is basically a nylon clip, is free to rotate about the ring and it serves to guide the yarn on to the bobbin. When the spindle rotates, the package will attempt to wind up the delivered yarn. Because of the high spindle speed, however, the tension rises quickly and the traveller is dragged round the ring. For each revolution of the traveller, one turn of twist is inserted into the yarn.

In the meantime, the roller system is delivering yarn which relieves, to some extent, the tension. Providing an appropriate traveller mass is chosen, the system assumes a state of equilibrium in which the traveller velocity is dictated by the yarn tension. The traveller lags behind the bobbin by an amount which is automatically sufficient to allow winding-on to take place. The overall arrangement allows the production of a twisted yarn which is, at the same time, conveniently wound on to a package.

$$\text{Turns per m} = \frac{\text{traveller revs min}}{\text{yarn delivery rate in m min}}$$

(For practical purposes, the traveller speed may be assumed to be equal to the spindle speed.)

For example, if the spindle speed is 6500 revolutions per minute and the yarn delivery rate is 13 metres per minute, the inserted twist will be:

$$\frac{6500}{13} = 500 \text{ turns m}^{-1}$$

Two-for-one twisting

The concept of two-for-one twisting is a simple one. If a yarn is held at two points while a third point is rotated, two turns of twist are inserted for every revolution of the third point.

The assembly wound yarn is withdrawn from the package by a rotating arm. The yarn passes through a hollow rotating spindle and through an outlet in the base and forms a balloon. The yarn then passes through a guide and is wound on to a package. Each revolution of the spindle inserts one turn of twist into the yarn as it passes down the hollow spindle and causes the yarn balloon to rotate, thereby putting another turn of twist in. The two turns are in the same direction, so two turns of twist are added for each revolution of the spindle.

The advantages of the two-for-one twisting system are that two turns of twist are inserted for every one revolution of the spindle, the take-up package can be a cone or cheese so eliminating the need for rewinding, there is a reasonably constant balloon tension, a large take-up package and a saving in floor space. The major disadvantage is the high capital cost.

Stage twisting

These systems carry out the twisting operation in two distinct stages:

Stage 1:   Assembling the component yarns with a small amount of twist just sufficient to bind the components together and prevent their displacement relative to one another during insertion of remaining twist.

Stage 2:   Insertion of remaining twist.

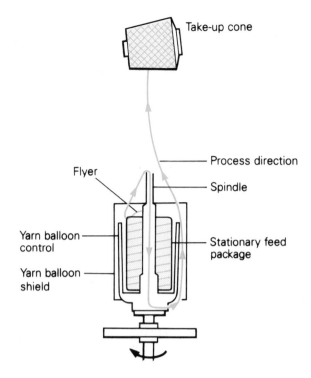

Figure 10.4 Two-for-one twisting.

A ring doubler is normally employed for Stage 1, with a very high delivery rate. An uptwister is used for Stage 2. Figure 10.5 shows the basic principle of stage twisting. The use of an uptwisting spindle eliminates the disadvantages of the ring and traveller (traveller speed restrictions, variations in yarn tension) but requires a package which can be unwound over end at high speed.

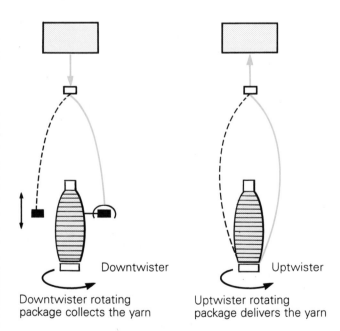

Downtwister rotating package collects the yarn

Uptwister rotating package delivers the yarn

Figure 10.5 Stage twisting.

End-uses for plied yarns

Table 10.1 Typical end-uses for plied yarns

2-fold	3-fold	multi-end
poplins	sewing threads	industrial yarns
voiles	industrial yarns	braids
gaberdines	canvas	electrical insulation
crepes	webbing	cords
lace	filter cloths	shoe laces
sewing threads	conveyor belts	embroidery
general purpose	hosiery	hosiery
		v-belt cords

End-uses for cabled yarns

Table 10.2 Typical end-uses for cabled yarns

Fine	Coarse
fine sewing threads	industrial cords
crochet yarns	heavy sewing threads
nets	tyre cords
re-enforcing threads	nettings
	fishing lines

Fancy yarns

Sometimes fabric producers require novelty or 'fancy' yarns to produce different textures and effects in their fabrics. Fancy yarns can be made from all natural fibres, all man-made fibres or blends of both. They can be from pre-dyed or undyed fibres and yarns.

Although they are very decorative, fancy yarns are not hard wearing if used alone and so are usually combined with straight hard-wearing yarns. As fancy yarns are more expensive to produce, this also helps to reduce fabric costs.

In weaving, heavier fancy yarns are used only in the weft, because they tend to unravel in the warp due to the stresses they undergo. Finer fancy yarns can be used in warp as they pass easily through the loom. Fabrics containing fancy yarns are used for many textile purposes, for instance apparel such as dress fabrics, or household textiles such as curtains and upholstery.

> **A fancy yarn** can be defined as one that differs from the normal construction of a single or doubled yarn by deliberately introduced irregularities in its construction.

The irregularities in a fancy yarn can be an increased delivery rate of one or more of its components, or the inclusion of periodic effects such as knops, loops, curls, slubs or the like.

Basic fancy yarn

Generally, fancy yarns contain two or more of the following: a base or core yarn, around which the end intended to create the fancy effect is wrapped; the effect yarn, which forms the design; and the binder which holds the effect yarn in place on the base to prevent it slipping while it is being wound, knitted or woven.

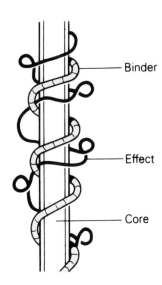

Figure 10.6   Basic fancy yarn.

Fancy yarn types

BOUCLE, GIMP AND LOOP

All these fancy yarns are produced by delivering the core and effect yarn at different rates. Boucle is a twisted core yarn, with the effect yarn wrapped around the core producing an irregular wavy surface. Gimp is the same as boucle but the effect yarn has a regular semi-circular appearance, while in loop, the effect yarn appears as well-formed circular loops.

Figure 10.7   Loop and gimp yarns.

ECCENTRIC

This is basically an undulating gimp yarn, produced by binding an irregular yarn in the opposite direction to the initial twist, creating graduated semi-circular loops.

Figure 10.8   An eccentric (slub gimp) yarn.

SNARL

This is made in the same way as a loop yarn, but using a highly twisted effect yarn which forms snarls rather than loops.

Figure 10.9   A snarl yarn.

KNOP (BUTTON)

This features prominent bunches of one or more of the component yarns at regular or irregular intervals.

Figure 10.10   A snarl or button yarn.

SPIRAL/CORKSCREW

A plied yarn, in which one of the components wraps around the other, rather than the components twisting regularly together under the same tension. A spiral yarn tends to have a higher twist than a corkscrew yarn.

Figure 10.11   A corkscrew yarn.

CHENILLE

This yarn has a cut pile effect which is bound to the core. This can be produced on either a specialised machine, used solely for producing chenille yarns, or it can be made on a loom. The warp threads in the loom are arranged in groups of two to six ends which are interlaced in a cross-weaving manner. The weft is inserted in the normal manner, between the warp threads which are spaced at suitable intervals to give the required length of pile. Each pick represents one pile thread and these are cut into warp-way strips to produce the yarn.

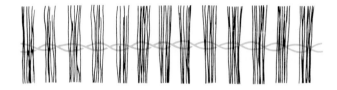

Figure 10.12 A chenille yarn.

SLUB

This is composed of short, abnormally thick places at regular or irregular intervals. There are basically two types of slub yarn; either the slub effect is spun into the yarn, or injected into the yarn.

Figure 10.13 A slub yarn.

CLOUD

A two-colour yarn, in which both yarns take it in turn to obscure or cloud the other, giving the appearance of an intermittent colour change.

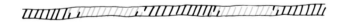

Figure 10.14 A cloud yarn.

FLECK

Small amounts of fibres of either different colours or lustre or both, are introduced into the yarn. This gives it a spotted and short streaky appearance.

Figure 10.15 A fleck yarn.

Production of fancy yarns

There are three methods used to produce fancy yarns: ring twisting, wrap spinning and a combination of wrap spinning and ring twisting.

RING TWISTING

In the case of ring twisting, production is carried out on either a fancy yarn doubler or a modified ring-spinning machine. Extra guides enable pre-spun yarns to be fed into the fancy yarn to give the desired effect.

There is usually a separate doubling operation to bind the effect yarn to the core where necessary.

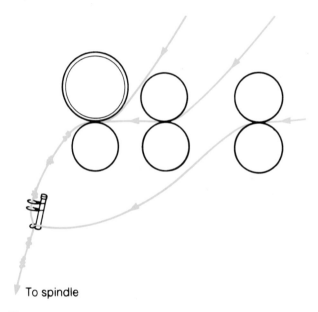

To spindle

Figure 10.16 Delivery of rollers of a ring doubler, modified to produce a fancy yarn.

WRAP SPINNING

Sliver is fed to a conventional roller-drafting system. When drafted, the fibres are guided in a straight line through the centre of the rotating hollow spindle. The wrapping yarn or binder is wound on to this spindle and feeds through the centre of its spindle with the drafted fibres.

The wrapping yarn is wound around the twistless core of the drafted fibres due to the rotation of the spindle. This permanent twist is inserted between the delivery rollers and the yarn guide at the bottom of the hollow spindle. The yarn is then wound on to a cone by the driving and traverse drum.

Fancy yarns are made by this method which can produce an effect yarn in one operation that would otherwise require several separate twisting operations on a conventional system.

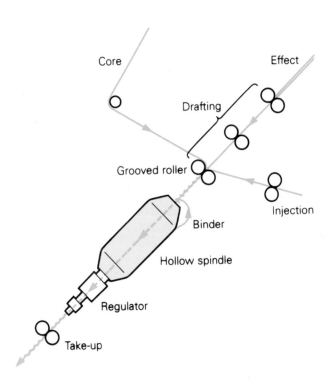

Figure 10.17 Fancy wrap spinner.

On fancy wrap-spinning machines there are also facilities to feed in effect yarns and inject slubs. They are set up to produce four main fancy yarn types, with an additional special yarn programme which can use the flexibility of the machine to produce a yarn using a combination of the other four yarn programmes.

1. Basic (boucle). This is produced by overfeeding between the front drafting roller and the delivery roller. This allows the central fibres of the yarn to form loops which are then bound to the core yarn by the binder.
2. Button (knop). The delivery roller is stopped momentarily to allow a short build-up of fibres producing the knop effect.
3. Flamme (stripe). This is like an elongated knop. The front drafting roller is slowed down to produce a slightly longer and more gradual effect.
4. Injected slub. There is a second mini-drafting system positioned behind the main drafting system. It can be programmed to run intermittently, injecting other fibres, usually from a roving bobbin, as required. These fibres then appear as slubs in the yarn.

In the case of button , flamme and slub yarns, the frequency of the effect can be regular or irregular. The designer can set the length of the effect and the length of the spaces between the effect.

These yarns can all be programmed directly into the machine via the keyboard on the control panel. The machine speeds are then altered electrically as all parts are driven by independent motors. The direction of twist is also set via the keyboard. The only caution here is to remember that the yarn on the hollow spindle has to be wound in the correct direction for the rotation of the spindle, otherwise it will not wind off correctly.

This electronic adjustment represents a huge saving in time, especially in the development stages. On a conventional ring twister, any alterations would have to be done manually by adjusting the gearing mechanisms that drive all the rollers and spindles. Any slight alterations represent both effort and down-time if they have to be done manually.

The other way of programming the machine is through a mini tape. This is ideal, as any yarn programmed can be recorded on mini tape to be used if a repeat is required.

WRAP SPINNING AND RING TWISTING

The initial effect and core yarns are produced on the fancy hollow spindle spinner. A further doubling operation on a ring twister secures or binds the effect to the core.

CHECK YOUR UNDERSTANDING

● Doubling produces yarns with characteristics that could not be obtained using single yarns, characteristics of uniformity, tenacity, balance, lustre and extension at break. These can be superior to the equivalent singles yarn.
● Twist direction is only important if the single yarn is to be doubled. The ratio of twist level in the doubled yarn to single yarn will determine the resulting yarn character in terms of maximum tenacity, maximum lustre, maximum balance and maximum extension.
● Ply yarns are produced by twisting two or more single yarns together in one twisting operation. Cabled yarns are produced by twisting two or more ply yarns together in two separate twisting operations.
● There are three main methods commonly in use for the production of doubled yarns: ring twisting, stage twisting and two-for-one twisting.
● There are many types of fancy yarn, all produced by introducing irregularities. They are loop, chenille, snarl, eccentric, slub, boucle, fleck, cloud, gimp, knop and corkscrew. Fancy yarns contain at least two of the following: a core, a binder and an effect.
● Three methods are commonly used to produce fancy yarns: ring doubling, hollow spindle spinning, or a combination of hollow spindle spinning and ring doubling.
● The end-uses of fancy yarns are almost exclusively in the apparel and household textile sectors.

REVISION EXERCISES AND QUESTIONS

1   What do you think the terms two-ply, three-ply, and four-ply refer to?

2   What would you consider to be the most important reason for using a ply or cabled yarn for the following end-uses? Embroidery thread; poplin or voile fabric; webbing; sewing threads; and hosiery.

3   Why is twist balance so important in knitting yarns?

4   How would you designate the following yarns?
    a) Three single 12 tex yarns have been plied together to form an S twist yarn with 400 turns per metre. The single yarn twist level is 700 turns per metre, Z direction. The resulting tex value is 35.
    b) Two 20s woollen count yarns are twisted together. Roughly, what would be the resulting count?

5   What is the major disadvantage of two-for-one twisting?

6   Why are fancy yarns rarely used to make up 100 per cent of a fabric?

7   Why is the linear density alone not enough to determine whether a fancy yarn will be suitable for a knitting or weaving machine?

Yarn testing

Introduction

Some form of quality control is needed at every stage of manufacture so that the finished product will be satisfactory to the customer and will hopefully lead to repeat orders. Testing is a means to this end, but two things must be remembered. No matter how well a material has been tested, this does not improve its quality because testing instruments cannot make decisions. Some person must interpret results and decide what action if any must be taken.

There are several reasons for testing. Selection of raw materials would be very much a matter of luck without fibre tests to determine the characteristics of that particular batch, monitoring and control of processing conditions are essential to the quality of the end-product, research and development of processes would not take place without some way of evaluating the processes, checking of the finished product is always a good idea even though this should be unnecessary if process control is efficient, and checking against customer specifications should be done at the beginning of the run to avoid rejection of the whole order.

Why test yarns?

Selection of raw material

The raw material of the spinner is the fibre. One thing that all textile raw materials have in common is their variability.

Prevention is better than cure, so it pays to test raw materials to keep the production process running smoothly. It is now possible with modern technology to test all the raw cotton bales in less than one day that are to be used by a spinning mill in a week.

Armed with this information, the technologist can select or reject individual bales of fibre.

Process control

If a process goes out of control, much time and money can be wasted producing sub-standard material. The earlier problems can be detected, the sooner the process can be brought back under control and faulty material isolated.

Standards must be set, with limits on either side of the standard. Material that falls within the limits is allowed to pass forward to the next stage in processing. In traditional mills, this monitoring is still carried out manually by operatives at set times in the day. In mills equipped with more modern machinery, there is electronic **on-line monitoring equipment** which is continuously assessing the process.

Research and development

If experimental work is being carried out, the effects of any alterations to the product or processing system must be assessed. Testing the material is the only reliable way of doing this.

Product testing

If process control was perfect, there would be no need to check the final product. This is last-resort testing, as if faults are found, it is usually too late to trace them back to the processing system and too much faulty or sub-standard material has been produced. It does, however, mean that a manufacturer's reputation can be saved by picking up the faulty goods before they are dispatched to the customer.

Specifications

Many customers will now supply the spinner with a specification. This will describe the yarn in technical terms and will give acceptance limits for each yarn parameter. For example, the linear density will be quoted, with the limit 20 tex, plus or minus two, which means the yarn must fall within the limits of 18 to 22 tex.

If the customer has given a specification, it is very likely that she will test the yarn – her raw material – against this. She will be entirely within her rights to return the yarn batch if it is not up to the agreed specification.

The main staple yarn parameters to be tested are linear density, twist direction, twist level, tenacity and regularity. The most important textured continuous filament parameter is the **crimp rigidity**.

Raw material impurity content

Trash content of raw cotton

The trash content of raw cotton is determined with the aid of a machine known as a trash analyser. The analyser takes advantage of the fact that fibres have a much higher surface area for a given mass than trash particles. A current of air is used. When the sample is fed into the machine, the air stream carries the fibres along with it horizontally while the trash falls down and in this way, the two are separated. The separated fibres (**lint**) may still contain some trash, in which case they are fed through the machine again. With older machines, the sample is only separated into lint and trash. The latest versions separate the trash into different types according to particle size.

To simplify the calculation, the original sample size is 100 grams. After separation, the trash is weighed.

Trash content (%) = trash weight.

If the trash content of samples is measured before and after processing, the cleaning efficiency of the process can be determined.

Grease and suint content of raw wool

The information required by the wool processor is the **yield of raw wool**. This is the per centage clean wool which will be obtained after the impurities have been removed.

The impurities in raw wool are removed by **emulsion scouring**. When determining yield in a laboratory, the impurities are removed using the same process but on a smaller scale. Wool absorbs a large amount of water vapour from the atmosphere, whereas the impurity does not. The amount of water vapour absorbed depends on the atmospheric conditions. This absorbed water vapour interferes with any method where weighing is involved. The best way to overcome this interference is to remove the water by drying and add a standard allowance to the final answer.

An outline of the procedure is as follows:

1. A small representative sample of raw wool is prepared.
2. The sample is dried thoroughly in an oven at 105°C.
3. The dried sample is weighed accurately in a weighing bottle to prevent re-absorption of water vapour.
4. The sample is scoured in a beaker using dilute soap solution and weak alkali as detergent.
5. The scoured sample is rinsed in warm water to remove traces of impurity and detergent.
6. The clean sample is dried thoroughly in an oven at 105°C.
7. The clean dry sample is weighed accurately in a weighing bottle.

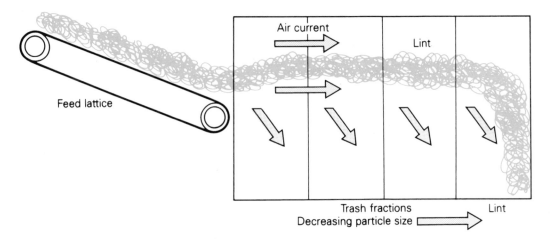

Figure 11.1 Schematic diagram of trash analyser.

The yield is calculated on a dry weight basis with a standard addition for absorbed water vapour.

$$\text{Yield (\%)} = \frac{m(1 + \frac{R}{100})}{M + \frac{Rm}{100}} \times 100$$

where M = dry weight of original greasy sample,

m = dry weight of scoured sample, and

R = standard regain allowance.

Linear density

Measurement of linear density and count

A hank of yarn is wound on a wrap reel and weighed on a sensitive balance.

It is inconvenient and unnecessary to wrap a whole length unit of yarn (one kilometre or 840 yards), so only a proportion is wrapped. This propotion is 100 metres when using the tex system (100 revs × 1 m) and 120 yards when using the cotton count system (80 revs × 1.5 yd).

The precise length of yarn in the hank depends on the winding tension, so the dimensions (girth) of the hank should be checked using a skein gauge. The skein gauge has a scale showing any deviation from the correct girth, allowing a correction to be made to the results.

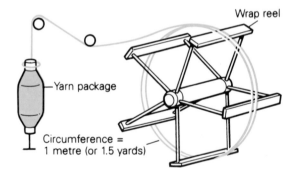

Figure 11.2 Measurement of yarn linear density.

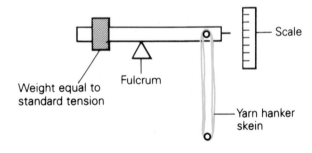

Figure 11.3 Skein gauge.

EXAMPLES OF CALCULATIONS

1. A 100 metre hank of yarn weighs 2.53 grams.

$$\text{The linear density} = \frac{2.53 \times 1000}{100}$$

$$= 25.3 \text{ tex}$$

2. When using cotton count, weight is usually measured in grains. As there are 7000 grains in 1 pound (lb):

$$\text{cotton count} = \frac{\text{yards}}{\text{grains}} \times \frac{7000}{840}$$

$$= \frac{120}{84} \times \frac{7000}{840}$$

$$= 12 \text{ N}_e$$

Simple balances (for example a quadrant balance) are calibrated in count or linear density units. Modern electronic balances are available which incorporate a microprocessor and printer. The microprocessor calculates count or linear density in any desired unit, calculates the variation within a large sample, and gives warning if the linear density is outside limits.

Twist

Twist testing is the measure of the number of spiral turns given to a roving or yarn in order to hold all the fibres together. Twist is put into a yarn to give it the desired characteristics. In some cases, strength is the most important factor, for example in single yarns used for a warp. In other cases the strength is not as important but the yarn must be soft and bulky, for example weft yarns. Sometimes the yarn needs to be very compact or even twist lively, for example crepe yarns.

Twist direction

For Z twist yarns, the spindle rotates in a clockwise direction. For S twist yarns the spindle rotates in an anticlockwise direction. In single yarns, the twist direction has no effect on the yarn characteristics.

Measurement of twist

Twist is not usually distributed uniformly along a yarn, because higher levels of twist are found in thin places. It is usually recommended that at least one metre is left between

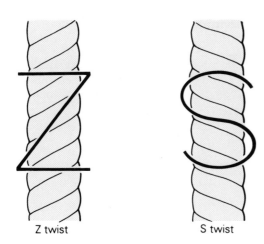

Z twist   S twist

Figure 11.4 Twist directions.

STRAIGHTENED FIBRE METHOD

A short length of yarn is clamped under a standard tension. The distance between the clamps must be shorter than the fibre length. It is usually set at either one centimetre or one inch. One of the clamps is rotated until a dissecting needle can be inserted at one clamp and run to the next clamp – in other words, until the fibres are parallel.

$$\text{Twist level} = \frac{\text{number of revolutions of clamp}}{\text{specimen length}}$$

TWIST CONTRACTION METHOD

When twist is inserted into a yarn, it decreases in length as all the fibres now run in a helical path rather than a straight path. When twist is removed during twist testing, the yarn increases in length again. This method uses this twist contraction as a means of measuring the twist level, rather than using the eye to see when all the twist has been removed.

A relatively long length of yarn (usually 25 centimetres) is clamped. One clamp is stationary, the other clamp is attached to a needle. The stationary clamp is rotated to remove the twist. The needle clamp moves over a quadrant scale as the yarn length increases. When all the twist has been removed, the clamp continues to be rotated, causing twist to be

consecutive twist tests to avoid this uneven distribution affecting results. Yarn can be withdrawn from a package in two ways: over the end of the package (over-end delivery), or from the side (unrolling delivery). It is recommended that for twist testing, yarn is withdrawn in the same way that it would normally be at the next stage of processing. Over-end delivery will affect the twist slightly, but unrolling delivery should not affect it at all.

There are two main methods of testing twist in single yarns, the straightened fibre method and the twist contraction method.

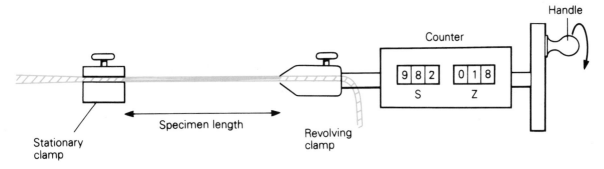

Figure 11.5 Straightened fibre method.

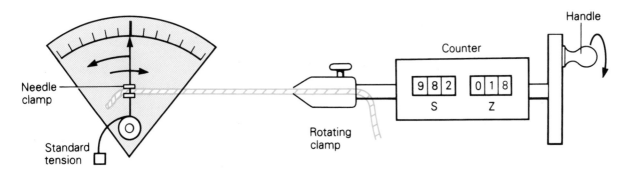

Figure 11.6 Twist contraction method.

inserted in the opposite direction. The yarn decreases in length again, causing the needle clamp to move back over the quadrant scale until it reaches its original position.

All the twist has been removed and as much put back in the opposite direction. The reading on the counter is actually twice the amount of twist in the yarn length.

$$\text{Twist level} = \frac{\text{number of revolutions of clamp}}{2 \times \text{specimen length}}$$

Yarn tenacity

The strength of a yarn is one of its most important characteristics, largely governing its performance in further processing. Measurement of the strength of a yarn is known as tensile testing.

Tensile testing is the loading of a yarn along its main axis. A weight or load is put on the yarn which measures the load in grams, kilograms or Newtons. The breaking load is the weight at which the yarn specimen breaks. The stretch or elongation in the yarn is also measured; the extension at break is the total increase in yarn length up to the breaking load. Extension is measured in centimetres or millimetres or given as a per centage.

Figure 11.7 Yarn tensile testing.

Load/elongation curve

The load and extension can be plotted on a graph. This is then known as a load/elongation curve which describes how the specimen behaves from zero load and extension up to the breaking point.

Yarn tenacity

If we wish to compare the results of tensile tests on yarns, the thickness and length of the yarn specimen must be taken into account. This will give the yarn tenacity. To compare results independently of their dimensions, we must use units of stress and strain rather than load and elongation.

STRESS

Stress is used rather than load because it takes into account the thickness of the material (a thicker material has a larger cross-sectional area and should therefore be able to bear more load than a thinner material). Stress is the load for a given cross-sectional area. As this is difficult to measure in yarns, the specific stress is used, which is the load for a given linear density.

$$\text{Specific stress} = \frac{\text{load}}{\text{linear density}}$$

Typically, the units of stress are grams per tex (g/tex), or grams per decitex (g/decitex). Using the correct SI units, load is measured in Newtons (N), the unit of force.

Force = mass × acceleration

Assume that acceleration due to gravity is 9.81 m s^{-2}

load (N) = mass (kg) × 9.81 (m s^{-2})

The SI units of specific stress are therefore Newtons per tex (N tex).

STRAIN

Strain is used rather than elongation because this measures the increase in length as a proportion of the initial length:

$$\text{strain} = \frac{\text{elongation (mm)}}{\text{initial length (mm)}}$$

Strain is a proportion and so has no units. It is sometimes quoted as the per centage extension:

per centage extension = strain × 100

MEASUREMENT OF YARN TENACITY

In the quality control laboratories of many spinning mills, the strength of a lea (120 yards) of yarn is tested, this being known as lea-strength testing. A hank of yarn, 120 yards long with its ends knotted together, is placed over the hooks of the testing instrument. The bottom hook moves down at a constant rate, so loading the hank. A number of the strands of yarn in the hank will break, until the point is reached where the remaining threads cannot bear any further load. This is noted as the breaking load. It has been a popular test because it is quick and simple, tests a relatively large sample of yarn and the broken hanks can be used for testing linear density.

For more accurate and flexible testing, single-thread strength testing is used. A load is applied to a single yarn specimen. Both breaking load and extension at break are noted. Some testing instruments will also automatically give a load elongation curve. If the instrument is also given the necessary information – yarn linear density and specimen test length – a stress/strain curve may also be possible.

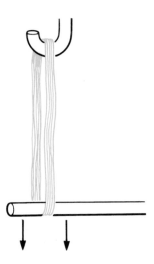

Figure 11.8 Lea strength testing.

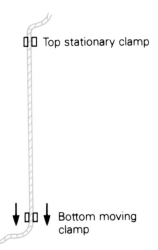

□□ Top stationary clamp

↓ □□ ↓ Bottom moving clamp

Figure 11.9 Single thread strength testing.

Yarn evenness

Growth in the case of natural fibres, and production factors in the case of man made fibres, give rise to variations in length, width and shape of fibres. The nature of this raw material makes manipulation of fibres very difficult.

Ideally, fibres are arranged parallel to the yarn main axis (length), laid end to end and spiral in form due to twist. In reality not all fibres are parallel, there are gaps between some fibre ends and overlaps of others, with folds and kinks instead of a regular spiral. Add to this the introduction of faults during processing and it is not surprising that unevenness or irregularity in yarn fineness occurs.

Yarns can be uneven or irregular in other ways such as strength, blend and twist, but this chapter will deal solely with yarn fineness irregularities.

Effects of yarn unevenness

> Yarn strength is affected by variation in fineness, which in turn affects further processing, such as knitting or weaving. Weaker yarn also means lower efficiencies during yarn production itself. In addition to the effects on yarn properties, irregularity adversely affects fabric properties such as visual appearance, dyeing ability or uniformity and fabric weight uniformity.

Woven fabrics tend to show bars across the width of the cloth due to yarn irregularity. This effect can be reduced or eliminated by **weft mixing** at the loom. This is using yarn alternately from different packages to form the weft. If the irregularity is relatively short and frequent, however, weft mixing will have no beneficial effect.

Knitted fabrics are the most susceptible to yarn irregularities, that is they are most noticeable in knitted fabrics, particularly in **weft knitted single jersey** fabrics. Carpets will display streaks due to yarn irregularity.

Twist tends to be higher at thin places in the yarn. When a dye or finish is applied to the fabric, penetration is less in areas of higher twist, which emphasises the yarn fault.

Fabric weight uniformity is dependent on yarn regularity. If the yarn weight per unit length varies, the cloth weight will vary. Weight uniformity is essential in fabrics for paper making and for filters.

Causes of yarn unevenness

> Irregularity in a yarn can be the result of two factors: irregularity in the fibre diameter or irregularity in the fibre arrangement.

Man-made fibres can vary slightly due to conditions during production, but natural fibres are subject to most variation. Climatic conditions, age, treatments used and variety of plant or breed of animal will give rise to greater variations in the fibre than varying conditions during man-made fibre extrusion.

The second factor is dependent on the machinery used to process the fibre and the staff who run, set up and maintain the machinery.

Methods used to describe yarn unevenness

If a strand of material is cut up into short equal lengths, the weight of each consecutive length could be found and plotted on a graph. By joining the points a trace is produced. This shows the way in which the weight per unit length varies about the mean value.

Figure 11.10 gives some idea of regularity, but it would be difficult to compare different yarns using a diagram alone. Using statistics, a number can be calculated that represents how even the material is.

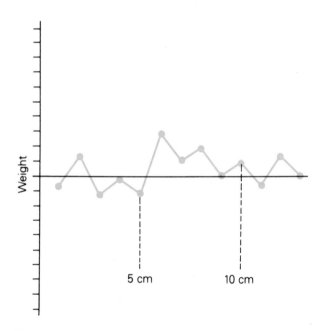

Figure 11.10 Weight of consecutive 1 cm lengths.

PERCENTAGE MEAN DEVIATION

The deviations of individual results from the mean result can be found. The mean deviation can be calculated and the percentage mean deviation (PMD) derived and used as a measure of irregularity. The higher the mean deviation (and so the PMD), the more the material is straying from the middle line. The higher the number, the more irregular the material.

All the numbers in the first column of Table 11.1 are weights of one centimetre of yarn. These have then been totalled at the base of the column and the mean value found by dividing this sum by the number of results:

$$\frac{0.35}{10} = 3.5$$

Table 11.1 Calculating deviation from the mean, example 1

yarn weight (mg cm – (x))	Deviation from the mean (x – x̄)
0.37	0.02
0.32	0.03
0.34	0.01
0.39	0.04
0.31	0.04
0.41	0.06
0.33	0.02
0.30	0.05
0.42	0.07
0.31	0.04
sum x = 3.50	sum of deviations = 0.38
mean x̄ = 0.35	

The second column shows by how much each individual result is different from this mean value of 0.35. Because we are after the difference between the mean and individual result, the sign – plus or minus – does not matter and so is left out. Again, the sum of all these differences is at the base of the second column (0.38).

The mean deviation is then found by dividing the sum of the deviations by the number of deviations:

$$\text{mean deviation} = \frac{\text{sum of deviations}}{\text{number of results}} = \frac{0.38}{10} = 0.038$$

This number on its own is difficult to compare with other mean deviations if we have yarns of different tex values. For ease of comparison, the mean deviation is expressed as a percentage by dividing by the mean value:

$$\text{percentage mean deviation} = \frac{\text{mean deviation}}{\text{mean}} \times 100$$

$$= \frac{0.038}{0.35} \times 100 = 10.86\%$$

STANDARD DEVIATION

Alternatively the standard deviation can be calculated. As before, the higher the number, the more irregular the material.

As for the mean deviation, the individual results are added up and the mean calculated. The second column is the individual result minus the mean value. The third column is the deviations squared, and remember that the sign – plus or minus – disappears when squared. These squared deviations are then totalled at the foot of the column (0.0176). The variance is found by dividing the sum of the squares by the number of results minus 1:

$$\text{variance} = \frac{0.0176}{(10 - 1)} = \frac{0.0176}{9} = 0.001956$$

The standard deviation is the square root of the variance:

$$\text{standard deviation} = \sqrt{0.001956} = 0.0442$$

The problem with the standard deviation is that you cannot compare yarns of different linear densities. To do this, the standard deviation must be related to the mean result. This is then known as the coefficient of variation.

COEFFICIENT OF VARIATION (CV)

The percentage mean deviation and the **coefficient of variation** are related, but only if there is a normal distribution of results, that is a random distribution. The coefficient of variation is usually expressed as a percentage: CV%.

$$CV\% = \frac{s}{\overline{x}} \times 100 \qquad \begin{array}{l} \text{Where } s = \text{standard deviation} \\ \overline{x} = \text{sample mean result} \end{array}$$

Using the figures from Table 11.2 :

$$CV\% = \frac{0.0442}{0.35} \times 100 = 12.63\%$$

Periodic variations

Not all variation measurements have a normal, random distribution. Some traces of variation show regularly spaced thick and thin places, known as **periodic variations**. These variations are described in terms of their amplitude and wavelength.

The amplitude is a measure of the size of the meander from the mean level and is usually expressed as a percentage of the mean level. The wavelength is the distance between thick or thin places.

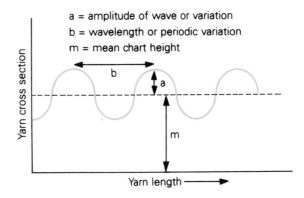

Figure 11.11 Periodic variations.

Limit irregularity and index of irregularity

The **limit irregularity** is the inherent irregularity in material with a random fibre distribution. It is the best possible regularity achievable. The **index of irregularity** (I) gives a measure of how far an individual yarn is from this ideal limit.

Table 11.2 Calculating deviation from the mean, example 2

Yarn weight (mg cm – (x))	Deviation from the mean (x + / − /$\overline{x}$)	Deviation^2
0.37	+0.02	0.0004
0.32	−0.03	0.0009
0.34	−0.01	0.0001
0.39	+0.04	0.0016
0.31	−0.04	0.0016
0.41	+0.06	0.0036
0.33	−0.02	0.0004
0.30	−0.05	0.0025
0.42	+0.07	0.0049
0.31	−0.04	0.0016
sum x = 3.50		sum of deviations^2 = 0.0176
mean $\overline{x}$ = 0.35		

$$\text{Limit } CV\% = \frac{k}{\sqrt{n}}$$

where $n =$ number of fibres in cross section

$k =$ constant dependent on fibre type

$k = 106$ for cotton

$k = 112$ for wool

$k = 100$ for man-made fibre

$$\text{Index of irregularity} \quad I = \frac{\text{Actual } CV}{\text{Limit } CV}$$

The closer the index is to one, the more ideal is the yarn. In practice, the index is always greater than one.

Short, medium and long-term irregularity

It is often useful to be able to classify irregularity as **short-term**, **medium-term** or **long-term**. This gives some indication of where in the processing sequence the irregularity occurred. While there is no rule on these class divisions, it is comman for variations to be classified by their wavelength expressed as a number of fibre length units:

short-term variation	1–10 times the fibre length
medium-term variation	10–100 times the fibre length
long-term variation	100–1000 times the fibre length

The amplitude of short-term variations is usually higher than those of medium- or long-term variations. This is because they are caused in the last machine and have had no chance of being reduced by drafting or doubling.

Count variation is classed as the variation between the weights of a **lea** (120 yards) of yarn.

Measurement of yarn evenness

Cutting and weighing is one technique which was used in the measurement of irregularity, but this is slow and labour intensive. Instruments have been developed which automatically produce a trace of variation and calculate either the PMD or the CV%.

SUBJECTIVE VISUAL ASSESSMENT

A single end of yarn is wrapped around a matt black board. This board has guides at both ends to enable a regular close spacing of the yarn, which imitates the appearance of a woven fabric.

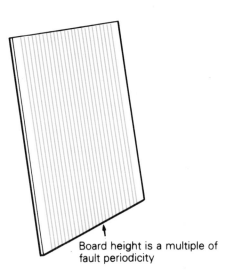

Figure 11.12 Taper black board.

The board is compared visually with photographed standard boards of yarns with varying degrees of regularity. This comparison should be done under good lighting conditions, that is a uniform, non-directional light, with the option of edge lighting that will highlight neps, for example.

Sometimes it is desirable to assess large quantities of yarn, like a whole package. A wrapping drum with a matt black surface can be used for this purpose. The drum diameter is usually in the order of one metre.

If a periodic fault is suspected, a tapered board may be used. The visual effect can be likened to a wood grain pattern. At the point where the peak of the pattern occurs, the board height is a multiple of the fault wavelength.

OBJECTIVE ELECTRONIC MEASUREMENT

A large length of yarn is run at a steady rate between the plates of an electronic capacitor. The mass of the yarn between the plates of this capacitor will alter its value. As the capacitor is of a fixed length, it is actually the yarn linear density which alters the capacitor value. Measuring of the capacitor's changing value is done electronically, and so very rapidly. It is the equivalent of cutting and weighing consecutive short equal lengths of yarn.

Modern **capacitance measuring instruments** will calculate the per centage mean range, coefficient of variation and number of imperfections (short lengths of very large variations in linear density) with a number of different options.

Measurement of the evenness of slivers and rovings is also possible with a change of material guides and size of capacitors.

The level of moisture in the material will affect the size of change in capacity, a high moisture content giving a greater change in capacity. If the moisture content is constant throughout the length of the material, this will have no effect on the coefficient of variation. It is consistency in moisture content rather than level of moisture content that is important.

This testing instrument has a number of outputs: diagram, spectrogram and imperfections. The diagram traces out the variations in the mass of the material against time. The spectrogram traces out the variations in the mass of the material against frequency or wavelength, rather than time.

The correct term for the curve which is produced by the spectrogram is **wavelength spectrum**. This enables the yarn manufacturer to see at a glance if there are any periodic faults in the material. If there is a periodic fault, then the variations in mass at that given wavelength will appear as an increased height in the curve at that wavelength. This is known as a 'chimney' in the spectrogram. The importance of a periodic fault is related to the height of the chimney in comparison to the height of the base at that point. If the chimney height is greater than half the base height, the fault may be considered to be significant. Imperfections are short lengths of large variations in yarn linear density. The testing instrument can be set to record imperfections at four levels of severity.

Crimp rigidity

This is one of the most important yarn characteristics for a textured continuous filament yarn. The yarn is wound into a hank in the same manner as it is for measurement of linear density. The number of strands in the hank is chosen so that a set load of 0.09 grams per decitex (0.1 grams per denier) can be applied, no matter what the yarn linear density.

The hank is then attached to two weights at one end, a small weight and a heavier one. The other end of the hank is supported by a clamp. The hank is lowered into a cylinder full of water at 20°C for two minutes. The scale within the cylinder is adjusted just before two minutes so that the bottom of the hank is level with zero on the scale. The heavier weight is removed while the hank is still in the cylinder, so reducing the load to 0.0018 grams per decitex (0.002 grams per denier). After a further two minutes, the position of the bottom of the hank is read off the scale.

The crimp rigidity is the reduction in the length of the yarn after the removal of the heavy weight, expressed as a percentage of the original length.

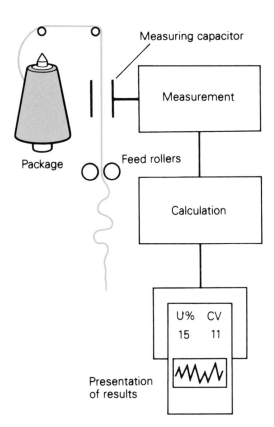

Figure 11.13 Electronic measurement of yarn evenness.

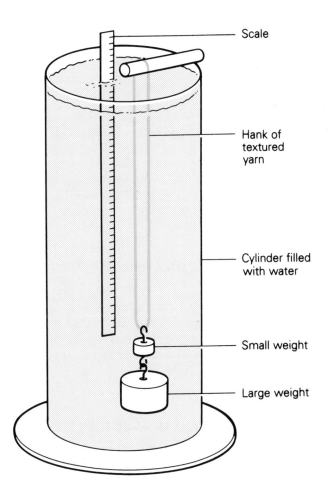

Figure 11.14 Crimp rigidity tester.

CHECK YOUR UNDERSTANDING

● There are many reasons for testing yarns: to select raw materials, to control processing, for research and development, to check the final product and to check against specifications.

● The main staple yarn parameters to test are linear density, twist, tenacity and regularity. The main textured filament yarn parameter to test is the crimp rigidity.

● There are direct and indirect systems for measuring linear density. In the direct system, the higher the number the thicker the yarn. In the indirect system, the higher the number the finer the yarn.

● Twist direction is unimportant in single yarns. Twist level can be measured using: straightened fibre method or twist contraction method.

● Yarn tenacity studies the load-bearing characteristics of a yarn. Methods used for testing yarn strength are lea-strength testing and single-thread strength testing.

● Crimp rigidity is a measure of the effectiveness of the texturing process.

● Yarn unevenness causes low productivity and so higher costs for the spinner, poor fabric productivity, and poor fabric appearance and performance.

● Yarn evenness is usually expressed as a percentage coefficient of variation (CV%). The higher the number, the more uneven the material. Modern evenness testing equipment will calculate the CV% and produce charts representing the material evenness.

REVISION EXERCISES AND QUESTIONS

1   a) Calculate the tex value of a yarn length of 100 metres weighing 5.8 grams.

b) Calculate the cotton count of a yarn length of 120 yards weighing 17 grains.

c) Which of the two yarns, a or b, is the finest?

2   Calculate the tenacity (in N tex) and the strain percentage of the following yarn:

9 tex combed cotton yarn, specimen length = 50 cm, breaking extension = 25 mm, breaking load = 160 grams.

3   What two factors cause yarn unevenness?

4   a) Calculate the index of irregularity for the following yarn:

200 cotton fibres in the yarn cross section, sd = 2.5, mean result $\bar{x} = 30$.

b) Is this a regular yarn?

Yarn preparation

Introduction

The yarn producer has several different customer types including weavers and knitters, wet processors, carpet manufacturers and sewing-thread manufacturers.

> Yarn preparation is the link between the yarn producer and the customer. Sometimes preparation is done totally by the yarn producer and sometimes it is done partly by the customer. Only rarely is it done totally by the customer.

The yarn producer has three basic products: spun yarn on ring tube or spool (spinners' packages) and continuous filament yarn on producer package (fibre producers' packages).

These packages are usually unsuitable for the customer. Yarn preparation is, as the name suggests, preparing the spun yarn for further processing. This can mean a number of different things which are totally dependent on which area of textile processing the customer is in. Some factors that must be considered are listed below:

1. package shape;
2. package density;
3. package weight;
4. yarn length on package;
5. package identification and transport;
6. yarn faults; and
7. frictional characteristics of the yarn.

The relative importance of these factors will change for each customer type.

This chapter will deal first with the production of single-end packages (containing only one yarn), and then with multi-end packages (containing many yarns).

Sequence of processes

In the production of woven fabric, two sets of threads are made to interlace at right angles to each other. The threads which lie vertically in the fabric are known as warp ends and those that are across the fabric are called weft picks. Knitted fabric consists of one set of threads only. If these threads form a series of loops across the fabric, a weft-knitted structure is produced. If they run in the lengthwise direction, the structure is said to be warp knitted.

When the threads are to be supplied as weft in either of these methods of fabric production, they will be supplied from packages containing a single thread which are commonly known as **cones**, or **cheeses**. If, however, it is to be supplied as warp, then a sheet of yarn is required, in which all the threads are parallel to each other. These are placed on a package known as a **beam**.

Figure 12.2 illustrates possible sequences of yarn preparation processes.

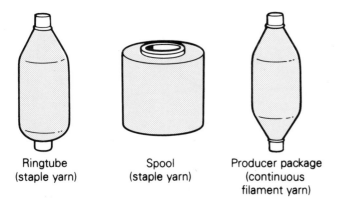

Ringtube (staple yarn)   Spool (staple yarn)   Producer package (continuous filament yarn)

Figure 12.1 Products of the yarn producer.

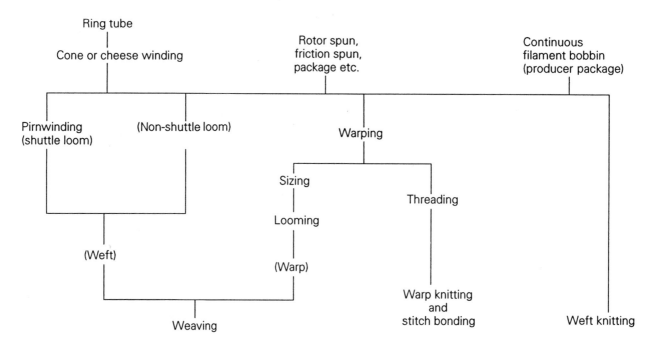

Figure 12.2   Sequence of yarn preparation processes.

There are two types of yarn preparation equipment: single-end winders which produce packages such as cheeses or cones, and multi-end winders which produce packages such as beams.

It can be seen from Figure 12.2 that, in many cases, the first stage in yarn preparation is to produce a cone or cheese which can either be used directly for weft knitting, or must be used as a supply package for making pirns or beams for weaving, or beams for warp knitting.

Single-end winding

There are three areas to cover under the title single-end winding: package factors, yarn factors and winding faults.

Package factors

PACKAGE SHAPE

The two most important types of single-end winders are cone and cheese winders. Both of these types of package have a **traverse length**, a maximum diameter and a **taper** (zero in the case of a cheese).

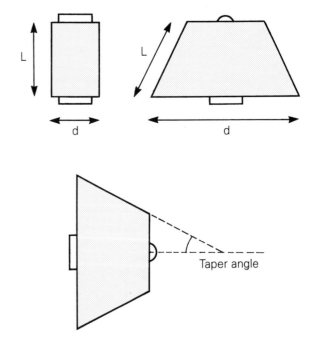

L = traverse length
d = maximum diameter

Figure 12.3   Package parameters.

Taper

Cones are preferred to cheeses in most cases because they cause less problems during unwinding. There are several different taper angle cones commonly in use:

3°30'	This cone holds more yarn than the other cones in common use, all other things being equal, and is suitable for most uses.
4°20'	Used commonly for wet processing (bleaching or dyeing).
5°57' and 9°15'	The yarn tension is critical in weft knitting. As yarn is removed relatively slowly from the package, a large taper is necessary to keep the yarn-unwinding tension constant.

PACKAGE DRIVE AND TRAVERSE MOTION

During winding the yarn undergoes two motions. It is wound around the package by the package drive and it is given a lateral motion to cover the package by the **traverse mechanism**.

> There are two ways to drive the yarn take-up package: by surface contact (drum winders), or by direct drive to the package spindle (spindle winders). There are three ways commonly in use to traverse the yarn to build up the package: **cam operation** (older system), **drum or rotary traverse** and **propeller** or **fan traverse** guide.

Cam traverse

The guide eye of the traverse motion oscillates from side to side along the traverse, laying the yarn in a helix pattern on the package. This oscillating motion causes a speed limitation to the machine (due to the acceleration, sudden stop and almost instantaneous change of direction of the guide eye), hence the introduction of alternative traverse methods.

Drum traverse

This type of traverse has become the more popular of these two methods due to the lack of speed limitation. The yarn is guided along the traverse and back by a groove in the driving drum, which is helical (only the yarn has to change direction). This helical pattern appears as cross patterns when viewed from the front of the winder. The drum is denoted as a 2-crossing drum, 2.5-crossing drum, or 3-crossing drum etc.

Propeller traverse

The propeller thread-guide system has two blades, rotating in opposite directions. They are set to cross over at the edges of the traverse. One blade will carry the yarn from the left of the traverse across to the right, where the opposing blade picks up the yarn and guides it back from the right across to the left again. This has no mechanical speed limitation, unlike the cam system. It works independently of the package drive, so can be used with delicate staple-spun yarns or continuous filament yarns, unlike the rotary drum system.

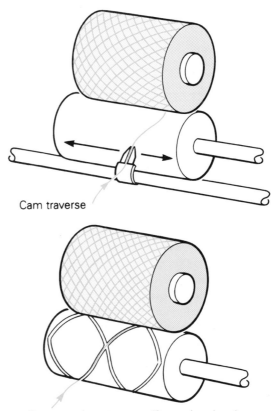

Cam traverse

Rotary or drum traverse (2-crossing drum)

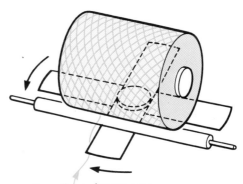

Propeller or fan traverse

Figure 12.4 Cam, rotary and propeller traverse motions.

PACKAGE BUILD – RANDOM AND PRECISION WINDING

There are also two types of package build. This is the number of coils on a package for a complete double traverse.

The **wind per double traverse** is the number of coils laid on the package during a double traverse, during the time it takes the yarn to go from one side of the package and return to the same side. It can be found nominally by counting the number of times the package must be revolved to traverse and return the yarn to the same point, or it can be determined more accurately by calculation:

$$\text{wind per double traverse } (w) = \frac{\text{package revs min}}{\text{double traverses min}}$$

> If the number of coils per double traverse at the beginning of winding the cone is equal to the number of coils per double traverse at the finish (remains a constant throughout the package build), the package is said to be precision wound. If the coils per double traverse decrease from start to finish of the package, then the package is said to be random wound.

It is possible to make both random-wound and precision-wound packages on each of the drum and spindle winders. Taking into account the different traverse mechanisms, there are several possible combinations. The most common type of random winder has a package which is driven by a drum that also has grooves in its surface which traverse the yarn.

The most common type of precision winder has a spindle drive with a separate cam or propeller traverse mechanism.

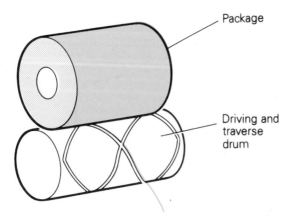

Figure 12.5 Random drum winder with rotary traverse.

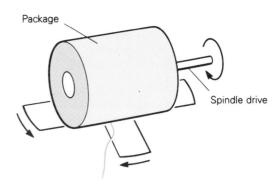

Figure 12.6 Precision spindle winder with propeller traverse.

Random winding

> The **random winder** is the most common type. It is suitable for most staple-spun yarns, but is unsuitable for continuous filament or delicate staple-spun yarns as the friction contact, especially at high speeds, causes yarn damage.

The yarn package is driven by contact with a driving drum, which may be metal or plastic. The yarn may be traversed by either the cam system, propeller system or by a grooved driving drum.

Precision winding

> In order to wind delicate yarns, such as continuous filament and fine or low twist staple-spun yarns, the yarn take-up package must be directly driven, rather than driven by friction as it is on a drum driven winder. This type of winder is known as a **precision winder**. The traverse mechanism must therefore be separate from the package drive.

The most common type of yarn traverse mechanism in this case is the cam traverse, although the propeller thread guide has gained popularity as it overcomes the speed limitation of the cam system.

Due to the increase in the yarn speed on a precision winder as the package builds, the yarn tension would also increase. This would result in a deformed package because of the differences in density from the inside to the outside of the package. To offset this effect, the method of controlling yarn tension is different from that of the drum winder. The disc tension device is used on drum driven winders, the gate tension device is used on spindle winders.

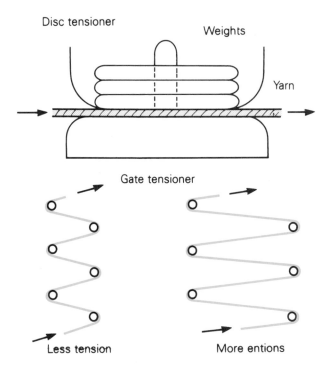

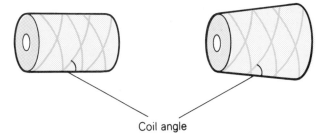

Figure 12.8 Coil angle.

Yarn factors

YARN CLEARING

Yarn from ring spinning and other unconventional spinning methods may contain faults that can be unacceptable, depending on the end-use.

These faults may be thick places, spinners' piecings, thin places, neps and trash. The size and quantity of faults in the yarn that are acceptable is totally dependent on what the yarn is going to be used for – a shirt cloth manufacturer will obviously need to have higher standards than a dishcloth manufacturer.

> Removal of unacceptable faults can be carried out at the winding stage; this is known as yarn clearing. Fault detection and removal used to be a mechanical process, but now the modern winding machine is equipped with electronic yarn sensors and automation to detect and remove faults.

Figure 12.7 Disc and gate tensioners.

The gate tension device is altered by a counterbalance weight which is linked to the increase in yarn diameter, so that the tension is reduced as the package builds to offset the tension increase due to the increase in winding speed.

There are more complex spindle winders that have a variable package drive to enable the yarn winding speed to be constant as the package increases in diameter.

COIL ANGLE

> The **coil angle** is the angle between the direction of the yarn on the package and the traverse direction. If this angle is too small, the coils on the edges of the package tend to slip inwards, creating a deformed package. If the angle is too large, the coils on the edges of the package tend to slip outwards causing the yarn to trap on the underside of the package during unwinding (known as **cobwebbing** or **stitching**).

The coil angle must therefore be limited if trouble-free unwinding is to be achieved. The values found from practice are an upper limit of 81° and a lower limit of 68° for staple yarns. Due to the lower friction characteristics of continuous filament yarns, these coil angle limits must be narrower – between 80° and 70°.

After fault removal or change of supply package, the yarn ends are joined together automatically, usually by either a knot or a **splice**. In splicing, the two ends of yarn to be joined are opened out by either a blast of compressed air, or a mechanical rubbing action. They are then placed together, and closed by the reverse action.

Obviously a knot is at least twice as thick as the nominal yarn diameter. In a sense, the fault is being replaced by another fault, namely a knot. The splice is a longer piecing than a knot, but can be the same diameter as the yarn. There may be a compromise between splice strength and splice appearance, but this is usually achieved satisfactorily for most end-uses.

Almost all automatic winding machines now use splicers for piecing rather than knotters, as a splice is considered far less objectionable than a knot.

The electronic sensor can be adjusted to remove faults over a given diameter and length. The sensors available to remove thin places are more expensive, so most manufacturers rely on yarn tension during winding to break any thin places.

When deciding on how sensitive the settings of the electronic sensor must be, the yarn manufacturer must take into consideration the fact that a knot is a fault. There is no sense in removing a fault that is smaller than a knot and then replacing it with a knot. The splice has solved this problem to a large extent, but the smallest of yarn faults will still be smaller than a splice.

Irrespective of what type of yarn sensor or piecing method is used, the sensitivity of settings is, and always has been, a compromise between quality and production. If the clearer setting is too critical, machine production will be low, causing an increase in costs. If the setting is too open, the yarn quality will not meet the customer's specification and could result in a rejected batch of yarn, or a cancellation of the order.

YARN LUBRICATION

For some end-uses, in particular yarn used for weft knitting, the frictional characteristics of the yarn must be modified, usually by the application of wax or oil.

The consistency of the yarn friction is as important as the level of yarn friction. If the yarn friction is not consistent, there will be differences in the yarn tension, resulting in tight courses which show up as bars in the fabric. In extreme cases, the yarn will break due to a sudden increase in tension, causing holes in the fabric or a press-off, where most or all of the needles on the knitting machine cast off their loop of yarn, causing a great deal of wasted machine time.

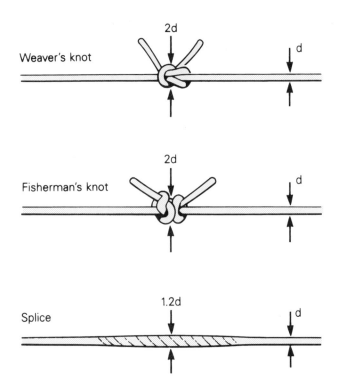

Figure 12.10   Relative diameters of knots and splices.

The friction properties of the yarn can usually be altered sufficiently by **waxing**. Modern automatic winders have a wax applicator, which is similar to a disc tension device. One side of the metal disc is replaced by a wax disc. The yarn runs over the surface of the wax which is rotated to avoid the yarn cutting into the disc. On spinning machines that directly produce a package suitable for the customer, a wax applicator is added to the yarn take-up mechanism.

Figure 12.9   Electronic clearer and splicer.

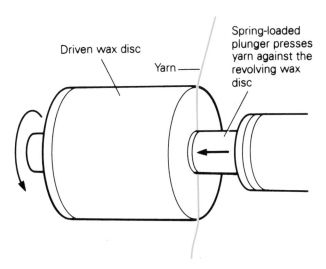

Figure 12.11 Wax disc.

Winding faults

PATTERNING

Patterning occurs when coils on adjacent layers are superimposed on each other, where the coils on the next layer are put directly on top of the previous coils causing a ridge on the package. This is undesirable, as it adversely affects the unwinding properties of the package and causes areas of very high density next to areas of very low density.

Patterning occurs when the wind per double traverse is exactly an integer.

$$\text{Wind per double traverse } (w) = \frac{\text{package revs min}}{\text{double traverses min}}$$

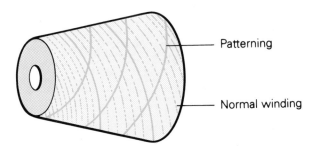

Figure 12.12 Patterning.

Spindle winders

As seen previously, the wind per double traverse (w) is a constant value on a spindle winder. When the winder is set up initially, it should be ensured that w is not an integer, so that patterning never occurs. If the value of w was set to an integer, patterning would occur continuously.

When w is set to almost an integer (a whole number plus or minus a small amount), it is possible to get the next layer of coils very close to the previous layer without them being superimposed. This is known as close winding and is used if a very dense package is required, when it is necessary to have as much yarn on the package as possible for a given volume, for example sewing thread. The major problem with close winding is that if the package is unwound at high speed, several layers of yarn may come off at once, causing a break. For package dyeing, open winding is preferred.

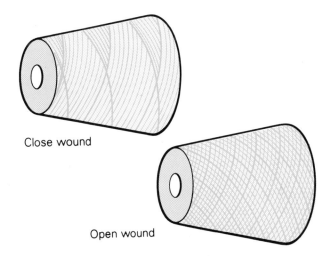

Figure 12.13 Open and close winding.

Drum winders

The wind per double traverse (w) with a random winder decreases as the package builds. Patterning will occur intermittently because w varies, so that every time w becomes an integer, patterning will occur for a period.

In order to avoid patterning, pattern-breaking devices work on the principle of continuous small variations in the winding speed. Some common methods are: lifting the package slightly off the driving drum at frequent intervals, so altering the ratio of traverse and surface speed of the yarn, (this alters the wind per double traverse); variation in the cam speed, usually by use of a split pulley drive (again this alters the traverse to surface speed ratio); variation of the driving drum speed, which causes the package to slip so altering the wind per double traverse.

COBWEBBING

If the coil angle is too large, the coils on the package tend to slip outwards. This is not too objectionable if it only happens on the nose of the cone. If this 'cobwebbing' occurs on the base of the cone, the yarn traps on the underside of the package during unwinding, rendering the package unusable.

Even if the coil angle is within the correct limits, cobwebbing can still occur for other reasons. If the yarn is not sufficiently tensioned the coils may slip, causing cobwebbing. The traverse guide must be set to the correct distance from the package to give adequate control, otherwise the coils will slip.

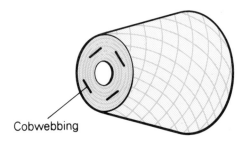

Cobwebbing

Figure 12.14 Cobwebbing.

HARD EDGES

This occurs to some degree in all cross-wound packages. At the reversal of yarn traverse direction there should ideally be only a small amount of yarn laid on the edges of the package. Because the yarn cannot instantly stop and change direction, there is a small delay in the traverse motion, causing more yarn to be laid down at the reversal point, that is at the package edge. This only becomes a real problem for wet processing packages, where the difference in package density from the edges to the centre would lead to uneven flow of dye liquor.

There is no complete cure for hard edges, but the problem can be minimised. If the traverse mechanism is by driving drum, small lateral movements to the drum will spread the reversal points over a greater area, so reducing the yarn build-up in one spot. If the traverse is by cam and guide eye, moving the camshaft or the shaft holding the packages will have the same effect. The guide eye can be fitted with a mechanism which spreads the traverse over three different lengths consecutively to achieve the same effect.

TWIST INTERFERENCE

At any point where the yarn may be caused to roll, twist interference can occur. As the yarn rolls, it untwists, causing a weak place. It is only usually a problem with low twist yarns.

It is always best to keep the yarn path as straight as possible with a minimum of contact points. Rotary traverse mechanisms can cause this problem as the yarn rolls in the grooves of the drum, so causing end-breaks later during unwinding. A separate traverse mechanism such as cam or propeller are better for delicate yarns.

Pirnwinding

The **pirn** (Figure 12.15) is the yarn package that is fitted into a shuttle in order to supply the weft at the loom. This stage in the preparation of weft yarn for weaving follows cone or cheese winding.

The shuttle, as a means of weft insertion, is losing popularity in the light of the success of the newer methods of weft insertion, but it will be a long time before it is completely obsolete.

In practice, a pirn should just fit into a shuttle, with a minimum of wasted space, but it should be realised that when a loom is designed originally, it will be based on the unwinding characteristics of the finest or weakest yarn that it is expected to weave.

> The extent of the long- and short-term yarn unwinding tension variations is paramount in determining the dimensions of a pirn. This is because, if the short-term tension variations are too great, it is possible that there will be an increase in the weft breakage rate and also, with filament yarns, **diamond barring** may result.

Long-term tension variations are created as the yarn is withdrawn from points nearer to the butt of the pirn, when it will be dragged along the stem of the pirn. If the pirn stem is too long or the yarn too fine, tension increases may develop and create an increase in the weft breakage rate and/or a fault

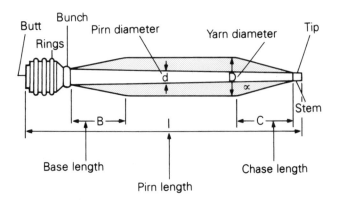

Figure 12.15 A pirn.

known as the **cop-end effect**. This fault develops as the weft crimps to a lesser degree, causing unwanted lines to be created across the fabric (**repping**) and the sides of the fabric to be pulled inwards. Immediately on replacing the old pirn with a new one, the crimp value and fabric width will return to normal, but the fault will recur at regular intervals throughout the fabric (coinciding with the length of fabric woven from a pirn).

In addition to these criteria, it is also important that the yarn build-up on the pirn should be correct, with the ring diameter being equal to the yarn diameter, the base length and the chase length being the same and the bunch containing a length of yarn equivalent to that of three to four pick lengths. This latter point is critical in ensuring that when pirn changes take place automatically, there is not an excessive amount of waste yarn on the pirn, but at the same time the yarn does not expire before the change takes place, as this will cause a fault known as a **broken pattern**. The chase angle (α) can also be critical. It is recommended that it should not exceed 8° for continuous filament yarns, 12° for medium-count staple fibre yarns and 15° for very coarse staple fibre yarns.

With the desirable chase angle, the empty pirn diameter (d) and the maximum yarn diameter (D) being known for a specific yarn, it is possible to determine the chase length (C) and so the base length, because these two should be equal:

$$\tan \alpha = \frac{D - d}{2} + C$$
$$\therefore C = \frac{d - d}{2 \tan \alpha}$$

The pirnwinding process was ideal for automation as, when the work was performed manually, it involved the operative in removing the full pirn from the spindle, placing an empty pirn on the spindle, trapping the yarn under the new pirn and recommencing winding, repairing yarn breaks, replacing empty supply packages with new ones, placing the wound pirns into boxes or on trays and generally supervising the machine.

As long ago as the 1950s, all of these duties had been automated and in the early 1960s Leesona introduced a pirnwinder that fitted onto the loom. The system was call Unifil and it became universally adopted wherever high rates of production were needed from a minimum of manpower. It takes many advantages to combat the expense of requiring one pirnwinding unit per loom, compared with the previous situation where one pirnwinding spindle could supply up to two looms. Unifil required that the winding rate need only exceed the weaving rate by about 20 per cent so that lower winding speeds created less wear. There was less yarn handling, fewer pirns were required per loom (12 or 14 compared with 300 to 400) and the empty pirns were stripped of waste yarn automatically at the loom so that the need for a separate pirnwinding department was eliminated.

Multi-end winding

Beams

> A beam consists of a large number of threads arranged in parallel order. The length of each thread is usually at least several thousand metres.

The empty beam package consists of a barrel with **flanges** at each end. The inside of a flange supports the threads on the beam as they build up on the barrel, while there may be a ruffle, a pike or both on the outside. The **pike** is usually used to mount the beam in the machine for winding and unwinding. The **ruffle** is usually used for unwinding only, but it can also be used as part of the braking system which applies tension during processing. It is quite common for a beam to have both a ruffle and a pike.

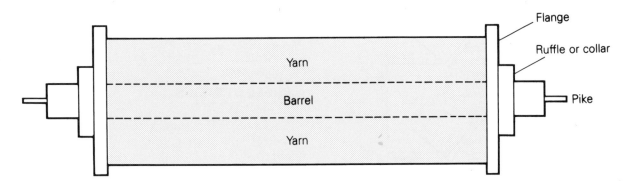

Figure 12.16 A beam.

Warping

This process is also known as beaming. To produce a beam which contains a large number of individual threads parallel to each other, it is necessary to place a large number of wound packages into a unit known as a **creel**. These creels consist of six to ten horizontal rows of packages, with the length of the creel being determined by the desired number of threads, commonly 400 to 900.

Many different warping systems have been used over the years, but the modern market is monopolised by just two: **high-speed beaming** and **section warping**.

When high-speed beaming is used to produce beams for the weaving process, the resulting package is a warper's beam which contains a fraction of the number of ends required in the final weaver's (loom) beam. At a later stage, the sheets from a number of these warper's beams are combined to give the required number of ends for the weaver's beam, and there will normally be a sufficient length

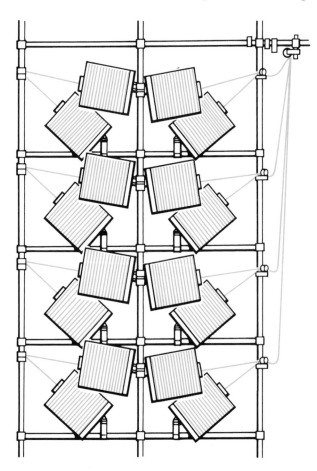

Figure 12.17   A creel.

of yarn to produce a number of weaver's beams from the one set of warper's beams. The system is widely used when long lengths of the same fabric are required and when the yarn will need an additional treatment, such as sizing before weaving.

High-speed beaming is also used to produce the beams that will supply warp knitting and stitch bonding machines, in which case it is the usual practice to clamp a number of the resulting beams side by side at the back of the fabric-forming machine.

Section warping (also known as horizontal mill warping) is used when there is no need for any additional treatment such as sizing, or when short runs or complicated patterns are being processed.

TYPES OF CREEL

A typical creel layout is illustrated in Figure 12.17. The packages are placed on spindles arranged back to back in a framework. The thread from each package is drawn forward to pass through a tension device, which is frequently of the disc type illustrated in Figure 12.7.

It is essential that the loading on the tension devices in a warping creel is correct and uniform throughout, necessitating frequent cleaning of the units so that the tension in each end of the warp sheet is the same.

Some modern creels now use electronic sensing devices in the guides in order to ensure a uniform tension throughout the warp sheet.

Each thread is then drawn forward to the front of the creel in a strictly controlled order which ensures that there is no crossing of the threads. At the front of each horizontal row of packages, on each side of the creel, there is a row of guides where each thread passes under a trip wire. If a thread breaks during the course of processing, this wire will fall to make an electrical contact and stop the machine before the broken thread becomes lost under subsequent layers of yarn on the beam. A light at the end of the relevant guide bar is illuminated in order to direct the operative to the source of the broken thread.

CREEL SYSTEMS

A major problem in creeling is the amount of time required at the end of a run, when it is necessary to break the old yarn, remove the old package from the creel, replace it with a new one and then tie the new thread to the end of the old one in the creel. This routine is necessary for every end in the creel and the creeling process takes even longer if the creel is empty to start with, as the thread from each package has to be passed through the guides in a specific sequence.

In an attempt to reduce the time required for this work, a number of modified creel systems have been developed. These are illustrated in Figure 12.18.

The **magazine creel**, shown at (a), allows the tail of yarn from the package that is supplying yarn to be tied to the leading end of yarn of the new package. Both packages are mounted on spindles which are aligned with the same guide and the transfer of feed from one package to the other is automatic. Although the space required for the creel is greatly increased, the system is ideal for mass production but does depend on a minimum number of yarn breaks on transfer, in order to achieve high efficiencies.

Duplicate creels are shown at (b). There are two creels per headstock and at the end of each run they are moved sideways so that a full creel is quickly positioned behind the headstock. It is possible that one of the reserve creel positions could be behind the running position of the creel. However, it is more usual for the headstock to move sideways as this requires less

space. It is clear that, whichever system is used, it is possible to be re-creeling in one position while warping is proceeding in the other position. This saves a lot of time, but it will be necessary to re-thread the warp at the beaming headstock before commencing the new run. This system is versatile. It is therefore popular for long runs and also where quality changes are frequent.

When **truck creels** are used, as shown at (c), the yarn packages are placed on spindles of trucks in a preparation area. A number of trucks are required per creel. At the end of a run, the yarn of each end is broken between the package and the guide, and the trucks are wheeled out from the centre of the creel to be replaced by the pre-loaded trucks. It is then necessary to tie the yarn from each new package to its corresponding end in the creel. The system is rather less efficient than the magazine creel but it is used in similar circumstances. An automatic version, which breaks out the old yarn and ties in the new yarn, is available.

The **reversible creel**, shown at (d), allows the position of the old packages and the new ones to be reversed at the end of

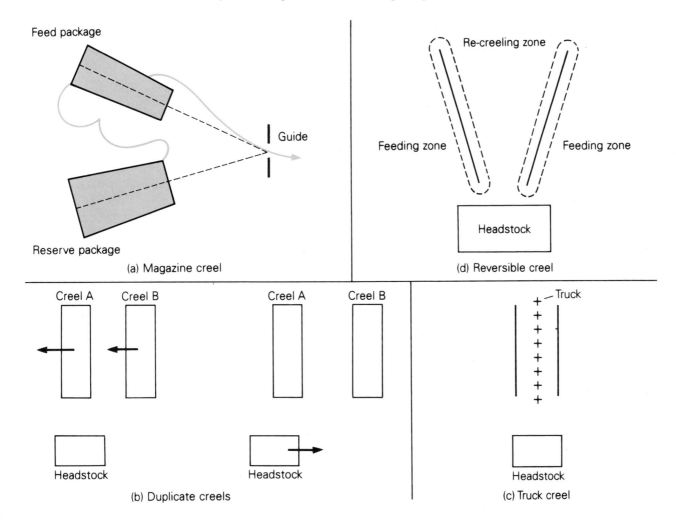

Figure 12.18 Creel systems.

a run. The vertical racks of packages are arranged in sections which can be turned inside out, or they are placed on a chain which carries the new packages from the creel's inside position to the outside, from where the yarn is fed to the headstock. The creel sides are arranged in a V-form, which leaves plenty of room for re-creeling in the inside position while the machine is running. It is a good system, but is not particularly popular in spite of allowing quite a degree of versatility.

HIGH-SPEED BEAMING

The sheets of yarn from the rows of guides at the front of the creel extend to the condensing rollers of the high-speed beamer, as shown in Figure 12.19, where they converge into

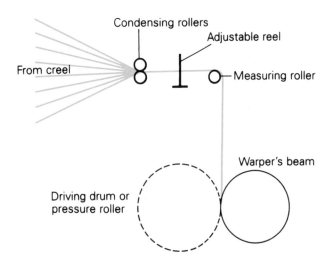

Figure 12.19   High-speed beamer.

one sheet. The ends are arranged one per dent (space between the metal guides of the **reed**) in the adjustable reed, which ensures that the threads are uniformly spaced across the warp sheet. The reed is also used to set the width of the warp sheet to the exact distance between the flanges of the beam.

The position of the first and last ends in the reed, in relation to the flanges, is critical in ensuring that the yarn does not build up or fall away adjacent to the flange (Figure 12.20). The correct build-up of yarn against a flange is shown at (a), while threads that create a larger diameter, as at (b), will be slack in subsequent processing, and those on a smaller diameter, (c), will be tight and may ultimately break. In both of the latter cases, there is the possibility that yarn on the larger diameter will roll sideways and become trapped under subsequent layers of yarn, so that it will not be able to be unwound satisfactorily.

The measuring roller also acts as a guide. It is connected to a measuring device, which is preset according to the length of yarn required on the beam. The counter of this measuring device then runs backwards and, when it reaches zero, the machine will be stopped automatically for a beam change.

Although beams were originally driven by frictional contact from a driving drum, it is now more usual to use a system of direct drive from a motor. The friction drive system had the advantage that the yarn speed would be constant throughout beam build-up, whereas, if the beam revolutions per minute were constant on the direct drive system, the yarn speed would increase as the beam diameter increased. This would cause the tension in the yarn sheet to increase and the yarn on the inside of the beam to be compressed and become damaged. By using a variable speed motor to drive the beam, it is possible to preset a desired yarn speed and, with this linked to a tension sensor, a uniform beam density can be ensured throughout.

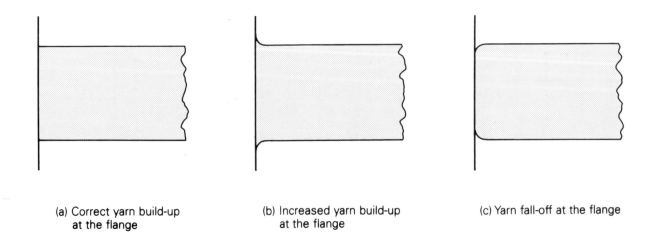

(a) Correct yarn build-up
at the flange

(b) Increased yarn build-up
at the flange

(c) Yarn fall-off at the flange

Figure 12.20   Yarn build at the beam flange.

SECTION WARPING

This is a two-stage process, as shown in Figure 12.21. In the first stage, the yarn from the creel has a similar sequence to that of high-speed beaming, except that there is the facility to insert a lease in the warp sheet. The purpose of the lease is to make it easier to find broken threads and generally make yarn handling easier. At this point, the lease consists of at least two cords, around which the threads pass in an under and over sequence, alternately, as shown in the inset. This 1 × 1 lease is the most common, but others are possible if they are more effective for the fabric being processed.

The sheet of yarn is placed on a horizontal mill (also known as a **drum** or **swift**) in sections. Each section contains a fraction of the number of ends required in the final sheet. If a pattern is involved, the order of the ends in each section is arranged to be similar so that, in any circumstance, the amount of re-creeling between sections is minimal. The length of yarn wound per section is sufficient for one or maybe two weaver's beams only. The number of sections, placed side by side, is dependent on the creel size and the number of ends in the final warp.

Each section is inclined to the vertical, with the first section resting on inclines (or wedges) at the end of the mill. This ensures that threads do not fall off the top outside edge of a section to become buried under the yarn of the next section build-up. To achieve this incline, it is necessary for either the mill or the headstock to move sideways. The rate at which this movement occurs is dependent on the angle of incline of the wedges, the thread spacing and the depth of yarn to be placed onto the mill.

$$\text{Total traverse per section} = \frac{\text{total depth of yarn on drum}}{\tan \alpha}$$

It is extremely important, when a new section is being started, that the space between the first end of the new section and the last end of the old section should be exactly the same as that between the threads within the sections. If it is not, then mounds or hollows will develop in the yarn build-up on the mill where sections meet, resulting in slack or tight ends on the resulting beam.

When all of the sections have been wound on to the drum, the second stage of the process can take place. This involves the sheet being pulled off the drum and onto a beam, during

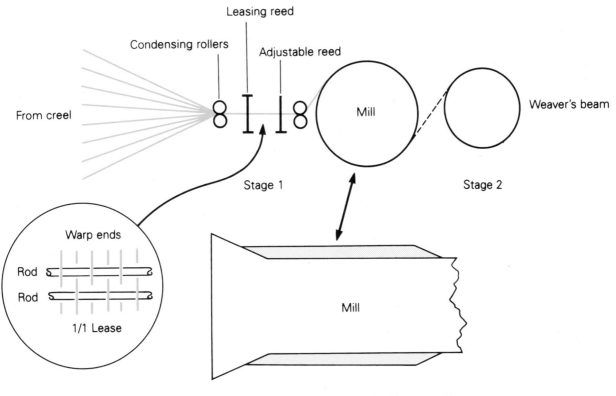

Figure 12.21 Section warper.

which time the mill or the beaming headstock will traverse in the opposite direction and at the same rate as that moved in the first stage.

PATTERNED WARPS

It is possible to process patterned warps on both the high-speed beaming and the section warping systems. Careful planning of the division of the pattern between the different sheets of the warper's beams or the sequence of the pattern in the sections of the mill is critical if the amount of re-creeling is to be kept to a minimum and crossing of ends in the warping machine is to be avoided. It is vital that the pattern sequence on the final weaver's beam is correct in order to minimise the possibility of crossed ends at the loom.

Sizing

In the sizing process, a coating of a starch-based adhesive is applied to the sheet of yarn to improve its weavability. Sizing increases yarn strength; it also reduces hairiness, which minimises the abrasion that occurs between the warp threads and the various parts of the loom, and between threads that are adjacent to each other.

A number of warper's beams are used to supply the yarn to the sizing machine, so that the eventual sheet placed on the weaver's beam will contain the correct number of ends. Only on very rare occasions is a beam from the section warping system sized on a beam-to-beam basis. This is because the density of the yarn in that warp sheet tends to be so high that it is difficult to ensure that the size liquor reaches all of the parts of every thread in the sheet. Also there is a tendency for the threads in such a dense sheet to stick together after sizing and so a fault, known as taped ends, can be created.

The basic ingredients of a size liquor are adhesives, lubricants and a solvent. Over the years, other classes of ingredients have been added to the size mix for a variety of reasons. These include: whiteners/blueing agents to improve the appearance of the fabric when it is to be sold in its loomstate; colour tints to assist in the identification of the yarns during weaving (for example S and Z twist yarns); deliquescents to attract moisture from the atmosphere surrounding the loom; weighting agents; antiseptics to discourage the formation of mildew when fabric may have to be stored in its loomstate for a period of time before being sold; and antistatic agents. The use of many of these latter agents is rare today.

When the size has been applied to the yarn, it is important that, in addition to improving the performance of the yarn in the loom, the size itself should have strength, be able to form a good film, have fluidity to aid penetration of the size into the yarn, be pliable so that it will not flake off as the yarn flexes and bends during weaving, be easily removed after weaving, and also be relatively inexpensive.

OPTIMUM SIZE PERCENTAGE

The percentage size to be applied to a warp in order to achieve a minimum number of end-breaks during weaving is dependent mainly on:

1. the end density (that is the number of threads in the warp sheet), as this will affect the amount of end-to-end abrasion that will take place;
2. the linear density of the warp, which greatly influences the strength of the yarn and will also affect the amount of abrasion; and
3. the pick density (number of weft threads per centimetre of fabric), which will affect the amount of abrasion between the warp ends and the reed as it reciprocates.

There are other factors which may also need to be taken into consideration, such as the fibre type, the yarn structure, the type of size and the type of loom.

Figure 12.22 shows a size-break curve. It clearly illustrates that the end breakage rate increases much more rapidly as a result of undersizing than is the case for a similar amount of oversizing. This is because undersizing leaves the yarn soft, creates increased amounts of dust and allows beads to form on the warp ends (usually behind the reed), all of which are major causes of yarn breakages.

The amount of size to be applied to a yarn is often determined by trial and error, but this is only possible when long runs are involved in mass production exercises. Companies usually have formulae that they apply whenever there is a change in fabric specification or size mix. These formulae will give good results but will normally err on the

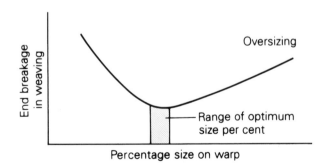

Figure 12.22   Size-break curve.

side of oversizing, because the consequences are relatively negligible for a slight amount of oversizing. However, when oversizing is excessive, the yarn will be brittle because of a loss in pliability and extensibility, and it is more expensive because extra size materials will be used.

It is usual to express the amount of size added to a warp as a percentage, which is determined at the machine by the size concentration and the size pick-up. These are defined as follows:

% size = the number of kg of oven-dry size solids on 100 kg of oven-dry unsized yarn;

% concentration = the number of kg of oven-dry size solids in 100 kg of paste;

% pick-up = the number of kg of paste on 100 kg of oven-dry yarn as it leaves the tip of the squeeze rollers.

THE SIZING MACHINE

There are four main parts to the sizing machine. They are identified in Figure 12.23 as the creel, the size box, the drying zone and the headstock.

The creel

This houses the warper's beams and should ensure that there is a uniformity of tension throughout the ends on the weaver's beam by strictly controlling the tension applied to the sheet of yarn from each back beam. It is also desirable that a creel should allow access to all parts of each beam so that repairs to broken threads can be carried out easily, and in some cases an economy of space might be necessary.

The beams can be tensioned in a variety of ways by creating a frictional drag on either the pike or the ruffle on the flange. Although hydraulic controls have been developed, spring- or weight-loaded friction pads or bands are still widely used.

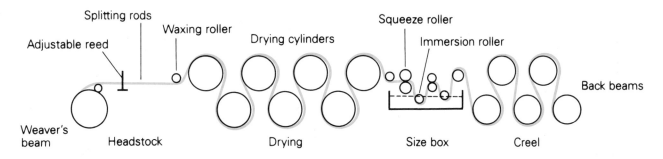

Figure 12.23 Multi-cylinder sizing machine.

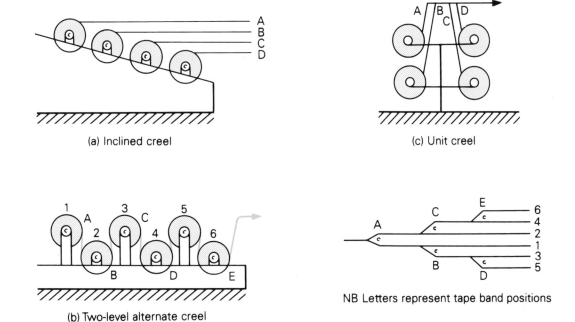

(a) Inclined creel

(c) Unit creel

(b) Two-level alternate creel

NB Letters represent tape band positions

Figure 12.24 Sizing machine creels.

Selvedge ends, which require little or no size because they are often produced from stronger, less hairy, folded yarns, are supplied from separate bobbins mounted on a framework above the sides of the creel.

The size box

A basic size box is illustrated in Figure 12.26. The sheet of yarn from the back beams is guided into the size liquor where an immersion roller ensures that there is an adequate facility for the yarn to be thoroughly saturated. The sheet then passes out of the liquor and over the size roller on which rests a squeeze roller, which is weighted but has a resilient surface. This squeezing action has a dual purpose, namely, to ensure that there is adequate penetration of the size liquor into the yarn and that excess size is removed.

Drying

Cylinders are preferred in modern machines because they are more efficient when used in multiples, although when compared with hot-air systems, they do tend to flatten the yarn and require more softener in the size mix in order to ensure an acceptable level of pliability.

The headstock

The headstock (as illustrated in figure 12.23) comprises a number of different parts that, in sequence, can be used for waxing, moisture regain measurement, sheet splitting, measuring and marking, beam (and so yarn) drive, and stretch control.

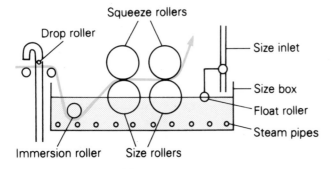

Figure 12.25   Beam tensioning systems.

Figure 12.26   Size box.

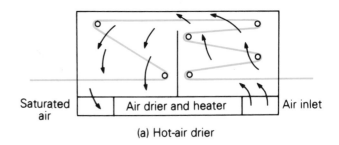

(a) Hot-air drier

(b) Multi-cylinder drier

Figure 12.27   Sizing machine dryers.

1. The amount of moisture in the yarn is measured either by the capacitance or the resistance methods. It needs to be strictly controlled, as underdrying may encourage mildew and cause ends in the weaver's beam to stick together (taped ends). On the other hand, overdrying lowers production, costs more for heat, and makes the yarn brittle, which increases the chance of end breaks and increases yarn abrasion against loom parts.

2. Wax can be applied to the warp sheet immediately in front of the moisture regain measurer. It allows a small amount of lubricant to be applied to the yarn, if desired. This will help to reduce friction between the yarns in the warp sheet as they change positions (during shedding) and also ease the passage of the warp yarn through the loom during weaving.

3. Splitting the warp sheet is essential to avoid taped ends at the loom. It is achieved by separating the yarn according to its back beam sheets and then placing one end from each of the sheets in a different dent of the adjustable reed, which is at the front of this section of the headstock. The adjustable reed (as in warping) ensures that the width of the warp sheet and the beam build-up, especially at the flanges, are correct.

4. A roller, which also acts as a guide, is used to measure the length of yarn passing through the machine. It can be connected to a unit that will mark the warp sheet at predetermined intervals according to the desired piece (cut) lengths, so that known lengths of cloth can be removed from the loom for subsequent processing, while the later pieces are still being woven.

5. Originally, a drag roller was used to drive the beam via manually adjusted conical rollers and a clutch. More

recently, a motor connected to the electronic unit has been used to control the speed of the beam and the other driven rollers in the machine.

6. A certain amount of stretching of the yarn is accepted as being essential to ensure control of the yarn sheet and also to avoid slack ends. The amount of stretch is usually controlled between 1.5 per cent and 2.5 per cent. A preset, positively infinitely variable (PIV) gearbox has been used in the past, but again the electronic unit is used on modern machines, in order to achieve the necessary control.

Threading and looming

Before beams can be used in either knitting or weaving, it is necessary for each thread on each beam to be placed in units that will control its movement during fabric formation. This process is known as threading for warp knitting, amd looming for weaving.

THREADING

This involves passing each end that is to be used in warp knitting or stitch-bonding through the eye of a guide. Many guides are mounted on a bar and the threading process needs to be carried out at the machine. Hence, it can only be done as a hand operation.

LOOMING

This involves either knotting the ends of the old warp to the corresponding ends of the new warp (if the production details of the two warps are identical), or drawing each thread through the eye of a **drop wire**, the eye of a **heald** and the dent of the reed.

Knotting is much quicker and so more economical, but drawing-in is essential when the new warp has a different specification to the one that has just finished weaving. Additionally, when a set of drop wires, healds and reed have been in use for a period of time, they may have to be removed from the loom in order to allow them to be cleaned thoroughly. Under these circumstances, the replacement warp will have to be drawn-in before it can be used. There are some looms which are so large that knotting cannot take place.

Knotting normally occurs at the loom in order to minimise the movement and setting-up of the drop wires, healds and reed. However, knotting may have to be delayed if two warps on different looms finish weaving at the same time. Careful planning in the weaving shed can minimise this machine interference problem.

Drawing-in at the loom only takes place in certain special circumstances (for jacquards and very wide weaving machines). Generally, it is better to carry out this operation in a separate area, as it allows the new warp to be pre-prepared and ready for placing in the loom as soon as the old warp has finished weaving and the loom has been cleaned. The warp threads are drawn through a set of drop wires, healds and the reed, which can then be transported on a gantry to the loom. It is a relatively simple task to then replace the old beam, drop wires, healds and reed. Planned maintenance of the loom and adjustments to the settings, if a fabric having a different specification is to be woven, can also be carried out at the same time.

In modern installations both drawing-in and knotting are mechanised, but there are certain circumstances where it is preferable to use a hand operation. Knotting can be replaced by twisting the corresponding ends of the two warps together, providing that the yarns are compatible, but this technique is rarely used unless there is only a small number of ends in the warp. In small weaving installations, where there are very few looms, it may not be economically viable to have a machine for drawing-in or even knotting. In this case, the work is likely to be done manually by operatives who are multi-skilled.

CHECK YOUR UNDERSTANDING

● Spinners' packages are generally unsuitable for the customer because: the length of yarn on the package is insufficient; the package shape is wrong for unwinding; the yarn friction is too high; there is a variation in package density, or the package density is wrong; and there are unacceptable faults in the yarn.

● There are two types of single-end winding machines used for producing cheeses and cones. They are the spindle-driven package and drum-driven package. There are two different package builds: random and precision.

● Yarn often needs to be cleared of unacceptable faults. The level of fault acceptance depends on the yarn end-use.

● Yarn sometimes needs to be lubricated to reduce the friction level.

● Faults can occur during winding. They include patterning, cobwebbing, hard edges and twist interference.

● Weft knitters use cones or cheese from single-end winders, and the yarn is always waxed for lubrication. Weft is supplied for shuttle looms by winding pirns from cones or cheeses. This yarn is never waxed. Non-shuttle looms can use cones or cheeses directly for weft supply.

● Both warp knitting machines and stitch bonding nonwoven machines use beams made from producer packages or single-end winders. Beams for weaving are also made from single-end packages.

● The two main methods of beaming or warping are high-speed beaming and section warping. During high-speed beaming, several warper's beams are produced which contain a fraction of the number of ends required on the weaver's beam, but many times the length required. These warper's beams are usually combined during the sizing operation to form the weaver's beam. Section warping is used where only short runs or complicated warp patterns are needed. These beams are not usually sized.

● Yarns are only sized for weaving. Size is a starch-based adhesive which increases the yarn strength and reduces hairiness, which in turn reduces abrasion between yarn/loom and yarn/yarn. Oversizing is less detrimental than undersizing.

● Threading of warp threads from beams through the guide eye of the warp knitting machine must be done at the machine and so can only be done by hand.

● Looming is either carried out by knotting the new weaver's beam to the old beam, or drawing-in each warp thread through a drop wire, heald and dent. Knotting is quicker but cannot always be done. Drawing-in is usually done off the machine, with new drop wires, healds and reed being threaded, then transported to the loom and dropped in to place.

REVISION EXERCISES AND QUESTIONS

1 What fabric-producing processes require beams of yarn?
2 Why are different cone taper angles necessary?
3 Why are spindle winders sometimes necessary?
4 What is close winding and where is it used?
5 Why is patterning a problem?
6 What determines the level of clearing that an electronic clearer should be set to?
7 Why is pirn unwinding tension so important?
8 How can creeling time be cut down during warping?
9 How are beams driven and why is it necessary to reduce this speed as the package builds?
10 Which warping system is used for patterned warps?
11 How is size applied to warps for weaving?
12 Why is it necessary to draw-in warps rather than knot the new warp to the old warp?

Weft knitting

Introduction

Knitting is the production of fabric by forming loops with yarn, which are interlaced in a variety of ways to form the fabric. Traditional hand knitting, using knitting needles or pins, is thought to have existed as early as the 5th century, although other simpler techniques of intermeshing and knotting of yarns existed much earlier.

The first real evidence of a production knitting machine was the stocking frame, invented by the Reverend William Lee in 1589. The invention laid the foundation for the development of both weft and warp knitting technologies. Lee's invention enabled the knitting of loops at ten times the speed of traditional hand-pin knitting.

The knitting industry is divided into two distinct sectors, weft knitting and warp knitting.

> In **weft knitting**, the loops are formed across the width of the fabric, and each weft thread is fed, more or less, at right angles to the direction in which the fabric is produced. It is possible to knit with only one thread or cone of yarn, though production demands have resulted in circular weft knitting machines being manufactured with up to 192 threads (feeders).

Compared with warp knitting, weft knitting is a more versatile method of fabric production in terms of both the range of fabric structures that can be produced and the yarn types that can be utilised. Weft knitting is the simplest method of converting a yarn into a fabric.

> **Warp knitting** is a method of producing a fabric by using needles similar to those used in weft knitting, but with the knitted loops made from each warp thread being formed down the length of the fabric; the loops (courses) are formed vertically down the length of the fabric from one thread as opposed to across the width of the fabric, as is the case of weft knitting.

In warp knitting, each warp thread is fed more or less in line with the direction in which the fabric is produced, and each needle in the knitting width must be fed with at least one thread at each course. Compared to weaving and weft knitting it is the fastest method of converting yarn into fabric, though modern developments in weft knitting machines mean that there is now very little difference in terms of production between the two forms of knitting.

The rest of this chapter will consider weft knitting.

Knitting terms and definitions

In order to discuss the different types of knitted fabric structures, certain terms must be understood.

Courses

Courses are rows of loops across the width of the fabric produced by adjacent needles during the same knitting cycle, and are measured in units of courses per centimetre.

Figure 13.1 shows a simple plain-knitted structure, indicating a course or row. The number of courses determines the length of the fabric.

Wales

A **wale** is a vertical column of needle loops. The number of wales determines the width of the fabric and they are measured in units of wales per centimetre. Figure 13.1 indicates the wales and also the needle loop.

Stitch density

Stitch density is a term frequently used in knitting and represents the total number of needle loops in a given area.

Stitch density is the product of the courses and wales per unit length and is measured in units of loops per square centimetre.

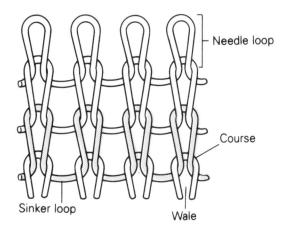

Figure 13.1 Plain single-jersey weft knitting.

Stitch length (ℓ)

The **stitch length**, measured in millimetres, is the length of yarn in the knitted loop. Stitch length is one of the most important factors controlling the properties of knitted fabrics. It can be determined by removing one course length (or part of a course length) from a fabric and dividing this length by the total number of needles knitting that length of yarn. Generally, the larger the stitch length, the more open and lighter the fabric.

The knitted loop

The unit of a knitted fabric is known as the loop. Figure 13.1 illustrates how the individual loops, both needle and sinker loops, are connected together to form the knitted structure. A large number of loops, which are suitably connected together, will produce a fabric in which the loops are arranged in horizontal and vertical rows. The loops in the horizontal rows are courses and are made consecutively from one yarn package, with one thread of yarn feeding all the needles in the knitting unit. A vertical row of loops linked together is called a wale. The loops in a wale are connected together by drawing each loop through the previous one. Figure 13.2 shows the **technical face** and **technical back** of a plain knitted (single-jersey) fabric. Technical in this sense means the machine back and front of the fabric rather than the side of the fabric used as the front or right side. It is more convenient to represent a knitted structure by using a conventional stitch notation, as illustrated, rather than by elaborate loop diagrams.

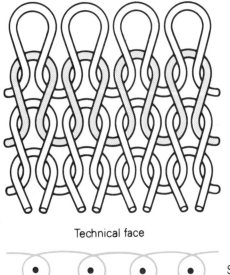
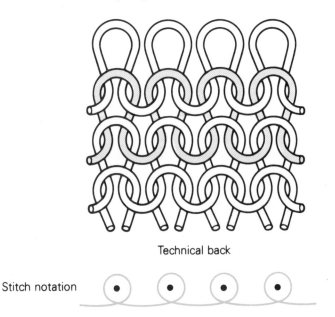

Figure 13.2 Technical face and back of plain single-jersey fabric.

Fabrics are produced either by forming loops on one side of the fabric only or on both sides. These two possibilities give four basic classes of weft knitted fabrics, namely **plain**, **rib**, **purl** and **interlock** which are widely used in their simple forms, but also provide a basis for the production of an infinite variety of weft knitted structures, by using types of stitches other than knit stitches. These other stitch types will be discussed later.

Properties of knitted fabric

There are four basic types of weft knitted fabric: **plain single-jersey fabrics** are the simplest form, knitted with one set of needles; **rib** or **double-jersey fabrics** are knitted using two sets of needles; **purl fabrics** are formed using a two-headed needle; and **interlock fabrics** are basically two rib fabrics locked together.

Plain single-jersey fabrics

> Plain single-jersey is the simplest weft knitted structure that it is possible to produce on one set of needles.

The structure is widely used in the manufacture of knitted outer-wear, footwear and all types of fashioned garments. The fabric can be unroved from either end and if a stitch is broken,

the wale will disintegrate causing the stitches in that line to undo or ladder. When the fabric is used for the manufacture of garments by cutting pattern pieces then sewing (known as piece goods), some difficulty can be experienced during making-up (sewing together the pattern pieces) because the fabric tends to curl at the ends and sides unless it has been heat set during finishing. Circular machines can be used to produce fabrics for garment manufacture without the need for side seams if the correct machine diameter is available, or for slitting to give a full open-width material, or to produce an endless succession of body lengths with each length being separated by a draw thread.

Rib fabrics

> The term rib is used to describe a knitted fabric with vertical rows (wales) of loops meshed in the opposite direction to each other.

Some loops knit to the front and some to the back, so that some wales look like the technical face of plain knitted and some like the technical back of plain. Figure 13.3 shows the structure of the simplest rib fabric, termed a '1 × 1 rib', having alternate wales knitted to the front and back (two sets of needles are required to produce rib fabric). The ribs tend to close up to create a double-faced fabric, which has the same appearance on both sides. The width occupied by a 1 × 1 rib fabric is about half the width of a plain fabric produced on the

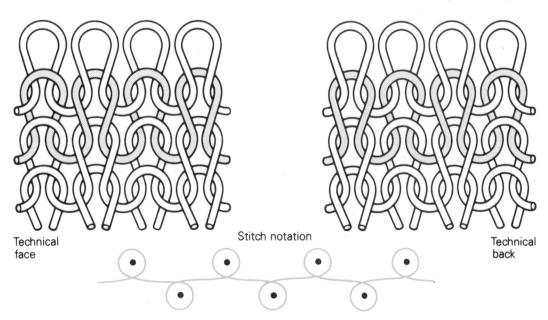

Technical face   Stitch notation   Technical back

Figure 13.3 Technical face and back of 1×1 rib double-jersey fabric.

same number of needles, but it does have nearly twice as much elasticity in the width. Lengthwise, the elasticity varies from moderate to high, depending upon the yarn used.

Rib fabrics do not curl and can only be unroved from the end knitted last, hence rib fabrics are suitable for waist bands, collars and cuffs as well as stretch-to-fit garments.

The conventional stitch notation for a 1×1 rib structure is also shown in Figure 13.3. Other rib structures, such as 2×1, 3×1, 4×1, 2×2 and more, are possible. To produce a 2×1 rib structure, for example, the knitted loops would have to be two knitted on the front and one knitted on the back of the fabric alternately.

Purl (links-links) fabrics

> 1×1 purl fabric has loops knitted to the front and back on alternate courses, in contrast to a 1×1 rib fabric which is knitted to the front and back on alternate wales.

Figure 13.4 shows a 1×1 purl structure. The fabric will not curl, both sides are similar in appearance, and it will extend easily in the lengthwise direction. It can be unroved from either end. Variations, such as 3×1 and 2×2 purl can be made and there is good scope for patterning. The fabric is commonly used for children's wear. The conventional stitch notation of a 1×1 purl structure is also shown in Figure 13.4.

Interlock fabrics

> Interlock structure consists of two 1×1 rib fabrics knitted one after the other by means of two separate yarns, which knit alternately on the face and back of the fabric and are interlocked together.

Interlock is a reversible fabric, which has a similar smooth appearance on each side. It does not curl, is firmer and less extensible than most weft knitted fabrics, and is heavier and thicker than rib fabric knitted with the same yarn. Consequently, fine yarns are usually used to reduce the area density of the fabric. Interlock is used for outerwear fabrics (dresswear and skirts), often using wool, acrylic and polyester yarns, while cotton and polyester/cotton blends are used for the production of underwear fabrics.

Knit, tuck and miss stitch types

Loop formation – knit stitch

To understand the different types of stitches, we need to look at how a simple knit stitch is formed. It is easier to understand if we assume that we have already made a loop, which is held in the hook of the needle.

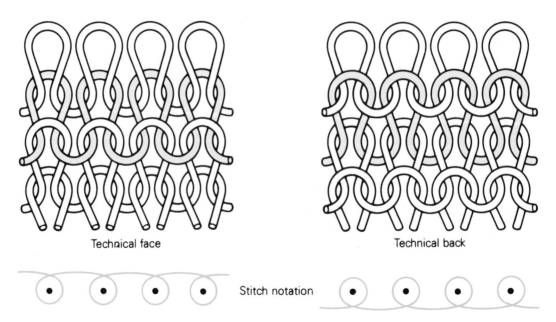

Technical face   Stitch notation   Technical back

Figure 13.4 Technical face and back of purl fabric.

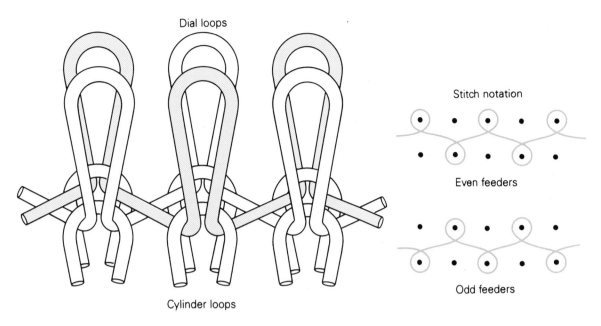

Dial loops

Stitch notation

Even feeders

Odd feeders

Cylinder loops

Figure 13.5   Interlock double-jersey fabric.

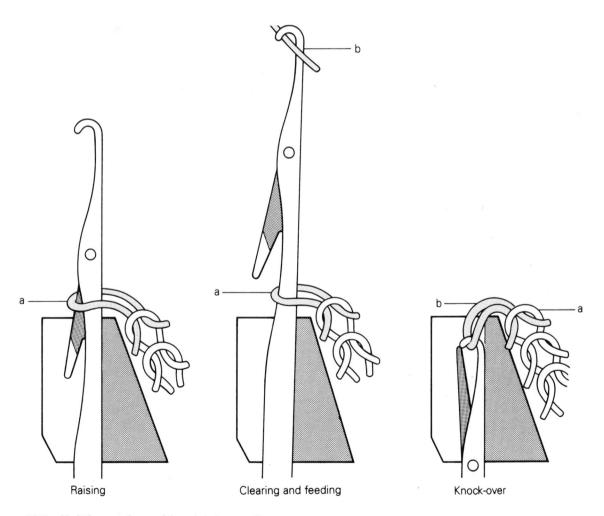

Raising

Clearing and feeding

Knock-over

Figure 13.6   Knitting action with a latch needle.

When a stitch has been formed, the needle rises to take the new yarn to produce another stitch. While this is happening, the fabric must be held down to prevent its rising with the needle. The loop (a) in the needle hook opens the latch of the needle as the needle rises. When the needle has risen to its **clearing** height the old loop is below the latch on the needle stem. The needle is now in position to receive the new yarn (b) before starting to move down. The needle begins to descend, causing the old loop (a) to close the latch, so trapping the new yarn (b). When the needle reaches its lowest position, the new loop (b) will have been drawn through the old loop (a) – known as **knock-over** – and the needle is now ready to rise so that the sequence can begin again.

The weft knitted structures described so far have been totally composed of knitted loops, which are produced whenever the needle clears the old loop, receives a new yarn and knocks over the old loop from the previous knitting cycle. Figure 13.7 shows the three possible positions of the needle at the time of **feeding** the yarn. They are referred to as knit, tuck and miss positions.

These different stitches are produced by controlling the height of the needles, and individual selection of needles enable knit, tuck or miss stitches to be formed.

Tuck stitch

A tuck stitch is made when a needle takes a new loop without clearing the previously formed loop, so that loops are accumulated on the needles.

The previously formed knitted loop is called the held loop and the loop which joins it is the tuck loop. The tuck loop will always lie at the back of the held loop.

The number of consecutive tucks on any one needle is limited by the amount of yarn that the needle hook can hold, with the maximum usually being between four and five loops.

Figure 13.8 shows a single tuck viewed from the technical face of the fabric, which is produced by raising the needle to the tuck position so that it is high enough to receive the new yarn without clearing the held loop.

Figure 13.9 shows a three-course tuck structure viewed from the technical back and, in addition, how this structure is represented using conventional stitch notation. Tuck stitches tend to reduce the length of the fabric and increase its width, resulting in the fabric being thicker with less extension in its width. The yarn in the tuck loop is able to straighten itself more easily than the yarn in the normal knitted loop, causing loops in the adjacent wales to be pushed apart. Relaxation in the width direction is consequently less than that of a plain knitted fabric produced under similar knitting conditions.

Miss stitch

A miss stitch is produced by a needle holding the old loop (the needle is not raised, which effectively means the needle is missed), while the two adjacent needles are raised and cleared to produce a new knitted loop.

The float will lie freely on the reverse side of the held loop, which is the technical back, and in the case of rib and interlock structures it will be inside the fabric. Figure 13.10 illustrates that the float will extend from the base of one knitted or tucked loop to the next.

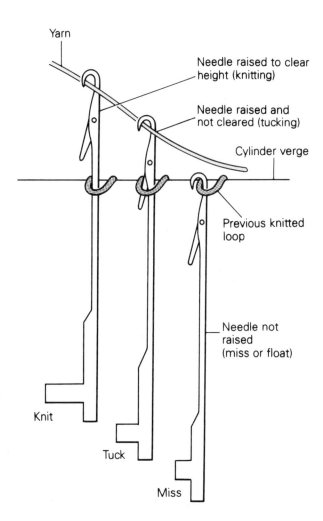

Figure 13.7 Three needle positions for the production of three needle types.

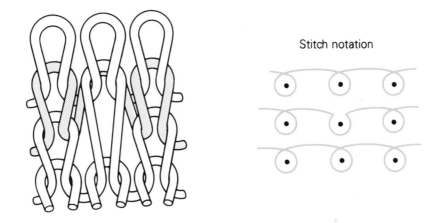

Figure 13.8 Single tuck stitch – technical face.

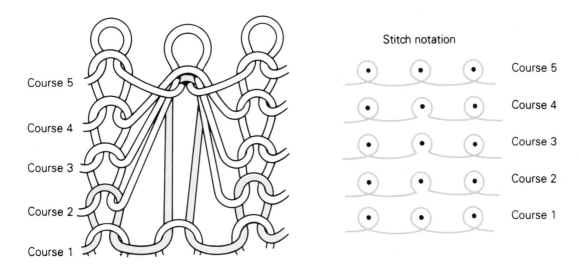

Figure 13.9 Three-course tuck – technical back.

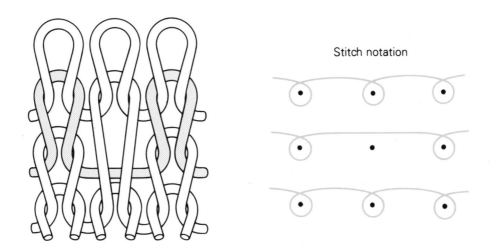

Figure 13.10 One needle float or miss stitch – technical face.

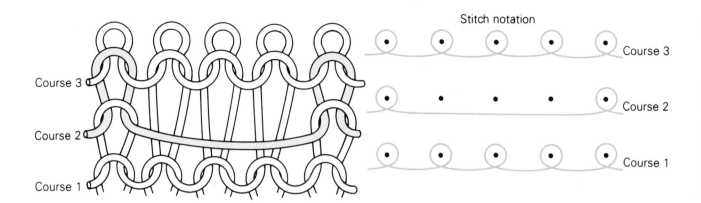

Figure 13.11 Three-needle miss – technical back.

Figure 13.11 shows a three-needle float viewed from the technical back, together with the conventional stitch notation used to represent this structure.

The introduction of miss stitches results in the fabric becoming narrower in width, since the wales are pulled closer together and the held loop 'robs' yarn from adjacent loops. This tends to improve fabric stability.

Knit, tuck and miss stitches can be used in any of the four fabric types – single jersey, rib, purl or interlock – to produce a wide range of structural effects.

Weft knitting machines

Knitting elements

Only one type of needle has been used in the descriptions of weft knitting so far. There are three commonly used metal needle types for the production of weft knitted fabrics: latch needles, which are self-acting; compound needles, which have two independently controlled parts; and bearded needles, the simplest in form but requiring another element to control them.

LATCH NEEDLE

The **latch needle** was developed in the mid 19th century and compared with the bearded needle, which evolved some 260 years earlier, it has the advantage of being self-acting, though

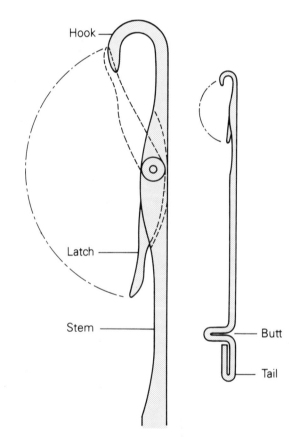

Figure 13.12 Latch needle.

it is slightly more expensive to produce. It is the most widely used needle in weft knitting. Figure 13.12 shows the main parts of the latch needle.

COMPOUND NEEDLE

Figure 13.13 shows the **compound needle**, which comprises two parts – the hook and tongue – that are controlled separately. This type of needle, though designed in the mid 19th century, did not really become popular until after the Second World War when it was used on warp knitting machines. Today the open-stem type compound needle is increasingly used for warp knitting in place of the bearded needle, but its use in weft knitting has been limited, though developments by leading weft knitting machinery manufacturers have resulted in its being incorporated into their machines.

The compound needle is expensive, with each part requiring separate and precise control. This is not a major problem in warp knitting since all the needles operate together, but it can create problems in weft knitting. The compound needle offers a much shorter, smoother and simpler knitting action in comparison to the latch and bearded needle, and this enables production speeds to be increased.

BEARDED NEEDLE

Figure 13.14 shows the **bearded needle** and its main parts. This needle is the simplest and cheapest to manufacture but it does require an additional element to close the beard during knitting. In the case of warp knitting, this is a presser bar. In weft knitting, the bearded needle is used mainly on straight bar machines, but there is an increasing demand for it to be replaced by either latch or compound needles, both of which enable much higher production rates to be achieved. The majority of modern high speed warp knitting machines now use compound rather than bearded needles.

Classification of weft knitting machines

Table 13.1 gives a simple classification of weft knitting machinery. These machines range from high production, limited capability, single-jersey types to versatile, multi-functional models with extensive fabric patterning ability.

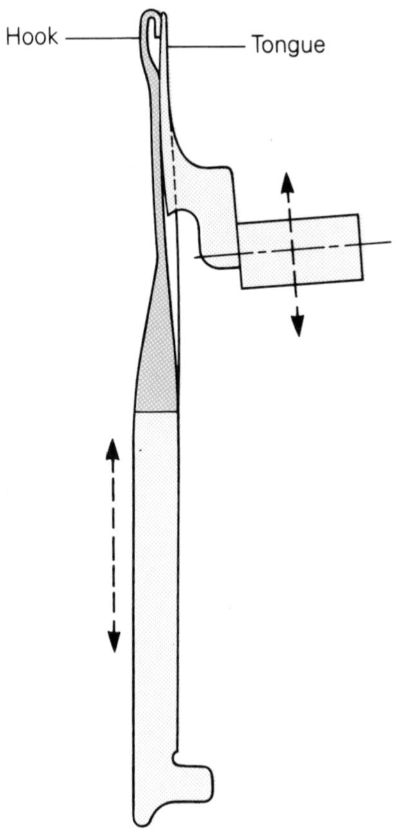

Figure 13.13 Compound needle.

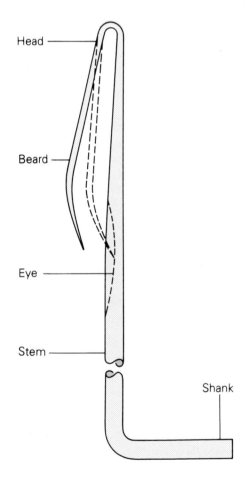

Figure 13.14 Bearded needle.

Table 13.1 Classification of weft knitting machinery

Straight bar (bearded needle)		Flat bar (latch needle)		Circular			
				(latch needle)		(bearded needle)	
one needle bed	two needle beds	one needle bed (domestic type)	two needle beds	one needle bed	two needle beds	double cylinder	one neddle bed
fully fashioned	—		v-bed; flat purl	plain single-jersey jacquard; pile; inlay; sliver knit	rib; interlock; double-jersey jacquard	purl	sinker wheel; loop wheel
shaped knitwear		knitwear	knitwear	garment or fabric	garment or fabric	garment or knitwear	fabric

In all cases these machines will employ one of the types of needle shown in the table to form the knitted loop. Machine types shown in Table 13.1 predominantly employ latch needles of one form or another.

From table 13.1 it can be seen that the simplest weft knitting machinery has one set of needles, arranged either in a straight line (flat bar/straight bar) or around a cylinder (circular). These machines are capable of producing single-jersey fabrics, but not double jersey, and can use a combination of three types of stitch: knit, miss or tuck.

With two needle beds, double-jersey fabrics such as rib and interlock can be produced on both flat bar machines and circular machines. In the case of circular machines this second needle bed takes the form of a dial, a flat disc placed on top of the cylinder. The second needle bed of a flat bar machine is placed at an angle to the first, and in the case of v-bed machines, the two beds form an inverted 'v' shape.

In the case of purl machines, two needle beds are used. They can be flat or circular and use special double hooked needles. In the circular version of the purl machine, the second set of needles is in the form of a second cylinder positioned above the first.

Knitting single-jersey fabrics with latch needles

Latch needles have an individual movement and slide up and down in grooves which are cut in the cylinder or needle bed. These grooves are called **tricks**. The sliding movement, up or down of the needle, is controlled by **cams** which form a track for the needle butt to follow. The stitch cam is adjustable, which means the stitch length or the length of the yarn in the knitted loop can be varied. Figure 13.15 shows a typical cam system and the sequence of actions that allow a loop to be formed on a circular single-jersey machine.

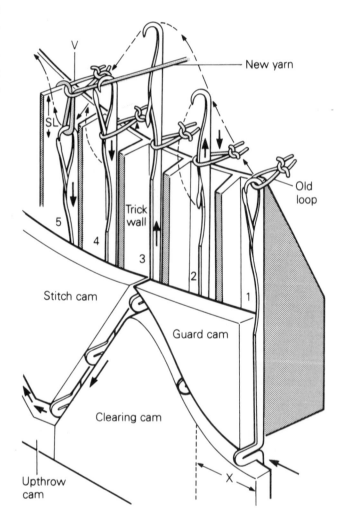

Figure 13.15 Knitting action of a latch needle circular machine.

As described earlier, the fabric must be held down while forming the knitted loop. On older machines, this was done by pulling the fabric down (the take-down mechanism), but most modern circular machines employ holding-down **sinkers** or plain web sinkers and are referred to as sinker-top machines. These machines have one needle for every wale in the fabric and, between each needle there is a sinker, which has two functions: to hold the fabric loops in a given position whenever the needle rises, and to provide a surface over which the needle draws the loop.

Figure 13.16 shows the knitting action of a latch needle machine employing sinkers. The principle of loop formation is similar to that already described, but in this technique sinkers are employed to aid loop formation.

In position (a), the sinker is in the forward position, with the throat of the sinker holding down the fabric as the needle starts to rise. At (b), the sinker is still forward as the needle reaches the clearing height, but then at (c) it begins to move back and the needle descends to collect the new yarn, while at (d), the old loop has closed the latch to trap the new thread and knockover is taking place. The sinker then moves forward (e) to hold down the fabric as the process starts to repeat itself. The movement of the sinkers is controlled by sinker cams. They are housed in a sinker ring and cap assembly, with the latter being finely adjusted to ensure that the sinker timing is correct. The sinker timing is influenced by the appearance of the knitted fabric.

Loop formation of a 1 × 1 rib fabric

Rib fabrics are generally produced on v-bed or circular machines. In both cases, loop formation is effectively the same, with v-bed machines having a front bed and a back bed, while circular machines have a cylinder and dial (or sometimes a superimposed cylinder, one positioned directly above the other).

Two sets of needles are used to produce rib structures, and Figure 13.17 illustrates the knitting action and loop formation on a circular cylinder and dial machine.

Position (a) shows the needles at the start of loop formation, while at (b) adjacent needles have been moved to the clearing height. At (c) the needles start their return movement and take the new yarn into the needle hook simultaneously. The needles now come under the control of the stitch cam (d), as the new loop is drawn through the old loop, with the old cylinder loop being knocked over. It can be seen that in position (d) the dial needle has not completed its knock-over. This is known as delayed timing, which is very popular in the production of rib fabrics, as the delay produces tighter fabric due to **robbing-back** (this is where some yarn is taken

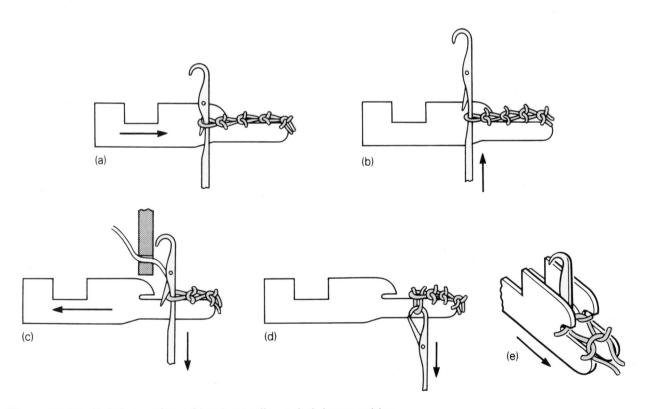

Figure 13.16 Knitting action of latch needle and sinker machine.

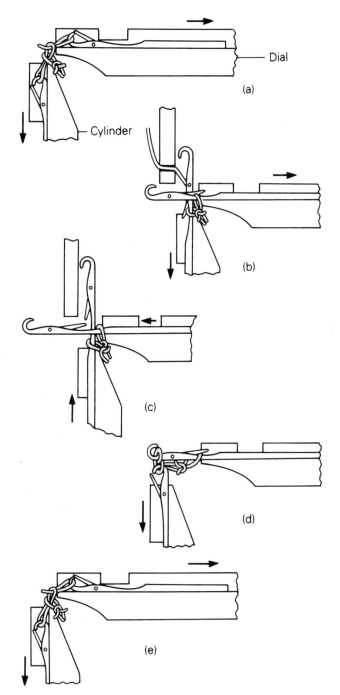

Figure 13.17 Loop formation of a 1 × 1 rib fabric on a cylinder and dial circular machine.

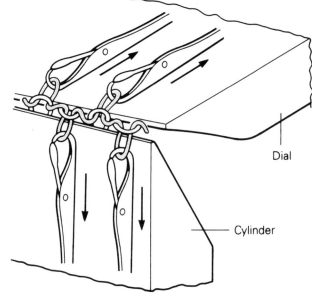

Figure 13.18 Needle arrangement for a 1 × 1 rib fabric.

Purl knitting

Flat purl knitting uses two horizontal needle beds and double-ended latch needles which may, according to the selection and type of fabric being made, be transferred from one bed to the other, knitting first on the hook at one end and then on the hook at the other.

Figure 13.19 shows the knitting action of a flat bed purl machine which has tricks in each of the needle beds. They are in line with one another to enable the needles to transfer from one bed to the other. Sliders positioned in each trick control the double-ended latch needle movement. Position (1) shows the needle knitting in the front bed under the control of the slider in that bed. In position (2), the needle has been moved to the centre, with both sliders engaging the needle hook. The sliders then start to move back, but the slider in the back bed is pressed down by a cam at point X, so that the front bed slider is freed from the needle hook and the needle is transferred to the back bed.

In position (3), the slider in the back bed has control of the needle and it can be seen that the yarn is fed to the opposite end of the needle, when compared to that of position (1). Position (4) shows that the slider in the back bed has moved the needle to the knock-over position to complete the formation of the purl stitch. It should be noted that a purl stitch is made when a loop is formed by one hook and then

from the previously knitted stitch to make the current stitch). Position (e) shows knock-over complete. If both the cylinder and dial needles knock-over together, to produce loops of equal size, it is known as synchronised timing and this could be shown diagrammatically by omitting position (d) from Figure 13.17.

Figure 13.18 shows the needle arrangement for a 1 × 1 rib fabric.

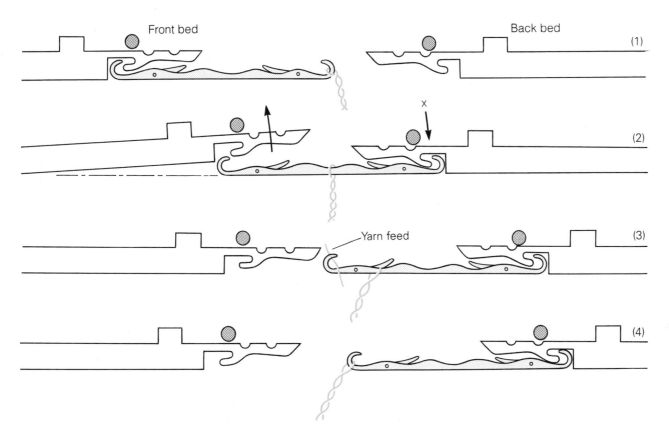

Figure 13.19 Purl knitting.

at the next course by the other hook of the same needle, so that one course is formed on the front bed and the next course is formed on the back bed to create a 1 × 1 purl structure.

The flat bar machine is also capable of producing rib structures, dependent on the slider set-out. Structures such as 1 × 1, 2 × 2 and 3 × 1 ribs can be made by ensuring that the same needles knock-over in the same direction as each course is knitted. The machine is consequently very versatile.

Interlock knitting

Interlock is a popular double-jersey structure produced on a cylinder and dial circular weft knitting machine.

Figure 13.20 shows the needle set-out on the machine, with long and short needles alternating on the cylinder. In the dial, the needles are set out exactly opposite to those on the cylinder. This means that, as a result of the special arrangement of the cams only one set of needles will knit at each feeder. To make this possible, there are two separate cam tracks with one controlling the short needles and the other the long ones. At the first feeder only long needles will knit, and

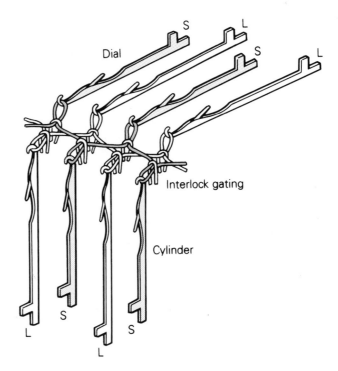

Figure 13.20 Needle arrangement for interlock fabric.

at the second feeder only short needles will knit so as to produce one actual course of interlock two feeders are required. Figure 13.20 illustrates the interlock structure.

End-products of weft knitted fabrics

Weft knitted fabrics are used as apparel, household, industrial and technical fabrics.

End-products of weft knitted fabrics

FLAT BAR MACHINES

Machine gauge: 5–14 needles per inch (npi)
Machine width: up to 78.7 inches
Needle type: latch
Needle bed type: single, rib and interlock
Products: jumpers, pullovers, cardigans, dresses, suits, trouser suits, trimmings, hats, scarves, accessories, ribs for **straight bar machines** (fully-fashioned machines).

CIRCULAR MACHINES

Machine gauge: 5–40 npi
Machine width: up to 60 inches
Needle type: latch, bearded (on sinker wheel and loop wheel), and some compound needle machines
Needle bed type: single, rib, interlock and double cylinder
Products: i   hose machines: seam-free hose, tights, industrial use dye bags, knit-de-knit yarns, industrial fabrics
                   ii half-hose machines: half-hose, stockings, children's tights, sports socks
                   iii garment blank machines: underwear, t-shirts, jumpers, pullovers, cardigans, dresses, suits, trouser suits, vests, briefs, thermal wear, cleaning cloths, industrial fabrics
                   iv fabric machines: rolls of fabric with the following end-uses: jackets, tops, sports and t-shirts, casual wear, suits, dresses, swim-wear, bath robes, dressing gowns, track suits, jogging suits, furnishing upholstery, industrial and technical fabrics, household fabrics.

STRAIGHT BAR (FULLY FASHIONED) MACHINES

Machine gauge: normally 21–30 needles per 1.5 inch
Machine width: from 2 to 16 section machines, each section up to 36 inches wide
Needle type: bearded and latch
Needle bed type: single and rib
Products: jumpers, pullovers, cardigans, dresses, suits, trouser suits, fully-fashioned hose, underwear, sports shirts, thermal wear.

Knitted loop length control

The control of loop length during knitting is of paramount importance. The need to control it precisely has led to considerable research into its behaviour as well as the development of devices and instruments for its control.

> The loop length is the fundamental unit of the weft knitted structure; its length and shape determines the fabric dimensions, which in turn can be affected by the yarn used and the finishing techniques employed, such as heat-setting.

Loop length

A number of individual loop lengths form a course length, and this ultimately influences fabric dimensions and other associated properties, such as fabric area density. Variations in course length within a fabric will result in a fabric fault known as **barre** (bars appear across the fabric). To reduce or even remove course length variation, a number of yarn measuring and control devices have been developed and, with the introduction of multi-feeder machines, it is even more important to control loop length.

DETERMINATION OF COURSE LENGTH

Course length measurements can be obtained by removing a number of courses from the knitted fabric, though this can be time consuming and only really serves as an indication of loop length after knitting. Determination of loop length at the start of knitting and control during knitting are essential to fabric quality. Two instrument types are available for use during knitting: yarn length counters and yarn speed meters, which indicate how much yarn is being used by each feeder while the machine is operating.

The yarn length counter is the simplest; it records the amount of yarn fed by a particular feeder for a given number of revolutions, with the course length being obtained by dividing the reading by the number of knitting machine revolutions. The yarn speed meter can be hand-held. It records the yarn feed rate in metres per minute and this reading is divided by the number of knitting machine revolutions per minute to obtain the course length.

Other types of yarn speed meters exist. One such example gives a direct reading of the yarn speed in centimetres per second.

CONTROL OF COURSE LENGTH

Modern circular weft knitting machines are fitted with a number of feeders, which at one time required individual stitch cam adjustment. The stitch cams caused the needles to pull yarn from the supply package, and variations in unwinding properties of supply yarns led to variations in loop length. Adjusting individual cams was not only time consuming, it led to stitch-length variation between individual feeds.

> **Positive feed devices** were designed to eliminate the problem of variations in unwinding properties and cam setting by strictly controlling the rate and tension of the supply yarn to the knitting elements.

All modern cylinder rotating, single-jersey machines are fitted with positive yarn feed devices, which feed the yarn to the needles at a constant rate to control the stitch length in the fabric. The function of the stitch cam is in this case reduced to that of a yarn input tension device.

The tape positive-feed system proved to be cheap and extremely effective. Each positive-feed wheel is driven by a continuous tape via a single pulley from the main machine drive. This ensures that yarn is fed at the same constant rate to each feeder so that adjustments in the rate of feed to all feeders are therefore easily and quickly made. Consequently, only one feeder unit needs to be checked for the correct yarn feed rate. If the diameter of the drive pulley is increased the rate of feed will increase, resulting in a larger stitch length.

Developments in positive-feed devices have resulted in ultrapositive-feed units. These units have a small yarn store in the form of a number of wraps of yarn around a wheel, reducing the possibility of yarn slippage and variation in tension from cone to cone at each feeder. It is possible to

have up to four tiers of tapes on machines producing more complex structures where course lengths vary at each feeder. Tape feed units are generally suitable for structures having a maximum of four different course lengths.

Another type of yarn furnishing device is the storage feeder, which is similar to a weft accumulator in weaving. This device supplies yarn at uniform tension, rather than a constant rate of feed, by withdrawing yarn from a cone or package and winding onto a store. These units are motor driven and wind yarn on to the store at the same time that it is being withdrawn, so that yarn and cone-to-cone tension variations are reduced. A store of yarn is created to reduce the possibility of a fault being introduced into the fabric if the yarn breaks or runs off at the cone.

Storage feed units tend to be expensive and, as a result, a number of other devices are available for the control of yarn tension.

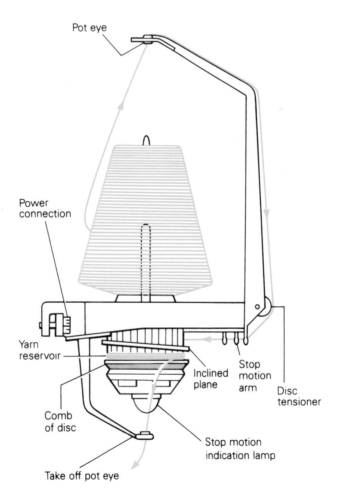

Figure 13.21 Iro storage unit.

Knitted fabric geometry

There has been considerable research into the behaviour of single-jersey structures in different states of relaxation. These relaxation states include dry-relaxed, wet-relaxed and fully relaxed. On the machine the fabric is under stress. After a time off the machine the fabric dry-relaxes. Wet-relaxed fabric has been soaked in water and the fully relaxed state is achieved by agitation during drying, which should give a true relaxed state to all fabric types. The fundamental principle of this work was to enable plain single-jersey fabric parameters to be predicted prior to actual knitting.

Tightness factor

Tightness factor is the ratio of the area covered by the yarn in one loop to the area occupied by that loop.

The expression developed for the calculation of tightness factor (K) is given below:

$$K = \frac{\sqrt{T}}{\ell}$$

where T = yarn linear density in tex

ℓ = stitch length in millimetres

For most plain fabrics, the mean tightness factor is between 1.4 and 1.5, although they can range between 1.2 and 1.6. Outside this range, fabrics are considered to be unsuitable for clothing applications.

Fabric area density

The calculation of fabric area density is important in that it can be used as a guide to quality control procedures. In its simplest form, fabric area density for plain single-jersey is as follows:

$$\frac{s \times \ell \times T}{100} = \text{g per square metre}$$

where s = stitch density (loops per square cm)

ℓ = stitch length in mm

T = yarn linear density in tex

Calculations for 1×1 rib fabrics can be done in a similar way to the above, but it must be remembered that the face wales of the rib need to be doubled because these conceal the alternate wales knitted on the back of the fabric. In the case of plain interlock, only the face of the fabric is analysed and the results are doubled to arrive at the fabric area density

(interlock is basically two 1×1 rib fabrics locked together). In practice, then, only one feeder is analysed for interlock fabrics.

It is normal practice to weigh a 10 cm × 10 cm piece of fabric and multiply by 100 to arrive at the actual area density in the correct units of grams per square metre. This is then compared to the calculated area density, and the percentage difference between the actual and calculated values should be less than three per cent. A re-check of the variables would be necessary if the difference was found to be greater.

CHECK YOUR UNDERSTANDING

● Knitting can be divided into two distinct sectors: weft knitting and warp knitting.

● The knitted loop is the fundamental unit of the weft knitted structure. Courses are rows of loops across the fabric width and wales are vertical columns of loops. Stitch length is the length of yarn in the knitted loop.

● There are basically four types of weft knitted fabric: plain single-jersey; rib; purl; and interlock.

● There are three types of weft knitted stitch: knit, miss and tuck.

● There are three commonly used needles: latch, compound and bearded. Weft knitting machines can be divided into three main classes: straight bar, flat bar and circular. All three types can have one or two needle beds.

● Control of loop length is vital in weft knitting because variations in course length cause barre fabric.

● Tightness factor is the ratio of the area occupied by the yarn in one loop to the area occupied by the loop. Weft knitted fabrics have tightness factors within the range of 1.2 to 1.6.

● Fabric area density can be calculated or the actual fabric area density determined by weighing a 10 cm × 10 cm piece of fabric and multiplying by 100 to get the standard units of grams per square metre.

REVISION EXERCISES AND QUESTIONS

1 What are the differences between warp and weft knitting?
2 What is the simplest knitted structure?
3 How could the stitch density be calculated?
4 What does the term 'technical face' mean?
5 Name two types of double-jersey fabric.
6 What is the difference between a tuck and a miss stitch?
7 Which weft knitting machine uses two needle beds but only one set of needles?
8 What is the difference in needle arrangement between rib and interlock machines?
9 How are loop length and course length related?
10 Why must yarn tension be carefully controlled during weft knitting?

Warp knitting

Introduction

> Warp knitting forms fabric by interlacing loops of yarn, but vertically down the length of the fabric in contrast to weft knitting. Each needle in the knitting width must be fed by at least one yarn and in line with the direction of fabric production. It is the fastest method of fabric production using mainly continuous filament yarns.

Warp knitting machines were invented in 1775, some 200 years after the first weft knitting machines. Man-made continuous filament yarns enabled bulk production of the simplest warp knitted fabrics after the first World War. There was phenomenal growth in the warp knitting industry between 1950 and 1970 due to developments in yarns available (synthetic continuous filaments), machine developments in both knitting and yarn preparation, and new fabric structures. After 1970, warp knitting declined with the reduction in sales of nylon shirts and sheets (due to their lack of comfort) which were the major products of warp knitting at that time. Textured polyester weft knitted fabrics started a boom period at the same time, contributing toward this decline. The inability of warp knitting machines to successfully process natural staple-fibre yarns, such as cotton and polyester/cotton, led to a fashion swing towards woven polyester/cotton fabrics for sheeting and shirting.

Gradually staple fibre yarns and needles capable of successfully knitting them have been developed for use in warp knitted structures, although warp knitting of 100 per cent cotton yarns has only recently become commercially feasible. Warp knitting has also expanded into geotextiles and lace fabrics.

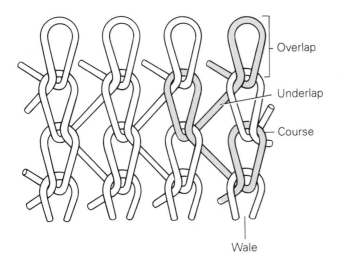

Figure 14.1 Single bar warp knitted fabric.

Warp knitted fabric properties

Warp knitted fabrics can be designed to exhibit a dimensional stability equal to that of a woven fabric or with elasticity comparable with that of weft knitted fabrics, while open work structures and designs can also be produced. It is possible to use an extremely wide range of yarns in various counts but continuous filament yarns are the most popular, particularly on Tricot – the simplest machines. Although single **guide bar** fabrics can be made, in which only one set of yarns is used, the fabric has a poor cover and is very unstable. Two bar machines (using two sets of yarns) are used for producing basic and simple fabric constructions for lingerie, or more rigid fabrics for shirting, fitted sheets and pillow cases. Raised loop fabrics are produced for nightwear, outer wear, upholstery and bedsheets, and plain and fancy net and mesh fabrics are made for curtains.

Types of machine

Two types or classes of machines are used for the production of warp knitted fabrics: **Tricot** and **Raschel**.

Table 14.1 gives a simple classification of warp knitting machinery, indicating the types of needles used and giving examples of products that can be produced.

There are a number of fundamental design differences between Tricot and Raschel machines. Tricot machines use both bearded and compound needles, with the latter becoming extremely popular since its shorter and smoother needle movement has enabled increased production speeds to be achieved. Usually two guide bars are used on Tricot machines, though up to five guide bars are possible. They are used for the production of apparel and household fabrics, particularly when bearded needles are used to process continuous filament yarns.

Raschel machines use latch and compound needles and are usually coarser in gauge than Tricot machines (gauge refers to the number of needles per inch). Raschel machines can have up to 78 guide bars and they are capable of processing both staple fibre and continuous filament yarns for furnishing, industrial and jacquard fabrics.

Figures 14.2 and 14.3 show sections through a Tricot machine and a Raschel machine respectively. They clearly show some basic design differences, in terms of the relative position of the warp beams, the number of guide bars used and the angle at which the fabric is taken up from the needles.

Fabric structure

To form warp knitted fabrics, each needle is supplied with a yarn. All needles knit at the same time, producing a complete course at once.

Warp knitting machines have straight needle bed(s) and can produce flat fabric on a single bed and a tubular fabric on a double bed machine. Yarn is supplied to the needles by a warp beam. From the beam, each yarn is threaded through the eye of a guide bar and the guide bar movement wraps the yarns around the needle to form the stitch. All needles operate at the same time, moving up and down to interlace the loops.

Table 14.1 Classification of warp knitting machinery

Tricot machines (bearded, needle)					
Single needle bar				**Double needle bar**	
2–5 bars lingerie shirts dresses	weft insertion 2–3 bars bed linen curtains lining	cut presser blouses curtains dresses	pile 3–4 bars bed linen bath robes gowns	gloves lingerie	

Raschel machines (latch/needle)					
Single needle bar				**Double needle bar**	
Standard Raschel 2–9 bars high speed	weft insertion 1–10 bars curtains industrial furnishings	lace 12–48 bars (fall-plate) curtain lace foundation garments		face-to-face plush (jacquard) 6–7 bars	cords trim bandages 4–8 bars
jacquard lace up to 78 bars (fall-plate) electronically controlled jacquard lace	special version up to 18 bars (fall-plate) weft insertion curtains			high pile fabric 6 bar	

In the Raschel double needle bar rightmost column: special version / split film / fruit and vegetable bags

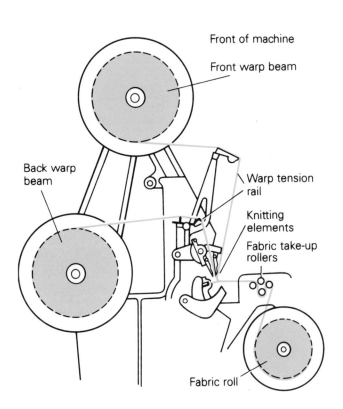

Figure 14.2 Two guide-bar Tricot machine.

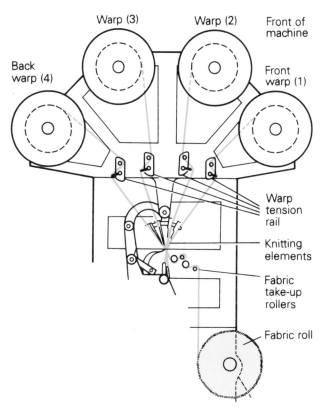

Figure 14.3 Four guide-bar Raschel machine.

The structure of a warp knitted fabric is dependent upon several factors. The number of guide bars used determines the number of separately controlled sets of yarns, with each guide bar feeding a set of yarn to the needles. The order of threading or sequence in which the warp threads are passed through the eyes of the guides alters the structure. It should be noted that if two or more guide bars are used it is not essential to provide each guide in each bar with a warp thread, but the arrangement must be such that each needle in the knitting width receives at least one warp thread at each course.

The lateral or lapping movement of the guide bars which wraps yarn around the needles also affects the structure. These movements are controlled from either interchangeable pattern wheels or from pattern chains consisting of varying heights of links which can be built up to give the required guide bar movements (see Figure 14.4).

The type and linear density of the yarns used will determine factors such as area density. Special mechanisms are available for producing held stitches, tuck stitches and figured fabrics, raised effects and full-width weft insertion, with the latter providing a means of creating fabric stability in the width direction.

There are two basic terms used in warp knitting to describe the sideways or lapping movement of the guide bars. These are overlap and underlap.

> The **overlap** is a lateral movement of the guide bar on the beard or hook side of the needle, and it usually extends over one needle space only. The **underlap** is the lateral movement of the guide bar on the side of the needle remote from the beard or the hook, and the extent of this movement is only limited by mechanical considerations.

Pattern chains

Figure 14.4 shows the pattern chain links which have been accurately ground to provide a smooth and accurately timed sideways movement, known as a **shog**, to produce overlap and underlap movements of the guide bar. The diagram shows the four different types of link available to produce the shog: A – straight; B – leading; C – trailing; D – leading and trailing. They also have numbers: 0, 1, 2, 3, 4 and so on, relating to the height of the links. Each successive link number will move the guide bar needle one space further than the previous number.

A pattern chain is built up of differing links with three links being required for each course of the structure being

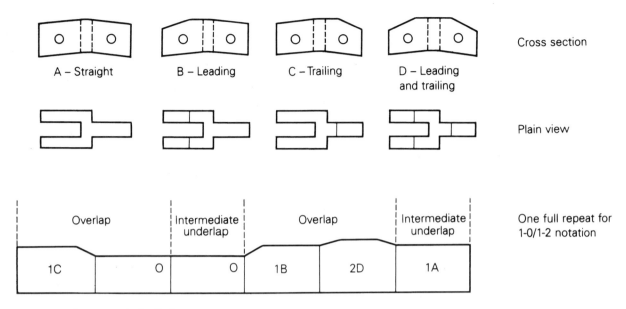

One full repeat for
1-0/1-2 notation

Figure 14.4   Pattern chain links.

produced. Two links will produce the overlap with a third link, known as an intermediate link, being added on most Tricot machines to allow time for the underlap to take place.

Loop formation

Knitting action – bearded needle Tricot machine

Figure 14.5 shows the position of the knitting elements of a Tricot warp knitting machine, while Figures 14.6 and 14.7 illustrate a sinker unit and a guide-bar unit respectively. The actual knitting cycle is shown in Figure 14.8.

In Figure 14.8, position (a) shows that the needle bar has risen to the centre of its vertical path. The fabric is held in the throat of the sinker to stop it rising with the needle and the guide bars will already have moved left or right one or more needle spaces for the first movement, which is known as the underlap.

At position (b) the guides have swung between the needles towards the back of the machine and stopped on the beard side. At this point the guides make a sideways movement of one needle space. This is called the overlap. These laps may be in the same or opposite direction for each guide bar, depending on the structure being produced. The guides then swing back to the front of the machine (c), with the overlap having wrapped a thread around the needle. This overlap thread usually stops on the beard.

The second rise of the needle takes place, which is sufficient to allow the thread to fall off the beard and onto the stem of

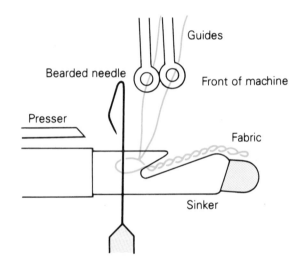

Figure 14.5   Knitting elements of a Tricot machine.

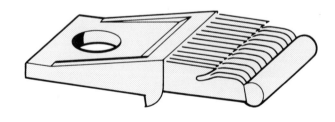

Figure 14.6   Warp knitting sinker unit.

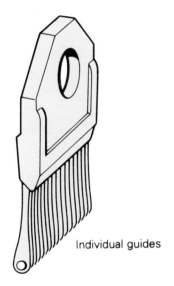

Individual guides

Figure 14.7 Warp knitting guide unit.

the needle (d) before it descends (e) until the tip of the needle is just underneath the top of the sinker. The presser then comes forward to close the beard.

At (f) the sinker moves backwards and, by its camming action, raises the old loop on the needle stem, onto the closed beard. The presser then moves back and the needle descends towards knock-over, which occurs at (g), when the old loop is thrown over the top of the needle and the new loop is pulled through the old loop. Finally, the sinker moves forwards to hold the fabric down and the guide bars are repositioned ready for the next course (the underlap).

Knitting action – latch needle Raschel machine

Figure 14.9 shows the main elements involved in the loop formation of a Raschel warp knitting machine and illustrates the sequence of events in one machine cycle. The guide bars

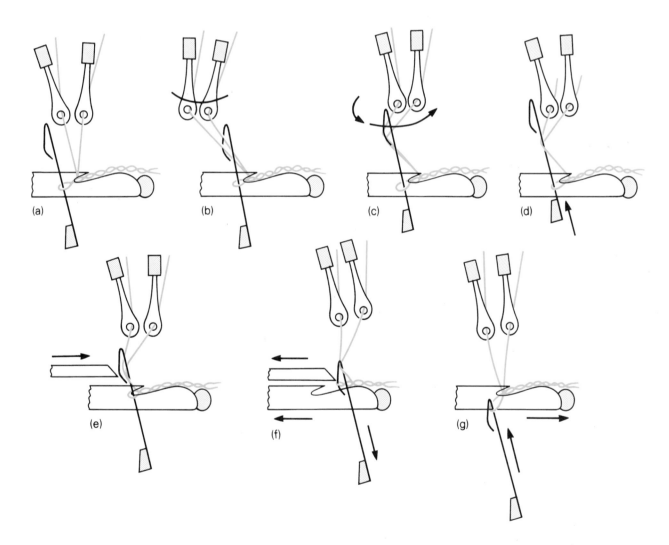

Figure 14.8 Knitting action of a bearded needle Tricot machine.

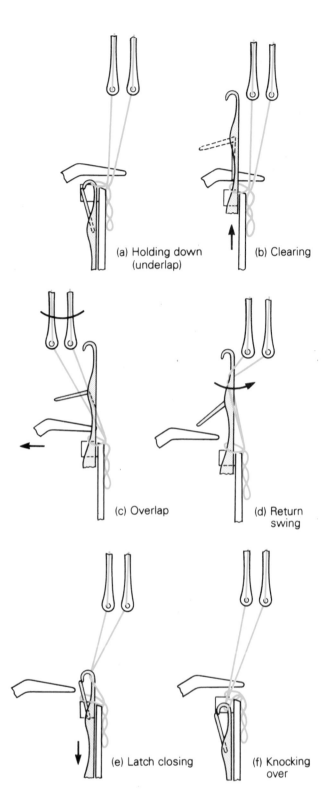

(a) Holding down (underlap)

(b) Clearing

(c) Overlap

(d) Return swing

(e) Latch closing

(f) Knocking over

Figure 14.9 Knitting action of a latch needle Raschel machine.

are at the front of the machine after completing their underlap at (a), with the web holders being forward to hold the fabric down as the needle bar starts to rise from knock-over.

At (b) the needle bar has risen to its full height and the old loop has slipped down the stem after opening the latches, which are prevented from closing by the latch guard. The web holders can then start to withdraw and allow the guide bars to form the overlap.

The guide bars have swung to the back of the machine (c) and will then move one needle space sideways to form the overlap before swinging back to the front of the machine (d), so that the warp threads can be laid into the needle hooks. The needle bar then descends (e) and the old loops contact and close the latches, so trapping the new loops inside. The web holders start to move forwards and, as the needle bar has continued its descent, its head has passed below the surface of the trick plate (f). This allows the new loops to be drawn through the old loops, which are cast off and, as the web holders advance over the trick plate, the underlap movement starts again.

Knitting action – compound needle Raschel machine

Figure 14.10 shows the various stages in loop formation for a compound needle warp knitting machine.

At (a) the needles are at the knock-over position after completion of the previous course, with the web holders positioned between the needles to hold the fabric down.

The needles have risen to the full height at (b), with the closing element having risen to a lesser extent, to allow the hook to open. The guide then swings between the needles towards the back of the machine for the start of the overlap (c), before making their sideways shog and swinging back to the front of the machine to complete the overlap (d). The web holders then begin to withdraw and the needle descends (e). This closes the element which descends at a slower rate to close the hook and trap the newly wrapped yarn. The guides then shog sideways to reposition themselves in front of the needle space ready for the start of the next course, and the underlap is completed.

At (f) the needle has descended to the knock-over position and a new course of loops has been produced.

Warp knitted fabric structures

To produce warp knitted fabric, the wales must be connected to each other. These connections are produced by traversing the guide bars between overlaps so that the threads wrap around different needles at different courses. These movements (underlaps) determine, by their direction and

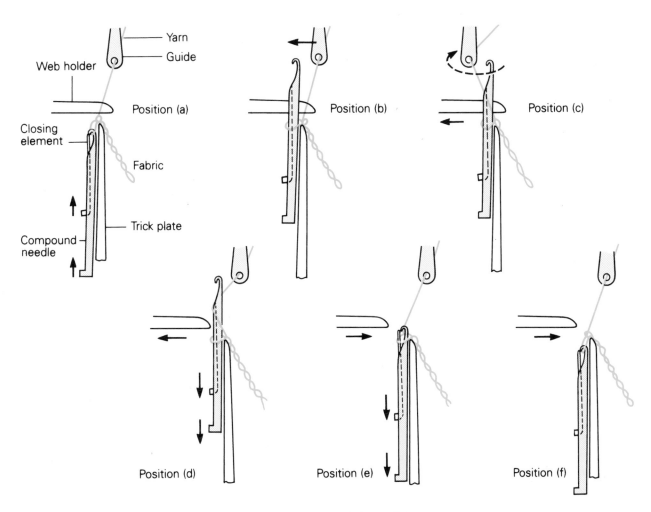

Figure 14.10 Knitting action of a compound needle Raschel machine.

size, the structure of the fabric, and since it is the underlaps that decide the structure of the fabric some form of notation must be used to record the movement of the guides.

Notation

The movement is plotted on point paper, where each dot represents a needle in the needle bar, and each row of dots represents a course, reading successive courses upwards on the paper, from bottom to top, and with the needle spaces being numbered from right to left.

Pattern chain notation

In addition to the notation for the fabric structure shown in Figure 14.11, notation is also used for the pattern chain.

The overlap movements are indicated by a dash, with the spaces that the guide bar has moved from and to. For

example, Look at Figure 14.11, part (g). The first overlap was caused when the guide bar moved from space 1 to space 2, which would be noted 1-2. The second overlap was caused when the guide bar moved from space 1 to space 0, noted 1-0. The underlap is noted by a solidus /, so the underlap was caused when the guide bar moved from space 2 to space 1, noted 2/1, then from space 0 to space 1, noted 0/1. The full chain pattern notation for (g) would therefore be 1-2/1-0/1-2/1-0, repeating to form the structure. Usually only one repeat of the pattern is given, 1-2/1-0.

As was mentioned earlier, the pattern chain is formed from individual links, two forming the overlap. A third intermediate link on Tricot machines allows time for the underlap. For example, for a two-course repeat 1-0/1-2 notation, the links used for the pattern chain for one full repeat would be as shown in Figure 14.12.

This would produce a smooth movement and would be repeated until all the links have been included to fill the pattern drum, which normally requires 48 links in total. With three links per course, 16 courses will therefore be required for one revolution of the drum.

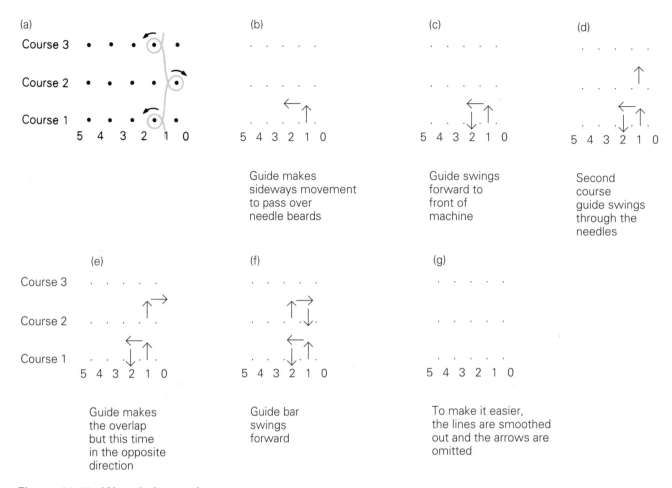

(a)

Course 3

Course 2

Course 1

5 4 3 2 1 0

(b)

5 4 3 2 1 0

Guide makes
sideways movement
to pass over
needle beards

(c)

5 4 3 2 1 0

Guide swings
forward to
front of
machine

(d)

5 4 3 2 1 0

Second
course
guide swings
through the
needles

(e)

Course 3

Course 2

Course 1

5 4 3 2 1 0

Guide makes
the overlap
but this time
in the opposite
direction

(f)

5 4 3 2 1 0

Guide bar
swings
forward

(g)

5 4 3 2 1 0

To make it easier,
the lines are smoothed
out and the arrows are
omitted

Figure 14.11 Warp knit notation.

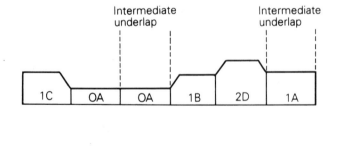

Intermediate
underlap

Intermediate
underlap

| 1C | OA | OA | 1B | 2D | 1A |

Figure 14.12 Links used for pattern chain.

Lapping movements

Figure 14.13 shows the lapping movement over the same
needles but in opposite directions. This produces what is
known as closed and open laps.

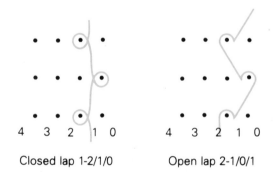

4   3   2   1   0

Closed lap 1-2/1/0

4   3   2   1   0

Open lap 2-1/0/1

Figure 14.13 Open and closed laps.

An **open lap** is produced when the underlap is made in the same direction as the preceding overlap and a **closed lap** is formed when the underlap is made in the opposite direction to the preceding overlap. An **open pillar stitch** (or chain stitch) is produced when only overlaps are made, so that it is an open lap stitch. **Miss-lapping** occurs when neither overlaps nor underlaps are made, while **laying-in** has no overlaps, only underlaps.

Miss-lapping and laying-in are made by the back guide bar and overlaps from the front guide bar are required to secure them into the structure.

The notation for this miss-lapping motion is 1-1/1-1, since there are neither overlaps nor underlaps. The notation for laying-in would be 0-0/3-3, as again there are no overlaps, but underlaps (underlaps being 0/3, 3/0).

When two or more guide bars are used, it is customary to show the guide bar movement separately. In Figure 14.15, for example, **locknit** is made on two bar machines. The front bar laps 1-0/2-3 and the back bar laps 1-2/1-0, as shown below.

Figure 14.16 illustrates the lapping notations for some basic, warp knitted, two guide bar structures. Variation in the construction of a warp knitted fabric allows the properties to be modified, with more elastic structures such as locknit being used for lingerie, while **queenscord** or **sharkskin** are used for shirts or blouses because they are more rigid.

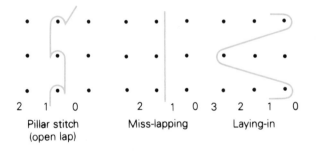

Pillar stitch (open lap) Miss-lapping Laying-in

Figure 14.14 Pillar stitch, miss-lapping and laying-in.

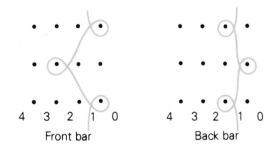

Front bar Back bar

Figure 14.15 Locknit.

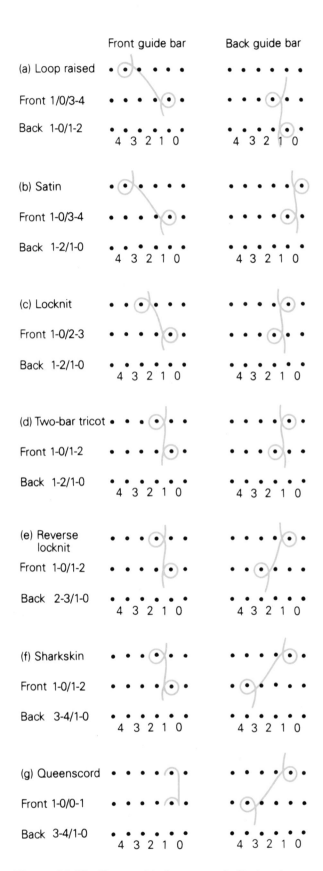

(a) Loop raised
Front 1/0/3-4
Back 1-0/1-2

(b) Satin
Front 1-0/3-4
Back 1-2/1-0

(c) Locknit
Front 1-0/2-3
Back 1-2/1-0

(d) Two-bar tricot
Front 1-0/1-2
Back 1-2/1-0

(e) Reverse locknit
Front 1-0/1-2
Back 2-3/1-0

(f) Sharkskin
Front 1-0/1-2
Back 3-4/1-0

(g) Queenscord
Front 1-0/0-1
Back 3-4/1-0

Figure 14.16 Two guide-bar warp knit structures.

Properties of two guide-bar structures

Basic rules

The following basic rules apply in the production of two guide-bar warp knitted structures.

1. When the guides swing through the needles to commence their overlap, the back guide bar will be the first to lay its underlap on the technical back and the front bar must be last so that its underlaps will be on top on the back of the fabric.
2. The front guide-bar thread will be the first to strike the needle on its return swing following the overlap and it will occupy a lower position on the needle, so that it will be prominent on the technical face of the fabric.
3. When the two guide bars underlap in opposite directions they will tend to balance the tension at the needle head and produce a more rigid upright overlap stitch.
4. When the front guide bar makes a shorter underlap it will tie the longer underlaps of the back guide bar securely into the rigid structure.

Full tricot

Tricot is the simplest two-bar structure (Figure 14.17). The two underlaps balance each other exactly as they cross diagonally between each wale producing upright overlaps. The structure tends to have poor cover and is prone to splitting between the wales during **stentering** or button-holing.

Locknit

This is the most popular two-bar structure. The longer underlaps of the front guide bar plate on the technical back of the fabric, as illustrated in Figure 14.18, improve fabric extensibility, cover and handle, so that the structure is ideal for use as a lingerie or intimate apparel fabric.

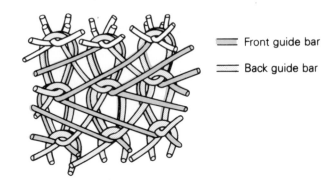

— Front guide bar
═ Back guide bar

Figure 14.18   Locknit.

Reverse locknit

This is not as popular as locknit. The shorter underlaps on the front guide bar reduce fabric extensibility and shrinkage in the finished width.

Sharkskin

The increased back guide-bar underlap of three needle spaces produces a more rigid and heavier fabric that is suitable for printed fabric products.

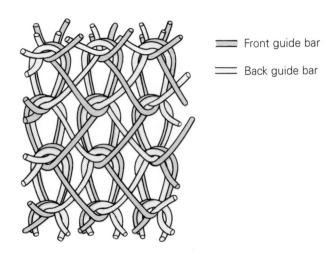

— Front guide bar
═ Back guide bar

Figure 14.17   Full tricot.

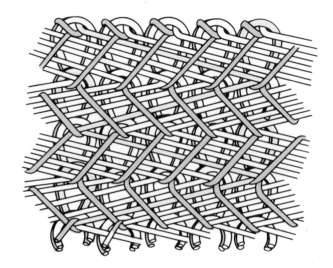

Figure 14.19   Sharkskin.

Queenscord

This structure has even more rigidity than sharkskin because of the pillar stitch produced by the front guide bar. This traps the back bar underlaps tightly to give minimal shrinkage.

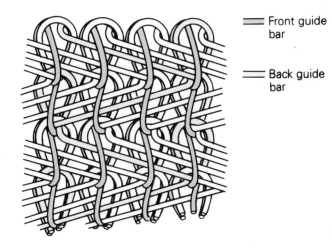

Front guide bar

Back guide bar

Figure 14.20 Queenscord.

Satin

Large underlaps are produced by the front guide bar, giving the structure greater elasticity than locknit. When the fabric is produced using a lustrous continuous-filament yarn in the front bar, the fabric has a high sheen.

End-products of warp knitted fabrics

Tricot machines

Type of needle:	compound or bearded
Machine gauge:	from 18 to 40 needles per inch
Machine width:	84 to 210 inches
Machine speed:	1000 to 3500 courses per minute
No. needle bars:	one or two
No. guide bars:	two to five
Products:	lingerie, shirts, outer wear, leisure wear, sportswear, car seat covers, upholstery, industrial fabrics, technical fabrics, bed linen, nets, towelling, linings and footwear fabrics.

Raschel machines

Type of needle:	latch or compound
Machine gauge:	from 6 to 32 needles per inch
Machine width:	75 to 230 inches
Machine speed:	500 to 2500 courses per minute
No. needle bars:	one or two
No. guide bars:	from 2 to 78.
Products:	marquisettes, curtains, foundation garments, nets, fishing nets, sport nets, technical fabrics, industrial fabrics, curtain lace, power nets, tablecloths, bed covers, elastic bandages, upholstery, underwear, drapes, geotextile fabrics.

CHECK YOUR UNDERSTANDING

● In warp knitting, loops of yarn are interlaced vertically down the length of the fabric. Each needle in the knitting width must be fed with at least one yarn at every course.

● Continuous filament yarns are mainly used on Tricot machines. It is the fastest method of fabric production.

● Tricot machines are the simplest, usually using only two guide bars. They use both bearded and compound needles.

● Raschel machines can have up to 78 guide bars, they are usually a coarser gauge and use both latch and compound needles. These machines are capable of producing complex structures.

● Beams of yarn supply guide bars which move laterally and swing backwards and forwards between needles in order to wrap yarn around the needle to form loops. All needles on a warp knitting machine operate simultaneously, moving up and down to interlace the loops.

● Overlap is the sideways movement of the guide bar on the hook side of the needle, usually moving one needle space only. Underlap is the sideways movement of the guide bar on the opposite side of the needle and can extend over several needle spaces.

● Pattern chains control the sideways movement, or shog, of the guide bars.

● Closed laps have overlaps followed by underlaps in the opposite direction. Open laps have overlaps and either underlaps in the same direction, or no underlaps at all. Laying-in has underlaps, but no overlaps; miss-lapping has neither underlaps nor overlaps.

● The relative timing between front and back guide bars in two guide-bar structures is such that on the technical back, the underlaps of the front guide bar show; on the technical face, the front guide bar overlaps are predominant.

REVISION EXERCISES AND QUESTIONS

1 Why was there a decline in warp knitting after 1970?

2 How has the warp knitting industry reacted to this decline?

3 With more than one guide bar, it is not necessary to provide each guide in each bar with a warp yarn. What is essential for the production of a fabric?

4 What would be the chain notation for the following structure?

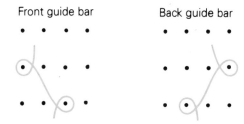

Front guide bar   Back guide bar

What is this structure called?

5 Which popular two guide-bar structure would you use if maximum rigidity was the priority?

6 What is the most popular two guide-bar structure and what is its major end-product?

7 When would miss-lapping and laying-in be used in warp knitted fabrics?

Woven fabric

Introduction

Woven fabric is produced by interlacing the threads running down the fabric (warp ends) with those lying across it (weft picks). The major reasons for variations in the appearance of woven fabric are the yarn structure and the fabric structure.

The aspects of yarn structure that are most likely to affect the final appearance and properties of the fabric include the degree of hairiness of the yarn, its smoothness and lustre, its extensibility and twist, while its strength will be critical in ensuring satisfactory performance in use. For example, fabrics produced from staple spun yarns will have a less regular appearance than those produced from continuous filament yarns, and their hairiness makes them appear less lustrous.

This chapter will deal with fabric structure and its affect on the resultant fabric properties. Woven fabric parameters will be dealt with first, followed by the basic weaves – plain, twill, satin and sateen, the instructions for setting up the fabric – drawing-in, denting and lifting plans, and finally ornamentation of the basic weaves.

Woven fabric parameters

There are four basic parameters that are essential for every woven fabric: thread density (**sett**), yarn diameter (**linear density**), yarn bending (**crimp**) and the order of thread interlacing (**weave**).

Sett

> Sett, or thread density is normally expressed as the number of threads per centimetre, although there are still times when threads per inch are used.

The main methods used to determine the thread density in a fabric is either to count them using a piece glass or to use line gratings.

A piece glass is basically a magnifying glass mounted within a stand, the base of which is cut out to precise measurements, for example 20×20 millimetres, 10×10 millimetres, 1×1 inch. Otherwise, it may be in the form of a cross, with each arm and each cross axis having a different measurement.

The method of using line gratings is described in Chapter 18.

Linear density/count

This provides a means of indicating the yarn thickness, but it must be realised that yarns having the same thickness may vary in their linear density (yarns may contain more or less air spaces between fibres, or the constituent fibres may be of different densities). The popular yarn count systems that have been used for many years include the cotton count, worsted, metric and denier. In 1956, the textiles industry agreed to adopt the tex system as the standard system but it is taking a long time to become widely accepted.

Crimp

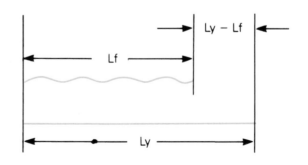

Figure 15.1 Crimp.

> Crimp refers to the amount of bending that is done by a thread as it interlaces with the threads that are lying in the opposite direction of the fabric.

Figure 15.1 shows the difference between the length of yarn (L_y) taken from a length of fabric (L_f), so:

$$\text{crimp } (c) = \frac{(L_y - L_f)}{L_f}$$

This will normally give values ranging from around 0.01 to 0.14, although there are circumstances where the values can be greater. The formula can also be developed to:

$$c = \frac{L_y}{L_f} - 1 \quad \text{or} \quad (c + 1) = \frac{L_y}{L_f}$$

This gives a value known as **crimp ratio**, which is often of more use. Often, it is generally considered most convenient and preferable to use per centage values:

$$\text{crimp \% } (c\%) = \frac{(L_y - L_f)}{L_f} \times 100$$

The use of calculations using the crimp formulae is essential in determining the amount of yarn that is required for a particular circumstance or in assessing how much fabric can be produced from a known length of yarn. Three examples are given below.

Example 1

Determine the length of warp required to produce 200 metres of fabric if the warp crimp is 7.5 per cent.

By expressing the percentage as a decimal ($7.5 \div 100 = 0.075$) and then using the second formula,

$$c = \frac{L_y}{L_f} - 1 \qquad \text{which may be rewritten as:}$$

$$L_y = L_f(1 + c)$$
$$L_y = 200(1 + 0.075)$$
$$L_y = 200 \times 1.075 = 215 \text{ m}$$

Example 2

What will be the final width of a fabric, if the width of the warp sheet is 1.20 metres and the weft crimp is five per cent?

In this case, the crimp % expressed as a decimal is 0.05 and the formula will be written as:

$$L_f = \frac{L_y}{(1 + c)}$$
$$L_f = \frac{1.2}{(1 + 0.05)}$$
$$= \frac{1.2}{1.05}$$
$$= 1.143 \text{ m}$$

Example 3

What is the percentage crimp in a fabric that is being analysed in the laboratory, if the fabric is cut at points 160 millimetres apart and the yarn length that is subsequently removed from the fabric is 176 millimetres?

Using the third formula: $c \% = \dfrac{(L_y - L_f)}{L_f} \times 100,$

$$= \frac{(176 - 160)}{160} \times 100$$
$$= \frac{16}{160} \times 100$$
$$= 10\%$$

A crimp tester can be used to determine the crimp per centage. The longer the length of yarn tested, the greater is the degree of accuracy.

Weave

> Weave refers to the order of interlacing of the warp ends and the weft picks.

Figure 15.2(a) shows a plan view of the most popular weave, which is called **plain weave**. This method of illustration clearly shows the order of interlacing in simple structures, but it can become quite complicated and also require a lot of space and time when larger weaves are being illustrated.

Cross-sectional diagrams (as shown at (b) in Figure 15.2) are sometimes used but they can become complex when more than one or two longitudinal threads are illustrated on one diagram. However, they are ideal for showing the basic structure of compound weaves.

The preferred method of illustrating weave structures is to use squared paper (also called point paper), which normally has eight small squares to each large square in both directions. The squared paper design for plain weave is illustrated at (c) in Figure 15.2. A square is filled in every time that a warp end passes over a weft pick, known as a warp lift. Any symbol can be used to indicate the lift.

A **weave repeat** is illustrated on the squared paper design.

> A weave repeat is the smallest number of threads required to show all of the interlacings in the pattern. It is usually considered sufficient to show one repeat only.

Weaves fall into three main categories, namely basic weaves (which are the most popular and include plain, **twill**, **satin**

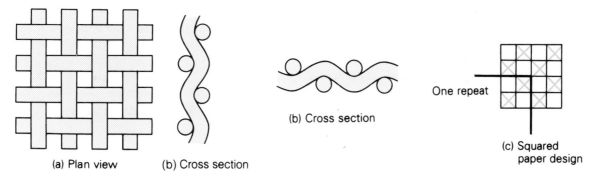

(a) Plan view   (b) Cross section

(b) Cross section

One repeat

(c) Squared paper design

Figure 15.2 Plain weave representation.

and those weaves that are developed from them), fancy weaves and compound structures.

Comparative or inter-related fabric parameters

It is not always convenient to quote the basic parameters of a fabric in order to give a clear picture of the fabric that is being discussed. It is often the case that reference to the fabric weight, cover factor or thickness may be more meaningful.

There are certain accepted abbreviations that will be used in the following sections.

Table 15.1 Abbreviations

ends per cm	n_1	picks per cm	n_2
warp count (tex)	N_1	weft count (tex)	N_2
warp crimp percentage	$c_1\%$	weft crimp percentage	$c_2\%$
warp weight in 1 m² of fabric (gm⁻²)	w_1	weft weight in 1 m² of fabric (gm⁻²)	w_2
warp cover factor	k_1	weft cover factor	k_2
total cover factor	k_c	fabric thickness	t
		fabric weight (gm⁻²)	w_c

FABRIC WEIGHT

Fabric weight (w_c) is the weight of yarn per square metre in a woven fabric, which is the sum of the weight of the warp (w_1) and the weight of the weft (w_2).

w_c = total length of yarn in one square metre

× mass per unit length of yarn,

where total length of yarn = total threads per metre × length of each thread, and length of each thread = 1 metre + crimp allowance.

$$w_1 = n_1 \times 100 \times \frac{[1 + (c_1\%)]}{100} \times \frac{N_1}{1000} \text{ g}$$

$$w_2 = n_2 \times 100 \times \frac{[1 + (c_2\%)]}{100} \times \frac{N_2}{1000} \text{ g}$$

Total fabric weight per square m $= w_1 + w_2 \text{ gm}^{-2}$ and weight per piece $= (w_1 + w_2) \times$ piece length × piece width g.

An example of a weight calculation is given below for a fabric 120 metres long, 1.3 metres wide and having 30 ends per centimetre of 12 tex warp and 24 picks per centimetre of 15 tex weft. The warp and weft crimp percentages are five per cent and eight per cent respectively. An accepted alternative method of stating these fabric particulars is 30×24; 12 tex × 15 tex; 5% × 8%.

Warp weight per square metre

$$= \frac{[30 \times 100] \times [1 + (5)]}{100} \times \frac{12}{1000}$$

$$= 37.8 \text{ gm}^{-2}$$

Weft weight per square metre

$$= \frac{[24 \times 100] \times [1 + (8)]}{100} \times \frac{15}{1000}$$

$$= 38.88 \text{ gm}^{-2}$$

Total weight per square metre

$$= 37.8 + 38.88 = 76.68$$

Piece weight

$$= \text{total weight per m} \times \text{piece length} \times \text{piece width}$$

$$= 76.68 \times 120 \times 1.3$$

$$= 11962.08 \text{ g} \quad \text{or} \quad 11.96 \text{ kg}$$

It is possible to calculate the piece weight of warp and weft directly, by including the length and width in the first calculations, if desired.

In addition to using this type of calculation from a design point of view, woven fabric weight calculations, incorporating crimp calculations, are important in determining the rate at which yarn will be consumed at the loom. Providing that the weaving efficiency is known, it is possible to establish the frequency with which new weft supplies will be needed, how long it will take to weave a piece of cloth or when a new beam will be required at the loom.

COVER FACTOR

> **Cover factor** (k) is defined as the area covered by yarn when compared with the total area covered by the fabric.

The warp cover factor can be found by using the formula:

$$k_1 = \frac{n_1 \sqrt{N_1}}{10}$$

Similarly, the weft cover factor can be found from the formula:

$$k_2 = \frac{n_2 \sqrt{N_2}}{10}$$

so the total cover factor is:

$$k_c = k_1 + k_2$$

If the same fabric that was used for the weight calculation ($30 \times 24; 12\,\text{tex} \times 15\,\text{tex}$) is considered, it is now possible to determine the cover factors.

$$k_1 = (30 \times \sqrt{12}) \div 10 = 10.39$$
$$k_2 = (24 \times \sqrt{15}) \div 10 = 9.30$$
$$k_c = k_1 + k_2 = 10.39 + 9.30 = 19.69$$

These values allow fabric technologists to develop a mental image of fabrics and acquire a knowledge of the most suitable cover factors related to specific end-uses. An awareness of the full cloth geometry theories makes it possible to engineer new fabrics or modify established fabrics theoretically rather than by the trial and error techniques that were used for so many years.

FABRIC THICKNESS

For a wide range of fabrics, this parameter is not important, but it becomes critical for fabrics that are to be used as belts and felts, and also in some types of pile fabrics. The subject is complex because of the thread flattening that occurs in two and three dimensional fabrics and because it is difficult to ensure that tufts and loops are vertical in pile fabrics.

Plain weaves

> Plain weave is the simplest and by far the most popular of all woven structures. It allows the maximum amount of interlacing of the warp and weft and so, for the same sett and yarns, a fabric produced from plain weave will have greater stability and firmness than fabrics produced from any other weave.

The order of thread interlacing for plain weave is illustrated in Figure 15.2, but many variations in the characteristics of the ultimate fabric can be created by having similar production details for warp and weft (**square plains**), by having a greater amount of warp (**warp-faced plains**) or weft (**weft-faced plains**).

Square plain weave

This is the most popular group. The fabrics are relatively featureless and have roughly the same production particulars for both warp and weft. Although they do not have to be exactly the same, they are sometimes divided into true square plains and approximately square plains. The end-uses for fabrics of this type include, in rising order of cover factors: surgical dressings for bandages; dairy cloths for cheese or meat wrapping; muslin dress fabrics; parachute fabric; handkerchief fabric; fabric for shoes or tents; sheeting fabric; canvas for transport covers; and fabric for use as ribbons in typewriters or computers.

There are some end-products of square plain fabrics that are produced in a range of cover factors, depending on the actual area of application. Filter fabrics and dress wear, in a wide range of different materials, are typical examples.

Most of the end-products given as examples were originally produced in cotton, but parachute and many canvas fabrics are now produced from continuous filament nylon, while others, such as sheeting, use blends of staple-spun polyester/cotton. In all cases, it is important that the properties of the fabric are appropriate for the end-product and, in this respect, two examples are discussed below.

1. Surgical dressing must act as a filter to ensure that dirt cannot get to the wound, but it must be sufficiently open in structure so that air can penetrate and encourage the

wound to heal. Additionally, it needs to be able to absorb blood and other fluids (hence the preference for cotton). It should be inexpensive since it is destroyed immediately after use, and also it should be lightweight. Appearance and strength are relatively unimportant. A typical quality would be 7.5×6; 13.4 tex $\times 11$ tex; $0.5\% \times 0.5\%$; giving a fabric weight of 17.4 gm^{-2} and a cover factor of $2.74 + 2.00 = 4.74$.

2. Nylon, which has a high work of rupture, is preferred for parachutes to enable the fabric to resist the insurge of air as it opens (pairs of double threads are now used at approximately eight millimetre intervals to act as rip stops in order to enhance this quality). It is also extremely important that the structure should allow air to flow through at a rate that will permit a controlled descent. Furthermore, nylon is resistant to attack by bacteria and can be compacted into a small space without creasing. A typical quality would be 41×36; 5 tex $\times 5$ tex; $4\% \times 6\%$; giving a fabric weight of 40.4 gm^{-2} and a cover factor of $9.17 + 8.05 = 17.22$.

Warp-faced plains

In this group of fabrics, the warp cover factor is much greater than that of the weft cover factor. This is normally achieved by having many more ends than picks per centimetre, although it is possible for the warp count to be coarser than that of the weft. It is also common to find that the warp crimp is high, while the weft crimp is very low, which results in the fabric having characteristic faint lines across its width.

A typical fabric in this group is **poplin** for shirtings, skirts and rain-wear. A typical construction for a polyester/cotton poplin shirting is 50×25; 16 tex $\times 15$ tex; $14\% \times 3\%$; giving a weight of 130 gm^{-2} and a cover factor of $20.0 + 9.7 = 29.7$.

Weft-faced plains

This is not a popular group of fabrics because, as it is normally produced with more picks than ends per centimetre, the rate of production in the loom will be greatly reduced in comparison with producing the warp-faced equivalent. It is difficult to detect the extremely faint lines running down the fabric.

The most popular fabric in this group is the **limbric**, which is used for dress prints. It has a soft, full handle due to the predominance of the weft, which is spun with fewer turns per metre than the warp because it is placed under less strain during weaving.

The difference in warp and weft cover factors and crimp values is normally less in weft-faced plains than in warp-faced plains. A typical construction for a cotton limbric

would be 26×40; 12 tex $\times 16$ tex; $4\% \times 8\%$; giving a weight of 102 gm^{-2} and a cover factor $9.0 + 16.0 = 25.0$.

Ornamented plain weave fabrics

It is possible to introduce ornamentation into plain weave fabric. In the warp only, stripes will be woven down the fabric, while in the weft only, the effect is a crossover (though this term is not common and the word stripe is often used). Weft 'stripes' are less popular except when used in conjunction with a warp stripe in order to produce a check effect.

The most popular means of producing these effects is by the use of different coloured threads, but variations in the sett, yarn linear density (including the introduction of fancy yarns), fibre type, yarn twist and yarn crimp are possible. The well-known seersucker effect is produced when the crimp is varied in stripes, which may differ in width as required.

Voile and crepe fabrics

These fabrics are produced using highly twisted two-fold yarns, with the doubling twist in the same direction as that of the single yarn. For voile yarns, the tex twist factor is usually between 5000 and 7000, while for crepe yarns it is nearer to 9000:

$$\text{turns per m} = \frac{\text{tex twist factor}}{\sqrt{\text{tex}}}$$

So, for a 15 tex voile yarn, the turns per metre could be:

$$\frac{50}{\sqrt{15}} = 1290 \text{ turns per m},$$

and for a 16 tex crepe yarn it will be:

$$\frac{70}{\sqrt{16}} = 1750 \text{ turns per m}.$$

Voile yarns are lively and are **gassed** (passed rapidly over a flame which burns off protruding surface fibres) after doubling to make them hairless. They are used in lightweight, semi-opaque fabrics for dress and blouse wear, saris and light filters.

Crepe yarns are very lively. Two threads S twist and two threads Z twist are inserted alternately in the warp only (for example, crepon) or weft only (for example, canton crepe), or in both directions (for example, georgette). The fabric is allowed to shrink by up to 25 per cent in wet processing so that the resulting fabric has a rough, irregular surface appearance that is popular for dresses and blouses. It also acquires an elastic property that makes it very suitable for support bandages. The fabric specification determines the end-use application.

Rib and matt weaves

These weaves are developed from the plain weave structure, as illustrated at (a) in Figure 15.3. When the lifting and lowering of the threads is extended in the warp direction, warp ribs are formed, while weft ribs are produced when the floats extend in the other direction. However, if the floats are extended in both directions for a number of threads, a matt (also known as a **hopsack** or **basket**) weave is produced.

WARP RIBS

A number of different warp-rib structures are shown at (b) in Figure 15.3. These weaves invariably demand a high warp sett and a much lower weft sett, which results in the weft lying virtually straight (having a low weft crimp), while the warp crimp will be high so creating prominent rib lines across the fabric. The resulting fabric has good drape properties, which make it ideal for curtains and other soft furnishing end-uses. **Repps** are undoubtedly the most popular fabrics in this group.

WEFT RIBS

Examples of weft rib weaves are shown at (c), but this is not a popular structure as it demands that a fabric has many more picks than ends per centimetre, which would require a much longer time to weave than the corresponding warp rib. The resulting characteristic of rib lines which run down the fabric are less prominent than those in warp rib structures and are not essential for any specific end-use. One weft rib is used for ladies' cotton dress prints. The fabric is woven using the 2 × 1 structure, with 18 tex warp for the two ends weaving as one (both twisted normally) and 21 tex warp (soft spun –

lower twist level) for the other end. The 21 tex soft-spun weft is a major reason for the ultimate soft handle and excellent drape.

MATTS

Two examples of matt weaves are shown at (d) in Figure 15.3. They have many characteristics that are similar to plain weave, though the thread groups tend to show more clearly as the size of the weave repeat becomes larger. They also require more threads per centimetre to approach the same stability as that achieved in plain weave fabrics. Typical end-uses for matt weaves include those where a degree of openness is required, such as sackings.

The structure becomes looser as the repeat size increases, until a stage is reached when it is impossible to achieve any degree of stability in the fabric. It then becomes necessary to introduce binding points into the weave, which may be arranged randomly to create a stitched matt or in an ordered manner, as illustrated in Figure 15.4, when the weave is said to be a fancy or figured matt.

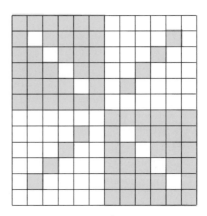

Figure 15.4 6 × 6 Fancy matt weave.

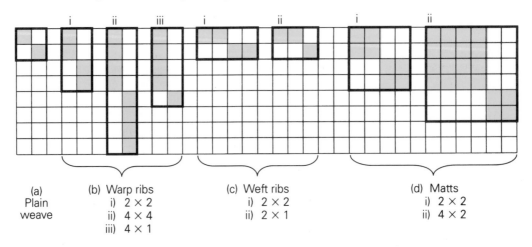

Figure 15.3 Rib and matt weaves.

Twill weaves

Twill weaves are characterised by diagonal lines in the fabric. These may run from bottom left to top right, in which case the twill is said to be a Z twill because its line is in the direction of the centre stem of that letter. Likewise, twills that run from bottom right to top left are known as S twills.

All of the ends in a twill weave lift alike, but each end starts its lift one pick higher or one pick lower than the end adjacent to it. This is referred to as a step of one and it is clearly illustrated in the 1/2 Z twill at (a) in Figure 15.5. The 2/1 Z twill, shown at (b), is an extension of that weave because each end is given an additional lift to that of the original twill.

The number of ends and picks in any twill weave is the sum of the numbers in the weave description, hence both the 1/2 and the 2/1 twills repeat on three ends and three picks. The former weave may be designated as either 1/2 or $\frac{1}{2}$.

Probably the most common twill weave is the 2/2, which is illustrated as a Z twill at (c) and as an S twill at (d) in Figure 15.5, while a 3/1 Z twill is illustrated at (e).

Twills in which the number of warp and weft lifts are equal are called **balanced twills**. The 2/2 weave is the most popular and it is used in such end-uses as linings (using continuous filament yarns), sheetings (using polyester/cotton blends), suiting fabrics (in worsted or polyester/wool blends), in dress wear in a wide range of different materials, or in gaberdines.

Unbalanced twills are created when there are more floats of one set of yarns on the surface. Warp-faced twills usually have more ends than picks per centimetre and in weft-faced twills there are usually more picks than ends per centimetre, which is the reason for this latter structure being much less popular. Warp-faced twills – often using the 2/1 or the 3/1 weaves – are the most popular and are used extensively in workwear (for example, drills and florentines), while the success of denim and jean fabrics, many of which are woven in these weaves, is well known.

Twist/twill interaction

The prominence of the twill line in the fabric is dependent on the direction of the twist in the warp and weft yarns, in relation to the direction of the twill. If the twist direction in both yarns is opposite to that of the twill direction then the twill line will be prominent, but if they are in the same direction, the twill line will be indistinct. If only one of the yarns is twisted in the opposite direction to that of the twill, only the twill line created by that yarn will stand out.

Figure 15.6 illustrates the yarn twist directions that will give the most prominent twill line for a 2/2 Z twill. The effect of using all of the twist combinations for this weave is given below. For a Z twist fabric:

S twist warp × Z twist weft = prominent twill
S twist warp × S twist weft = warp twill prominent
Z twist warp × Z twist weft = weft twill prominent
Z twist warp × S twist weft = twill indistinct

The consequences of using the various twist combinations with a 2/2 S twill can be determined in a similar way.

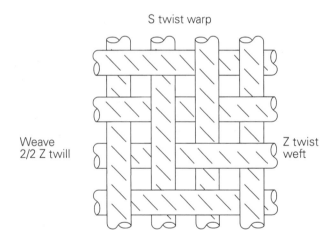

S twist warp

Weave
2/2 Z twill

Z twist
weft

Figure 15.6 Twist/twill interaction.

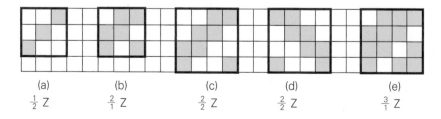

| (a) | (b) | (c) | (d) | (e) |
| $\frac{1}{2}$ Z | $\frac{2}{1}$ Z | $\frac{2}{2}$ Z | $\frac{2}{2}$ Z | $\frac{3}{1}$ Z |

Figure 15.5 Basic twill weaves.

Developed twills

Twill weaves have a great potential for the introduction of ornamentation into the fabric. The most popular developments are pointed, herringbone, diamond and elongated twills, but zigzag, combined, broken, figured and curved twills can also be designed. Only the first four of these structures will be described and they are illustrated in Figure 15.7.

POINTED TWILL

This weave is created by reversing the direction of the twill (for example, the 3/3 Z twill shown at (a) in Figure 15.7) at a predetermined point, which is often the end of a repeat, to give the effect shown at (b). A neat point of turn-back is essential and this is achieved by excluding the first and last ends of the original twill in the reversed twill line. Hence, the number of threads per repeat in the direction of the wave will always be:

$$(2 \times \text{threads per repeat in basic twill}) - 2$$

Another problem associated with this weave is the fact that the longest float in the same direction will be equal to:

$$(2 \times \text{the longest float in the basic weave}) - 1$$

This may create unacceptably long floats, hence the herringbone twill, which avoids this problem, is often preferred.

HERRINGBONE TWILL

When the twill direction is reversed in this weave, the lift is also reversed – the lift of the first end of the reversal is a negative image of the last end of the basic twill shown at (c) in Figure 15.7. It is clear that the longest float is now equal to that of the longest float in the original twill and that the repeat size is double that of the original twill.

This is a very popular weave for use in suitings and also in fabrics for overcoats.

DIAMONDS

Diamond effects can be generated in a number of ways. At (d) in Figure 15.7, the basic 3/3 twill has been turned over sideways (as in the production of the waved twill), and it is then turned over downwards in the same manner in order to complete the diamond effect. It is also possible to follow the same principles

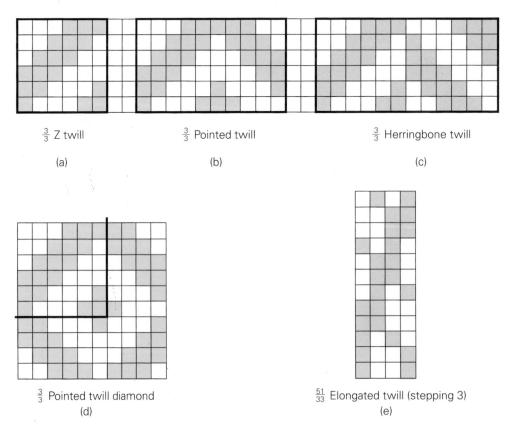

$\frac{3}{3}$ Z twill $\frac{3}{3}$ Pointed twill $\frac{3}{3}$ Herringbone twill

(a)   (b)   (c)

$\frac{3}{3}$ Pointed twill diamond $\frac{51}{33}$ Elongated twill (stepping 3)

(d)   (e)

Figure 15.7 Developed twills.

that were used in the production of the herringbone twill to create a herringbone diamond.

ELONGATED TWILLS

When a basic twill weave is produced with an equal number of ends and picks per centimetre, the twill line will be at an angle of 45° in the fabric. It may be desirable to change this angle to give the warp greater or less prominence. The former is generally adopted because the fabric can be woven with a much increased warp sett, which is preferred to having a higher weft sett. An alternative technique is to modify the step of the twill in either direction.

Because the warp yarns are usually stronger and more abrasion resistant, it is more usual to step upwards to create a steep angle. The properties of the resulting fabric are then enhanced further by having more ends than picks per centimetre. Whip cords and cavalry twills produced in this manner are popular for trouserings and an appropriate weave is shown at (e) in Figure 15.7, where a basic $\frac{51}{33}$ Z twill stepping three has been used.

Satins and sateens

The characteristic feature of satin and **sateen** fabrics is a smooth, lustrous surface created by extensive floating (lengths of yarn with no interlacing) of the warp (satin) or weft (sateen) on the face side of the fabric. One side of the fabric will normally be more lustrous than the other. This is a consequence of a satin fabric generally having many more ends than picks per centimetre, while in a sateen fabric the pick density will be higher.

Once again the situation exists where the satin is more popular than the sateen because it will take less time to weave. Another feature of these weaves is that each thread in the repeat is bound only once and binding points should not touch. To meet this criterion, the following steppings are unacceptable:

1. one;
2. the number of threads in the repeat;
3. the number of threads in the repeat minus one;
4. a factor of the repeat size (for example, two and four in an eight-thread repeat);
5. a number that has a common factor with the repeat size (for example, six has two as a common factor with eight).

Consequently, only the numbers highlighted are acceptable steppings for the repeats below:

4-end repeat – 1 2 3 4
5-end repeat – 1 *2 3* 4 5
6-end repeat – 1 2 3 4 5 6
7-end repeat – 1 *2 3 4 5* 6 7
8-end repeat – 1 2 *3 4 5* 6 7

The method of constructing an eight-end sateen weave using this information is illustrated in Figure 15.8. Initially, it is useful to indicate the extent of the weave repeat. The bottom left-hand square should then be filled in and using one of the acceptable steppings (three or five), the number (three in this case) should then be counted sideways and the square above the selected number filled in as illustrated. This procedure should be continued until the repeat is completed, as shown at (a). It would be acceptable to count upwards. The sateen weave without the numbers is shown at (b) and the satin weave, which is a negative image of this weave, is shown at (c).

Satin fabrics are popular for use in linings, lingerie, ties, dresses, curtains, quilts, bed and chair covers, and also for some denim fabrics. A typical quality for a continuous filament viscose lining fabric would be 66 × 30; 8 tex × 11 tex; 4% × 2%; 90 grams per square metre; 18.7 + 10.0 = 28.7 cover factor.

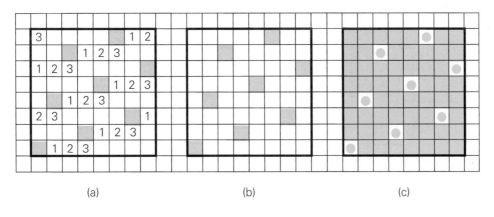

(a)   (b)   (c)

Figure 15.8 Construction of satin and sateen weaves.

Satin and sateen weaves can be made to interchange positions in a random pattern order in the production of **damask** fabrics for table linen and, in conjunction with other weaves, to produce **brocade** fabrics.

Both satin and sateen weaves are used extensively in conjunction with other weaves to create decorative effects in the form of stripes or checks for use in shirts, blouses, tableware and handkerchiefs, but in these circumstances the lack of availability of the four-end and six-end weaves creates a problem. Satin weaves repeating on an odd number of threads do not bind effectively with plain weave, which repeats on two threads and, when larger weave repeats are used, the capacity of the mechanism that controls the weave can become restrictive. Under these circumstances, modified four-end and six-end weaves have been developed. They are termed **irregular satins and sateens.**

Irregular satins and sateens

The method of constructing these weaves is a little more complex than that used for the standard weave.

It is again preferable to indicate the repeat size and fill in the bottom left-hand square. A step of two (or four) is then used for the six-end weave to the halfway stage in the repeat, followed by a step that is half the repeat size. The repeat is then completed by using the initial step but counting in the reverse direction. The stages are illustrated at (a) in Figure 15.9 for the six-end weave and at (b) the sateen weave is illustrated, while the satin weave is shown at (c). A similar sequence is shown at (a), (b) and (c) in Figure 15.10 for a four-end irregular satin weave, which uses a step of one (or three). In this latter weave, it is impossible to produce a design in which binding points do not touch.

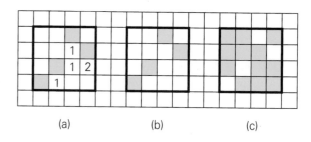

Figure 15.10 Four-end irregular satin and sateen.

Drawing-in, denting and lifting plans

These plans form an essential link between the designing of a fabric and the working parts of the loom.

Drawing-in plans

Drawing-in plans indicate the order in which the warp ends are drawn through the eyes of the healds, which are mounted in heald frames in the loom. Healds control the movement of the warp threads to form a **shed**, through which the weft picks pass and it is in this way that the yarns are interlaced to form the woven fabric. As has been shown, different weaves are different interlacings of warp and weft threads.

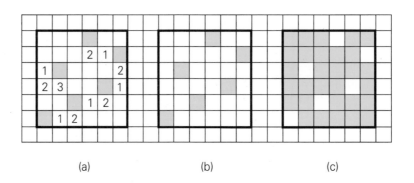

Figure 15.9 Six-end irregular satin and sateen.

Each end will be drawn through the eye of one heald and healds that lift alike (which are raised at the same time) will be placed on the same heald frame, while healds that lift differently will be placed on different heald frames.

The drawing-in plan is placed directly beneath the design. Each row in the drawing-in plan represents one heald frame and a cross is placed on the appropriate row, directly under the end to which it refers. The first end is usually designated to be controlled by the first or front heald shaft. If the second end lifts differently, the cross under that end is placed on the row representing the next heald shaft and so on, as shown at (a) in Figure 15.11. However, if the second end lifts exactly like the first, its cross will be placed on the same horizontal row, as shown at (b). The process is continued until every end in the design has been designated to a heald frame.

The drawing-in plan shown at (a) is said to be straight, while that at (c) is called a pointed or V-draft and those with no strict sequence (as at (b)) are usually said to be fancy.

Denting plans

Denting plans describe the arrangement of the warp ends in the reed (**dents** are the gaps between the metal reed wires). Denting plans are entirely dependent on the end density and the number of dents per centimetre in the reed, though there are some fabrics that require precise positioning of the dent wires in relation to the weave.

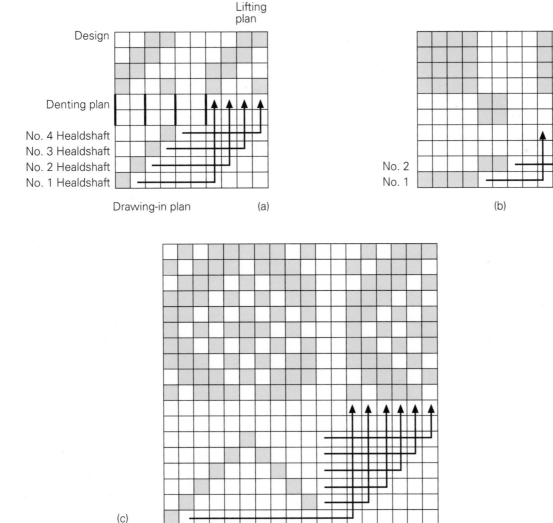

Figure 15.11 Drawing-in, denting and lifting plans.

As an example only, the method of indicating two ends per dent is illustrated at (a) in Figure 15.11.

Lifting plans

> **Lifting plans** indicate how each heald shaft is lifted on each pick in the design.

The lifting plan should be situated to the right of the design with the corresponding picks on the same horizontal row. It is then helpful to indicate which heald shaft in the drawing-in plan relates to each vertical row in the lifting plan by drawing arrowed lines, as shown in each of the examples in Figure 15.11. These lines are not essential but they help to avoid mistakes and may become unnecessary with experience. It is traditional for the first heald shaft to be at the left-hand side of the lifting plan.

As each arrow is traced from its cross in the drawing-in plan and the lift of the end(s) to which it refers in the design are indicated above the arrow tip (for example, at (a), the lift of the end above the cross on the first heald shaft is 2/2 and it is this lift that is inserted above the arrow tip). This procedure continues until the lift of each heald shaft has been inserted in the lifting plan.

Ornamentation of basic weaves

Combining a number of different weaves is one method by which fabrics can be ornamented, while the introduction of colour in relation to the precise lifts of the weave provides an alternative method. Both of these methods of figuring normally utilise the basic weaves, though they can be used with other weaves.

Combined weaves

This technique is usually used to create stripes down or across the fabric, or a combination of the two will produce checks. Freely drawn designs using this technique are possible. They are known as brocades and need to be produced with the aid of a jacquard. This is the most versatile patterning system available to the weaver.

To create the desired effect in good quality fabric, it is necessary to ensure that there are a maximum number of good binding points where the weaves change (in other words, there should be an interlacing between warp ends and weft picks at this point); that the first and last ends of a repeat join correctly; and that all of the weaves in a vertical stripe repeat on the same number of picks. Likewise, all of the weaves in a horizontal stripe must repeat on the same number of ends.

The combined weave effect for a stripe having four ends of plain weave, four ends of 3/1 Z twill and four ends of plain weave is shown in Figure 15.12. It should be noted that the fourth (plain end) binds correctly with the fifth end on the fourth pick, but an unavoidable bad binding point occurs on the second pick, as indicated (this is acceptable so long as the number of bad binding points are kept to a minimum). The last end of the repeat joins perfectly with the first end of the next repeat and four picks of plain weave are necessary because the twill repeats on four picks. (There is also a bad binding point between the eighth and ninth ends on the first pick.)

The drawing-in, denting and lifting plans have been produced to illustrate that it is usual for the heald shafts at the front of the loom to control the ends that are making the

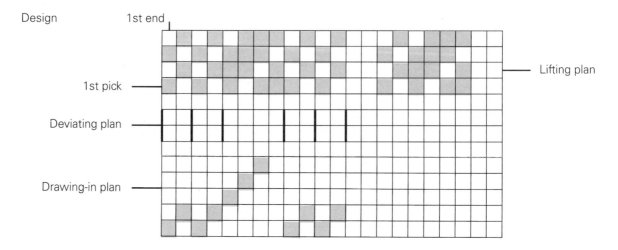

Figure 15.12 Combined plain weave and twill stripe.

most interlacings and that the weave having fewer intersections is likely to be woven with more ends per dent. Additionally, if there is a great difference in the crimp per centage in the two weaves, it will be necessary to supply the warp yarn from two separate beams.

At (a) in Figure 15.13, the design for a combined weave having four ends of plain weave, six ends of six-end satin and four ends of plain weave is shown. It should be noted that the order of the binding points in the six-end satin weave has been rearranged from that shown in Figure 15.9, to ensure a maximum number of good binding points with the plain weave, while retaining a perfect joining of the last and first ends in the repeat.

The check effect produced at (b) demonstrates that stripes down the fabric should be produced in satin, while those across are produced in sateen. It is usual for the satin to be on the surface where the two stripes cross. Once again the binding-point sequence for the satin and sateen weaves is different from that previously illustrated in Figure 15.10.

Just as it is necessary to have more ends per dent in satin stripes to avoid looseness as a consequence of fewer interlacings, it is necessary to increase the density of the picks in sateen stripes. This is done by preventing the cloth take-up motion from advancing the cloth during weaving. The action is known as **pick cramming** and it is achieved by means of a retarding motion, which is made to act on at least every other pick and, in many instances, on two out of three picks. In this way, the cloth will only be advanced once every two or three picks rather than every pick.

A suggested denting plan is indicated in both Figure 15.12 and Figure 15.13.

Colour and weave effects

These are the visual effects created when different coloured threads are woven into a fabric in a precise order related to the weave. The procedure to be used in order to predict the effect in the cloth is illustrated in Figure 15.14. At (a) the weave and the sequence of colours in the warp and weft, one-end blue (Bl.), one-end black (B), are shown. The influence of the warp colours on the fabric surface is shown (b) where only the ends are lifted, while (c) shows the influence

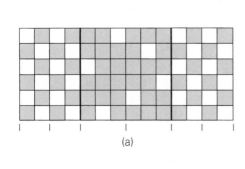

(a)

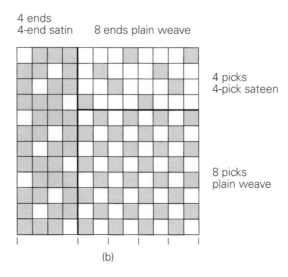

4 ends
4-end satin   8 ends plain weave

4 picks
4-pick sateen

8 picks
plain weave

(b)

Figure 15.13   Combined plain weave and satin stripes.

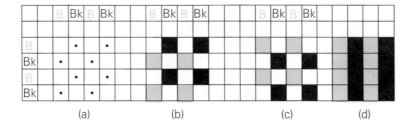

(a)   (b)   (c)   (d)

Figure 15.14   Production of a colour and weave effect.

of the colours where the weft is on the surface. The final effect, in this case known as a hairline, is produced at (d) by combining (b) and (c).

It is possible to produce a wide range of colour and weave effects, but the most popular are detailed below and illustrated at (a), (b) and (c) in Figure 15.15.

(a) Crowsfoot – 2/2 matt   four threads black;
                            four threads red in warp and
                            weft.

(b) Dogtooth – 2/2 twill   four threads black;
                            four threads white in warp and
                            weft.

(c) Basket – plain   one thread black;
                      one thread white;
                      one thread black;
                      one thread white;
                      two threads black;
                      one thread white;
                      one thread black;
                      one thread white;
                      one thread black in warp and
                      weft.

One repeat of a colour and weave effect often fails to give a true impression of the final effect and so four repeats of each effect are illustrated in reduced size below their respective design.

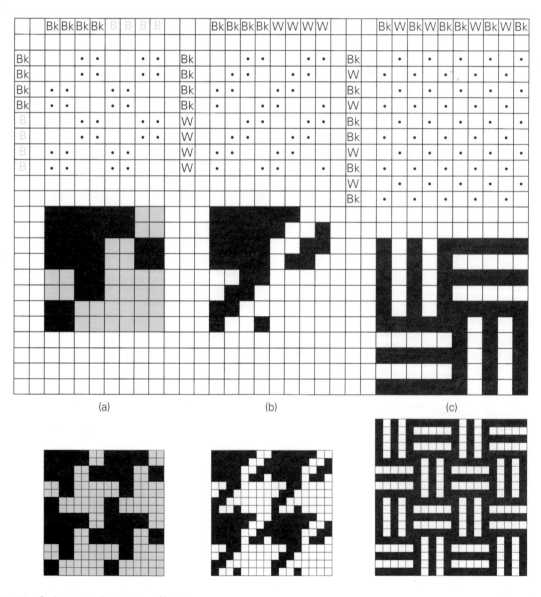

Figure 15.15 Colour and weave effects.

Other weaves

Many other weave structures are available, most of which are based on at least one of the basic weaves (plain, twill, satin or sateen). These include simple fancy weaves (for example, huckaback, mock leno, honeycomb, crepe and Bedford cord) and compound structures including brocade, extra yarn figuring, double and multi-ply cloths, leno and pile fabrics (for example, terry, velvet, carpets, velveteen). Each of these weaves produces effects and properties that make the structure of the fabric particularly suitable for specific end-uses.

The rest of this chapter will look briefly at some simple fancy weaves.

Huckaback

This is based on a plain weave foundation, which gives both stability and good wearing properties. Long floats are introduced to the weave to give good moisture absorbency properties to the fabric.

Figure 15.16 is a six-pick repeat huckaback, which is used for coarser qualities, while the ten-pick repeat shown in Figure 15.17 is used for finer qualities of fabric.

One drawback to using this weave is that the ends tend to form groups of five. This can be counteracted by paying attention to the denting plan. Placing the centre three ends of this group of five in one reed dent with the two ends at

Figure 15.16   Six-pick repeat huckaback.

Figure 15.17   Ten-pick repeat huckaback.

either side of this in the next dents, creates a denting order of two and three ends alternately. Ends that pass through the same dent tend to group together, so a denting order of this kind will counteract the tendency of this particular weave to group five ends.

Mock leno

This weave is used to give a perforated fabric which imitates an open gauze fabric, or a distorted thread effect which imitates a net fabric. (True leno fabrics create a hole effect by crossing over warp threads transversely.)

With a huckaback weave, we try to counteract the thread grouping effect caused by the weave, whereas here we encourage end and pick grouping to give a hole effect. Figure 15.18 shows one example of a mock leno weave, used to produce an imitation open gauze. One end-product of this is embroidery fabric.

Figure 15.18   Mock leno.

Honeycomb

Ridges and hollows are formed by this weave, giving a cell-like appearance to the fabric. Floats of warp ends and weft picks on the fabric surface give it good moisture absorbency so it is used for towels and table linen.

There are two distinct classes of honeycomb weave: ordinary, where both sides of the fabric have a similar textured effect; and Brighton, which has only one textured side to the fabric.

ORDINARY

Figure 15.19 is an example of an ordinary honeycomb weave repeating on eight threads.

If a large honeycomb is required, a double row of base marks is used to give dimensional stability to the fabric, as shown in Figure 15.20, which is a weave repeating on 16 threads.

Figure 15.19   Ordinary honeycomb.

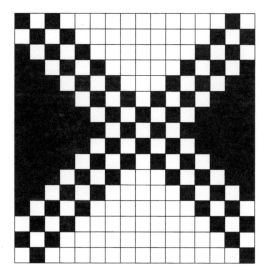

Figure 15.20   **Ordinary honeycomb with double base marks.**

BRIGHTON

The number of threads in a repeat must be a multiple of four for a Brighton honeycomb weave.

If the 16-thread repeat Brighton honeycomb weave in Figure 15.21 is compared with the 16-thread ordinary honeycomb weave in Figure 15.20, it is found that the ordinary weave produces one large cell only, while the Brighton produces two large and two small cells.

Crepe

This weave gives the fabric a surface texture, giving the appearance of small dots. A similar effect can be produced by using crepe yarns (very highly twisted) in a plain weave, alternating the twist direction of the warp ends.

One way of producing a crepe weave is to use a sateen weave as a base, with additional interlacing points and either regular or irregular sateen bases can be used for this.

Figure 15.22 is an example of a crepe weave based on a regular sateen, which has the same appearance on both sides

of the fabric. Figure 15.23 is still based on a regular sateen, but more warp ends are brought to the fabric surface on one side of the fabric.

Figure 15.24 is an example of a crepe weave based on an irregular six-thread repeat sateen.

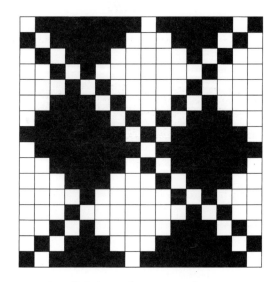

Figure 15.21   Brighton honeycomb.

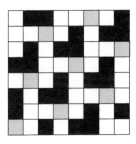

Figure 15.22   **Crepe weave based on an eight-thread regular sateen.**

Figure 15.23   **Crepe weave based on an eight-thread regular sateen.**

Bedford cord

Raised longitudinal warp lines are formed in the fabric, with fine sunken lines between them. Figure 15.25 shows one

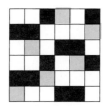

Figure 15.24 Crepe weave based on a six-thread irregular sateen.

Figure 15.25 Ordinary Bedford cord.

example of a Bedford cord; the number of ends between the pairs of plain weave ends can be varied to give cords of different widths.

▮ CHECK YOUR UNDERSTANDING

● Two major factors determine the appearance and characteristics of woven fabrics – yarn structure and fabric structure.

● There are four essential fabric parameters: sett (thread density); linear density of the yarn; crimp (bending of the yarn); weave (interlacing of the warp and weft threads).

● Inter-related fabric parameters such as fabric weight, cover factor and thickness are sometimes more meaningful in practice.

● Fabric weight (w_c) = total length of yarn × mass per unit length. This combines the fabric parameters of sett, linear density and crimp.

● Cover factor is the area covered by the yarn compared to the total area covered by the fabric.

● Fabric thickness is usually not important; it can be critical for felts and belts, but is a complex subject.

● The weave or interlacing arrangement of warp and weft threads is shown on squared design paper. A square is filled every time a warp end passes over a weft pick – usually only one repeat of the pattern is shown.

● Plain weave is the simplest interlacing arrangement possible. Square plain weaves have the same warp and weft specification; warp-faced plains have a greater cover factor in the warp, while weft-faced plains have a greater cover factor in the weft. This weave can be ornamented by altering the sett, crimp, yarn linear density or type, or introducing coloured yarn or highly twisted yarn. Matt and rib weaves are developed from plain weave.

● Twill weaves show diagonal lines in the fabric and may be S or Z twill. A one-step twill will have ends lifting one pick

sooner or later than the adjacent end. The prominence of a twill is dependent on the direction of twist in the warp and weft threads: if the twist in warp and weft is opposite to the twill direction, the twill line will be most prominent. Twills can be ornamented, for example pointed twills, herringbone, diamonds and elongated twills.

● Satin weaves have extensive floats of warp ends on the fabric surface, while sateen weaves have extensive floats of weft picks. True satin/sateens cannot be produced on four- or six-thread pattern repeats and irregular satins or sateens are used to overcome this problem.

● Drawing-in plans indicate the sequence in which warp ends are drawn through the heald eyes. Heald shafts lift the warp ends and so control the interlacing of warp and weft threads.

● Denting plans determine the arrangement of the warp ends in the reed.

● Lifting plans show how each heald shaft should move at each pick.

● The basic weaves (plain, twill, satin/sateen) can be ornamented by combining different weaves or using colour in relation to the weave.

● Many other weaves are available to produce effects and fabric properties particularly suited to the specific end-product. They are usually based on one of the basic weaves

▮ *REVISION EXERCISES AND QUESTIONS*

1 How can a plain weave fabric be affected by the yarn structure?

2 Calculate the length of warp required and the fabric width from the following:
   length of fabric required = 500 m
   width of warp sheet = 1.5 m
   warp crimp = 6.5%
   weft crimp = 5.5%

3 A fabric is composed of 40 tex weft yarn, with a crimp of 6% and 15 picks per centimetre; a 30 tex warp yarn with a crimp of 4.5% and 20 ends per centimetre. Calculate the fabric weight and cover factor and state the fabric particulars in the accepted way.

4 Why are weft-faced plains, twills, ribs and sateens not as popular as their warp-faced equivalents?

5 Complete the drawing-in, denting and lifting plans for the following weave:

$\frac{3}{3}$ Twill

Weaving

Introduction

Weaving is carried out on a machine traditionally known as a loom, though it has more recently been called a weaving machine, to indicate the high standard of precision engineering that is used in its manufacture today.

Figure 16.1 shows a cross section through a typical loom, with the warp ends being contained on the weaver's beam at the back of the loom. From this point each end successively passes through the eye of a drop wire (which is an essential part in stopping the loom in the event of a break in any of the warp ends), through the eye of a heald (with groups of healds mounted within heald frames), and through gaps (known as dents) between the wires of the **reed**, which is basically a closed comb. In front of the reed, the warp and weft combine at the fell to form fabric which is drawn forward to be stored on the cloth roller.

Weaving mechanisms

Primary motions

Every loom requires three primary motions to produce woven fabric: shedding, weft insertion and beating-up.

Shedding is the name given to the motion which moves the healdframes up and down in order to separate the warp sheet into two layers and create a triangle in front of the reed (referred to as the 'shed') through which the weft can be passed. **Weft insertion** (originally referred to as picking) is the means by which the weft is projected through the shed. This was traditionally by shuttle, but more recently it is done by projectile, rapier, air jet or water jet. **Beating-up** is where

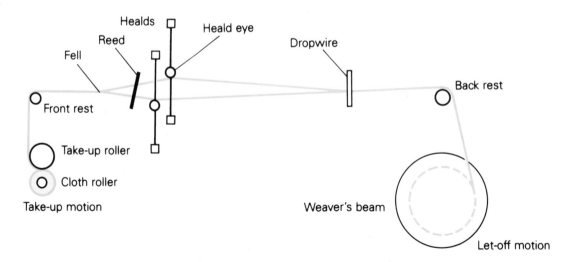

Figure 16.1 Cross section of a loom.

182

the reed, mounted in a reciprocating sley, pushes the weft into the fell of the cloth to form fabric. This requires considerable force, hence the term beating-up.

Secondary motions

> There are three secondary motions in weaving: **let-off**; **take-up**; and **weft selection**.

Secondary motions are also critical in allowing weaving to take place and in controlling the quality of the final fabric being produced. The let-off motion ensures that the warp ends are controlled at the optimum tension for the fabric that is being woven. The cloth take-up motion withdraws cloth from the fell and then stores it at the front of the loom. A weft selection or patterning mechanism is only necessary when it is desired to vary the weft being inserted.

Ancillary motions

Ancillary motions are widely used on modern weaving machines.

> Ancillary motions include: **warp stop motions**; **warp protectors**; **weft stop motions**; **weft replenishment**.

Weft stop motions halt the loom in the event of a break in the weft yarn, while warp stop motions halt the loom when a drop wire falls as the result of an end break. Warp protector motions stop the loom before beat-up in the event of the shuttle or projectile failing to complete its traverse from one side of the loom to the other and weft replenishment ensures a continuous supply of weft yarn to the loom whenever a supply package becomes exhausted.

The mechanisms of a loom are driven by shafts which rotate at speeds appropriate to the frequency with which a mechanism operates. The main shaft of the loom (often called the crankshaft because of the bends in the shaft) is responsible for the beat-up action which must take place after each weft insertion and so it will make one revolution per pick inserted. It is also the source of drive for any other mechanisms that operate on a one-pick cycle, such as weft insertion on non-shuttle looms. However, it may be necessary to introduce additional shafts, rotating at the same speed, to drive the mechanism from a convenient point on the loom. Mechanisms that operate once every alternate pick (for example, the picking mechanism on a shuttle loom, some shedding motions or a mechanical warp stop motion) need to rotate at half the speed of the main shaft. The bottom

shaft provides this source of drive on a shuttle loom, while an auxiliary shaft may be needed for further appropriately reduced speeds.

Basic loom design

There has always been a desire to produce woven fabric at the quickest rate possible. Accordingly, it has been common practice to quote the speed of a loom in picks per minute, though this fails to take into account the effect that loom width has on fabric production. For a number of years it has been widely accepted that the amount of weft inserted per minute provides a truer guide to the rate at which a loom produces fabric.

> Metres of weft inserted per minute = picks inserted per minute × reed space.

There are several major factors that need to be considered by a company when it is deciding to install new weaving machines:

1. The type of yarn to be woven. This is important because looms that are to weave continuous filament yarns will require many different features to those weaving staple fibre yarns.
2. The width of fabric to be woven. The loom must be able to weave the maximum desirable width required, so it will always be able to weave narrower fabrics.
3. The method of weft insertion to be used. This is determined by the suitability of the weft insertion media to the type of yarn, the fabric structure, the patterning required from the shedding and weft insertion systems, the type of **selvedge** (fabric edge) that will be produced and the amount of waste created.
4. The shedding system: this is mainly decided by the range of weaves to be used and the versatility required from the system.
5. Mechanisms to create specific fabric features, such as leno (warp ends are crossed over), terry (loop pile fabric), velvet (cut pile fabric).
6. The speed of the weaving machine and its ability to produce the required quality of fabric.

Shed size

In the initial stages of designing a loom, it is necessary to ensure that the size of the shed is large enough to allow weft insertion to take place. In the case of the shuttle each end is tapered, as illustrated in Figure 16.2, and this makes it possible for the shuttle to enter a partly opened shed and leave a shed that is closing. At both these points the top warp sheet will have to bend round the front wall of the shuttle and when this occurs, it is referred to as the bending or **shuttle interference** factor.

The size of shed required for a shuttle is much greater than is the case for some other weft insertion methods, such as projectile or rapier, and so a smaller shed depth and less sley movement are possible in these non-shuttle looms. Yarn type must also be borne in mind; hairy staple fibre yarns will tend to cling together when the warp sheets cross during shedding and slackness in some of the warp ends may cause them to sag. The two warp sheets will therefore have to separate to an extent that is sufficient to create a clear shed for weft insertion.

Loom settings

Uniform end spacing is an essential aspect of good woven cloth quality. However, it may not be possible to achieve this

naturally if there is more than one end per dent in the reed, as the ends will tend to group accordingly and the position of a reed wire will tend to create a space between groups of ends.

Some of the settings of the loom mechanisms, and the time of their action within the loom cycle, are important and may even be critical. Adjustments to the height of the back rest and specific timings associated with the shedding and weft insertion mechanisms can minimise this problem.

Back-rest height

It is reasonable to assume that the tension in the upper and lower warp sheets formed during shedding should be the same throughout weaving. In this case the centre shed line, which bisects the shed angle behind the fell, would be in the position shown in Figure 16.3: inclining downwards towards the back rest.

Uniformity in end spacing at the loom can be improved if one of the warp sheets is under greater tension than the other. This is particularly true when staple-fibre yarns are being

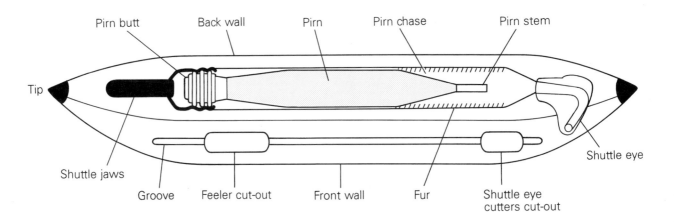

Figure 16.2 A shuttle.

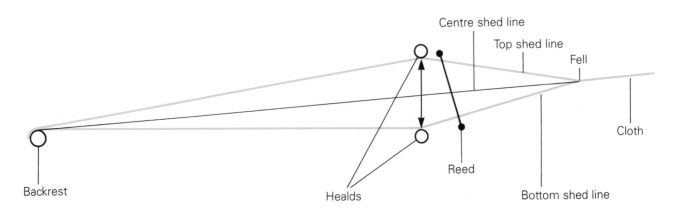

Figure 16.3 Cross section through the warp shed.

woven, as the ends are much less likely to slide naturally towards uniform spacing. Under these circumstances, it is common practice to raise the height of the back rest from that indicated to create a slack top shed and a tight bottom shed. It is not usual to produce a tight top shed by lowering the back rest, as this would limit the space available for the beam and also the slacker ends in the bottom warp sheet may be displaced by the shuttle or rapier as they traverse the loom. The alternative practices of adjusting the height of the healds in the loom or the height of the cloth fell are also available, especially for non-shuttle looms.

Loom timing

> The sequence in which the loom mechanisms operate is referred to as the timing of the loom and the rotational movement of the main shaft of the loom is used as the method of describing this timing.

Accurate settings become possible by making reference to the 360° movement of the main shaft. The beat-up position is often used as the start point – 0° – for this purpose because it offers a precise point on all looms, though some machines prefer to use other readily identifiable points. All references to timing in this chapter will assume 0° occurs at beat-up.

Figure 16.4 shows the two main forms of timing diagram. At (a), a circular diagram is illustrated in which it is necessary to indicate the direction of rotation. This is a popular technique but it fails to identify accurately timings that occur less frequently than once per pick, in which case the linear timing diagram shown at (b) is preferable.

Clearly, beat-up must occur when the sley is in its most forward position, at 0°. The timings for shedding and weft insertion vary considerably depending on the type of yarn being woven and the mechanisms that are being used on the loom. At this stage, it is sufficient to say that the healds are likely to be crossing at around 345° to 0° on a loom weaving continuous filament yarn, and at 270° to 330° for looms weaving staple-fibre yarns. There is a period of time when the healds remain widest apart and this may extend from 72° to 180°, but is commonly around 120°. This dwell period is invariably displaced equally and directly opposite to the healds level time. Picking commences at around 60° on a shuttle loom, but the shuttle may not start to enter the shed until about 105° at the earliest, while it will leave at around 240°. In Figure 16.5, typical timings for a loom weaving continuous filament yarns are shown at (a) and those for a loom weaving staple fibre yarns are given at (b).

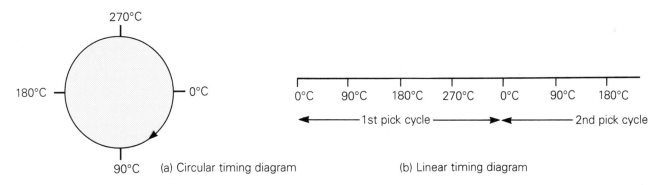

(a) Circular timing diagram

(b) Linear timing diagram

Figure 16.4 **Loom timing diagrams.**

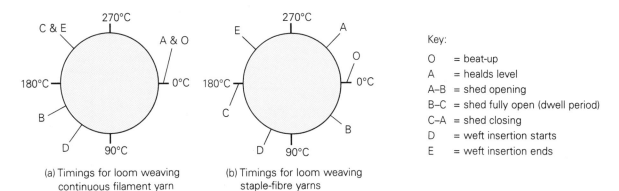

(a) Timings for loom weaving continuous filament yarn

(b) Timings for loom weaving staple-fibre yarns

Key:

O = beat-up
A = healds level
A–B = shed opening
B–C = shed fully open (dwell period)
C–A = shed closing
D = weft insertion starts
E = weft insertion ends

Figure 16.5 **Loom timings.**

Shedding

> Shedding systems raise and lower the ends in the warp sheet to the pattern required in the fabric and as determined by the drawing-in plan. This is done by moving heald frames up and down using **cranks**, **tappets** or **dobbies**, but in **jacquard** systems the heald eyes are moved up and down individually within each repeat.

The simplex heald type is shown at (a) in Figure 16.6, while a duplex type, which allows more healds per centimetre, is shown at (b).

The maximum number of healds per centimetre is limited to between 10 and 25, depending on the linear density of the warp yarn being woven. If the number of ends per centimetre that have to be controlled by one heald frame exceeds this number, it is necessary to use more than one heald frame working in unison. This is most likely to happen with plain

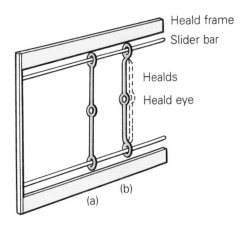

Figure 16.6 **Heald frames and healds.**

weave and if the heald frames are to be driven by one connection from the same source, it is necessary to replace the standard 'straight' drawing-in plan with a modification known as **skip draft**. These are illustrated at (a) and (b) in Figure 16.7 for four and six shafts respectively weaving plain. In both cases, the front healds will lift alike, as will the back ones.

Types of shed

If a heald frame is driven in both directions then the action is said to be positive, but if it is only driven in one direction and returned by springs or weights then it is negative. Positive shedding is generally preferred because it maintains good control of the heald frames, so allowing higher speeds to be achieved. In certain looms – such as jacquards – negative shedding is unavoidable, while in some narrow fabric looms where the loads on the heald frames are small and the speeds are exceptionally high, negative shedding is preferred to minimise wear.

> The four types of shed are: bottom closed; centre closed; fully open; and semi-open.

In Figure 16.8, each arrow represents the movement that will be made by one heald during one pick cycle. Closed sheds are formed when all of the threads in the warp sheet return to the same position after each pick. With **bottom closed** sheds (a), all the selected ends move twice the depth of the shed per pick so that there is a lot of wasted movement and so lost time. There is also an imbalance in the load on the machine. This type of shed is now found only on hand looms. The **centre closed** shed shown at (b) gives a balanced action, but there is wasted movement whenever an end is required to be in the same position for consecutive picks. The **fully open** shed shown at (d) is the ideal, as the

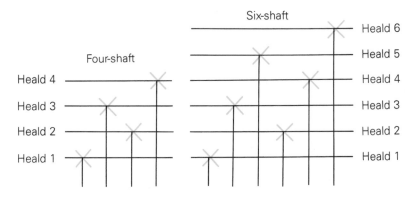

Figure 16.7 **Skip drafts.**

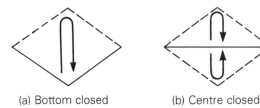
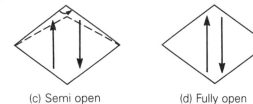

Figure 16.8 **Types of shed.**

ends either move or stay as required so that maximum speeds become possible, while (c) illustrates the **semi open** shed that some mechanisms produce because they are incapable of retaining the top shed line. In most cases their performance is very similar to that of an open shed.

Shedding systems

For any shedding system, it is essential to know the number of different lifts that can be controlled and the maximum number of picks that are possible in a repeat. Other important points are the degree of mechanism complexity; the ease with which the pattern can be changed; the system maintenance; the extent to which faults are possible; the speeds attainable; the cost; and the fabrics to which each system is suitable. A comparison of the available systems is given in Table 16.1.

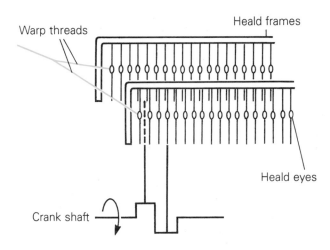

Figure 16.9 **Principle of crank shedding.**

CRANK SHEDDING

Cranks are used in this system of shedding. They are mounted on a shaft, the speed of which has been reduced so that it makes one revolution per two picks. The heald shafts will be raised and lowered in opposition to each other on a two-pick cycle and so the system is only suitable for plain weave.

CAM SHEDDING

Cams or tappets can be negative or positive in action. The cams act negatively, as they push the bowl to drive the heald shaft in one direction and normally rely on springs for the return action. The mechanism illustrated in Figure 16.10,

Table 16.1 Comparison of shedding systems

	Crank	Cam	Dobby	Jacquard
Maximum number of different lifts	2	6–10	16–28	5376 or 8000; 1344 is standard
Maximum picks per repeat	2	8	24 000+	20 000+
Degree of complexity	Minimal	Minimal	Quite complex	Simple in principle but many parts
Ease of pattern change	Not possible	Can take time	Very quick	Very quick
Amount of maintenance	Minimal	Low	Low to medium	Highest
Likelihood of faults	Very low	Low	More possible	Greatest likelihood
Capital cost	Lowest	Low	Quite high	Highest
Typical maximum revolutions per minute	900+	800+	800+	700+

however, achieves a positive action because the downward drive given to one heald shaft is used to generate an upward action of the other heald shaft via the roller motion at the top of the heald shafts.

This roller reversing motion has been very popular over the years because of its simplicity, though it does highlight the problems that arise in ensuring the angle (α) formed by the shed at the fell is constant. To achieve this, the back heald

shaft needs to move through a greater distance (h_2) than the front one (h_1). This is achieved by ensuring that the throw of the tappet (c_2) controlling the back heald shaft is greater than that of (c_1), which controls the front heald shaft, to an extent that depends on the distances of the heald shaft connections from the tappets and the treadle fulcrums, as well as the distance of the heald shafts from the fell. Additionally, the diameters of the reversing rollers (d_2 and d_1) need to be modified by the same ratio.

Cords, leathers and wires are used for the connections from the treadles and the rollers of the reversing motion to the heald shafts in all systems using negative-type cams. This is not ideal because regular adjustments to the settings are necessary as the cords and leathers stretch or are affected by heat and moisture in the weave room, which is often called the **weaving shed**.

The use of positive cams for shedding is gaining popularity as the desire to run looms at higher speeds increases. For many years, the grooved (or plate) cam illustrated in Figure 16.11 has been used. In the diagram, the bowl has been forced to its furthest distance from the centre, causing the lever system to move in the directions illustrated by the arrows. This results in the heald shaft being moved up. When the bowl is moved nearer to the cam centre, the direction of all the movements will be reversed and the heald shaft will be moved down. An increase in the amount of movement given to the heald shafts – as they are positioned further from the cloth fell – is made possible by adjusting the points of connection of the various levers. Also, as all of the connections are of a rigid nature, there are no longer any problems associated with cords and leathers, though wear within the groove is likely to occur after a prolonged period of running if cleaning and lubricating is not carried out on a regular basis.

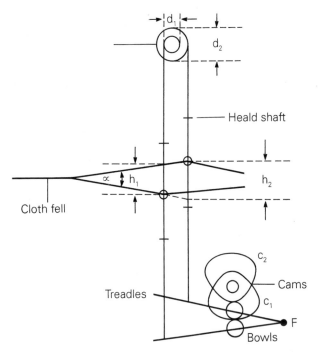

Figure 16.10   **Cam shedding with roller reversing.**

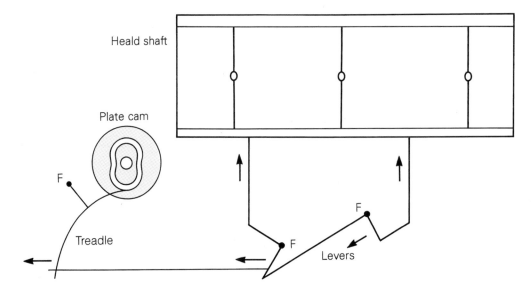

Figure 16.11   **Plate tappet system.**

Conjugate or matched cams (illustrated in Figure 16.12) involve two cam profiles machined from one piece of metal which act on two bowls mounted on a treadle that has its fulcrum point between the bowls. Both bowls remain always in contact with their respective profile so that when one bowl is pushed outwards by its cam profile, the other bowl will follow the other cam profile inwards. The consequence of the lower cam bowl being pushed away from the camshaft results in the movements indicated by the arrows in the diagram, and when the upper bowl is pushed outwards the heald shaft will move up.

Once again, adjustment to give an increased lift to the heald shafts as they are positioned further from the fell is easily achieved with the linkage connections. Again there are no cord or leather parts to be maintained. This type of shedding system is designed to run in an oil bath so that the problems of wear and regular lubrication are minimised.

DOBBY SHEDDING

Dobby systems normally control a maximum of 16 to 32 heald shafts, though units have been produced with up to 36 heald shafts.

Figure 16.13 is a diagram of a negative dobby in which there is a set of feelers, hooks, baulk, jack, cords, rollers and return springs for each heald shaft. Additionally, there is a single drive to the two griffes, each of which extends the entire depth of the dobby.

Although this type of dobby has been superseded in most areas, it does illustrate the principles in a simple manner. It is driven from the bottom shaft of the loom via an eccentric which causes the griffes to move in and out alternately and so create a balanced double action. Selection is made by the presence or absence of pegs in lags positioned under the outer end of the feelers (a square filled in on design paper represents the position where a peg is required in a lag so that a heald shaft will be lifted). When the outer end of the feeler is lifted by a peg the inner end, and so its hook, is lowered. If there is no peg, then the weighted outer end of the feeler will not be lifted and the inner end will push the hook into a raised position.

When the T-lever pulls a griffe outwards, it will pull any lowered hooks and so their baulk which will fulcrum against the stop at its other end. This will cause the jack to be displaced and pull the heald shaft upwards via the cords and rollers. The springs will be stretched and will return the heald shaft when the griffe makes its return movement. Any unselected hooks will remain undisturbed and the springs will hold the heald shaft in the down position.

Because there is a gap between the hook and the griffe to allow selection to take place, the outward moving griffe must move a short distance before it engages with any selected hooks. In the meantime, the inward moving griffe will have started its movement and the heald shaft will move down slightly before being lifted to the top position again, if it is required to be retained in the up position for two consecutive picks. Theoretically a semi-open shed is formed, but the movement is so slight that, basically, an open shed is created.

A modern, positive dobby, as illustrated in Figure 16.14, utilises many of the developments that have taken place and have been incorporated in negative dobbies. These include cam drive to the griffes and punched pattern card selection.

Cam drive to the griffes generally uses grooved cams, though a negative profile cam (acting in conjunction with

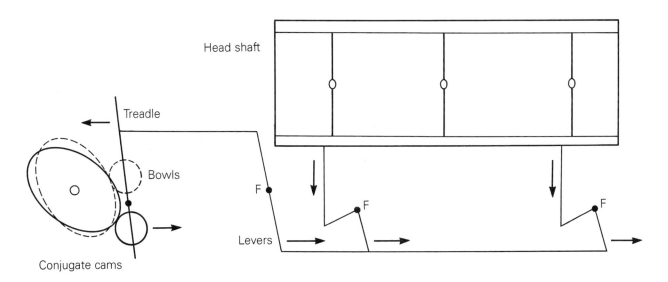

Figure 16.12 Conjugate cam shaft.

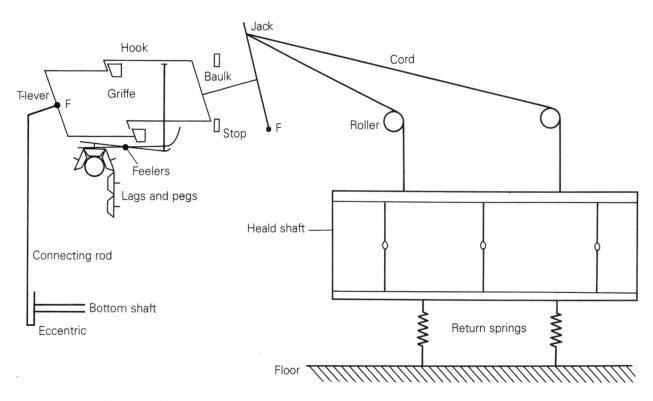

Figure 16.13 Negative dobby.

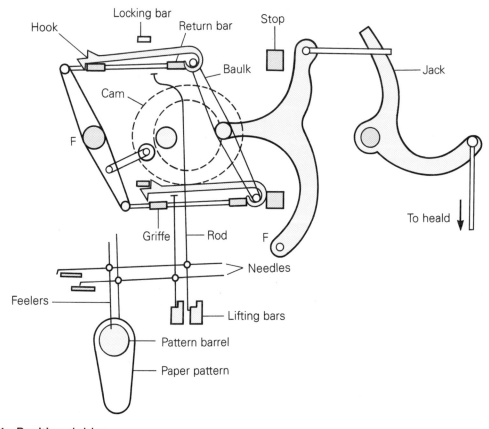

Figure 16.14 Positive dobby.

springs) and conjugate cams have been used. The advantage of this type of drive is that the cam can be profiled to allow the healds to dwell in their widest apart position for a predetermined period of time. This produces a clearer shed for a longer period of time – for weft insertion – without having to give an excessive lift to the heald shaft. Additionally, the outward moving griffe can be made to start its movement before that of the inward moving griffe to ensure that a true open shed is produced. There are fewer moving parts, especially in the area around the side of the loom so that less space is needed and the machine is safer.

Punched pattern selection uses an endless length of paper (or, more recently, plastic sheet) into which holes are cut to achieve the same objective as the pegs in lags. When a needle is lowered through a hole that has been punched in the pattern the rod is pulled sideways and the hook will remain in its lowest position, so that when the griffe moves outwards it will be pulled and the heald shaft will be lifted. However, if the pattern is uncut, the needle will be supported and the rod will remain on the lip of a lifting bar which rises by cam action once every two picks. This movement pushes any unselected hooks upwards so that they will be clear of the outward moving griffe and the heald shafts will remain in the down position. Punched patterns can be prepared in less time than a lag and peg pattern – except for the shortest of patterns – and subsequent patterns can be cut automatically using a copying unit. Less power is needed to drive the dobby and less storage space is necessary at, and away from, the loom. This system has been popular for many years but the patterns cannot be disassembled and reused, as is the case with lags and pegs.

The desire for higher speeds and the demands of heavier lifts, especially on wider looms, made a positive dobby essential. Such a dobby requires a positive cam drive to the griffes and the return springs must be eliminated. Return bars, introduced as an extension to the griffes, push any displaced baulks back to their original position adjacent to the stop in order to lower any heald shafts that have been lifted. Additionally, projections were added to the top of the hooks. These engage behind fixed (locking) bars when an unselected hook is pushed upwards. If this did not happen, the unselected heald shaft could not be held down and it would drift into a mid-shed position as a result of the influence of the tension in the warp sheet and the absence of springs, so that weaving would be impossible.

One of the later developments uses a rotary, instead of a reciprocating, action to generate the lift given to the heald shafts. This makes higher speed possible with less wear.

Further developments have taken place, including the use of computers into which the desired lifting plan is fed. This is then entered onto a disc that is subsequently fed to the dobby, where the pattern is read and memorised by an electronic system. This system eliminates the possibility of miss-lifts resulting from broken pegs and torn pattern sheets. As a disc

can be removed from the dobby after the pattern has been memorised, it can be used for a number of looms so removing the need to make duplicate patterns.

JACQUARD SHEDDING

The basic principles of a jacquard are shown in Figure 16.15. Rows of eight, twelve or sixteen needles are repeated to create the ultimate capacity of the machine.

Each individual pattern card contains the selection for one pick, with a hole being cut whenever an end in a repeat is required to be lifted. The cards are connected in sequence by lacing string and are mounted on the cylinder which moves in and out every pick. As it moves in, the cylinder will push any needles that encounter uncut card, causing the needle and its hook to be displaced sideways and the spring to be compressed. However, if a needle penetrates one of the holes that has been cut in the card, the needle and hook are undisturbed and the hook remains upright. As the griffe moves up, it takes with it the undisturbed hooks and so lifts the neckcord, harness cords (one for each repeat of the pattern) and the heald, which then form part of the top shed line. The

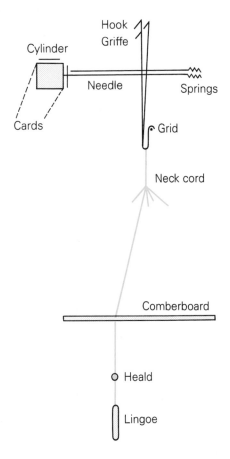

Figure 16.15 Single lift jacquard shedding.

ends controlled by a displaced hook are held down by the weight (known as the lingoe) because the hook has not been lifted. As the griffe starts to fall, the lingoe pulls down all the parts that have been lifted while the spring returns the displaced needle and hook. The action is therefore negative and, as the griffe cycle is completed within a one pick cycle (single lift), an undesirable closed shed will be formed.

The cylinders, which may have four, five or six sides, are turned through one section after each pick, so that the next card in the pattern chain is presented for the selection of the next pick.

When each needle is made to control two hooks that are lifted by two separate griffes operating alternately, a double lift is achieved (Figure 16.16). This gives a more balanced movement and allows higher speeds to be attained, though Figure 16.17 shows that when it is required to lift an end for two consecutive picks, the descending hook will start to fall at approximately the same time as the newly selected hook starts to move up. This results in the two hooks being level at the mid-shed position and so the top shed line cannot be retained between picks two and three. A semi-open shed is created.

A further slight increase in machine speeds is claimed when a cylinder is placed at each side of the jacquard. This requires one set of needles and hooks to be controlled from the left side of the machine and the other set from the right side. The hooks that control the same end are adjacent in the machine and are joined at the neck cord. Care is needed to ensure that the cards are presented in the correct sequence because the odd-numbered cards are mounted on one cylinder and the even ones on the other. If they get out of sequence, a fault known as weaving on the wrong card occurs.

Cylinders may be placed over the front and back of the loom or at the sides. The former is called the **straight tie** and the latter the **cross tie**. The merits of the two systems are debatable, but the former is probably more popular.

The position of the individual heald eyes is controlled by passing the harness cords through holes cut in a unit known as a **comberboard**. The order of tying up these harness cords between the needles and the healds is critical and dependent on the arrangement of the needles in the jacquard and the way in which the cards are cut prior to weaving. An example of a possible end-numbering sequence for the holes in the comberboard is shown at (a) in Figure 16.18. At (b), a range of repeat arrangements is shown. The straight tie-up (i) is used for labels and woven pictures; the repeating tie-up (ii) is for curtains, ties, carpets, and dress wear; and the pointed tie-up (iii) is used to enlarge the repeat for curtains. The border tie (iv) is used for tablecloths and towels, with the centre section using any of the other tie-ups. The values of x and y are dependent on the repeat size.

Coarse pitch jacquards are normally limited to maximum repeat sizes of 400 or 600, although 96, 200 and 900 have been used. The distance between needle centres is 0.25 inch (4.2 millimetres). A major factor in the wider acceptance of the fine pitch jacquard was the need for larger repeat sizes in

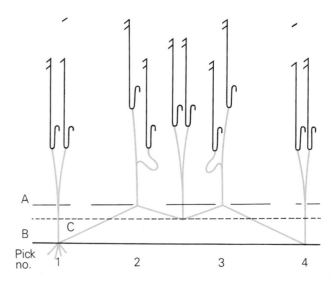

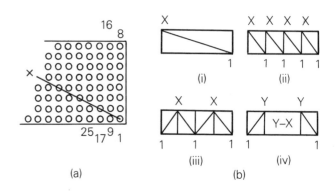

Figure 16.17 Double lift jacquard shed formation.

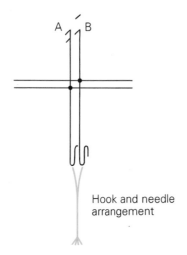

Figure 16.16 Double lift jacquard shedding.

Figure 16.18 Jacquard harness tie-ups.

a similar or smaller space. Ultimately, the endless paper jacquard which uses a modified system of selection, has a distance between needle centres of eight millimetres. It gained universal acceptance with its maximum capacity of 1344, though 1200 is more usually accepted because it is divisible by the more popular basic weave repeat sizes of two, three, four, five, six and eight.

An open shed can' be made available by adding an additional latch to each hook. This will rest on a fixed griffe when the hook is lifted. It will remain there for as long as is necessary until it is displaced sideways as the result of uncut card causing the needle to be pushed sideways, when its latch will be clear of the fixed griffe and so be free to fall.

Individual light springs or elastics have replaced lingoes in recent machines to ensure the quicker action that is necessary for high-speed weaving.

As with dobby machines, computers are now widely used for designing, and the ultimate pattern details are stored on a disc. This disc is then used to feed an electronic memory unit connected to the jacquard, and when the memory has been stored the disc can be removed and used to feed the pattern to other machines. The electronic jacquard has required a modification to the hook unit and the method of generating the lift.

A fixed block containing a solenoid has a modified hook at each side (see Figure 16.19). These hooks are raised on

alternate picks by the griffes. If the solenoid is not energised the hook will fall with the griffe. However, if it is energised for a selection, the hook will be attracted inwards and will be held in the cut-out at the top of the block, so that when the other hook rises the roller unit will rotate and rise to lift the harness cords that are suspended from it. The trapped hook will be released when the solenoid is de-energised because there is no selection, and the hook will be lowered by the falling griffe. An open shed is formed because both hooks will be trapped in the raised position if a lift is selected on successive picks, but shedding is still negative because the healds are returned by light springs or elastics.

Weft insertion

> Weft insertion can be carried out by various means: shuttle, projectile, rapiers (single or double, rigid or flexible), water jet or air jet.

Shuttle insertion

The basic principles of the main systems are illustrated in Figure 16.20, and although the shuttle has been superseded in modern industry by projectiles, rapiers and jets, there are still a large number of shuttle looms in use today.

The shuttle carries a pirn (Figure 12.15) from which yarn is released as the shuttle reciprocates across the loom. This endless length of yarn allows an ideal selvedge to be formed at both sides of the loom (Figure 16.39 (a)), but unfortunately the weight of the shuttle – and so the energy needed to send it across the loom and then stop it at the other side – is high. In addition, it needs to be controlled as it traverses the loom so that maximum weft insertion speeds rarely reach 500 metres per minute. In total, however, it is the most versatile method of weft insertion and can be used to produce any type of woven fabric.

Projectile insertion

A similar type of mechanism can be used to pick and check a reciprocating gripper shuttle (projectile), which inserts single lengths of weft picked from supply packages at each side of the loom. This system requires a fringe selvedge at each side of the loom and only achieves weft insertion rates of around 400 metres per minute. Nevertheless, it is the most successful method for weaving wiry types of yarn or extremely coarse yarns.

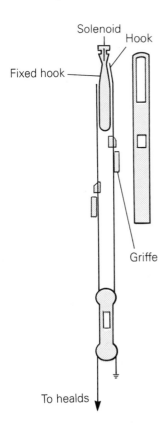

Figure 16.19 Electronic jacquard.

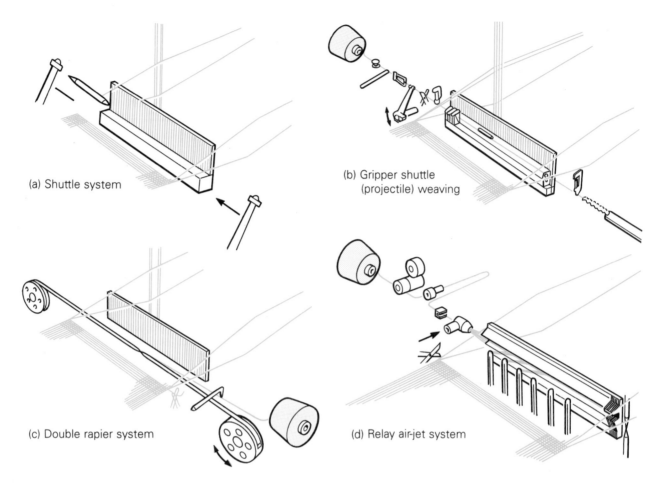

(a) Shuttle system

(b) Gripper shuttle (projectile) weaving

(c) Double rapier system

(d) Relay air-jet system

Figure 16.20 Weft insertion systems.

Sulzer, a Swiss machine manufacturer, introduced a loom in the early 1950s which used a number of projectiles operating in sequence. Each projectile grips the weft at the left-hand side of the loom and carries it to the right-hand side (Figure 16.20 (b)), where it is released. The projectile is then ejected onto a return conveyor chain which carries it back to the left-hand side of the loom at a much lower speed. On one of the most popular widths of loom – 3300 millimetres (130 inches) – up to 17 projectiles are used in sequence. The projectiles need to be steered through the shed by a series of guides and the protruding weft at each side of the loom is pulled in to form a tuck selvedge (Figure 16.39 (b)). Weft insertion rates of up to 1100 metres per minute are achieved, but the system is not suitable for the production of warp pile fabrics. It is, however, a very appropriate system for high rates of production with a degree of flexibility in its product range.

Rapier insertion

Many companies have used a wide range of concepts in attempting to produce rapier looms. The main variations are between rigid or flexible; single or double (the latter of which has a choice of loop or tip yarn transfer); the method of mounting the rapier drives on the loom frame or on the sley; and the method of controlling the rapier head as it traverses the sley. Figure 16.20 (c) shows a double flexible rapier system using tip transfer of the weft.

The variations are extensive and only selected examples will be considered but, in general, rapier weft insertion cannot be achieved at speeds as high as those achieved by projectiles, and are normally at a maximum of around 800 metres per minute. However, weft patterning is achieved more easily and without the need to reduce machine speed, so rapier weft insertion is very popular in fancy weaving, especially when pattern changes are frequent.

Rapier systems generally produce fringe selvedges, though one technique did allow a conventional selvedge at one side of the loom. Tuck selvedges can now be produced, although this will require a slight reduction in the machine speed which can be offset if making-up costs are reduced, as is the case when producing soft-furnishing fabrics. Probably the greatest limitation to the further development of rapier looms is the width restriction, though working widths well in excess of 3000 millimetres are now available.

Air-jet and water-jet insertion

Air and water have vied with one another as the most desirable media for jet weaving. In the era of single jets, water had the advantage in achieving greater widths, though air-jet looms could run at higher speeds of around 400 picks per minute, compared with around 330 for water-jet looms. The water jet proved to be ideal when hydrophobic yarns were being woven and it is still used to weave nylon fabrics for tarpaulins, anoraks, parachutes and overalls, at weft insertion speeds in excess of 1400 metres per minute. However, if sizing became necessary – as with staple fibre yarns or weak continuous filament rayons – difficulties arose and the air-jet system was more popular. In this case, it was particularly suitable for low sett fabrics such as gauzes and scrims, and the system is still used to produce fabrics of this type at speeds of 800+ picks per minute. The introduction of a series of intermediate air jets at intervals across the loom allowed higher speeds to be achieved while weaving a wider range of fabrics and without a width restriction. Weft insertion rates of 1500+ metres per minute are achieved. This system (illustrated in Figure 16.20 (d)) has now gained wide popularity and its versatility is being extended to include weft patterning as well as dobby and jacquard shedding, with the option of fringe or tuck selvedges.

Techniques to insert weft continuously have been developed in both flat and circular form. In the former system, a technique has still to be developed that will allow fabric to be produced without **broken patterns** (a portion of weft being missing within the length of one pick when the weft yarn breaks). Many circular looms have been produced for the manufacture of hosepipes, sacks and more, but they are unsuitable for other types of end-product and their wider acceptance is, therefore, very restricted. This principle allows very high rates of weft insertion (in excess of 2000 metres of weft per minute) to be achieved, without the high dynamic forces that are required in shuttle and projectile weaving and the complex mechanisms that are essential in high-speed rapier and jet weaving machines. Patterning, however, is not possible.

Weft insertion velocities

The rate at which fabric can be woven is determined by the speed at which a loom can run (picks per minute, P), which is governed by the width of the loom (reed space in metres, R), so that it is often of more value to refer to the rate at which weft is inserted. Hence:

weft inserted per min $= P \times R$ m per min

The average rate at which weft is inserted on the loom is also influenced by the fraction of the pick cycle that is

available for this purpose. This latter value can vary from around 120° to 135° of crankshaft rotation when using shuttles or in some single-jet looms, and to around 240° in some rapier looms.

The average weft velocity is influenced by the method of weft insertion and by the different conditions that may exist for any one method. Figure 16.21 illustrates typical velocity curves for a relatively high-speed example for each method of weft insertion.

Problems can arise when these velocities are exceptionally high – especially at the commencement of weft insertion – due to the thread of weft being snatched from the supply package at a very high initial velocity. This problem, however, does not exist in shuttle weaving where the yarn basically does not have a velocity in relation to the shuttle which is carrying it.

Although many early projectile and some early rapier looms operated without too much difficulty, the weft breakage rate increased as loom speeds increased and, with certain yarn types, it became necessary to introduce units known as **weft accumulators**, which have become essential in many modern high-speed, non-shuttle looms.

These units withdraw yarn continuously from the supply package and store it on a drum or in a tube. The yarn is then pulled from the storage unit, under virtually no tension, when

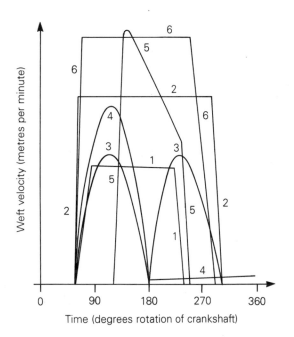

Figure 16.21 Weft insertion velocities.

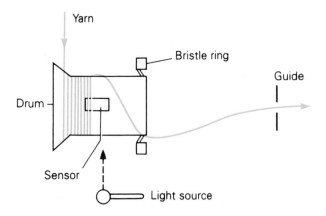

Figure 16.22 Weft accumulator.

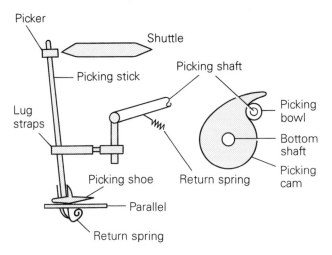

Figure 16.23 Shuttle picking mechanism.

it is required for weft insertion. Figure 16.22 shows a drum-type storage system which has a bristle ring to remove any snarls from the yarn before it is placed in the fabric. If a tube is used, air suction performs a similar function. It is possible for such units to measure the exact length of yarn required for each pick and this is generally desirable on single-jet looms, though most other systems operate effectively if there is a store of yarn on the drum that is slightly longer than the next pick length required. In this case, it is necessary to have a sensor to switch on the winding unit after yarn has been withdrawn and to switch it off when a sufficient amount has been wound on for the next pick.

In Figure 16.22, the yarn will be wound on to the drum from the side and unwound over the end of the drum. This will affect the amount of twist in the yarn. In the rare cases when this is critical, it is necessary to have a stationary drum and a revolving guide to place the yarn on the drum so that the change that occurs in the yarn twist during winding on to the drum will be nullified as it is wound off.

Shuttle weft insertion

PICKING

In the case of the shuttle loom, it is necessary to have a picking unit at each side of the loom. Picking cams must be placed on a loom shaft that is operating at half loom speed and these cams should be set at 180° to one another so that they will operate on alternate picks.

At the time of picking, the picking cam will force the picking bowl upwards to cause the picking shaft to turn sharply. This will pull the lug straps and the picking stick inwards so that the picker will project the shuttle across the loom. Springs return the parts of the mechanism (Figure 16.23)

If the picking stick had only one fulcrum at its base, the picker would move in an arc and the shuttle would not be

projected along the correct, roughly parallel path. To combat this, the lower end of the stick is attached to a curved shoe which rocks on a flat plate so that the fulcrum moves progressively forwards as the picker moves inwards to generate the parallel movement required. Many later models used a double-link system attached to the bottom of the stick for the same purpose. This gave a more positive control but it had to use a shorter picker action so that picking forces were higher.

When a loom is turned by hand, the shuttle is only pushed out of the shuttle box, but when it is running at its normal speed, the shuttle will traverse the full width of the loom. This is because the picking stick bends and the lug straps stretch as the cam acts on the bowl, due to the inertia of the shuttle. The action is very similar to that of a catapult. Figure 16.24 shows the difference in the nominal (loom turned by hand) and the actual (loom running normally) displacement of the picker.

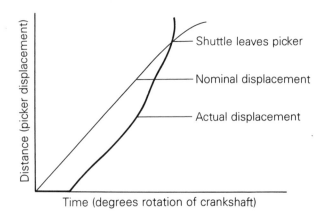

Figure 16.24 **Nominal and actual picker displacement.**

CHECKING

When the shuttle reaches the opposite side of the loom it has to be stopped. This is done by a checking mechanism, which involves a shaped swell pressing the shuttle against the box front as it enters the box, to create a braking action (see Figure 16.25). The shuttle should still have some velocity when it strikes the picker (which has a buffer to assist in checking and to protect it from becoming damaged), to ensure its rest position will always be constant in the shuttle box. This is essential so that the picking stroke and shuttle velocity are the same for every pick.

Projectile (torsion rod) picking

Weaving machines which use this method of weft insertion are frequently known as Sulzer looms after the name of the company which developed them and totally monopolised the market.

The weft is supplied from cones mounted at the left-hand side of the loom, from where it passes through a series of guides and brakes to a feeder. This in turn ensures that the weft is placed in the jaws of the projectile, which is then fired across the loom. As the projectile is much smaller than a shuttle (889 ×14 ×6 millimetres) and much lighter in weight (40 grams), it is necessary to control its path across the width of the loom. This is done by a series of guides (one of which can be seen mounted on the sley in Figure 16.32) set at 9.5 millimetre intervals. The projectile is stopped in the receiving unit at the right-hand side of the loom by upper and lower brake pads. It then releases the weft before, ultimately, being ejected onto a chain which carries the projectiles back to the picking side of the loom at a much slower rate. The weft is cut at the left-hand side of the loom and prepared for the next pick, while the tails of weft that are left protruding at each side are pulled into the shed formed for the next pick by oscillating needles which enter the shed from below to create a tuck selvedge.

Each loom requires a projectile for every 254 millimetres, or part of 254 millimetres, of reed space plus an extra projectile for the picking unit and three for the receiving unit, so a loom weaving a fabric having a 2845 millimetre reed space will require $(2845/254) + 1 + 3 = 16$ projectiles.

As the projectile is only picked from one side of the loom, only one mechanism is required and the picking cam can be mounted on the main shaft of the loom which is making one revolution per pick. As the cam rotates (see Figure 16.26) it will act on the toggle lever bowl and push the toggle lever until the bowl and the two ends of the link form a straight line slightly to the right of the toggle lever fulcrum. This leaves the mechanism in a balanced state. When this position is reached, the link will have pushed the torsion lever and inserted approximately 32° of twist in the **torsion rod**. This position is maintained until the cam bowl meets the lip of the toggle lever, when the whole system collapses. As the rod untwists it causes the picker to send the projectile across the loom at a velocity that is totally independent of the loom speed.

When compared with the shuttle loom, the projectile achieves a substantially higher weft velocity. To do so it requires a much higher rate of acceleration, but because the projectile is so much lighter in mass the picking force required is much lower.

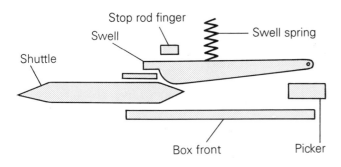

Figure 16.25 Shuttle checking.

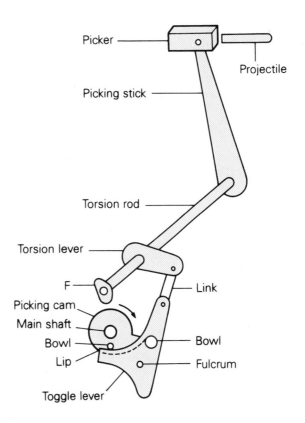

Figure 16.26 Torsion rod picking.

Rapier weaving

The sequence of actions in the most popular rapier systems are shown in Figure 16.27. At (a), a single rapier is used, which crosses the loom to pick up the weft from the supply package and pull it into the shed during its return movement. Such systems have limited popularity, but are used for the processing of special yarns and fabrics such as glass and paper.

At (b) two rapiers are used. One carries the weft to the centre of the loom where it meets the other and transfers the grip-hold on the tip of the yarn. The second rapier then completes the pick insertion as the rapiers are withdrawn. Initially, there was a problem with dropped picks on transfer, but this has been overcome by the use of precision engineering so that tip transfer is the most popular system in use today.

The loop transfer system shown at (c) only cuts the weft after every second pick, with the loop of yarn that is formed in the first part of the cycle being transferred at the mid point and then being straightened out in the second half of the cycle. This allows a conventional selvedge to be formed at one side of the loom. In this system, all of the yarn for each pick is withdrawn from the supply package in the first half of the pick cycle so that the yarn velocity, and thus the yarn

tension, is very high (as shown in Figure 16.21). In the second half of the pick cycle it is zero. This system has lost popularity in the light of the improved design of looms using tip transfer.

Many methods have been developed to drive the rapiers. The use of a crank and connecting arm gives the rapiers a movement that approximates to simple harmonic motion. This creates undesirably high values so that a quicker movement in the early and late stages of weft insertion becomes preferable to reduce the peak velocities. The crank and connecting arm system is now only used on the very slowest systems (for example, single rigid rapier looms). Modern looms tend to prefer cam drives or four-bar linkage systems.

The higher speeds generated in the movement of the rapier in the early part of its movement result in the rapier head moving faster at the time that it picks up the weft yarn. This creates a greater tendency for the yarn to be snatched and broken at this point. Weft accumulators are essential in order to minimise this possibility.

The design of the rapier driving system influences whether the rapier housing is mounted on the loom frame or the sley. The latter avoids the need to have the sley dwelling in the back position, so that the resulting smoother sley movement avoids excessive machine vibrations and so wear on the loom parts.

Whichever system is used, it is necessary to ensure that the path of the rapier head is controlled accurately, especially when the two heads of the double rapiers must meet perfectly for tip or loop transfer. Some systems allow a heavier rapier head to run on a small raceboard, while others use an extended guide unit situated just outside the selvedge. Modern high-speed rapier looms, however, tend to prefer a series of guides similar to those of the Sulzer projectile loom.

Jet weaving

When single jets were used, the main problem was to keep the jet concentrated sufficiently in order to carry the yarn across the loom. This was easier with water than air. In the latter case, a number of ideas were used in which supplementary devices were introduced. The most successful was a series of closely set guides called constrictors which were similar in shape and size to the guides used on the Sulzer projectile machine.

As a single jet projects the weft across the loom, two factors occur which limit the distance that it can travel. In the latter stages of the pick cycle, the yarn begins to buckle in front of the jet nozzle because the yarn projected in the early stages of that pick eventually loses some of its velocity. In addition, the leading tip of yarn curls up as it continually meets an undisturbed wall of air. Increased widths become possible when the rate of air feed from the nozzle is slowed down to avoid the buckling and the yarn feed is stopped by a clamp

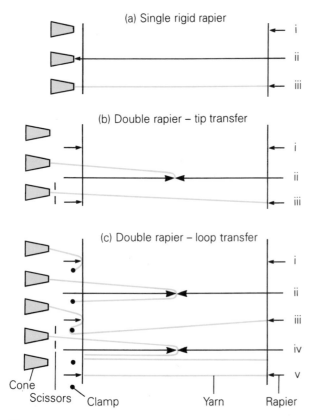

Figure 16.27 Rapier systems.

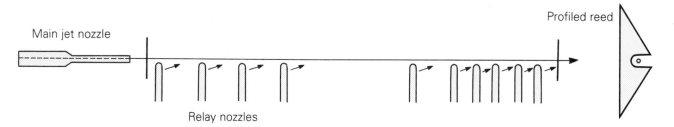

Figure 16.28 Relay air-jet system.

just before weft insertion is complete, so that inertia in the weft creates a thrust which causes the leading tip to straighten out.

Figure 16.28 shows the arrangement of supplementary jets in a relay jet loom. The main nozzle is responsible for the initial weft insertion, but its force is supplemented by the relay nozzles which are made to act in groups and in succession. These nozzles are spaced at 75 millimetre intervals across the width of the loom, except at the receiving end where the frequency is doubled. The system is so effective in maintaining the necessary force in the jet stream that the method of weft insertion does not create a restriction on the loom width.

Figure 16.29 shows the period of time for which the supplementary jets are operating in relation to the distance across the loom. In areas A and B there are five relay nozzles in a block, while the remainder contain four, with closer setting of the nozzles in blocks E and F. Another factor that assists in keeping the air-jet stream concentrated is the modified shape of the reed, as shown in Figure 16.28, where the dot indicates the yarn path.

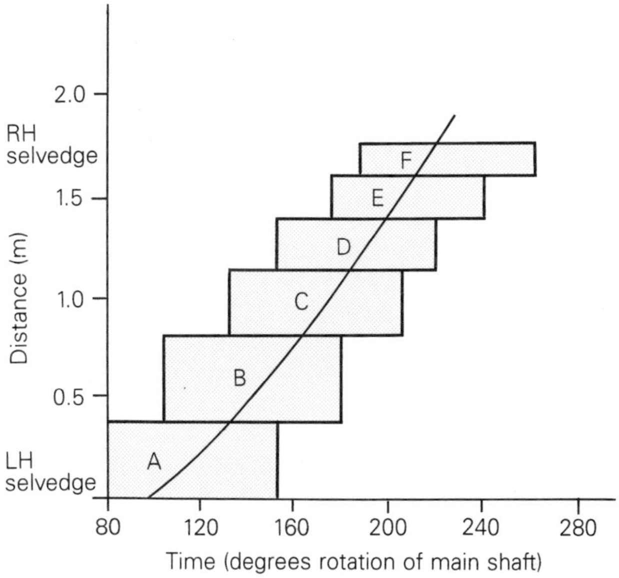

Figure 16.29 Sequence of relay jet actions.

Beating-up

The reciprocating reed is responsible for pushing the pick into the fell of the cloth for beat-up. It also holds the warp ends at a designed, usually uniform, spacing in the fabric and supports the shuttle (or, in some cases, the rapier) as it traverse the loom.

The sley, which carries the reed in its upper framework, is driven from the crankshaft. Crankarms connect these cranks to the sword pins mounted in the rear of the sley so that the rotating action of the crankshaft is converted to a reciprocating movement of the sley (Figure 16.30), which oscillates on its rocking rail.

If the cranks and swordpins coincided, the sley would move with simple harmonic motion (SHM), but the introduction of crankarms causes a deviation that is known as eccentricity. Figure 16.31 shows a SHM curve and, slightly above it, an

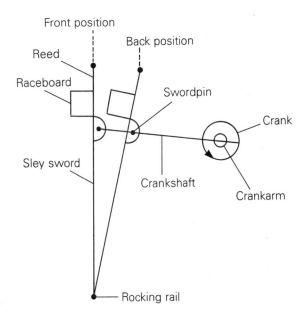

Figure 16.30 Crank-driven sley.

eccentric curve, e. This eccentricity is useful in weaving because it allows the sley to move more slowly through its back position when the weft insertion medium is traversing the loom (more time is available for weft insertion) and at a quicker rate through the front centre position, so generating more force for beat-up.

When it becomes necessary to mount the weft insertion and receiving units on the loom frame, as in projectile and some rapier and jet looms, it is necessary to allow the sley to dwell in its back position for part or, in many cases, the whole of the time of weft insertion. This demands that the sley must be driven by cams, and the Sulzer method using conjugate cams is shown in Figure 16.32.

Not only does the cam action cause the sley to reciprocate but it also allows the reed and any guides that are mounted in front of the reed to fall slightly as the sley moves forward, so that the guides pass underneath the cloth fell and do not interfere with beat-up.

Secondary and ancillary motions

Warp control

> The sheet of warp yarn is controlled by keeping it under tension. This is necessary to allow the warp sheets to separate cleanly, form a shed and resist the reciprocation of the reed.

The amount of tension applied to the warp affects the end breakage rate, the warp and weft crimp ratios and thereby the width and length of the fabric, the general appearance of the fabric and the selvedge.

Mechanisms to ensure that the warp is under the correct tension will restrict the rotation of the beam either by applying a braking force (negative let-off) or by driving the beam through a mechanism (automatic let-off). The negative let-off has been widely used but it required adjustment during the weaving of the beam so has been replaced under most circumstances. However, it is simple and robust and is still used for sample looms, hand looms and selvedge bobbins. Figure 16.33 shows the cross section through a beam similar

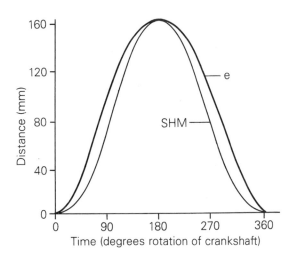

Figure 16.31 Sley displacement.

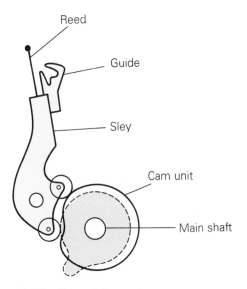

Figure 16.32 Cam-driven sley.

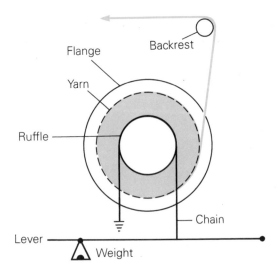

Figure 16.33 Lever weight and chain negative let-off motion.

to that illustrated in Figure 12.16, but with the lever, weight and chain tensioning unit in place.

As the beam diameter decreases, adjustments to the warp tension must be made regularly and manually at times when the operative assesses that it is necessary, to keep the warp tension constant.

A wide range of automatic let-off motions have been developed. Initially they were complex because they needed to take into account the warp tension variation from pick to pick as well as the longer-term tension variations. Modern let-off motions have eliminated these problems by using a roller around which the warp sheet angle is constant, in order to assess the yarn tension (see Figure 16.34). Slight variations in the position of the roller are signalled to an electronic unit through which a motor is switched on to turn the beam and release yarn. As soon as sufficient yarn has been released, the roller will rise against the warp sheet and the motor will be switched off. The degree of sensitivity is, necessarily, very acute as only minute lengths of yarn normally need to be released for each pick.

If the width of the fabric is correct, according to specification, when it is removed from the loom it can generally be assumed that the weaving tension of the warp is correct, as this will indicate that the crimp ratios of the warp and weft are as specified. It is not usual to measure the warp tension in the weaving shed, though a number of different instruments are available. However, they are generally unreliable if they are based on a single end because there can be a large amount of end-to-end tension variation. Similarly, full width tension meters are too bulky and a reliable system has not been developed. The most convenient systems act on a strip of warp yarn containing a known number of ends, though again the results can be variable and unreliable.

Cloth control

> There are three aspects of controlling the cloth once it leaves the fell: the temple (a cloth control guide, one at either side of the loom) is essential in holding the cloth correctly just in front of the fell; the pick density is determined by the speed of rotation of the take up roller; and the cloth must then be stored at the loom until the desired length has been woven.

Temples are necessary because, as the sley recedes, there is a tendency for the cloth to contract widthwise as the weft crimps around the warp. If this is allowed to happen at too early a stage, the ends at the selvedge will bend round the last dents in the reed to an excessive amount. This can cause an increase in the end-breakage rate and also damage to the reed at this point. The temples hold the cloth to the weaving width in the reed for a distance into the fabric to prevent this occurrence. Rubber covered rollers are used when weaving continuous filament yarns, while spiked rollers or a series of spiked rings are the most popular when weaving staple fibre yarns.

Pick density has been controlled, for many years, by a series of gear wheels. A typical example is shown in Figure 16.35, in which the number of teeth in the change wheel equals the number of picks per inch in the fabric.

Any damaged teeth or eccentric wheels within the system will cause periodic irregularities in the fabric's pick spacing. An additional problem existed with the large number of change wheels that had to be held in stock because this was costly and required a large amount of space and organised storing.

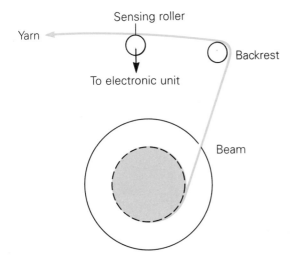

Figure 16.34 Position of sensing roller in an automatic let-off motion.

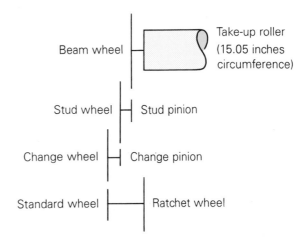

Figure 16.35 Seven-wheel take-up motion.

In more recent years, modified mechanisms used more than one change wheel to reduce the stock required per loom, while a system known as a **vernier take-up** has been introduced which can vary the amount of throw generated by a cam in order to adjust the pick density. Both of these latter systems are popular on modern looms.

The systems available for cloth storage are dependent on the type of yarn being processed, on the bulk of the fabric and the cloth inspection system used. At (a) in Figure 16.36, a typical cloth wind-up arrangement for use when weaving cotton and other staple fibre yarns is illustrated. The cloth roller is driven by frictional contact with the take-up roller, with contact being maintained by spring loading. This technique can damage fabrics at the nip point where the friction drive occurs, especially those produced from continuous filament yarns, in which case the arrangement shown at (b) is preferred. Many variations are possible, but there is usually some sort of spreader bar to minimise the possibility of the fabric becoming creased on the cloth roller.

Fabric batching systems, as shown at (c), are used when long lengths of cloth are required for the next stage of processing, such as for denim and thick fabrics for coating (for example, tarpaulins for lorry covers), or when the rate of fabric production is very high, as is the case in the weaving of tyre cord which has only around one pick per centimetre. The position of the cloth roller is ideal for fabric inspection at the loom. An alternative to a large cloth roller is to pass the cloth through a hole in the weaving shed floor and then collect it in a large container in the room below, from where it can be wheeled directly to the next stage of processing. Although this system allows the fabric to be inspected shortly after weaving – so that faults can be quickly identified and rectified – it has not gained wide popularity because of the large amount of space it requires.

Weft patterning

Yarns of different colour, texture, construction and material can be introduced into the warp in the loom simply by arranging the pattern sequence when making the warp and then ensuring that it is correct when drawing-in. Basically, there are no restrictions.

It is not possible to introduce such variations into the weft because there is a limit to the number of different wefts that can be supplied and, in some cases, the sequence in which that limited range can be introduced to the loom.

In shuttle looms, it was usual to have two, four or six different shuttles (and so the capability of using two, four, or six different yarns) in a unit known as a compound box at the side of the loom. Although it was possible to have such units at both sides, the mechanism was complex; most looms accepted a compound box unit at one side only. The unit rose and fell to achieve the required selection of wefts, and in this case, a six-box unit was possible but the demand was very limited and the four-box unit became the most widely accepted. With boxes at one side of the loom only, it was not possible to insert single picks or odd numbers of picks from one weft. Also, such looms could not use the wefts from the top and bottom boxes on successive picks and a reduction in loom speed of around 15 per cent was necessary in comparison to the single shuttle version of the loom. Multi-box looms started to lose popularity from the mid 1960s, with the advent of non-shuttle looms for weft patterning.

The weft patterning mechanism on the projectile loom operates by oscillating a multi-feeder unit, which replaces the single feeder unit in order to position the selected weft opposite the projectile in the picking unit. These units may have two, four or six feeders, and single picks of each weft

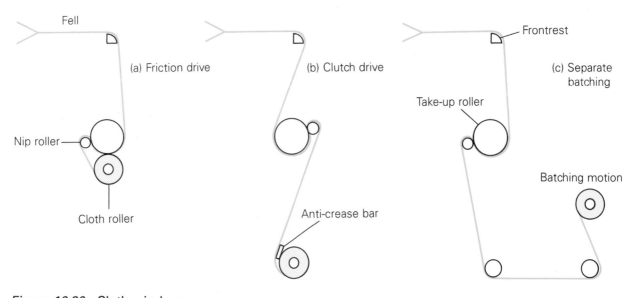

Figure 16.36 Cloth wind-ups.

can be inserted. Selection was originally from a separate pattern chain (which had a restricted pattern length) or directly from the dobby or jacquard. Weaving machines using these mechanisms were used widely in the worsted and fancy cotton weaving sectors of the trade, despite having to run 10 per cent to 15 per cent slower than the single colour version of the loom.

In rapier weaving, the weft is picked up by a guide which moves the yarn across the path of the rapier head just outside the selvedge on the supply side of the loom. To vary the weft that is being inserted, there must simply be a separate guide for each different yarn. Six is the common number, but there are no problems if eight guides are required. The system is simple and no extra time or energy is required for the guide movement, so there is no need to reduce the loom speed according to the number of wefts being used. Consequently, maximum speeds are always possible. This factor, coupled with the much improved performance of rapier looms, has virtually eliminated the use of the shuttle and projectile when weft patterning is required.

Selection of the guide that is to present the weft to the rapier head can be made by the shedding mechanism, which is ideal because the shedding pattern and the weft sequence cannot get out of synchronisation. It does mean, however, that the figuring capacity of the shedding mechanism may become restricted because there are fewer healds available for shedding. This can be critical in dobby weaving but may be insignificant in a jacquard loom where extra hooks are normally available in addition to the shedding requirements.

Weft patterning is being developed for relay air-jet looms, where up to four jets pointing at the entry point of the shed can be introduced. Selection determines which of the jets will operate and so which weft will be inserted on each pick.

Weft stop motions

> If part of a pick is missing because the weft has broken during weft insertion, a fault is created known as a broken pattern. If a number of picks are missing, the loom is said to have been **weaving without weft.**

It is desirable that a weft break should be detected as soon as possible. Shuttle looms use forks situated either at the side of the loom, between the selvedge and the entrance to the shuttle box, or in a cut-out near to the centre of the **raceboard**. In both cases, if the weft is present the full movement of the fork is restricted and the loom is allowed to continue running, but if the weft is broken, an extension from the undisturbed fork is picked up as the result of a cam-generated action. This ultimately results in the loom stopping.

As the side weft fork is positioned at one side of the loom only and requires a full pick cycle to bring the loom to a stop, it is possible that up to two picks could be inserted before the loom is brought to rest. It is then necessary to go through a process known as **pickfinding**.

> Pickfinding is finding the correct shedding position and returning the cloth fell to its true weaving position.

Finding the correct shedding position is not too difficult, but returning the cloth felt to its true resting position demands the greatest skill from a weaver because, if the cloth fell position is incorrect when the loom is restarted, a thick place or a thin place will be created.

A centre weft fork should be fitted, preferably with an efficient loom brake, so that when a weft break is detected, the loom will be brought to rest on that pick. If this is achieved, pickfinding will not be necessary. When the weft fork is centrally positioned, it must be set precisely and work efficiently to avoid damage to delicate wefts and also ensure that unwanted loops are not created in the middle of the fabric.

Originally, the projectile loom used a fork, as did some of the rapier and single-jet looms, but a more recent device has gained wide acceptance in non-shuttle looms because of its simplicity and effectiveness. It uses a **piezo** element mounted in a ceramic guide, so that as the yarn is pulled from the supply package and passes over the ceramic surface, it creates a vibration which generates a pulse in an electronic unit. If this unit fails to receive a signal when the weft is being inserted, it will act through the electronic unit to stop the loom before beat-up can occur. As there are times during the pick cycle when yarn is not being pulled through the guide, and in multi-coloured looms there are guides through which yarn is threaded but which are not being used, it is necessary for the electronic unit to recognise that the signal it receives is for the weft being inserted. Although this mechanism is more expensive, it is simple, takes up little space at the loom and is extremely efficient. It has therefore gained very wide acceptance with all non-shuttle methods of weft insertion.

Warp stop motions

In order for these mechanisms to operate, it is necessary for each end to be drawn through the eye of a drop wire. There are many different styles of drop wire and examples of some of the more popular types are shown in Figure 16.37.

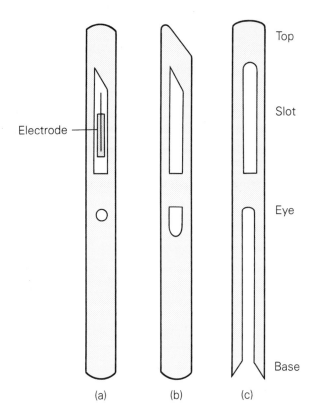

Electrode —

Top

Slot

Eye

Base

(a)   (b)   (c)

Figure 16.37   Drop wires.

The drop wires will vary in dimensions and weight according to the type of warp yarn, loom and fabric being woven.

The drop wire is supported by the warp end during weaving but, when an end breaks, it will fall on to the stop motion bar. In the case of a mechanical warp stop motion, the bar is serrated with the outer bars being stationary, while the centre bar reciprocates. The fallen drop wire will restrict the movement of the centre bar and ultimately stop the loom through a series of levers. The mechanism is robust but it cannot be guaranteed to stop the loom within four picks, it has never been popular for fabrics that show faults easily or for quality fabrics.

Electrical warp stop motions rely on the fallen wire making contact across the two parts of the electrode that are normally insulated from one another. This resulting contact completes an electric circuit and so energises a solenoid which causes the loom to be stopped quickly via a mechanical action or through an electronic signal. This mechanism is quick acting, but with early designs there was a chance that a faulty contact may cause a spark and so a fire hazard existed. Later models have minimised this problem so that modern machines invariably use the electrical system.

The time at which the loom is brought to rest is normally arranged to coincide with the heads' level position so that there is an easy access to the healds for repairing the broken ends and re-drawing them through the heald eyes without the weaver having to adjust the loom position.

Warp protectors

Warp protectors are only necessary in looms which use a free-flying media to insert the weft, such as a shuttle or a projectile. They stop the loom before beat-up can occur if the media fails to be arrested in the correct position after it has traversed the loom.

The fast-reed warp protector on a shuttle loom utilises the movement given to the stop rod finger (Figure 16.25) when the swell is pushed back as the shuttle enters the box. This will cause a metal arm, called a dagger, to be lifted and pass over a metal block, known as a steel, which is mounted on the loom frame. If the shuttle fails to enter the shuttle box, the dagger will not be lifted and it will strike the steel to bring the forward movement of the sley to an instantaneous halt. Springs are incorporated to absorb the sudden shock of this action.

If the advancement of the sley had not been stopped and the shuttle had come to rest in the confines of the shed, a large number of ends would have broken. This is known as a **smash** and a great deal of the weaver's time and skill is required to repair it. There is also the possibility that, depending on the position of the shuttle, extensive damage could occur to the reed, temple and/or shuttle.

Early loose-reed warp protectors became obsolete but the principle was revived by Ruti, a Swiss textile machine manufacturer, in the 1960s. It operated in a similar way as the fast-reed mechanism, except that it was the pressure of a trapped shuttle forcing the lower baulk of the reed backwards which resulted in the loom being brought to a stop.

A later range of shuttle looms incorporated electronic warp protectors in order to eliminate the vicious **bang-off** that occurs when the sley's movement is halted instantaneously. This system requires the shuttle to carry a magnet which responds to signals, emitted by sensors, mounted in the sley around its centre position. If a signal is not returned or is late, the loom is brought to rest before beat-up, with the reed a short distance from the cloth fell and before the trapped shuttle can do any damage. The success of non-shuttle looms prevented wider adoption of this principle.

The warp protector of the Sulzer loom requires a finger to be lowered on to the projectile at a precise time in the pick cycle. If the projectile fails to complete its traverse, then the increased downward movement of the finger will cause a mechanical action to apply the brake. The action is repeated a few degrees later in the pick cycle to verify that the projectile is still present in the receiving unit and has not rebounded into the shed.

Weft replenishment

This is achieved by nose-to-tail magazine creeling of the cones (see Figure 12.18(a)) supplying the weft in non-shuttle looms. The cones are situated in a framework at the side of the loom from which the weft is being inserted.

In non-automatic shuttle looms the pirn was changed by hand when the weft on the pirn was almost used up, while with automatic looms the shuttle or the pirn is changed without the need for attention by the weaver. The bobbin change mechanism, which ultimately became universally accepted, requires a feeler motion to detect that the weft on the pirn is nearly exhausted and then a means to change the empty bobbin in the shuttle for a new one containing yarn (see Figure 16.38).

An automatic system of loading the bobbins into a slide instead of the magazine was developed but was never accepted on a wide basis. However, the Unifil system, in which individual pirn winders were fitted to each loom to replace the magazine proved to be very efficient and the idea was widely accepted because it saved on labour and was very attractive from both the quality and economic aspects.

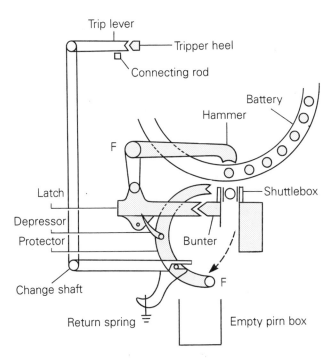

Figure 16.38 Automatic bobbin change mechanism.

Selvedges

At each side of a length of woven fabric there is a selvedge and its function is to stop the outside ends fraying from the body of the cloth. It provides strength to withstand the strains of weaving, which arise as the cloth contracts in width due to weft crimping in front of the fell, and also those strains that occur as a result of the stenter pulling during wet processing after weaving.

A regular selvedge is always a good indication of good woven cloth quality. It also provides a means of identifying the fabric by coloured threads, special weaves or woven descriptions such as the manufacturer's or designer's name.

A **hairpin selvedge** is formed naturally when the weft is supplied endlessly from a pirn in a shuttle because the yarn is continuous and forms loops round the last ends in the fabric, as illustrated at (a) in Figure 16.39, providing that the outside ends change position after each pick. No extra mechanism is required to form a selvedge.

When other systems of weft insertion are used, in which the weft is cut after each pick, an alternative means of locking the outside ends becomes necessary.

The **tuck selvedge**, as illustrated at (b), was first introduced on the Sulzer projectile loom. It produces a neat edge to the fabric and so eliminates the need for hemming in certain end-uses. The increased weft density within the selvedge can be a problem, but the attributes of this selvedge are such that it is now available on many modern rapier and jet looms.

Fringe selvedges have been used as centre selvedges on shuttle looms for many years, but their use only became essential for outside selvedges with the advent of the rapier and fluid-jet methods of weft insertion (and for projectile looms in some special instances). The **leno selvedge** shown at (c) in Figure 16.39 gives good strength and involves a simpler mechanism than that required for the helical selvedge shown at (d). However, its appearance is not so neat, so the **helical selvedge** is often preferred for fabric sold by the metre.

It is not possible to control accurately the length of each pick in rapier and fluid-jet weaving, so it becomes necessary at one or both sides of the fabric (depending on the method of weft insertion and machine maker) to have a longer fringe of yarn that is unsightly. This must be trimmed close to the edge of the fabric to create a neat appearance.

In order to make the severing action possible, it is necessary to trap the protruding pieces of weft between additional (catcher) threads, which normally weave plain. This produces a **dummy selvedge**, as shown at (c). The protruding weft is then held under control and can be fed to a point, as indicated, where it can be severed by means of a heated wire

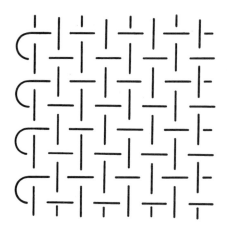

(a) Hairpin selvedge

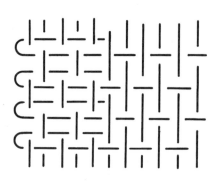

(b) Tuck selvedge

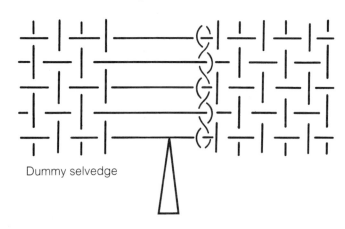

Dummy selvedge

(c) Leno selvedge

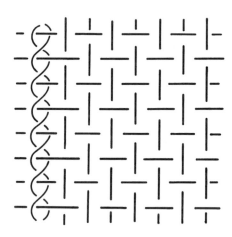

(d) Helical selvedge

Figure 16.39 **Woven fabric selvedges.**

(if thermoplastic yarns are being woven), or cut. In the latter case, six to twelve ends will be needed in the dummy selvedge to resist the scissor action.

The amount of weft waste created is not generally considered to be critical, but narrow shuttle looms will normally make less waste than their non-shuttle loom counterparts. The situation is reversed for wide looms.

■ CHECK YOUR UNDERSTANDING

● There are three primary motions needed to produce a woven fabric: shedding, picking and beating-up.
● Let-off, take-up and weft patterning (when desired) are secondary motions for weaving; ancillary motions used on modern weaving machines are weft stop motions, warp stop motions, warp protectors, weft replenishment.

● The operation of loom mechanisms are usually shown on a timing diagram which can be linear or circular. The degrees of the main shaft are used as the reference point.
● Shedding is the raising and lowering of warp ends to allow interlacing with the weft picks. This is done by raising and lowering heald frames or individual heald eyes which hold the individual warp ends.
● There are four types of shedding mechanism: crank, cam (or tappet), dobby and jacquard. Crank, cam and dobby create the shed by moving heald frames which contain many individual heald eyes, while a jacquard moves individual heald eyes.
● There are five main weft insertion methods: shuttle, projectile, rapier, air jet and water jet.
● Shuttle looms are the most versatile, they can produce any type of woven fabric, but the weft insertion rate is usually less than 500 metres per minute.

● Projectile looms are flexible, but are not suitable for pile fabric production. The loom width can be the largest of any loom, with weft insertion rates of 1100 metres per minute.

● There are several ways of inserting weft with rapier looms: single or double rapier, flexible or rigid. Weft insertion rates are lower than the projectile (800 metres per minute) but weft patterning is easier on this type of loom.

● Water jets weave hydrophobic yarns at rates of 1400+ metres per minute, with air jets achieving 1500+ metres per minute, but not restricted to hydrophobic yarns.

● The reed beats each pick into the fell of the cloth and holds the warp threads at a set spacing. The sley carries the reed and is driven by the crankshaft or cams. It is delayed to allow more time for weft insertion and sometimes dwells for most of weft insertion.

● The warp let-off motion controls the tension in the warp ends which is necessary to form a clean shed. There are negative and automatic let-off motions available. Incorrect warp tension will lead to incorrect warp and weft crimp levels.

● The take-up motion determines the pick density by winding up the cloth at the correct rate.

● Weft patterning (or insertion of different yarns) on a shuttle loom is usually carried out by a compound box containing four or six shuttles at one side of the loom only. Projectile looms employ a multi-feeder unit, rapier looms use a series of guides – one for each weft type – while weft patterning for air-jet looms is still being developed.

● Weft stop motions halt weaving when a sensor does not detect weft yarn. Older systems are purely mechanical, but a modern system uses a vibration sensor linked to an electronic control unit.

● Warp stop motions use warp pins to sense broken ends. Again, modern systems use electrodes, stopping the loom through an electronic signal.

● Warp protectors are only necessary with a free-flying weft insertion element such as a shuttle or a projectile. If the element is not sensed at the end of the shed before beat-up, the sley is stopped. If a shuttle was still in the shed at beat-up, many ends would be broken (known as a smash) and the reed damaged.

● On non-shuttle looms, the weft is replenished by use of magazine creeling. The automatic shuttle loom replaces the pirn without the aid of the weaver.

● The selvedge prevents the outside ends of the cloth from fraying, especially during wet processing. Shuttle looms form a selvedge automatically. Other types of selvedge are the hairpin, tuck, leno and helical.

REVISION EXERCISES AND QUESTIONS

1 What is the shed?
2 What is the fell?
3 Which secondary motion is not essential?
4 What factors need to be considered when choosing a loom?
5 Which weft insertion method requires the largest shed size?
6 How can grouping of warp ends be minimised?
7 When is a skip draft used?
8 Why is a fully open shed preferred?
9 Why do back heald shafts need to move through a greater distance than front heald shafts?
10 If a shuttle is the most versatile method of weft insertion, why are other methods used?
11 What advantage do rapier looms have over projectile looms?
12 Water-jet looms are only used for weaving hydrophobic yarns. Can you guess why?
13 Why are weft accumulators used in weaving?
14 Why is the reed sometimes made to dwell during the loom cycle?
15 In practice, warp tension is not measured during weaving. What is used to indicate that the warp tension is correct?
16 Why are temples used?
17 What are the restrictions on warp patterning?
18 What term is used for missing and broken picks in the cloth?
19 What looms use warp protectors?
20 Which selvedge is used on projectile, rapier and jet looms?

Non-woven fabrics

Introduction

One of the oldest non-woven fabrics is felt, which is 100 per cent wool fibres, or a blend containing wool fibres treated with heat and moisture, then agitated. The entanglement of the fibres forms a fabric which is resilient and absorbs liquids, air waves and vibration. Wool and hair fibres, due to their unique surface scales, are the only fibres with this ability to **felt**.

> A non-woven fabric is a manufactured sheet, web or batt of directional or random orientated fibres, bonded by friction and/or cohesion and/or adhesion, excluding paper.

The definition in the box excludes stitch bonded fabrics and composite fabrics (both discussed later in this chapter). Some experts class these as non-wovens, while others call them 'formed fabrics' or 'bonded fabrics'. For the purpose of this chapter, non-woven fabrics are those which can be produced by a variety of processes other than conventional weaving or knitting. Their production tends to require fewer preparation processes.

Fabric properties of non-wovens range from crisp to fluid, soft-to-the-touch to harsh, impossible-to-tear to extremely weak. This leads to a wide range of end-products – nappies, filters, teabags, geotextiles (support/separation/filtration fabrics for civil engineering) – some of which are durable, others disposable.

The first stage in the manufacture of non-wovens is the production of a web. The fibres in this web must then be bonded by some means and there are several basic methods available for the binding of a fibrous web to produce non-woven fabric. Some of these are: felting, adhesive bonding, stitch bonding, thermal bonding, needle punching, hydroentangling and spinlaying.

Figure 17.1 shows a simplified classification of the techniques available.

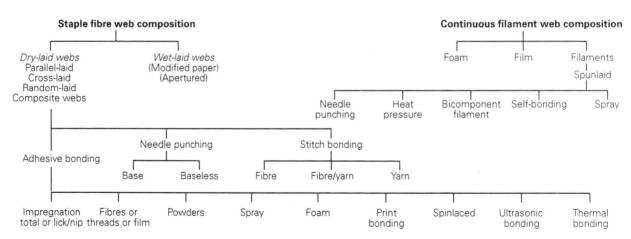

Figure 17.1 Classification of the types of non-woven fabrics.

Webs

> Staple fibre webs can be either wet-laid or dry-laid. Wet-laid webs are randomly orientated, while dry-laid webs can be orientated in one direction, more than one direction or randomly oriented.

In wet-laying, short fibres are suspended in water, drained and dried, leaving the fibres randomly orientated. Dry-laid webs can be layered so that the fibres are orientated in one direction, or more than one direction. Producing a dry-laid web in which the fibres are randomly orientated is more difficult (because the normal carding action orientates the fibres to some degree in the machine direction), but is possible.

> Continuous filament webs are called **spun-laid** or **melt-blown**. The filaments produce a randomly orientated web.

Both staple-fibre webs and continuous filament webs need to be bonded together by some means.

Staple-fibre webs

Staple-fibre webs may be wet-laid – in which case the fibres will be randomly orientated – or dry-laid, where fibre orientation can be parallel, cross-laid or again random.

Wet-laid webs

Wet-laying systems are very similar to the paper-making process. The fibres are dispersed in water and then laid on a wire mesh to filter the liquid and form a web, which is transferred to a drying felt before finally being heat-cured in a continuous process. This produces a web in which the fibres are randomly orientated. These webs are then superimposed on one another in a parallel fashion, hence the term **wet-laid parallel-laid webs**. It is the combining of the web that is directional, not the fibres within each web.

In paper making, very short cellulosic fibres of about 2.5 millimetres in length are used, but by using blends of cellulosic and synthetic fibres of slightly greater length, it is possible to produce papers which resemble fabrics. The cellulosic content minimises cost and ensures a degree of absorbency in the product, while the synthetic content, usually polyamide, increases the tear strength and resistance of the product to creasing. Papers of this type require the addition of up to 15 per cent of a bonding agent such as polyvinyl acetate to render them suitable for textile purposes. Alternatively, a polypropylene component, which subsequently melts during calendering, may be introduced as a bonding agent.

Wet-laid parallel-laid webs account for 15 per cent of web production and are produced on modified paper machines. The advantages of low cost and high production rates are offset by the limitations on fibre length (this technique is only successful with short fibres) and the papery handle of the web.

Modified synthetic fibres have been developed for incorporation into papers intended for textile end-products, including a bonding polyamide which is self-crimping and melts partially when the paper is subjected to heat treatment, and a polyester which shrinks up to 50 per cent when subjected to dry or steam heat. The introduction of synthetic fibres of this nature into a paper structure confers softness,

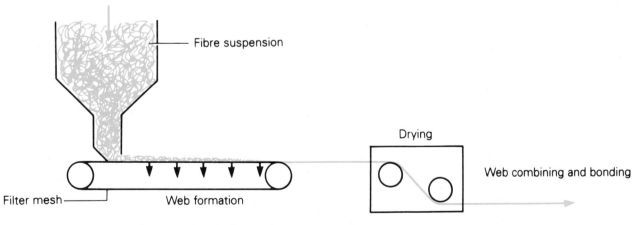

Figure 17.2 Principle of wet-laid web formation.

bulk and pliability, which represent some of the basic properties that distinguish a fabric from a paper.

> The wet-laying technique is particularly appropriate for large-scale production of a particular quality in order to be economical. This technique lends itself to the production of fabrics of low cost and limited durability.

Disposable end-products include handkerchiefs, napkins, towels, tablecloths, polishing cloths, nappies, aprons, gloves, tea bags and surgical gauzes, while more durable applications include interlinings, filter cloths and carpet underlays.

Dry-laid webs

PARELLEL-LAID WEBS

Several carding machines are placed one behind the other in a long line. The web from the first card is allowed to fall on to a conveyor which runs along the full length of the production line underneath the cards. As the web from the first card passes under the second, the web from the second card is superimposed upon it. This process is repeated along the line until a fleece of the correct mass per unit area is achieved.

> The parallel-laid web system is used extensively in the production of fleeces for relatively lightweight adhesive-bonded non-wovens, such as cleaning cloths.

However, the parallel-laid web system suffers from three disadvantages. The first is that even though some widthway stretching of the fleece is possible, it cannot be increased above the width of the carding machine. The second

disadvantage is that the fibres in the web lie predominantly in the machine direction which means that the web is five or six times stronger along its length than across its width. The third disadvantage is that the mass per unit area of the final fleece is limited because it is not economical to use more than twelve cards in a line.

CROSS-LAID WEBS

In cross-laying, the web is deposited on an inclined lattice as it leaves the card and is subsequently laid in a cross-wise manner on a wider lattice which is moving in a direction at right angles to the original direction of lay.

This cross-layer enables three important characteristics of the resulting fleece to be controlled:

1. the width of the fabric, with cross-laid fleeces of up to 15 metres in width being possible;
2. the mass per unit area of the fleece, which is dependent on the take-off speed, so that a slow take-off allows many layers to be superimposed and produces heavy fabrics, while a fast take-off produces fewer layers and a more open zig-zag of lay to create lighter fabrics;
3. the strength characteristics of the fleece, as cross-laid fabrics are stronger in the cross direction than in the machine direction, though the ratio can be varied by altering the angle of lay and the subsequent drafting of the cross-laid fleece.

> The cross-laid web technique overcomes the difficulties encountered with parallel-laid webs and has an added advantage. By stretching the cross-laid web, the ratios of the strengths of the fleece in the machine and cross directions can be controlled to suit the requirements of the end-product.

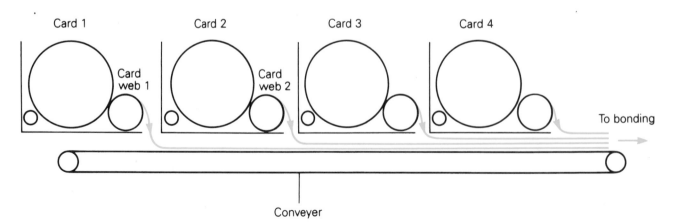

Figure 17.3 Principle of dry-laid parallel-laid web formation.

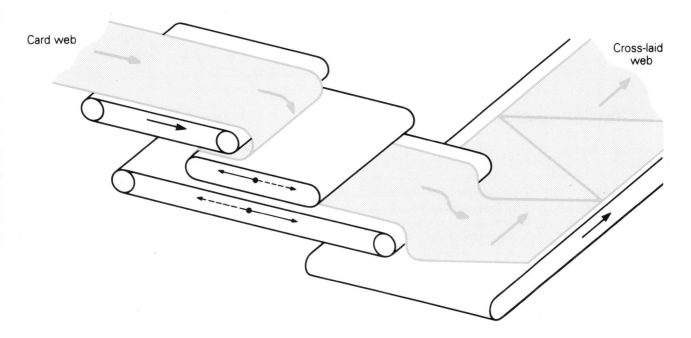

Figure 17.4   Principle of dry-laid cross-laid web formation.

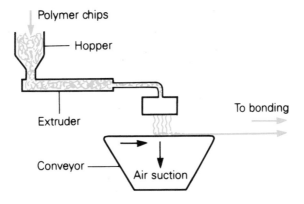

Figure 17.5   Principle of dry-laid web formation.

RANDOM-LAID WEBS

An alternative means of producing fleeces is offered by machines using aerodynamic feed of the fibres. In this case, loose fibres from a carding cylinder are carried in air currents and deposited onto a **condenser cage**, from which they are drawn off in sheet form. The condenser cage is basically a hollow cylinder formed from a mesh; this enables air to be drawn through the mesh into the centre of the cylinder, but fibres in the air current cannot pass through the mesh and collect on its surface.

The air- or random-laying technique allows fabrics with a wide range of mass per unit area to be produced, in which fibre orientation can be made very much more random than is the case with traditional web-layering. Short fibres can be processed easily, allowing textile waste materials to be used in non-wovens.

Random-laid webs are made as a single layer and are claimed to have equal properties in all directions. However, they are the most expensive to produce when compared to parallel-laid webs, which are the cheapest, and cross-laid webs, which lie between the two from the production cost point of view.

Continuous filament webs

Spun-laid webs

In this technique, a melt solution of a fibre-forming polymer is extruded through a system of spinnerets into a high-velocity current of air or other gas. The fibres formed are deposited on to a support, which may be a conveyor, a **scrim** (a very open-weave fabric) or a screen drum (condenser cage), to form a web. If necessary, the extruded filaments are drawn and internally orientated prior to web fromation, either by rollers or high-velocity air currents, in order to increase their strength. The support then carries the web to a bonding stage where consolidation of the web occurs.

Spun-laid fabrics tend to have low bulk, and high tensile and tearing strength. This leads to numerous industrial applications such as protective clothing, filters, packaging, and geotextiles.

Melt-blown webs

These are produced initially in the same manner as spun-laid webs, with polymer extruded through holes in a spinneret into a high velocity current of air. The difference between these two methods is an increased force used in the air current which breaks the filaments rather than just drawing them, to produce staple fibres of varying lengths. This is consequently not a true continuous filament web.

Non-woven fabric-forming techniques

> Several methods are available for bonding the fibres within a web to form a non-woven fabric: adhesive bonding; thermal bonding; needle punching; hydro-entangling; and stitch bonding. In some cases, a combination of these methods is used.

Adhesive bonding

Fabrics can be produced by total saturation of the dry-laid web of fibres in suitable adhesives. This is the simplest technique of applying adhesives to such webs, which are often lightweight (under 50 grams per square metre). The webs are immersed in a bath containing adhesive, where the amount taken up by the web is controlled by the concentration of adhesive in the bath and by the degree of squeezing applied to the impregnated material when it passes between two pressure rollers as it emerges from the liquor. Typical adhesives used are polyvinyl alcohol, polyvinyl chloride, polyvinyl acetate and acrylic binders, though numerous other adhesives are available depending on the type of fibre and the end-use for the final product. Figure 17.7 illustrates the principle of saturation adhesive bonding.

The saturation technique of adhesive bonding is very suitable for the production of stiff, highly compacted products.

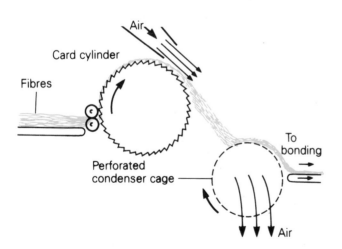

Figure 17.6 Principle of spun-laid web formation.

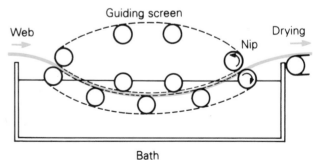

Figure 17.7 Saturation adhesive bonding.

For very open and bulky products, such as fillings for anoraks, the spray bonding technique is used, with the adhesive being dried and cured after treatment.

Spray bonding is now being replaced by a foam-impregnation processes for lightweight webs.

When bonding by means of spraying, the binder is introduced into or on to the textile structure by means of sprayers arranged over the moving web. The binder is distributed on the surface layers and does not penetrate far into the structure, which is normally quite thick.

Advantages of spray bonding are an exact measure of the amount of binder applied, uniform binder distribution and a soft fabric handle. This high-speed process is carried out by the Fleissner static-foaming box shown in Figure 17.9, where foam is produced directly at the foam padder, with the binder and compressed air being supplied in metered quantities. The foam is applied over the full width of the fabric by means of an adjustable slot in the foam box.

Adhesives of a much simpler kind rely on the fact that they melt and resolidify at temperatures high enough to enable the product to be used for many purposes without the adhesive remelting. Such thermoplastic adhesive must melt or become sticky at a temperature that is low enough to avoid damaging the fibres or the actual web, when they are used in the production of adhesive bonded non-wovens in the form of fibres, films and powders.

One method for depositing a thermoplastic polymer bonding powder is by depositing the powder on to the web through a stencil using air and a vacuum to carry the powder into place. Softening of the adhesive binder is achieved by hot air or stream ovens in the case of open, lightly compacted products or by heated rollers if dense, compact materials are required.

The formation of the strong bonds between the fibres occurs as the softened thermoplastic adhesive material resolidifies on cooling. This can be accelerated in continuous processes when chilled embossed rollers can be used to create bonds, under tightly controlled conditions, in webs which have been preheated by passing them through suitable ovens.

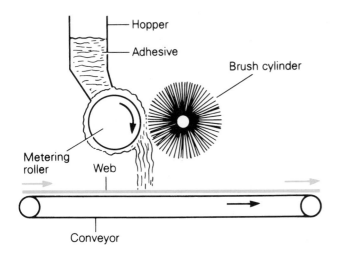

Figure 17.8 Spray adhesive bonding.

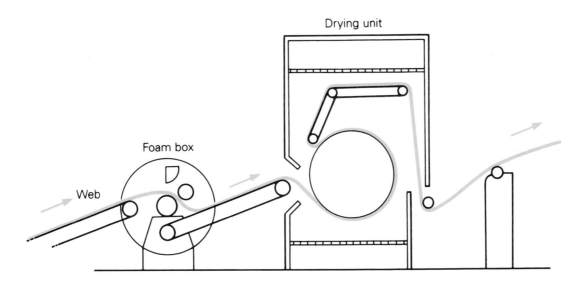

Figure 17.9 Adhesive bonding using a foam box.

DISCONTINUOUS BONDING

Where reasonable strength coupled with adequate draping characteristics are required, a more sophisticated means of applying the adhesives must be used. To improve the textile-like handle of the non-woven material, binders are applied to the web in restricted areas only, leaving areas completely unbonded. This is known as discontinuous bonding.

Discontinuous bonding can be achieved by printing the bonding agent on to the fabric, by adding thermoplastic fibres or by the introduction of powders, granules or rods which are then fused under conditions of high temperatures and low pressures, resulting in a fabric which will have innumerable anchor points.

In print bonding, the non-woven fabric typically contains about 20 per cent binder, though this can be reduced by printing the cloth with cellulose xanthate solutions, making it possible to produce miniature patterns. The patterns vary, with one of the more popular designs being the cross-hatch design. When stressed crosswise, this design produces a fabric with a bulky, three-dimensional structure, as found in disposable cloths.

Thermal bonding

Thermal bonded fabrics are produced by using heat in a variety of ways, often in addition to other bonding processes such as needle punching.

Webs of fibres with a low melting point, such as polypropylene, can be fused by the direct action of heat via a calender or oven system. Alternatively, per centages of binder

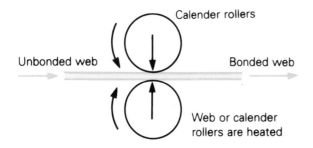

Figure 17.10 Thermal bonding.

fibres, powders (a combination of thermobonding and adhesive bonding) or bicomponent fibres can be blended with more thermally stable fibres to form selective bonds by melting at crossover points on heat treatment.

Thermal bonded fabrics are used in military applications such as explosion-suppression structures in the fuel tanks of helicopters, which have 99 per cent air by weight of fabric in order to reduce the possibility of an explosion when the fuel tank is pierced by a bullet.

Bicomponent fibres, pioneered in the UK by ICI Fibres, have individual fibres made of two types of polymer lying either side-by-side or in a cone/sheath formation. The web, composed of cone/sheath bicomponent fibres, is heated at a temperature above the melting point of the sheath polymer so that strong inter-fibre bonding takes place wherever two fibres are in contact. This process is sometimes referred to as melding and the fabrics have applications in civil engineering, milk filters, work wear and aprons, coverstock and a range of protective clothing.

Needle punching

Needled or needle-punched fabrics are produced when barbed needles are pushed through a fibrous cross-laid web, forcing some fibres through the web where they remain when the needles are withdrawn.

The needles are normally triangular in cross section, with three barbs on each of the three corners at different distances along the edge, as shown in the inset in Figure 17.11. This illustrates the main parts of a needle-punching machine.

If sufficient fibres are suitably displaced, the web is converted into a fabric by the consolidating effect of these fibrous plugs or tufts. This action occurs in needle-punching machines where a board, usually containing several thousand barbed needles, is reciprocated at speeds of up to 2000 strokes per minute, depending on the machine width. This action normally occurs in a vertical direction and some machines may have two sets of needles, one operating downwards and the other upwards, so that both sides of the web are needled.

Some webs can be superimposed with a woven or non-woven scrim fabric to assist fibre interlocking and fabric consolidation. This is a common method of production for needlefelts for use in filtration applications.

Fabric properties are generally dependent on a number of factors, the two main ones being punch density and needle penetration. The needle density, when increased, will increase fabric density and strength up to an optimum point after which further needling will result in a decrease in the breaking load of the fabric. Needle-punched fabrics are also

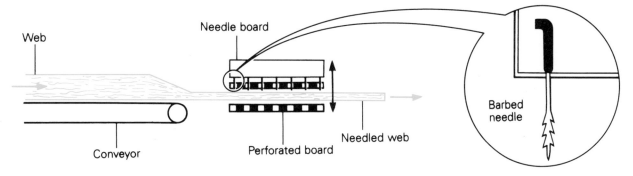

Figure 17.11 Needle bonding.

used for blankets, shoe lining materials, paper makers' felts, floor coverings, medical fabrics, heat and sound insulation, air filters and in geotextiles.

Hydroentangled

> Hydroentangled non-woven fabrics rely on the mechanical entanglement of staple fibres for their coherence. Fibre entanglement is achieved by using jets of water under pressure and a further measure, such as adhesive bonding, is usually needed to fully bond the web.

These fabrics have a softer handle and better drape than those of fully bonded, non-woven fabrics. Their disadvantages are a lack of liveliness, poor recovery from deformation and a difference in the properties between the machine and cross directions. Hydroentangled fabrics are commonly made from polyester fibre and their end-products include home furnishings, such as curtains and tablecloths, industrial fabrics especially coated, and garments.

Stitch bonding

> Stitch bonding invariably uses a cross-laid web, which is fed directly to the stitch bonder in a continuous process. The machine used in stitch bonding is basically a modified warp knitting machine which bonds the fibres by knitting columns of stitches down the length of the web.

In some cases, the web is fed initially to a needle puncher to achieve a light needling operation (known as tacking), before the rolls of fleece are passed to the stitch bonder. Tacking

enables the fleece to unroll easily and improves the mechanical interlocking between the fibres. This is of vital importance because a very serious shortcoming of many stitch bonded fabrics is that, under heavy or severe use, they tend to lose fibres from the web which can occur because the mobility of the knitted structure cannot provide sufficient anchorage of the fibre in the fleece. Other steps to minimise this weakness include the use of fibres of longer staple length and the inclusion of some relatively low melting-point fibres, which can provide additional bonding during subsequent heat setting.

The Maliwatt Stitch Bonder is shown in Figure 17.12. The web is fed to the machine in a vertical direction via a lattice arrangement. During stitch bonding it is normally supported, while the needles contained in the needle bar penetrate the web (a). When the needle emerges through the web, the yarn guides lay threads into the open hook (b) and, as the needles retract, the hook is closed by the tongue (c). The closed needle draws the new loop through the web and then through the loop of the previous course (d), which is held around the needle stem. Course spacing during knitting is largely governed by the take-up tension applied to the fabric by the take-up roller.

The structure and performance of stitch-bonded fabrics are affected by a large number of variables, some of which are controllable, for instance web area density, fibre characteristics and course spacing. Maliwatt machines are used to produce curtain drapes, mattress tickings and fabrics for the automotive industry, such as surface covers for various moulded components, parcel shelves and headliners. Other types of machines are available for the production of specialised fabrics, such as medical and electrical products.

Bonding of spun-laid webs

There are several possibilities for bonding spun-laid webs. The filaments may be: self-bonding (fibres which bond together when heated under pressure); subjected to heat, a bonding agent (usually in powder form) and pressure; interlaced by needle punching; or sprayed with adhesive to

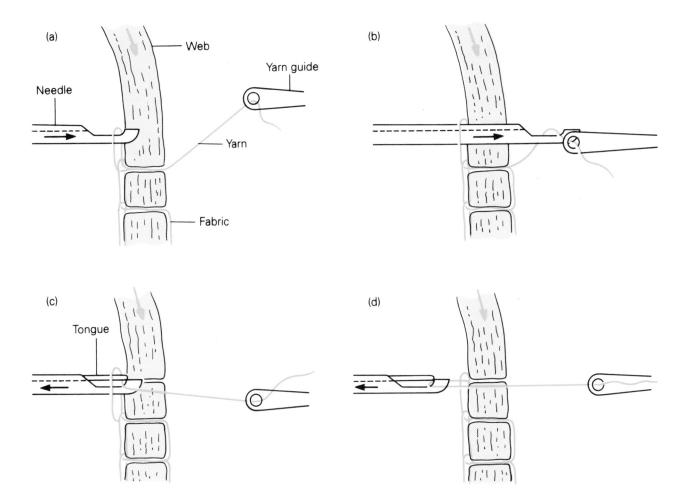

Figure 17.12 Stitch bonding.

make the filaments bond. **Bicomponent** filaments can also be used to produce a bonded fabric, with one of the components being thermoplastic to facilitate heat bonding and the other component having properties that will enhance the quality of the final fabric. The fabric area density in these processes is controlled by the speed of the lay-down belt.

Tyvek is an example of a self-bonded spun-laid fabric, in which extremely fine polyethylene fibres form a continuous network. Considerable variation in the fabric characteristics can be obtained by varying the bonding pattern. A dense, smooth and relatively stiff product is created if the sheets are bonded over their entire area, while bonding at discrete points gives a high mobility, softer and more flexible product. End-products include medical and surgical gowns, and protective clothing for use in the handling of harmful chemical substances.

Typar is a self-bonded spun-laid polypropylene made from coarse fibres originally developed for carpet backing. It is widely used in geotextiles, for drainage, erosion deterrent, the separation of layers or segments of soil construction systems and reinforcement of load-bearing structures.

Composite fabrics

Composite fabrics are two or more layers of fabric, or in the case of non-wovens, a fabric or backing (which may be a film or foam) and a fibrous web. Examples include spun-laid webs with a scrim base and needle-punched web and scrim compounds.

CHECK YOUR UNDERSTANDING

● Non-woven fabrics are produced by methods other than conventional weaving or knitting. Some experts class stitch-bonded fabrics as non-wovens, while others class them as formed or bonded fabrics.

● There are several ways to form a web for a non-woven

fabric. Staple-fibre webs can be wet-laid or dry-laid, while continuous filament webs are spun-laid or melt-blown.

● Wet-laid fabrics have a random fibre orientation, though the webs themselves are arranged in a parallel fashion.

● Dry-laid webs can have fibres orientated in one direction only (parallel-laid), in more than one direction (cross-laid), or randomly arranged (random-laid).

● Spun-laid webs are formed from randomly arranged filaments, though some orientation can be introduced.

● The above webs all need to have their component fibres bonded in some way. There are several ways of bonding, including adhesive bonding, thermal bonding, needle punching, hydroentangling, spinlaying and stitch bonding.

● Adhesive bonding can be by total impregnation of the web by adhesive, spray or foam-impregnation, or discontinuous adhesive application such as print bonding.

● Thermal bonding is application of heat or heat and pressure to melt either the fibre itself, part of a bicomponent fibre, or some binder in powder or other form.

● Needle punching entangles fibres by forcing them from the surface layers of the web through to the centre or opposite side using a needle with barbs. Fabrics can be needled in one direction or by using two sets of needles from both faces of the fabric at once.

● Hydroentangled fabrics are bonded by interlacing of fibres by high-pressure water jets. Usually a further bonding, such as adhesive, is needed.

● Stitch-bonded fabrics are held together by yarns stitched through the fibre web.

● Non-woven composite fabrics are composed of a web and a woven scrim or a base fabric such as a film or foam.

REVISION EXERCISES AND QUESTIONS

1 Why are stitch bonded fabrics not classed as non-wovens by all experts?

2 Why is it more difficult to produce a randomly orientated dry-laid web than an orientated web?

3 How are dry-laid non-wovens produced with fibre orientation in more than one direction?

4 Which method of dry-laid web formation is least expensive?

5 What advantage does the discontinuous adhesive bonded fabric have over the total adhesive bonded fabric?

6 What is the difference between hydroentangled and needle-punched methods of web bonding?

7 How does self-bonding differ from other types of thermal bonding?

Fabric testing

Introduction

As with yarn testing, which was discussed in Chapter 11, fabric testing does not in itself improve quality, it merely indicates the level that has been achieved. However, it is essential to know if, for example, the fabric produced falls within the customer's specification. If it does not, a repeat order would be highly unlikely and rejection of the current order is possible.

The same reasons for testing exist with fabrics as with yarns: selection of raw materials (in this case usually yarns); monitoring and control of processing conditions; research and development; checking of the finished product against customer specifications.

Checking the finished fabric parameters is dealt with first in this chapter, followed by yarn testing from the fabric manufacturer's point of view and finally the fabric dimensions.

Fabric analysis

It is often necessary to analyse a small sample of fabric for its structural parameters.

> The information needed to reproduce the fabric as closely as possible is: construction; yarn linear density; yarn crimp; thread densities; course length and stitch length (knitted fabric).

Construction

It is necessary to know the method of fabric construction – whether the fabric is woven, knitted or non-woven – and the structure, for example twill weave, purl fabric. This is determined by viewing the fabric using a **piece glass** or a low magnification microscope, if available. Using a combination of experience and powers of observation, the method of production can be determined.

Yarn linear density

The technique used here is different from that used to determine the linear density of yarn in package form.

From the definition of linear density, mass per unit length, two measures are required: one of weight and one of length. Since the amount of yarn available is likely to be small and not in a suitable state for convenient measurement of length, the results will not be very accurate. A sample of fabric is taken, placed on a flat surface, and two parallel slits are made in it at a convenient distance apart. This distance should be as large as possible to make length measurement as accurate as possible.

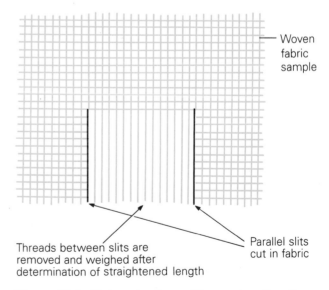

Woven fabric sample

Threads between slits are removed and weighed after determination of straightened length

Parallel slits cut in fabric

Figure 18.1 Determination of linear density of yarn in fabric.

Fifty threads are removed from the area between the slits and weighed. The distance between slits is not the length of the yarn because the yarn contains crimp due to interlacing of the threads in the case of woven fabric. The straightened length of the yarn is measured using a crimp tester. This applies a small tension to straighten the yarn without stretching it (see yarn crimp).

If the fabric is knitted, because of the very high crimp content due to the knitted loop shape, it is best to measure the straightened length of the yarn directly by straightening it under tension on a course length tester (see course length and stitch length below).

The linear density is calculated as follows:

$$\text{linear density (tex)} = \frac{\text{mass (g)} \times 1000}{n \times \text{straightened length (m)}}$$

where n = number of lengths removed and weighed.

With woven fabric, the warp and weft yarn linear densities must be determined separately as they are often different.

Yarn crimp

Yarn crimp is estimated by taking a small number (say, ten) of the threads removed from a known length of fabric and determining their straightened lengths under a small tension using a crimp tester. When using a crimp tester the tension on the yarn should be adjusted to suit the linear density of the yarn being tested.

$$\text{Crimp \%} = \frac{(\text{straightened length} - \text{crimped length})}{\text{crimped length}} \times 100$$

This procedure is repeated for each length of yarn and the mean crimp percentage calculated.

Thread density

This is the number of threads per unit length and width in the fabric. There are two methods of measurement: direct and indirect measurement.

The fabric sample is placed on a flat surface, making sure it is not under tension or distorted. A piece glass is placed on top and the fabric viewed through the lens. A magnified image of the fabric is produced. If the fabric is woven, the number of threads occupying the length and width of the piece glass square can be counted with the aid of a dissecting needle to pinpoint the individual threads in warp and weft. If the fabric is knitted, the number of loops in each direction (courses and wales) are counted.

If the piece glass is 2.5 centimetres square, the threads in one direction of woven fabric will be determined by:

$$\text{thread density} = \frac{\text{threads counted}}{2.5} = \text{threads per cm}$$

INDIRECT MEASUREMENT – WOVEN FABRIC

This is carried out using an optical device known as a **taper line grating**. This is a flat sheet of glass with a large number of straight lines engraved on it in a tapered fashion so that their density increases from left to right. When this is placed on top of a simple woven construction the threads interfere with the line grating and an optical pattern is produced. The pattern is used to indicate the thread density (for example, 55 in Figure 18.3).

Course length and stitch length

These are important parameters to measure with knitted fabric.

COURSE LENGTH

If the fabric has been knitted on a flat machine, a thread is removed from the full width of the fabric. If it has been knitted on a circular machine the fabric sample is slit along

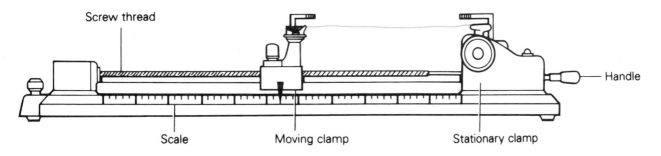

Figure 18.2 Crimp tester.

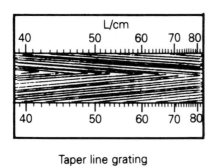
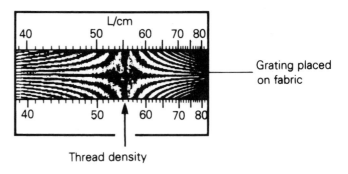

Taper line grating

Thread density

Grating placed on fabric

Figure 18.3 Taper line grating for determination of woven thread density.

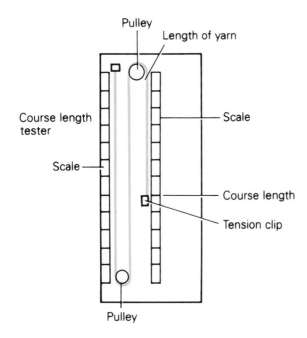

Figure 18.4 Determination of course length.

its length, opened out, and a thread removed from the full width of the sample.

The straightened length of the thread is then measured using a course length tester. This allows a long length of yarn to be measured under sufficient tension to remove the crimp created by the loop distortions.

STITCH LENGTH

First, the course length is measured as described above. If only a small sample of fabric is available a procedure similar to that for determining linear density is used. Two parallel slits are cut in the fabric a convenient distance apart. A length of thread is removed from between the slits and its straightened length measured using a course length tester. The stitch length is then calculated:

$$\text{stitch length} = \frac{\text{course length}}{\text{number of loops in fabric width}}$$

$$\text{or stitch length} = \frac{\text{straightened length}}{\text{number of loops in thread}}$$

Incoming yarn

If the characteristics of the incoming yarn are not correct, the dimensions and properties of the fabric are unlikely to be correct.

Linear density

The incoming yarn will be on some sort of package which makes it relatively easy to determine the linear density. A hank of convenient length is wound using a wrap reel. The hank is then removed and weighed. This technique is described in detail in Chapter 11.

$$\text{Linear density (tex)} = \frac{\text{mass (g)}}{\text{length (m)}} \times 1000$$

Coefficient of friction

Friction between the yarn and guides or other machine parts during processing causes tension. If the tension is excessive it results in yarn breakages and reduction in efficiency. This is especially critical during knitting and yarn for machine knitting is consequently waxed or oiled to reduce its coefficient of friction.

The coefficient of friction of the incoming yarn should be checked before it is used, by means of a yarn friction tester using the **capstan** or **coil friction** principle. The yarn, under slight tension, is fed round a cylinder made from the same material as the guides. The difference between input and output tension, which in turn is caused by friction, causes rotation of an indicator over a scale. The position of the indicator on the scale shows the coefficient of friction.

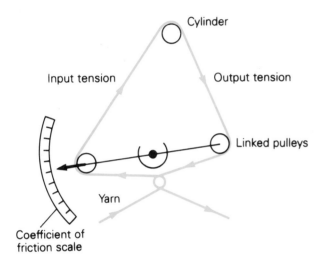

Figure 18.5   Determination of yarn friction.

Fabric dimensions

Length

It may be necessary to measure the length of a large piece of fabric in order to know how much has been produced by the manufacturer or how much has been delivered to a customer.

> The strains imposed during manufacture and processing may affect the length of a fabric and some recovery may occur during storage. Before measurements are made the fabric should be unrolled and stored without tension, preferably in a standard atmosphere.

Due to the flexibility of fabrics, a small tension during measurement causes an increase in dimensions and results cannot be expected to be very accurate.

The fabric is placed on a large table under minimum tension and folded so that it contains no creases. Starting at one end, marks are made on the selvedge every five metres using a metre rule as a measure. The end portion is measured to the nearest ten millimetres and the total length is calculated:

$$\ell = 5N + f \text{ m}$$

where ℓ = total length,

$\quad N$ = number of marks,

$\quad f$ = length of end section.

Devices are available for rapid measurement of fabric length. The fabric is passed continuously through rollers which grip the selvedge, causing the rollers to rotate and operate a length meter.

Width

It is important to know if the width of a fabric is correct so that when it is made into garments the patterns will fit across the width without too much waste. Some finishing processes change the width of the machine state (grey) fabric. Again slight tension during measurement can cause inaccuracies.

The fabric is placed at full width on a large table so it is free from creases. The width is measured using a metre rule, at ten places spaced equally along the piece, taking care not to stretch the fabric. The accuracy of measurement depends on the width of the fabric.

Thickness

Specimens of fabric are placed between two small flat plates (feet) and the distance between the plates is measured. A small pressure is applied to flatten the surface fibres but not enough to compress the fabric. The pressure applied depends on the type of fabric under test. There are also different standard presser foot areas for different types of fabric (thin fabrics: small area; thick fabrics: large area). With modern instruments the feet are initially set wide apart. The specimen is placed between them and the distance gradually decreased, so increasing the pressure on the specimen. When the pressure reaches a preset value, a light switches on. The thickness at this pressure is measured by a dial gauge operated by the moving foot. The gauge is sensitive to 0.001 millimetres.

Mass per unit area

As absorbed moisture affects both mass and dimensions, it is important to precondition samples and carry out measurements in a standard atmosphere.

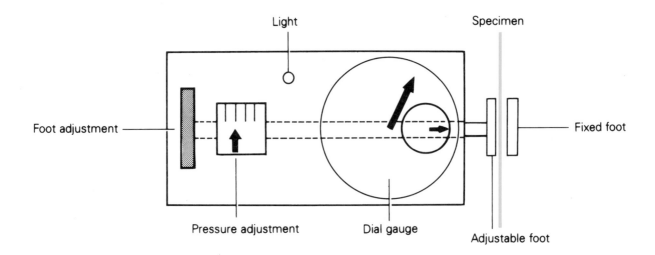

Figure 18.6 Fabric thickness gauge.

Mass per unit area is expressed in grams per square metre (g m^{-2}) but it is not necessary to measure a square metre of fabric. A relatively small specimen is cut out, usually 10×10 centimetres, with the aid of a template. Circular cutters are also available which cut out the same area ($10 \times 10 = 100$ cm^2). The specimen is then weighed accurately. Using this area of specimen:

mass per unit area = specimen mass (g) $\times 100$ (g m^{-2})

CHECK YOUR UNDERSTANDING

● Fabric tests are carried out to: select raw materials; monitor and control processing; assist in research and development; and check the finished product.

● Fabric analysis involves: fabric construction; component yarn linear density; crimp; thread density; course length and stitch length for knitted fabrics.

● In any fabric manufacturing process, the incoming yarn is tested to determine the actual linear density. In the production of weft knitted fabrics the frictional characteristics of the yarn are vital – usually a coefficient of friction test is carried out.

● Fabric dimensions – length, width, mass per unit area and sometimes thickness – are usually checked against the original fabric specification.

REVISION EXERCISES AND QUESTIONS

1 Calculate the linear density given the following information:
    50 threads of 23.5 cm length weigh 0.5 g
2 Calculate the crimp given the following information:
    straightened length = 33.2 cm
    crimped length = 30 cm
3 Calculate the stitch length given the following information:
    course length = 450 cm
    number of loops in the fabric width = 900
4 Calculate the mass per square metre given the following information:
    a 10×10 cm square of fabric weighs 2.65 g

Wet processing

Introduction

The wet-processing sector of the textile industry covers all the processes on a textile that involve some form of wet or chemical treatment. Processes such as bleaching, dyeing, printing and finishing are carried out at various stages during textile manufacture. These processes all involve some form of chemical action on the material.

It is the chemical basis of the wet-processing sector that largely distinguishes it from the other sectors of the textile industry such as yarn, fabric and garment production. These functions are based on mechanical principles rather than the chemical principles involved in wet processing.

The basic operations

The wet-processing sector can be divided into three distinct sections: preparation processes; coloration processes; finishing processes. These are represented along with their aims in Table 19.1.

This chapter will briefly look at these three types of process, when they happen and how the industry is organised. Later chapters will cover the processes in greater detail.

Preparation processes

Textiles are often in a very impure state when they arrive at the coloration stage. If the fibre used in the textile is from some natural origin, for example cotton or wool, it will still contain a great deal of the impurity that the fibre acquired while it was growing in a field or on a sheep. These impurities must be removed before dyeing or printing processes can take place as they would not only spoil the appearance of the textile but would either make the coloration processes impossible or, at the very least, difficult to perform.

Man-made fibres contain very much less impurity than natural fibres but they too need to be cleaned up and, in some cases, have their physical properties adjusted before they can be wet processed successfully.

Table 19.1 The three functions of the wet-processing sector

Preparation processes	Coloration processes	Finishing processes
These processes exist to ensure that the textile has the right physical and chemical properties to enable it to be coloured or finished.	These processes exist to provide the the textile with colour either for aesthetic reasons or for some functional purpose determined by the product.	These processes exist to provide the the textile with the properties that the end-use demands and which have not already been provided by any earlier processes.
Examples: Scouring Bleaching Heat setting.	*Examples:* Dyeing Printing.	*Examples:* Water repellency Flame retardancy Handle modification Anti-soiling finish.

Dyeing and printing

The purpose for which the textile will be used determines why we colour it in the way we do. It is very easy to jump to the conclusion that textiles are only coloured to make them more attractive. Of course, this is often the case but it is not the only reason. We do not print fabric for military uniforms with camouflage designs for aesthetic reasons; we do it for very good functional reasons.

Finishing processes

As the name suggests, finishing processes come at the end of a series of wet processes, typically right at the end of the whole processing sequence of the textile. They are often the last thing which happens to a textile before it becomes the raw material of another industry, for example the clothing manufacturing industry. The finishing process is usually the last chance to make sure that the textile has either the properties required by the end-product or those required by further processing operations.

When a textile reaches the finishing stage, processes which have gone before may have impaired or even destroyed some of the desirable properties of the fibre, so the finishing processes carried out must attempt to reintroduce these properties or to increase them if they have been reduced in some way. One example of this might be that a given textile develops a very harsh handle as a result of the way that it has been dyed, and finishing processes will therefore have to put the softness of handle back again. Alternatively, we may require properties in the final textile that were never present at any time previously.

Cotton is a fibre used for nightdresses and curtain or upholstery end-products, but it burns very easily. By appropriate finishing of a cotton textile, it can be given a high resistance to burning. Another example is absorbency. Cotton is used for towels and for raincoats, and these end-products obviously require totally opposite abilities to absorb or repel water. The correct finishing processes can help the textile either absorb or repel water.

Wet processing and the manufacturing sequence

In the processing of a textile from the original loose raw fibre to the final end-product, the wet processes could occur at several stages. Consider for a moment the sequence of processes shown in Figure 19.1.

The yarn manufacturing processes occur at only one point in this sequence, as do the fabric production operations of

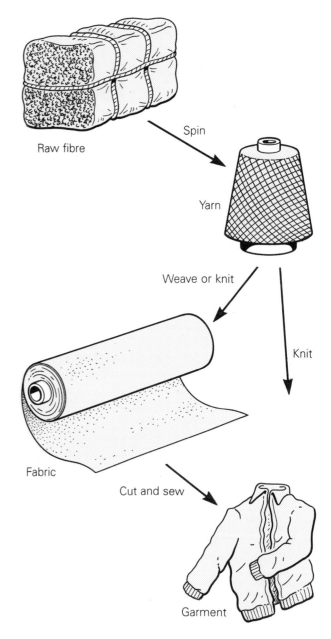

Figure 19.1 Textile processing routes.

knitting and weaving. A yarn spinner always has the same raw material – fibre. A fabric producer nearly always manufactures product from yarn.

> The wet processor could have several types of raw material: fibre; yarn; fabric; garment.

To spin a coloured yarn it is necessary to have coloured fibre from which to spin it or coloured yarn to weave or knit coloured fabric. The textile can be left undyed until it becomes a garment at which point the garment is dyed, or the fabric may be dyed and the garment produced by cutting it up and sewing the parts together.

> No matter at which stage it occurs, wet processing will still involve preparation, coloration and finishing operations.

Finishing operations can be carried out on a yarn after the yarn has been dyed but before the fabric has been produced from it. The fibre can even be finished twice, for example a finish is applied to the yarn after dyeing it to make it easier to knit, but having been knitted, the fabric needs finishing to prevent it from shrinking excessively or to make it softer.

The ability to process a textile in any of the physical forms which might exist – that is at any point in the processing sequence – is one of the principal distinctions between wet processing and fibre, yarn, fabric or garment manufacture.

To cope with this diversity of raw materials, wet processors will normally specialise in one or more of them. Typically, there are dyers of loose fibre (**loose stock**), yarn dyers, dyers of fabric (**piece dyers**) and garment dyers. This specialisation is necessary because different textile forms require different kinds of handling to avoid damage. Specifically designed machinery is needed in each case.

Industrial organisation

There are two organisational structure types: **vertical** and **horizontal**. This does not refer to the shape of the factory but to the ways in which the various parts of the structure relate to each other.

Vertical organisations

> A company which is structured in such a way that it takes in a basic raw material and performs all of the necessary processing functions to convert it into the finished product is said to be vertical or vertically organised.

A textile company that takes in raw fibre and by spinning, weaving, wet processing and making-up, converts it into an end-product such as bed sheets, is said to be a vertical organisation and the wet processing function that exists within it is also vertical. Figure 19.2 shows this diagrammatically.

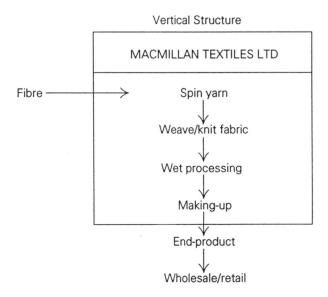

Figure 19.2 Macmillan Textiles Ltd is a single company performing all of these functions.

Horizontal organisations

> A company that only performs part of the overall manufacturing process, the products of which become raw materials for the next company in the processing sequence, is said to be a horizontal organization.

Horizontally organised companies are not part of a single organisation (if they were, the organisation would be vertical). They are independent firms unconnected with each other except that they are all involved in the chain of processing from raw material to finished product. Each separate company sells its product to the firm carrying out the next process.

A horizontal structure is more complex than a vertical one. Within the textile industry they can be so complex that it can be a very difficult task to trace the processing route that fibre has taken to end up as the finished product and this becomes a serious problem when a fault has occurred in the processing somewhere along the line and the attempt is being made to find out where.

Taking Figure 19.3 as an example, the spinning company (Ring, Traveller & Co.) produces yarn which it sells to anyone who wants to buy it (in this case, a weaver and a knitter). The products of these two firms (the loomstate or greige fabrics) may be bought by organisations known as converters (more correctly, **merchant converters**). They become the new owners. Converters do not carry out any processing

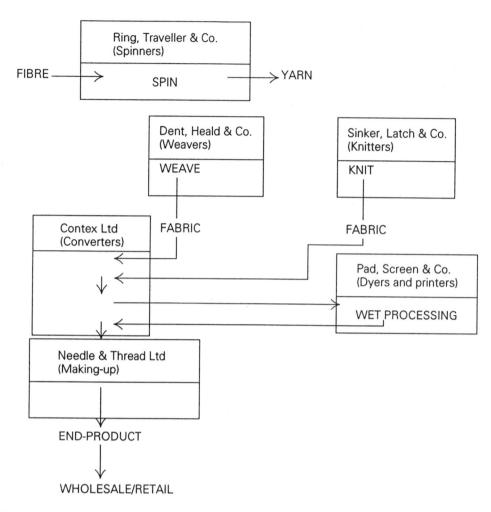

Figure 19.3 A structure involving six individual companies.

themselves but will have the fabrics wet processed as and when they find buyers for the finished fabric.

The goods may be returned to the converter by the wet processor or they may be passed on directly to the converter's customer, who is usually a making-up organisation.

Whether the wet processor is working in a horizontal or vertical organisation makes a considerable difference. In a vertical company, the goods that the wet processor is processing are owned by and have been produced by the same organisation so that whatever information the processor needs about the goods is available. Quality standards have been set in the full knowledge of what the capabilities are of both the preceding processes and the ones which follow wet processing. The properties that the end-product is required to have are known and the wet processor is free to design the processing to provide them. It is possible to operate with relatively high running costs for some stages if this maximises the profitability of the operation as a whole. In other words, the fabric producer could afford to run at a slight loss if this enabled the wet processor to make a large saving.

An independent wet-processing company operating in a horizontal structure will have little knowledge of the previous history of the goods received for processing and only information from the supplier or from an analysis of the textile performed in the laboratory will be available. The converter will usually have sold the textile before the wet processor is asked to process it. A technical specification will already exist and there will be very little opportunity for the wet processor to discuss what is or is not technically possible, or what it is economically efficient to do.

In a vertical organisation, it is likely that the product will be manufactured before a buyer is found for it and it is easier, in this situation, to find buyers for goods that are not of first quality by selling them at a lower price. The horizontal wet processor who processes goods which fail to meet the customer's specification has failed to produce goods that the customer has already sold at an agreed price. The wet processor will not be paid for doing this and must make a profit out of the work done. It cannot be in the independent wet processor's interests to make a loss in order that some other company in the processing sequence can make a profit.

Being in a vertically or horizontally structured operation is critical for the operation of a successful wet-processing business. On one hand it would seem that being an independent horizontally organised wet processor is potentially far more risky than being vertically structured. This may be so but the independent companies are usually specialists in a particular processing technique and may therefore be able to command a premium on the work they carry out.

Horizontal arrangements are more complex than straightforward vertical organisations, but most actual structures are more complex than either of them. An organisational structure may involve both vertical and horizontal aspects. For example, in Figure 19.4, Motivate Ltd can be considered to be a largely (but not entirely) vertically operating company. However, the company also operates partly in a horizontal fashion.

As well as using the yarn that it produces for its own fabric production, Motivate Ltd sells yarn to other companies (one of which is shown – Sinker, Latch & Co.). Its wet-processing department operates vertically when it is processing the company's own fabric, but horizontally when it takes in other fabrics, such as the input shown from the converter Contex Ltd. Fabrics from the converter are produced by another weaver (Dent, Heald & Co.). Note that the fabric produced by Sinker, Latch & Co. is wet processed horizontally by another dyer (Pad, Screen & Co.) but is then returned to Motivate for making-up in their own organisation.

There are several good reasons why Motivate should operate in this way. Imagine a situation in which Motivate operated entirely vertically. It produced its own yarn, which was then converted entirely into woven fabrics, dyed and made up. Suppose that at some point in time the demand for

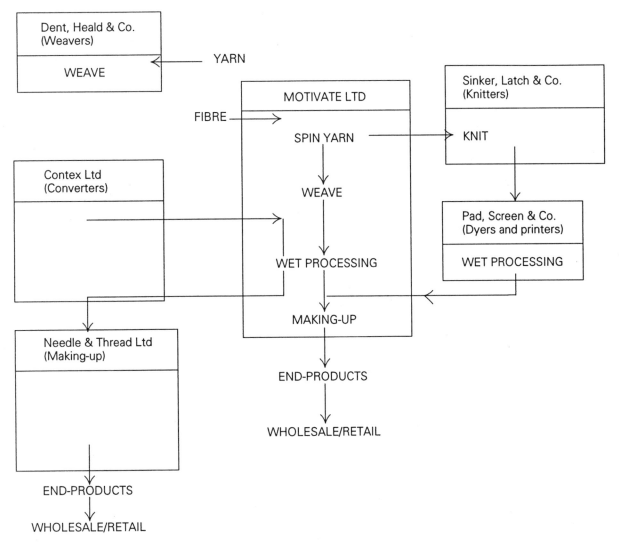

Figure 19.4 A structure with both vertical and horizontal elements.

fabrics produced by weaving decreased and the demand for knitted fabrics increased. Motivate would be faced with either installing knitting machinery and the wet-processing equipment needed to deal with knitted fabrics (knitted fabrics and woven fabrics require different types of dyeing and finishing equipment) or they could find an alternative structural answer. Figure 19.4 represents one such possible alternative.

By selling yarn to a knitter (Sinker, Latch & Co.) and using another dyer already equipped and specialising in knitted fabrics (Pad, Screen & Co.), the fabric is produced in its finished state and can then be made up by Motivate and marketed by them as if it were entirely their own production. Since the demand for their own woven fabrics had fallen, Motivate would have a wet-processing department equipped to deal with only woven fabrics which was then under utilised. The possibility exists, therefore, for them to take in other people's woven goods for processing and so to keep their wet-processing department functioning profitably. Consequently, they wet process woven fabrics on behalf of Contex Ltd.

Batch and continuous processing

> Wet processing is carried out using two very general techniques or a combination of the two. These are: **batch processing** and **continuous processing**.

Batch processing

The total amount of textile is processed at the same time in a suitable machine. The textile is loaded, this load being one batch of material and will remain in the machine until the process is complete, when it will then be unloaded. It is like loading laundry into a domestic washing machine. Each load of clothing is a batch and the next batch cannot be started until the first batch is completed and removed.

Continuous processing

The textile passes continuously through the processing liquid which is replenished as the textile absorbs it. Typically, the textile will pass on continuously to the next machine in the sequence to bring about the desired reaction with the textile. In a continuous process the various operations necessary to complete the treatment have to be identified and machinery designed to carry them out so that the textile can enter the sequence of operations and pass from one step to the next in a continuous way until it comes out at the other end with the full process completed.

Although both approaches can, in general, be used for most wet processes, it is often the case that either one or the other will be chosen. Occasionally, a process is designed to include both batch processing steps and continuous sequences.

Many of the operations necessary to prepare, dye or print and finish fabrics can be performed continuously simply because a fabric lends itself to be handled in a continuous way by machinery. However, yarn and garments are normally batch processed because it is difficult to devise simple techniques for handling these products in a continuous way through a series of processes. The reasons which determine whether batch or continuous techniques are chosen might also relate to technical difficulties of one technique or the other, or perhaps the cost implications.

It is generally true that the larger the amount of textile that is to be processed, the more likely it is to find a continuous way of doing it. Machinery designed to perform these continuous operations is usually large, technically complex and therefore very expensive. It is necessary to keep such machinery fully utilised if it is to repay the investment made in it. Larger quantities of textile will keep such machines running and usefully employed for longer.

If the wet processor's customer only requires a small amount of the material to be processed, it will probably make more sense to carry out a batch operation. To process small quantities on a conventional continuous machine is not an efficient use of it. The machine would probably spend as much time being cleaned and adjusted to perform the next run of goods as it would processing material. Batch machinery, on the other hand, can normally be reset very quickly to the processing conditions required for the next batch.

CHECK YOUR UNDERSTANDING

● Wet processing involves some form of wet or chemical treatment.

● Wet processing can happen at various stages in the manufacturing sequence.

● The basic operations are: preparation processes; coloration processes; finishing processes.

● Preparation processes are necessary to ensure that dyeing or printing can take place efficiently.

● Dyeing and printing are carried out for functional reasons as well as aesthetic reasons.

● Finishing processes are used to reintroduce, increase or create desired properties in the end-product.

● Wet processing can be carried out at various stages: on fibre (loose stock); on yarn; on fabric (piece dyeing); or on garments.

● The wet-processing industry is organised in one of two basic ways: horizontally or vertically. In reality, a company can operate vertically and horizontally.

● Vertical organisations process the basic raw material through to the finished product. Horizontal organisations only perform one part of the total manufacturing process.

● There are two general techniques used to wet process materials: batch or continuous processing. As the names suggest, batch processing tends to be shorter runs carried out in discrete stages, while continuous processing tends to be large runs in which the material passes from one stage to the next continuously.

1 Why is it necessary for wet processors to specialise in one part of the industry?

2 Why is it sometimes necessary for a vertically organised wet processor to act like a horizontal organisation?

3 Why are garments usually processed in a batch rather than continuously?

4 Why is coloured yarn sometimes necessary? At what stage other than yarn dyeing could wet processing be carried out and the same effect be achieved?

5 What advantages are there to being horizontally organised rather than vertically organised?

Preparation processes

Introduction

Preparation processes are used to remove impurities from natural fibres and any added substances from earlier stages of processing. These added impurities might also be present on man-made fibres. If **dyestuffs**, **pigments** or finishes need to be applied, impurities must be removed first.

Natural fibres contain many impurities which form part of the raw fibre. Both cotton and wool contain fats and waxes and these effectively waterproof the fibre. There are many other substances which form part of the natural impurity in these two fibres but it is the fatty content which is the main problem.

Some examples of added impurity that might be present in any fibre type are sizes and spinning lubricants. However, because of their origin, man-made fibre **substrates** (material on which wet processes are carried out) generally contain less impurity than natural fibre substrates. The preparation processes designed to remove impurity from the textile will therefore normally be less severe for a man-made fibre textile than they would for a natural one.

> Several stages are involved in the preparation of a textile for dyeing or printing but it is not necessary to subject all textiles to all stages.

There is little point in wasting time and money bleaching a product to a good level of whiteness if it is going to be dyed black afterwards, though bleaching is sometimes used to remove other types of impurity.

Preparation of woven cotton fabrics

This section considers essentially only woven fabrics; the processing of knitted fabrics is only referred to when the procedures are significantly different. Other cellulosic fibre textiles can also be processed in the ways described in the following section.

Typically, a woven cotton fabric would be prepared by a sequence of processes as shown below:

Singe
↓
Desize
↓
Scour
↓
Bleach
↓
Mercerise

The end-use of the textile will determine whether all of these stages are necessary. In some cases, the stages may occur in a different order or two stages may be combined into one.

Singe

> Surface hair removal is usually the first stage in a preparation sequence and can be carried out by the process of singeing.

Woven cotton fabrics are normally singed but knitted fabrics are not. The most widely used type of **singeing** machine allows the fabric to pass at great speed through a naked gas flame so that the surface fibres or hairs are burnt away. To be suitable for singeing, the fibre must be one that does not form hard, black residues when it burns or one that does not easily melt. Cotton and other cellulosic fibres behave ideally on singeing because they form a light, dusty ash which is easily removed afterwards. Wool, on the other hand, forms a hard residue and fabrics composed of synthetic fibres, for example acrylic, may discolour and distort when singed.

There are several objectives of singeing woven fabrics. First of all **wettability** is improved. Surface hair helps to trap air in the fabric when it is immersed in water so that it takes longer for water to enter the fabric since it must first displace the air. Singeing, therefore, helps to increase the fabric's wettability. It also creates a smooth surface for printing . It may be possible to print fine detail on a hairy surface but once the hair moves again after printing, the detail will become fuzzy and indistinct. Emphasis of the woven structure of the fabric, if that is desirable, can be brought about by singeing. A hairy fabric which has been dyed may have a cloudy or frosty appearance; the projecting dyed hairs give the fabric surface the appearance of being paler than the body of the fabric, and singeing can prevent this.

The tendency of blend fabrics composed of cellulosic and synthetic fibres (mainly polyester) to form **pills** can be minimised. Pills are the little balls of fibre that arise on the surface of some fabrics as a result of the abrasion that occurs during usage.

Singeing is a continuous process carried out on dry open-width fabric. It may be done on one side only or on both sides of the fabric but in every case it is necessary to do it at very high cloth speeds. Speeds of 150–400 metres per minute are typical to avoid scorching the fabric. The aim is to run at a speed which ensures that the projecting fibres will have burned down to the surface of the fabric but that there is no burning of fibres which are locked within the yarn and which

are not projecting. The exact running speed is largely determined by the amount of hairiness and the construction of the yarn and fabric. In general, the higher the yarn twist and the tighter the cloth construction, the more severe the singeing treatment can be.

Immediately after passing through the singeing region of the machine, the fabric is quenched by running it through water or a steam box to extinguish any remaining sparks and embers.

Desizing

> Sizes are applied to the warp yarns of woven fabrics to assist in the weaving process but must be removed prior to dyeing or printing in a process known as **desizing**.

Cellulosic and man-made fibre woven fabrics will always contain size of some type or other. Sizes will not be found on knitted fabrics because it would have the opposite effect in a knitting process that it has in weaving. In weaving, the size increases weaving efficiency by enabling the yarn to withstand the stresses encountered in the loom; such high levels of stress are not present in a knitting process so the size is unnecessary. If it were present, size would make the yarn stiffer and so the formation of the knitted loops would be more difficult.

Cellulosic and cellulosic fibre blends with man-made fibres are usually treated with starch-based size. These products have only very poor solubility in water and so are difficult to remove using just water and detergent.

Man-made fibre fabrics may be sized with a variety of water-soluble sizes, the main ones of which are polyvinyl alcohol and polyacrylic acid types.

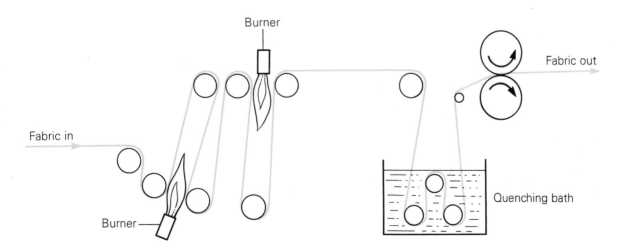

Figure 20.1 Singeing machine.

Both cellulosic and synthetic fibre fabrics may be sized with mixtures of starch-based and water-soluble types. In this case, they are treated as if they were sized with starch alone since the processes available to remove starch will also remove the water-soluble types.

The removal of starch sizes can only be performed if the starch is degraded in some way and converted into products with a higher degree of water solubility than the starch itself has.

Size has to be solubilised or broken down into molecularly smaller fragments and the key steps in the process, irrespective of what the desizing agent is, are as follows: impregnate the fabric with the desizing agent; allow time for the agent to be adsorbed into the size and to degrade or solubilise it; and wash out the degradation products.

Starch can be degraded by a variety of different agents discussed below.

BACTERIA

Cloth is wetted out in water and allowed to lie damp for several hours. Bacteria present in the atmosphere at all times will, under damp and warm conditions, degrade the starch. The process is a biochemical action, referred to as **rot steeping** and it is a very difficult process to control. If the bacteria are allowed to progress too far the cellulose itself will start to degrade. The fabric must be washed after the breakdown of the size is complete.

ACIDS

Cold solutions of dilute sulphuric or hydrochloric acids (0.5 per cent–1.0 per cent concentration on weight of fibre) can be used. The cloth is soaked in the acid then left for two to three hours at room temperature. This method has the advantage that it also removes any metal contamination that may be present in the fabric, which could be a serious problem when the fabric is bleached because the presence of very small amounts of metal in fabric can cause the bleaching action to go out of control and seriously damage the fibre. The use of acid is also cheap since there is no heat involved and the acids are relatively cheap.

There are, however, serious disadvantages to the use of acids for the removal of starch sizes. The chemistry of starch and cellulose is very similar and while acid will degrade starch by hydrolysing it, the fibre is also affected in the same way. It is vital to ensure that the acid is neutralised quickly and fully once the starch has been attacked. It is because of the risk to the fibre that this method, though practised by some wet processors, is not a popular one.

OXIDISING AGENTS

Some oxidising agents, particularly hydrogen peroxide, will degrade starch without any serious attack of the cellulose as long as reasonable care is taken with the process. The fabric is soaked in a hot solution of the oxidiser and batched up (rolled up) for several hours or steamed for 20 minutes or so at 100–105°C. Since hydrogen peroxide is used as a bleach for cellulosic substrates, and as a bleaching process would normally follow desizing, the two processes might be combined into one. This is sometimes done where the amount of size to be removed is not large. A more common practice is to economise by using an **enzyme** desizing process under conditions which are milder (and therefore use less chemicals and heat) and which result in incomplete desizing. The removal of size is then completed in the bleaching process by the oxidising action of the hydrogen peroxide bleach.

ENZYMATIC DESIZING

Enzymes are biochemicals which have a specific action on only one type of compound and which bring about a chemical change in it. They are contained within all living systems and carry out many functions, for example, their role in the digestion of food. One family of enzymes, known as the **amylases**, have an action on starch and nothing else and they convert starch to a variety of different sacharrides (sugars). If they could be used to act on the starch size of a woven fabric they would, by converting it to sugars, produce a water-soluble product that could be easily washed out.

Each enzymatic product that is available to the wet processor must be used under precisely the conditions specified by the producer. It is particularly important that the maximum temperature recommended for their use should not be exceeded as this will denature the enzyme and it will fail to function. This process is not reversible.

In general, bacterial amylases function best with an electrolyte, so common salt is often added to the enzyme liquor. The water should also be slightly hard and since it is usual to have very soft water in a wet processing plant a small amount of a soluble magnesium or calcium salt is often added to the liquor to artificially harden the water.

Enzymatic removal of starch is certainly the safest method with regard to fibre damage as it is the only method which acts only on the starch.

Scouring

Scouring is designed to: remove any remaining water-soluble impurities; remove natural fats and waxes contained in the fibre; partially break down any fragments of cotton seed or husk which still remain trapped in the fabric; and provide a general cleaning-up process to remove soiling and staining developed during transport and storage of the goods.

Removal of these impurities greatly improves the absorbency of the fibre, which is essential if dyeing and printing are to be successful.

ALKALI SCOURING

The traditional scouring process for cotton goods involves a treatment with sodium hydroxide solution at quite high temperature. This process depends on a clever use of the chemical properties of the fats and waxes found in the fibre. To understand this we need to look at how soaps are manufactured. Raw materials such as animal fats or vegetable oils are treated with a strong alkali such as sodium or potassium hydroxide and one of the products of this reaction is the sodium or potassium salt of the fat or oil that was present at the start. This salt is the soap and this type of reaction is known as a **sapication**. When alkali acts on the fats and waxes contained in cotton, it produces a soap in exactly the same way. The original fatty impurities are insoluble but the resulting soaps are soluble, so not only is water-insoluble impurity converted to a soluble one but the soluble product formed is a soap which has detergent properties and which can help in the removal of the dirt and other insoluble impurities. In reality, there are several different fats and waxes contained in the fibre so a variety of different soaps will be formed.

The process can be performed under a variety of different conditions. Using a dilute solution of sodium hydroxide (approximately one per cent weight per unit volume (w/v)) at a temperature around 100°C, complete removal of the impurity may take up to ten hours. However, if a more concentrated alkali solution is used (eight per cent w/v) at a temperature of 120°C, the process is completed in as little as a few minutes (two to twenty minutes depending on the amount of impurity present and the area density of the fabric).

It is fairly rare nowadays for the slower low temperature method to be used because it is so time and energy consuming. It is more important to ensure that the impurity remaining in the textile is completely uniformly distributed, rather than that all the impurity is removed. An uneven or patchy distribution of impurity leads to uneven wettability of the goods, resulting in patchy dyeing or printing. However, the amount of impurity remaining in the fibre must still be low. If it is not, problems usually arise later.

Some wet processors still feel that the only way of ensuring an even distribution of impurity is to ensure that it is all removed.

One important aspect of the scouring process is the necessity to exclude air when the process is carried out above 100°C. If this is not done the scouring conditions will result in oxidation of the fibre. It is the combined effects of alkali, air and high temperatures that cause the oxidation.

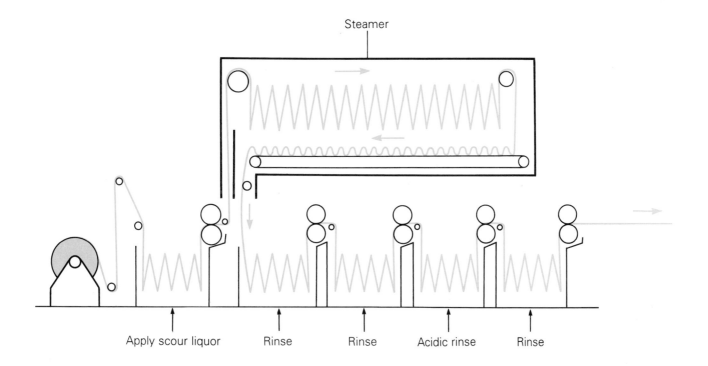

Figure 20.2 Continuous scouring range for cotton.

SOLVENT SCOURING

An alternative to the alkali saponification scouring process is a process referred to as solvent dewaxing or solvent scouring. Although the fats and waxes may not be soluble in water, they are soluble in organic solvents such as trichloroethylene. This compound is the solvent used by dry cleaners.

Knitted fabrics are typically scoured under milder conditions than those used for woven fabrics. The more open structure of knitted fabric enables impurity to be removed more easily than is often the case for a woven fabric. In some cases, say when the fabric is to be dyed under alkaline conditions, scouring may be omitted for a knitted fabric, the alkali present in dyeing being sufficient to saponify fatty impurity.

While this technique might efficiently remove the fats and waxes, it does not assist in the removal of seed fragments and husk. This process was very popular some ten to twenty years ago and was considered by many to be likely to replace conventional alkali scouring, though this has not proved to be the case.

Bleaching

The scouring process for cotton removes the wax and the majority of other impurities, leaving the material in a more absorbent condition, but scouring only partially removes cotton seed and husk, and has little effect on any natural colouring matter that may be present in the fibre.

> Bleaching completes the purification of the fibre by ensuring that seed and husk are fully broken down and removed and that colouring matter is destroyed or at least converted to colourless products.

In all cases, the bleaching of cellulosic fibres is carried out with oxidising agents, usually one of the following: sodium hypochlorite (NaOCl); hydrogen peroxide (H_2O_2); sodium chlorite ($NaClO_2$).

Each one of the above has advantages and disadvantages and it is usual for a wet processor of cotton to opt for the one which best suits the equipment and substrates that are being processed. Some wet processors choose to use two of them. This is normally done by carrying out two bleaching processes with two different bleaches, each of which might be better regarded as acting as a partial bleach so that the full bleaching action is only provided when both have been carried out. The two which are most commonly combined in this way are hydrogen peroxide and sodium hypochlorite. Note that they are not combined together in the same liquor but that two separate bleach liquors are applied one after the other.

SODIUM HYPOCHLORITE NaOCl

The goods are typically soaked in a cold solution of sodium hypochlorite under slightly alkaline conditions (pH 10 to 11) at a concentration of about two to four grams per litre. The goods are stored for several hours at room temperature until bleaching is complete.

It is essential that the impregnated fabric remains alkaline. If the pH falls to 7 (neutral), the sodium hypochlorite converts to hypochlorous acid. In this the cellulose is rapidly degraded and its strength falls dramatically.

> Remember: in the extreme case where the pH falls to below 7, chlorine gas is given off and this must be avoided because of its extreme toxicity.

Other precautions which must be taken are: protection of the impregnated fabric from direct sunlight which will greatly accelerate damage to the fibre by the bleach; neutralisation of the bleached fabric with dilute acid to ensure that the goods are not dried in an alkaline condition; and removal of residual chlorine remaining in the fibre after bleaching by treatment in a solution of a reducing agent such as sodium bisulphite (failure to do this can result in the formation of acid in the fibre during drying of the bleached goods, which then causes rapid fibre degradation).

HYDROGEN PEROXIDE (H_2O_2)

This is now probably the most commonly used bleach for cotton. It is considered to be easier to use than hypochlorite as it does not produce any toxic by-products and the effluent from the process is not as potentially damaging to the environment. However, it is necessary to carry out the process at a high temperature, which is clearly a disadvantage in terms of energy conservation and cost compared to hypochlorite.

A concentration of two to four grams per litre of hydrogen peroxide is used in a liquor adjusted with NaOH (sodium hydroxide) to pH 10 to 11.

One serious drawback with hydrogen peroxide is its relatively poor chemical stability. Both bacteria and small amounts of metals such as iron or copper present in the textile or the processing water can cause rapid catalytic decomposition of the peroxide. When this happens, the oxidising action of the peroxide is greatly speeded up with the production of oxygen which is then lost to the atmosphere. This loss of hydrogen peroxide as oxygen effectively means there is less available to bleach the textile. The oxidising process can be accelerated by catalysts to such an extent that complete oxidation of the fibre occurs and it becomes so weak as to tear or to create holes in the fabric.

To help prevent this effect, sodium silicate and a compound known as ethylene diamine tetraacetic acid (EDTA) are usually added to the bleach liquor. These additives prevent catalysts such as metals from catalysing the peroxide decomposition. To provide further protection, it is important that the machinery is constructed from a corrosion-resistant metal such as a high-grade stainless steel.

At a processing temperature of 95–100°C, the process may take two to three hours. This may be carried out as a batch operation, but if the temperature can be raised to 110–120°C, as for example by using a steamer, the processing time comes down to a few minutes. This would therefore provide a method of continuous bleaching.

This bleaching agent is used hot and under alkaline conditions so its use could be capable of acting both as a bleaching and a scouring treatment. Cotton goods are often treated by this combined scour/bleach technique but usually with the NaOH concentration increased a little above that which would be used for a bleach-only process.

Knitted cotton goods are often not bleached before dyeing or printing but when they are it is often by a combined-scour method using hydrogen peroxide as the bleaching agent.

COMBINED HYPOCHLORITE AND PEROXIDE

When this technique is employed, it is usual to perform the hypochlorite bleach first. The advantage of this is that hypochlorite will kill any bacteria in the fabric and so prevent their action as catalysts on the peroxide bleach which follows.

A bleach using peroxide alone is often considered to be too cream-coloured for goods which are not going to be dyed or printed but are going to be sold as whites. The combined bleach produces a truer neutral white.

Peroxide alone is perfectly adequate for goods which are to be dyed or printed. Remember, one of the reasons for bleaching in such cases is not just to provide a good base colour for dyeing but is also to ensure maximum absorbency and freedom from seed and husk. These will be more important than the base colour for all but the palest of shades.

SODIUM CHLORITE

Although capable of bleaching cellulosic fibres, this product is often not a popular choice. There are certain major problems associated with its use.

> Remember: sodium chlorite produces chlorine dioxide gas (even under the correct conditions of use) which is highly toxic. Machinery must therefore be efficiently ventilated and this adds to its cost.

Many individuals find the smell of sodium chlorite repulsive and even nauseating. It is extremely corrosive to the machinery, even when it is constructed from normal grades of stainless steel, and it is necessary to use machines made with molybdenum or titanium stainless steels to avoid the problem. These are significantly more expensive.

If applied before scouring, this bleach will partially attack the wax and fats and so it may prove possible to employ much milder scouring conditions than would otherwise have been necessary. This is clearly a saving.

Mercerisation

Mercerisation is a preparation process which is only applicable to cellulosic fibres, and cotton in particular. Blends of cotton with other fibres may be mercerised but only if the other fibre is able to withstand the severe conditions that mercerising imposes. Cotton/polyester blends are mercerisable but a cotton/wool blend is not. The process is not a purification process when carried out in the usual way.

> The main purpose of mercerisation is to alter the chemical and physical properties of the fibre. It gives the following cotton properties that the fibre would not otherwise possess. It is more lustrous; stronger; has a greater capacity to accept dye; is more absorbent; has a softer handle; and is more extensible.

The process is named after John Mercer who, in 1884, made a study of the effects of strong caustic liquors (NaOH) on cotton. Mercer's work was followed up by Lowe who demonstrated in 1890 that the lustre of cotton could be greatly increased if the textile was kept under strong tension while it was treated with the sodium hydroxide. In the absence of this tension cotton undergoes a very pronounced shrinkage in strong NaOH.

It has been shown subsequently that the increase in lustre occurs because of two effects.

1. The cotton fibre deconvolutes. In the unmercerised (natural) state, cotton is a fibre with twists in it (convolutions), but after mercerising the convolutions are no longer present. The fibre has a smoother surface which is a better reflector of light, and it therefore looks more lustrous.

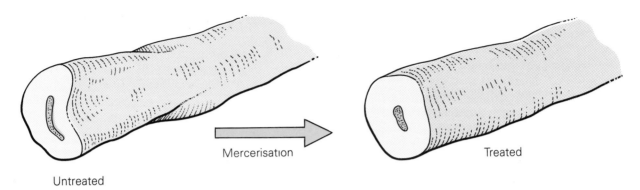

Untreated   Mercerisation   Treated

Figure 20.3 Mercerised and unmercerised cotton fibres.

2. The cross-sectional shape changes. Although cotton has a variety of different cross-sectional shapes in its natural state, on average, we might describe the shape to be 'bean' or 'ear' shaped. After being mercerised, the cross section becomes much rounder, making a more reflective fibre and hence the lustre increases.

It is important to note that the lustre is only achieved if the caustic treatment is accompanied by tension. In the absence of tension, the other useful characteristics will be obtained but lustre will not. With tension all of them are obtained.

DEAD COTTON

It is quite common to dye a 100 per cent cotton fabric and find that the result is unsatisfactory because it looks as if the textile contains some fibres which are very much paler than the rest. If it is a fabric, for example, little bundles (or neps) of these fibres may be seen on the fabric surface and this is normally undesirable. Dyers refer to this as being due to the presence of **dead cotton**, but it is really due to the presence of immature fibre.

Immature fibres are finer than mature fibres, they are more convoluted and contain less internal cellulose. It is their fineness and convolutions that cause them to bundle together during yarn manufacture, forming neps, yet it is their lack of internal structure that causes them to dye paler. Some dyestuffs will exaggerate this speckled appearance, while others will minimise it.

It is impossible to entirely remove immature fibres during yarn manufacture and although a severe scouring treatment can remove a few neps, some will remain in the resulting prepared textile. The problem arises when a particular type of dye is to be used because it is the only type that will give the necessary colour fastness but is also the type that exaggerates the dead cotton. The answer to this problem is to mercerise.

By swelling the immature fibres and giving them a rounder shape and a greater reflectivity, the fact that they are paler is less obvious. The swelling action opens up the internal structure of the fibre and makes it easier for dye to gain access, and the increased reflectivity enables the paler fibres to reflect the colour of their surrounding, more mature, darker neighbours. The overall effect is that they can no longer be seen or at least not as obviously. This effect is actually the combined effects of increased lustre and increased capacity to accept dye.

THE MERCERISATION PROCESS

The substrate is soaked in 18 to 30 per cent NaOH (usually about 22 per cent) at 13–15°C. Time is then allowed for the absorption of the alkali and the NaOH is then washed out with the substrate maintained under tension.

Cotton and its blends can be mercerised in both yarn and piece forms. These are dealt with separately below.

YARN MERCERISATION

There are two methods: mercerisation in hank form using NaOH and continuous cone-to-cone mercerisation using liquid ammonia. These two techniques are shown diagrammatically in Figure 20.4.

HANK MERCERISATION

Hanks are loaded on to the pairs of tension rollers as shown in Figure 20.4. These rollers then start to move apart in a vertical direction to apply tension to the hanks and, at the same time, the sprays release the NaOH of mercerising strength on to the yarn and the squeeze rollers rise to squeeze the hanks and assist the absorption of the alkali. Throughout this caustic impregnation the tension rollers continue to increase the tension on the hanks, and it may reach as much as 20 tonnes total tension by the end of this stage of the process. The tension rollers also rotate alternately clockwise and

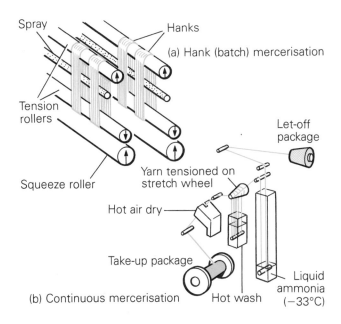

Figure 20.4 Yarn mercerisation.

anticlockwise to ensure an even distribution of the alkali or the wash water and acid which will follow.

The sprays then spray hot water followed by cold water – with the tension still on – in order to remove the caustic. Finally, as the tension is released, acetic acid is sprayed on to neutralise the NaOH.

In modern machines the whole sequence is controlled automatically and it simply requires that hanks be loaded on and off. Typically, machines consist of four pairs of tensioning rollers rather than just two as shown in the Figure 20.4.

CONTINUOUS YARN MERCERISATION

From the Figure 20.4 it is clear that this process is continuous, unlike hank mercerisation which is a batch operation.

The stretch wheel is a device which causes the yarn to be held back slightly and this mean that the take-up package is therefore winding on yarn somewhat faster than it is leaving the let-off package. This results in a stretch being applied of about five per cent and this, of course, provides the necessary tension for mercerisation to be effective.

It takes about one second for the journey through the process, and the output is about 200 metres of yarn per minute. Figure 20.4 shows just one treatment station and actual machines consist of many repeats of what is shown in the diagram, arranged side by side.

Continuous mercerisation by a process of this type is considered to produce a more uniform treatment than hank mercerisation, though the latter is more economical for small production lots.

WOVEN FABRIC MERCERISATION

Again there are two types of process available. In this case, however, they both utilise NaOH as the alkali. They differ essentially only in the way that the fabric is tensioned. The two types are the chain, or English, merceriser and the chainless merceriser. These two processes are shown diagrammatically in Figure 20.5.

THE CHAIN MERCERISING PROCESS

The fabric is immersed (dipped) twice and squeezed (nipped) twice in a machine known as a double-dip/double-nip pad mangle. This, coupled with the air passage over cylinders, ensures good absorption of the caustic. The fabric is maintained under tension by a series of clips which grip the selvedges and at the same time the fabric passes under water sprays to wash the alkali out again.

The fabric would shrink in width if the selvedges were not gripped. The tension exists because the clips are holding the fabric at around its loomstate width. As you might expect, it requires considerable force to do this and the clips are designed to keep a very firm hold on the fabric selvedges.

THE CHAINLESS PROCESS

In Figure 20.5 you will see that there is no pad mangle for the application of the NaOH. Instead of allowing the cloth to shrink and then creating tension by pulling the width out again, this machine keeps continuous tension on the fabric right from the first contact with the caustic through to the end of the rinsing stage.

To achieve this, the mangle is replaced with impregnation tanks through which the cloth passes in contact with bowed rollers. These rollers are also used at the rinsing stage to maintain the tension. The curvature of these rollers results in a pull on the fabric in the direction of its selvedges but at the same time the cloth will be attempting to shrink in width as a result of the swelling action of the alkali. There is, therefore, an outward pull due to the curvature and an inward pull due to the caustic and the result is exactly what is wanted, namely, considerable tension on the cloth.

SLACK MERCERISING

In the classic mercerising process that has been described so far (either for yarn or piece), it is vital to keep up the tension during the rinsing stage. The tension must be maintained on the goods until the concentration of alkali in the fibre is quite low. In the case of NaOH mercerisation, the tension

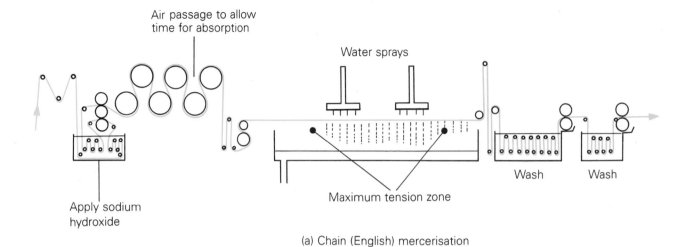

Figure 20.5 Fabric mercerisation.

must remain until the concentration in the fibre falls below 4.5 per cent. If this is not done, not all the effects of the process will be obtained. There will not be any increase in lustre nor any significant increase in strength. There will, however, be an increase in the absorbency and uptake of dyes. If only these effects are required, the process may be carried out with a lower caustic concentration and less or no tension. This is then usually referred to as **slack mercerisation** or **causticisation**.

KNITTED FABRIC MERCERISATION

Mercerisation involves placing the textile under tension. This can be done quite easily for a woven fabric, but it is much more difficult to apply the required amount of tension to a knitted fabric without distorting the fabric structure in a serious and perhaps irrecoverable way. This is not to say that knitted piece

goods cannot be mercerised but that the techniques for doing so are very specialised and difficult to carry out. Typically, the process would be carried out with the fabric in tubular form on machinery specially designed for the purpose, and sodium hydroxide is used as described above. The process is only performed to a limited extent.

Preparation of wool textiles

Cropping

Wool fabrics and wool-rich blends are not normally singed to remove surface hair. The problem with protein fibres is that when they burn they form a hard, black cinder-like residue which is much more difficult to remove from the fabric

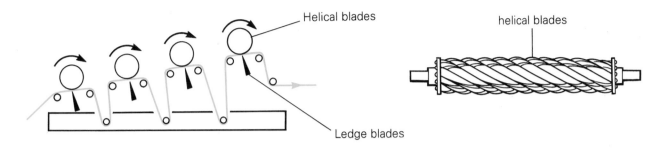

Figure 20.6 Cropping.

surface than the soft, pale dusty ash obtained with cellulosic fibres.

The alternative method for removing surface hair on wool fabrics is to take it off by some mechanical method. The technique used is **cropping**, also referred to as shearing.

A cropping machine is fitted with a series of helical blades which rotate at very high speed. The fabric passes beneath these blades and the hair is removed by the cutting action created between the rotary blade and the stationary ledger blade beneath the fabric.

Several sets of these blades are arranged in series within the cropping machine so that the hair is not taken off in a single pass but after being acted on by each of the sets of blades.

The process is much slower than singeing and is more commonly used as a finishing technique where it can be used to produce a controlled removal of hair from a fabric. Although slow, cropping enables a controlled removal of hair (singeing cannot produce a hairy surface of a defined pile height). Any fibre type might therefore be cropped as a finishing process even if it was singed in preparation processes. Wool and other hair fibres would normally be cropped before dyeing or printing and could, of course, be cropped again afterwards in finishing.

Scouring

Wool is scoured in loose stock, yarn and piece forms not just so that it can be dyed or printed in these forms, as would be the case if we were considering cotton, but also so that impurity can be removed which would hinder the next manufacturing stage. It is very difficult to construct a yarn from raw wool unless the natural impurities of the raw loose fibre are removed, and it might prove necessary to remove added impurities from the yarn (such as oil applied before carding) prior to weaving or knitting it or from the fabric prior to dyeing or printing it. Some examples of the

natural impurities found in wool are wool grease (lanolin), suint (sweat), vegetable matter, parasites, branding fliuds, pesticides and veterinary products.

Yarn or fabric may contain impurities which have been added to improve textile processing even though the natural impurity will have been removed prior to the yarn or fabric stages. Added impurities include: spinning lubricants and other aids such as anti-static agents; and oils and/or waxes used to lubricate the yarn during weaving or knitting.

Wool warps are not sized. There is consequently no need for the desizing processes required in the preparation of cellulosic and man-made fibre woven fabrics.

Because of the need to scour wool in its raw state to make it possible to spin, it follows that all wool will be scoured at least once, even if the eventual end-product is not going to be dyed or printed. Suppose we have the situation in which a wool yarn is to be dyed and then woven to produce a colour-woven fabric. A sequence of events will occur along the lines of that shown in Figure 20.7.

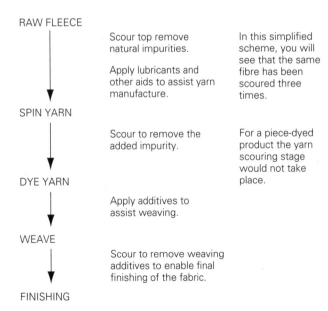

Figure 20.7 Possible processing stages for a colour-woven wool fabric.

SCOURING OF LOOSE WOOL

The technique consists of passing the wool through a series of several long narrow tanks containing soap or nonionic synthetic detergent and sodium carbonate (soda ash) at 45–55°C. This is often referred to as a soap and soda scour. The tanks are referred to as bowls and the series of them together as a scouring set. In the traditional type of scouring set, the fibre passes through the bowls propelled by a slight flow of liquor and by the action of harrows. Figure 20.8 shows one bowl of a traditional scouring set.

One of the problems with this traditional approach is that the fibre may tangle, which can lead to fibre breakage during subsequent carding. This has influenced the development of alternative types of machine, examples of which are shown in Figure 20.9.

This method of removing the wool grease and the dirt trapped in it depends on the ability of the detergent to emulsify the grease and so is known as **emulsion scouring**. It does not chemically alter the grease, unlike the action of NaOH on cotton wax which, of course, chemically converts it to a soluble soap.

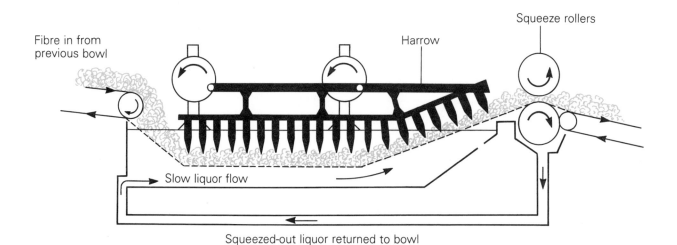

Figure 20.8 Raw wool scouring bowl.

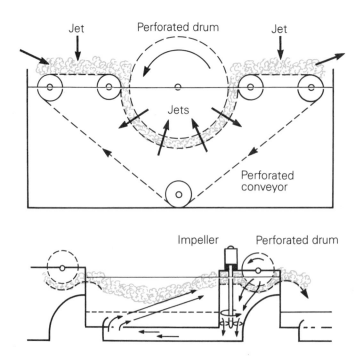

Figure 20.9 Alternatives to the traditional scouring bowl.

In stage 1 of Figure 20.10, detergent molecules enter the grease layer leaving their head groups out and in the water to which they are attracted. In stage 2, the grease has left the fibre surface, partly due to the heat of the process (scouring is normally done at 40–60°C and the grease melts at around 50°C) and also by the stirring action of the machine. It is then held in the form of droplets surrounded by molecules of detergent. Because the head groups repel each other, the droplets are prevented from recombining and are said to be emulsified. Note that the detergent molecules are still arranged at the fibre surface so the droplets are also prevented from redepositing onto the fibre by the same force of repulsion.

WOOL YARN SCOURING

Worsted spun yarns usually contain about three per cent of combing oil plus some general dirt acquired during processing. If it is to be dyed in package form the yarn can be scoured in a synthetic detergent and sodium carbonate in a conventional package dyeing machine (which dyes yarn on cone or cheese). If the yarn is to be dyed in hank form it can be scoured in the hank dyeing machine, but a continuous-tape scouring machine is sometimes used. These are arranged in trains like loose wool machines and are used in a very similar way. The basic difference between tape scouring machines and loose wool scouring sets is the manner in which the textile is transported through the process (see Figure 20.11).

With woollen spun yarns, the amount of lubricant used is often much greater (5–15 per cent). This may be a synthetic lubricant or the more traditional olein (crude oleic acid) plus a little mineral oil. A continuous-tape machine could again be used but the detergent is often omitted and just the sodium carbonate used. This is because the action of the carbonate (alkaline) on oleic acid is to form a soap by saponification.

PIECE SCOURING

Wool piece goods are generally scoured in rope form in relatively small batches – only a few pieces at a time. Continuous machinery is available but in most markets the batch sizes are too small to make continuous methods

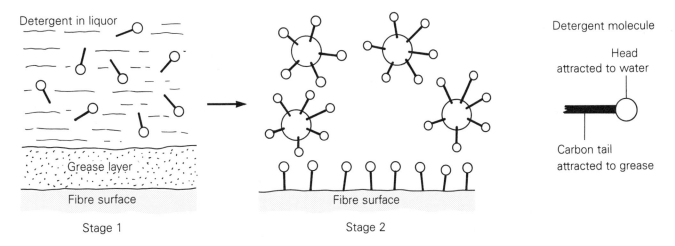

Figure 20.10 Emulsion scouring.

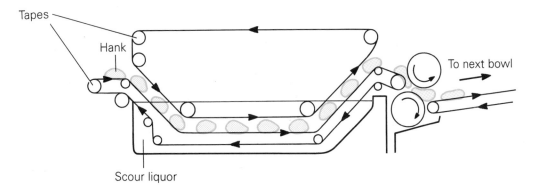

Figure 20.11 Wool tape scouring machine.

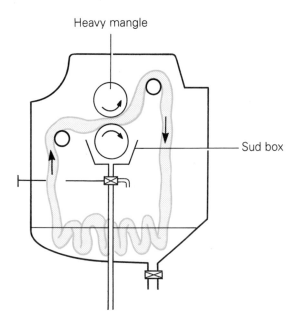

Heavy mangle

Sud box

Figure 20.12 **Dolly scouring machine.**

feasible. Batch scouring of wool piece goods in rope form is carried out in a dolly scouring machine (see Figure 20.12). One to four pieces are run side by side, each piece sewn into a continuous loop.

During scouring, the liquor squeezed out by the mangle can be returned from the sud box to the bottom of the machine. During rinsing, it can run to waste via the drain. Detergent and alkali are used, so this is again an example of an emulsion scour.

Carbonising process

> **Carbonising** is a chemical treatment of wool with strong acid designed to remove any remaining vegetable impurity.

Carbonising is normally carried out either at the loose wool stage or on the fabric. The action of the acid is to hydrolyse the vegetable matter to a dark, brittle hydrocellulose which can be removed mechanically by crushing it between rollers and then dusting the debris out of the wool in a rotating cage. It can be removed from piece goods by passing the fabric between flanged rollers.

The goods are impregnated with five to six per cent hydrochloric or sulphuric acid or a salt which will produce strong acid when the goods are dried, for example aluminium or magnesium chloride. After application of the acid or the acid salt, the fibre is dried and baked and it is at this point that the hydrolysis occurs.

As a final step in the carbonising process, the goods must be neutralised and rinsed.

Wool finds its way back into the textile industry when it is recovered from old clothing or from off cuts of the clothing industry. These rags are shredded and reduced back to fibre, but they often contain some cellulosic fibre such as from cotton sewing threads. Carbonising of the wool rags can be used to remove this cellulosic fibre contamination.

Wool bleaching

There are some important differences between the methods used for bleaching wool and the methods already described for cotton.

> Only oxidising agents are used to bleach cotton. With wool, it is possible to use reducing agents. Cotton is usually bleached before dyeing or printing, irrespective of the shade that it will eventually be dyed and, of course, when the intended end-use calls for white. Wool is also bleached for a white end-use but, when dyed, it is normally only bleached if the intended dyed shade is particularly bright and/or pale.

Bleaching using reducing agents

The bleaching action of the reducing agents used for bleaching wool is probably due to the action of bisulphite ions (HSO_3^-). In practice, there are basically two methods: either by exposing the wool to sulphur dioxide gas (SO_2); or by treating the wool in a liquor containing reducing agents, such as sodium bisulphite ($NaHSO_3$), sodium dithionite ($Na_2S_2O_4$), sodium metabisulphite ($Na_2S_2O_5$), sodium or zinc formaldehyde-sulphoxylate ($NaHSO_2CH_2O$ or $Zn(HSO_2CH_2O)_2$).

The use of reducing agents for the bleaching of wool is relatively limited. The principal reasons for this are because the use of sulphur dioxide gas often results in an unlevel appearance and the whiteness achieved with reducing agents is not permanent (the original colour of the fibre tends to return on exposure to air, especially when the wool is exposed to strong sunlight). This latter effect is due to an oxidation process which reverses the original reducing action.

BLEACHING USING OXIDISING AGENTS

Only one oxidising agent is normally used, namely hydrogen peroxide. There are good reasons for this. Sodium hypochlorite, widely used for bleaching cellulosic fibres, turns wool yellowish, while hypochlorite has a degrading effect on wool, causing significant decomposition of the fibre protein. Sodium chlorite does not have any advantages over hydrogen peroxide and has all the disadvantages discussed in the section devoted to bleaching cotton. Furthermore, it tends to produce white with a pinkish tone.

Compared to the use of reduction bleaches, hydrogen peroxide is more expensive, but the white it produces is permanent and has the added advantage that it will bleach even naturally black or brown wools which reducing bleaches will not.

Typically, cotton would be bleached with H_2O_2 at a pH of 10 to 11, but this is too high for wool. A pH of 8.5 to 9 is about as high as can be permitted without serious fibre damage being the result.

With cotton, the pH would be brought to 10 to 11 using NaOH and/or Na_2CO_3, but fine adjustments of pH with these alkalis is difficult. The maintenance of a constant pH during bleaching is vital for wool and it would therefore be better if the liquor were buffered (a pH buffer is a chemical that helps maintain the pH level). Fortunately, sodium silicate, which is added to provide the liquor with some stability against the catalysing action of metals that may be present (see peroxide bleaching of cotton) also has the necessary buffering ability.

Certain phosphate compounds are also able to function in this dual way. There are several commercial stabilising products available on the market which are mixtures of such phosphates.

Another difference between the use of hydrogen peroxide on cotton and wool is the temperature of the process. For cotton, 80–90°C would be typical, but for wool 40–50°C is used.

After bleaching, the goods are neutralised in acetic (ethanoic) acid to ensure that the wool is not left in an alkaline condition.

BLEACHING WITH HYDROGEN PEROXIDE UNDER ACID CONDITIONS

If it were possible to use H_2O_2 under acid conditions, this would be much less likely to cause fibre damage. This is possible but it is a very slow process if carried out in a conventional way because H_2O_2 is chemically very stable under acid conditions and therefore only functions very slowly as an oxidiser.

One technique used is to immerse the wool in a liquor and the unusual thing is that the goods are then dried. The bleaching action will continue over a period of about 48 hours or so in this dry state. It must be remembered that wool has a high moisture regain and will therefore contain moisture even when it feels dry.

This technique can be applied in the last bowl of a raw wool scouring set so that the bleaching process continues in the dry state during carding and spinning of the fibre.

A further advantage of hydrogen peroxide under acid conditions is that it can be used to bleach wool fabrics containing dyed and undyed wools. If a fabric is constructed with undyed yarns and some yarns which have been dyed with acid dyes, the undyed yarns can be bleached to white without loss of dye from the dyed fibre.

It is also claimed that the bleaching of wool under acid conditions produces a softer handle than the alkaline process.

Felting and milling

FELTING

The ability to felt is a characteristic of the hair fibres. No other fibres are able to do it and wool stands out, even among the hair fibres, as one with a marked tendency to felt.

> Felting is the tendency of the fibres to form matted entanglements such that a woven fabric, for example, can become so matted that the warp and weft yarns are no longer visible. The result is a fabric which is apparently composed entirely of an entangled web of fibres and the fabric is referred to as a felt.

This tendency to felt is both a benefit and a problem depending on what it is intended to produce. By deliberately inducing felting, the air spaces between fibres within the fabric get smaller. It becomes more difficult for air to pass through the fabric and, since air is a good thermal insulator, fabric which has smaller air spaces will be warmer to wear than fabric with bigger spaces (assuming that there is the same amount of fibre in each case). Felted fabric has a different appearance to unfelted and induced felting may therefore be carried out for purely design considerations.

Felting is always accompanied by shrinkage of the fabric because the fibres move closer together. If shrinkage occurs due to felting that was not intended, it will alter the appearance of the article and also reduce its size. This can be the case, for example, when wool articles are laundered under conditions which are too severe; the wool felts in a way that is undesirable.

All hair fibres have a scaly surface and wool especially so. Two other fibre characteristics are needed before we have the basis for a theory to explain the felting process. These are high fibre elasticity and high crimp.

There have been many attempts to explain felting behaviour, not all of them successful and there are still aspects of it that are not clear. It seems probable that the precise explanation is different when felting occurs under different conditions but one explanation is given here.

The cuticle scales on wool fibres overlap each other and do so in a relatively regular manner. These overlaps point in the same direction, rather like the tiles on a roof. Two fibres are located closely alongside each other as shown in Figure 20.13.

Suppose fibre A and fibre B were actually touching rather than slightly separated as they are drawn and the attempt was made to slide them along each other. It would be easier to slide fibre A to the right and fibre B to the left than it would be in the opposite directions. Both fibres would move easier in their root directions than in their tip directions.

It is clear that moving in the tip direction would be more difficult because the scale overlaps of one fibre would obstruct the movement of the other fibre. It is expected that wool fibres contained within a fabric will find it easier to move in the direction of their root ends, provided that there is some force at work causing them to move. If they have moved in their root directions they will become locked in a new location, because to move back again would involve them moving against the overlaps of the scales. The scales are able to function as ratchets, allowing movement of the fibre in the root direction and restricting it in the tip direction.

The fibre crimp is the waviness of the fibre and it is reasonable to expect that the more crimped the fibre, the greater will be its ability to form entangled structures. Straighter fibres would have a greater ability to slide out of a tangle. The fibre elasticity is a different matter. Elasticity influences the ability of tangles, once formed, to join up and so form larger tangles.

Wool has an elastic recovery of 1.0 at 35 per cent extension in water at 20°C. Under these conditions, it is perfectly elastic. Consider the diagrams in Figure 20.14. They represent the

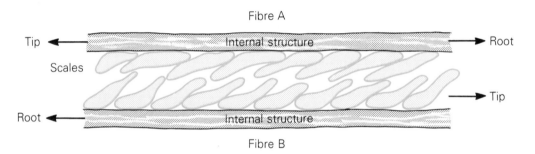

Figure 20.13 Wool fibres side by side.

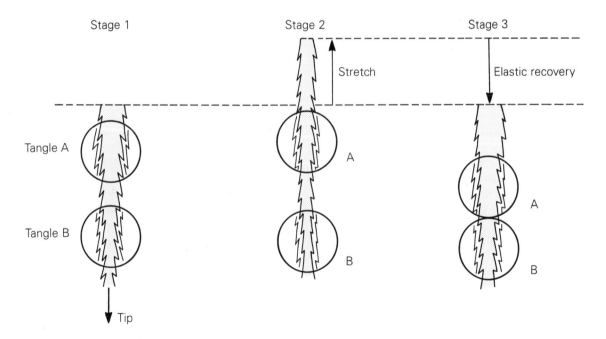

Figure 20.14 Fibre elasticity and the felting process.

ability of a wool fibre which connects two tangles to pull them closer together as a result of the connecting fibres' elasticity.

In Figure 20.14, the connecting fibre can pass through tangle A in which we imagine it is only loosely held. It can only pass in the root direction due to the locking of scales. We imagine it to be completely locked in tangle B and incapable of moving through it. Stage 1 represents the starting point. Stage 2 shows that as a result of agitation of the fabric in which these two tangles exist, the connecting fibre has become stretched and has passed further through tangle A in its root direction. In stage 3 the stretching force has now been removed temporarily so the connecting fibre springs back because of its excellent elasticity. It cannot travel back through tangle A because of the scale obstruction, so tangle A is pulled closer to tangle B.

This process can be repeated many times until the two tangles combine into one. Tangle A could have been moved closer to tangle B for a different reason. If a compression force (squeezing force) is operating on the two tangles as opposed to the stretching force described above, it is possible for tangle A to be pushed along the connecting fibre in the direction of tangle B. Of course, compression would not push B along the fibre towards A because this would require that B should move against the obstruction of the scales in the connecting fibre.

Forces of either stretch or compression will therefore result in increased entanglement of the fibres.

MILLING

> **Milling** is the process of deliberately felting wool goods to achieve the effects of felting.

A traditional machine used for the performance of this process on piece goods is the one shown in Figure 20.15.

The cloth is in rope form and it passes continually around the machine until the desired degree of felting is achieved. The fabric passes through the spout which guides it into the mangle which, in turn, forces it into the stuffing box. The fabric undergoes some degree of stretch as it rises up to the spout and in the stuffing box it undergoes compression.

The top of the stuffing box is hinged and may have different amounts of pressure applied to it. This determines the resistance that the box places on the cloth and so the amount of compression introduced to it.

The fabric is maintained in a wet condition by being repeatedly wetted in the bottom of the machine. The liquor usually contains soap which acts as a lubricant to encourage fibre movement within the fabric.

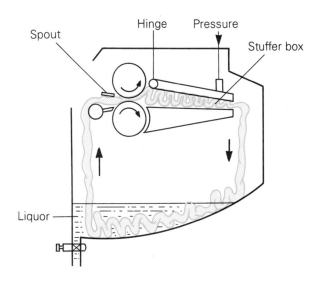

Figure 20.15   A rotary milling machine.

This machine looks similar to a wool scouring dolly (the dolly does not have a stuffing box but is of very similar construction). It is possible, because of this similarity of design, to carry out a combined scouring and milling process in the milling machine. The dolly machine provides a means of scouring fabric which is required not to felt.

The machine showed in Figure 20.15 is typical of the traditional rotary milling machine. More modern designs are much the same except that the design of the stuffing box is usually more sophisticated, as shown in Figure 20.16.

Modern machines also have controls for such things as monitoring the cloth length (as milling proceeds, the fabric gets shorter) and stopping the process when a preset length is reached. This length will therefore correspond to a given degree of felting. The machine can stop at a piece-to-piece sewing for ease of unloading, though the sewings can be hard to find after felting has occurred. The fabric speed, liquor temperature and pH, and the mangle and stuffing box pressures can all be controlled.

MILLING OTHER FORMS OF WOOL

If it is required to mill wool in a form other than piece goods like socks or jumpers, the rotary milling machine will obviously not be suitable. These items are now milled in machines closely resembling large versions of the domestic front-loading washing machine. Felting occurs because of the stretch and compression induced when the individual items collide with each other and the walls of the rotating drum that they are in. These machines are not specifically designed for milling nor is it their only use. They may be

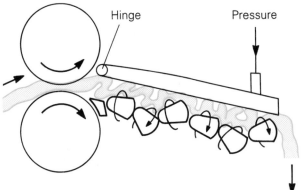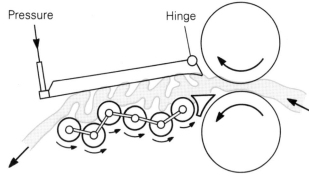

Figure 20.16 Alternative milling methods.

used as scouring, dyeing or even finishing machines for knitwear and are consequently not confined solely to the processing of wool; they are able to perform these processes on a variety of different fibre types. Only with wool are they able to function as milling machines.

Setting of wool

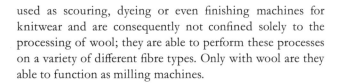

After the scouring process has been carried out on wool fabrics, the appearance and behaviour of some fabrics is unsatisfactory due to distortions of the structure, such as waviness (**cockling**) of the selvedges brought about by uneven stretching and compression forces introduced by the scouring machine. This distortion can be avoided by setting the cloth. Setting is achieved by subjecting the fabric to the combined effects of heat, moisture and pressure.

Remember, wool is a hair fibre and we are all familiar with the idea of setting hair fibres. We know that our own hair can be set into a particular position by wetting it and then drying it while it is held in the position we want. A wool fabric which is creased or cockled can be pressed flat while it is warm and wet and it will then retain the flattened, smoothed-out appearance.

However, we also know that when we set a wave in our own hair using only a wetting, shaping and drying process, the wave will come out again after a while and especially so if the hair is wetted again. By treating the hair chemically after shaping, however, it can be 'permanently' waved. The comparison of human hairdressing with wool setting is a close one. There are chemical methods for treating wool which will provide it with permanent freedom from distortion and shrinkage or stretch, but these are often carried out as finishing processes after dyeing. The setting processes carried out in the preparation of the fabric are of the non-permanent kind and are intended to ensure that the fabric goes forward into subsequent processes in an undistorted form.

There are essentially two techniques for setting a wool fabric during its preparation stages, known as **crabbing** and **blowing**.

CRABBING

The fabric is wound on to a roller under tension after first passing through a trough of hot water. A second roller presses down on the roll of cloth to apply the necessary smoothing pressure.

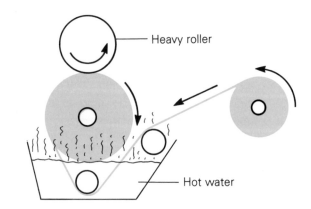

Figure 20.17 The crabbing machine.

BLOWING

The fabric is wound under tension on to a hollow perforated cylinder through which steam is then blown for one to three minutes.

The setting effect is at its maximum when the fabric pH is about 9 so it may be necessary to adjust this by a suitable wet treatment prior to setting. The set achieved will remain in the textile, provided it is never wetted again at a temperature equal to or higher than that at which it was introduced.

Preparation of man-made fibre textiles

The amount of preparation required on a man-made fibre product is usually considerably less than that necessary for the natural fibres such as cotton or wool. The main reason for this, of course, is that they contain far less impurity. Industry has no control over the natural impurities present in natural fibres, but if the fibre is a product of a process devised by people, it seems only sensible to produce it in a form which is as pure as possible in the first place.

A man-made fibre may be of high purity when it first enters the textile processing industry but it then begins to acquire impurities. The fibre may have lubricants or anti-static agents added to assist in spinning the yarn or knitting a fabric. It may have size added to the warp yarns if it is woven. These will normally have to be removed just as they would from a natural fibre, but at least there will not be the additional burden of natural impurities.

Desizing and scouring

If a starch size is present, an enzyme desizing process will be satisfactory and will be performed in much the same way that it would on, say, a cotton fabric. It is more likely, however, that a woven fabric composed of nylon, polyester or acrylic will have been sized with a water-soluble size. In such cases, a mild scour in a non-ionic synthetic detergent, perhaps with the addition of a little alkali at about 50–60°C followed by very thorough rinsing, is usually adequate to remove the size, any other lubricants and general dirt. A knitted fabric would not contain size but the same scouring process is likely to be carried out to remove the lubricants and dirt.

Again, if we are going to make a fibre, it seems not only sensible to make one free from impurity but also one of a good standard of whiteness.

> It is generally unnecessary to bleach the man-made fibre before dyeing or printing it. Only if the textile is used in an end-use requiring it to be white and of a very high standard of whiteness would bleaching be contemplated.

Setting processes

Some of the man-made fibres have the properties of thermoplastics, that is when they are heated they soften and can be moulded. Their tendency, in the absence of any tension preventing it, will be to shrink when they reach the temperature at which they soften. Man-made fibres which behave in this way are synthetics and modified regenerated cellulose fibres. This property enables us to have a very effective setting process for these fibre types.

> A fabric can be exposed to dry heat or steam at a temperature above the softening temperature while being held flat and to a particular width. If we continue to hold the width fixed while the fabric cools, the fabric will be very resistant to stretch or shrink in the width at any subsequent stage of processing so long as the setting temperature is not reached or closely approached. This is known as **heat setting**.

The set conferred on these fibres has greater permanency than the set on wool due to crabbing or blowing processes.

Flourescent brightening agents

If a brilliant white finish is required in a textile, the bleaching methods described so far in previous sections will be insufficient to achieve the effect. These methods rely upon the chemical degradation of impurities that are themselves coloured and reducing the whiteness of the textile. Once they have been destroyed, no further improvement in whiteness is possible.

Some means is needed to 'add' whiteness to the textile to enhance it to a level above that which is achieved by bleaching and this can be done by using substances referred to as **fluorescent brightening agents** (FBAs). These can be thought of as being white dyestuffs with the ability to fluoresce.

> Fluorescence is the ability of a substance to absorb radiation (in this case, light) and to re-radiate it at a longer wavelength.

The FBA which has been applied to the textile has the ability to absorb white light plus the additional characteristic of being able to convert any ultra-violet radiation present into visible light at the blue end of the visible spectrum.

The human eye cannot detect the ultraviolet, so when the FBA converts ultraviolet into visible light, there will apparently be more light which the eye can detect coming from the textile than there is detectable light shining on it. The sensation this produces is that the textile looks considerably whiter.

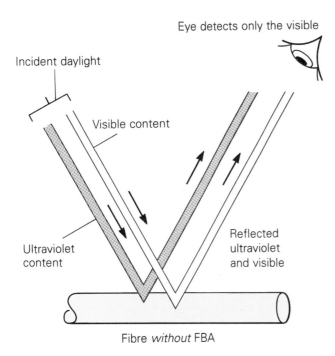
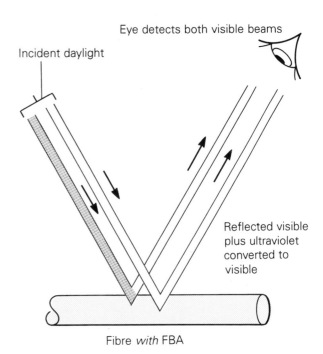

Figure 20.18 Fluorescent brightening agent.

Fluorescent brightening agents are available for all the major fibre types. They are applied by methods very similar to dyeing techniques and can usually be added to a bleaching liquor so that destruction of coloured impurity and enhanced whiteness happen simultaneously.

Fibre damage

The processes carried out to prepare textiles for subsequent wet processes such as coloration are potentially very damaging to the fibre if they are not adequately controlled. Some of the processes such as bleaching cannot be carried out at all without some adverse effect on the fibre occurring. We clearly must have ways of determining the extent to which a fibre has been damaged by the processing it has received and must know if the amount of damage is within limits that can be tolerated. When we speak of fibre damage, we should not assume that we are only interested in changes which are so serious as to ruin the fibre.

Detection of damage

Chemical and physical damage to textile fibres can be detected by using a combination of staining and microscopy. A sample of the suspect fibre is treated with a stain under specified conditions and then observed under the microscope. Areas of damage appear coloured and there are several stains available. The one used depends on the nature of the suspected damage and the type of fibre. Interpretation of the results requires skill and experience.

DETECTION OF DAMAGE TO COTTON

Samples of damaged fibre are treated with a solution of Methylene Blue dye under different conditions. Staining of the fibres indicates acid damage or oxidation damage, depending on the conditions of the test.

A sample of fibre is treated with a sodium hydroxide solution and then placed in a solution of Congo Red dye. The sample is mounted in sodium hydroxide solution for microscopical examination. The sodium hydroxide swells the fibres, making the damaged areas more accessible to the dye. Staining of the fibres in discrete areas indicates damage caused by mechanical means, heat, oxidation, acid or mildew, depending on the conditions of the initial treatment of the sample in the test.

DETECTION OF DAMAGE TO WOOL

A small sample of fibres is mounted in acidified Methylene Blue dye solution and heated. The slide is then observed under the microscope. Staining of the fibres indicates chemical damage by acid, alkali, chlorine or oxidation. The precise cause of the damage cannot be determined.

A sample of fibres is purified, neutralised and treated with a weak acid. The sample is then treated with a solution of Kiton Red G dye and observed under the microscope. Specific areas of staining indicate chemical damage by chlorine.

Quantitative estimation of damage

An estimate of the amount of chemical damage which has occurred to the fibres can be determined in various ways depending on the type of fibre.

METHODS BASED ON VISCOSITY MEASUREMENTS

Fibres are made from high molecular mass polymers. If a polymer is dissolved in a suitable solvent it produces a solution with a very high viscosity compared with that of the solvent (the viscosity of the solution depends on various factors which must be standardised in a test otherwise they will affect the results). If the polymer has been chemically damaged, a reduction in molecular mass may occur which results in a reduction in the viscosity of the polymer solution. The amount of reduction depends on the amount of chemical damage. If the viscosity of a solution of damaged fibre is measured and compared with that of a solution of undamaged fibre, a measure of the amount of damage can be obtained. Mechanical damage does not cause any reduction in molecular mass, so viscosity methods can be used to distinguish between chemical and mechanical damage.

Synthetic fibres: a sample of fibres is dissolved in a suitable solvent to give a solution of standard concentration. The viscosity of this solution is determined using an Ostwald **viscometer**.

The rate at which the solution flows is proportional to the viscosity. The time taken for a given volume to flow through the capillary tube is measured. This is carried out by filling the top reservoir and measuring the time taken for the meniscus to fall between the two timing marks as the solution flows through the capillary tube into the lower reservoir. This procedure is then repeated using pure solvent.

The relative viscosity is calculated as follows:

$$\text{relative viscosity} = \frac{\text{viscosity of solution}}{\text{viscosity of solvent}}$$
$$= \frac{\text{time of flow of solution}}{\text{time flow of solvent}}$$

The relative viscosity will have a value greater than one.

The relative viscosity of the sample can be compared with the relative viscosity of a sample of undamaged fibre (if

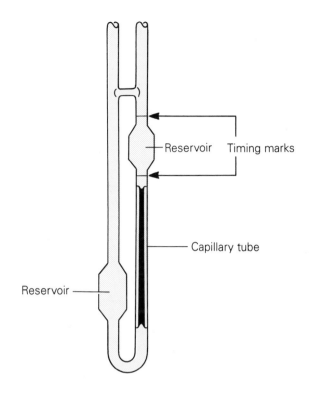

Figure 20.19 Ostwald viscometer.

available). A low value indicates chemical damage. The nearer the value is to one, the greater the damage.

Cellulosic fibres: traditionally, chemical damage to cellulosic fibres is estimated using fluidity measurements. Fluidity is the opposite of viscosity, so fluidity measurement is another form of viscosity measurement.

$$\text{Fluidity} \propto \frac{1}{\text{viscosity}}$$

A sample of fibres is dissolved in cuprammonium hydroxide solvent to give a solution of standard concentration. The solvent is unstable so various precautions have to be taken during preparation of the solution. The solution is prepared in the viscometer to exclude any air which may cause chemical damage by oxidation.

The fluidity (1/viscosity) is determined using a Shirley viscometer (Figure 20.20).

The principle of this viscometer is the same as the viscometer used with synthetic fibres. The time taken for a given volume to flow through a capillary tube is measured. This is carried out by having the reservoir full of solution and then measuring the time taken for the meniscus to fall from the top to the bottom, timing marks as the solution flows out through the capillary tube.

Calculation of the result is different to that with synthetic fibres. The fluidity is calculated from:

$$\text{fluidity} = \frac{\text{viscometer calibration constant}}{\text{time of flow (in seconds)}}$$

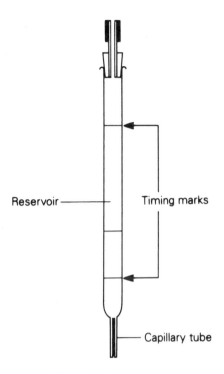

Reservoir — — Timing marks

— Capillary tube

Figure 20.20 Shirley viscometer.

The fluidity value of the sample is compared with that of undamaged cellulose which is known from experience. The higher the value, the greater the chemical damage.

CHECK YOUR UNDERSTANDING

● Preparation processes remove natural and added impurities from the textile substrate.

● A typical preparation sequence for cotton substrates would be singe, desize, scour, bleach and mercerise.

● Singeing removes surface hairs to give a clear rather than frosty appearance to dyed fabrics, better pattern definition to printed fabrics, to show woven structure and remove any pills from the fabric surface.

● Desizing can be carried out by bacteria, acids, oxidising agents or enzymes. Enzymes are considered the safest as they only act on the starch itself.

● Scouring removes water-soluble impurities, waxes and fats and soiling due to transport. It partially removes vegetable matter.

● Bleaching converts natural colorants to colourless products and helps break down any remaining vegetable matter. One or two of sodium hypochlorite, hydrogen peroxide and sodium chlorite are commonly used.

● Mercerisation swells cellulosic fibres, making the fibre more lustrous, stronger, giving it a greater capacity to accept dye, more absorbency, a softer handle and making it more extensible. Mercerisation can improve the appearance of

cotton fabric with a high per centage of immature fibres by the increased lustre and dye acceptance.

● Wool fabrics are cropped to remove surface hairs.

● Scouring of wool can occur at three stages: loose stock, yarn or piece. Loose stock is scoured to enable successful spinning.

● Carbonising is treating the wool with a strong acid to remove remaining vegetable impurity and is carried out on loose stock or piece.

● Felting is the ability of hair fibres, particularly wool, to matt into an entangled mess. It is deliberately done in the milling process, using hot water, detergent and agitation.

● Wool fabrics are given a temporary set during either crabbing (passing the fabric through hot water) or blowing (using steam).

● Man-made substrates are very rarely bleached.

● Heat setting can stabilise fabric dimensions but can only be carried out on thermoplastic fibres.

● Flourescent brightening agents are used to convert ultraviolet light into visible light to make the substrate appear brighter.

● Fibre damage during wet processing should be assessed. Certain dyes can be applied and the fibres viewed under a microscope to detect damage. Fibre viscosity measurements can give an idea of the extent of the fibre damage and also show if it is chemical or mechanical in origin.

REVISION EXERCISES AND QUESTIONS

1 Why is it necessary to remove impurities from a substrate?
2 Why are wool fabrics not singed?
3 What process is necessary immediately following singeing?
4 Why do knitted fabrics not need the desizing operation?
5 Why must care be taken in controlling the temperature during enzymatic desizing?
6 How does traditional alkali scouring work in principle?
7 Why must the fabric remain alkaline during bleaching with sodium hypochlorite?
8 Why must the substrate be under tension while mercerising?
9 How does mercerisation improve the appearance of cotton cloth with a high level of immature fibre present?
10 What is the advantage to removing surface hair by cropping rather than singeing?
11 Why is wool yarn sometimes scoured, rather than scouring in piece form?
12 When is wool felting a problem?
13 Why is it sometimes necessary to set wool fabrics in the preparation stages?
14 What tells the wet processor whether the damage is chemical or mechanical?

Coloration processes

Introduction

Textiles are usually coloured to make them attractive or for functional reasons, for example military camouflage and florescent jackets for road repair workers. Life would be more hazardous and certainly dull if textiles were only used in their natural colours.

There are two ways of adding colour to a textile substrate – **printing** or **dyeing**. Printing adds colour to the surface in discrete places, whereas dyeing completely covers the substrate with colour.

The substances used to colour textiles can be classified as **dyes** or **pigments**.

> Pigments are not water soluble and possess no specific attraction for any particular fibre type. They usually adhere to the surface of the fibre.

Most modern pigments used on textiles are organically based synthetic colorants, though inorganic salts such as the oxides of iron and lead have also been traditionally used to colour textiles and, in fact, titanium dioxide is still used as a basis for pigment whites.

> Dyes are water soluble. Certain dyes are attracted to certain fibre types. They are usually adsorbed into the fibre.

Although textile dyes were originally of natural extraction, being derived from a number of vegetable and animal sources, modern dyes are synthetic organic colorants. Dyes can be classified in a number of ways depending upon their ionic character, chemical type or application method. Each of these different types of dye classification is discussed in the following section. The chapter then covers dyeing, printing and evaluation of both.

Classification of dyes

Ionic class

Dyes are molecularly designed to be soluble in water, since water is usually used to transport the dye on to and into the fibres from the dyebath. Certain dyes possess molecular groupings on their structure to aid their solubility in water. These solubilising groups ionise (convert to charged molecules) in water during dyeing, to create either positively or negatively charged dye ions – **cations** (positive) or **anions** (negative).

Solubilising groups able to form dye anions include the sodium carboxylate ($-COONa$) or more usually the sodium sulphonate ($-SO_3Na$) radicals (molecules with at least one unpaired electron). The dye molecule (shown as D below) containing one or more of these groups will readily separate to form a coloured anion within the dyebath, as:

Similarly, the quaternary ammonium group ($-NR_4$) when bonded to a halogen atom (Cl or Br) forms a useful dye solubilising group, which will create a coloured dye cation within the dyebath. This is shown as:

The success of water as a solubilising medium for dyes is due to its highly polar character. Oxygen's high tendency to attract electrons (its high electronegativity) compared to hydrogen means that the covalent bonding electrons in water are unequally shared between oxygen and hydrogen atoms. They are drawn, or polarised, towards the oxygen atom, giving the latter a negative character (σ^-) compared to the hydrogen atoms' electropositive character (σ^+):

The positive or negative dye ions will therefore each be surrounded by a sheath of water molecules attracted to the charged site:

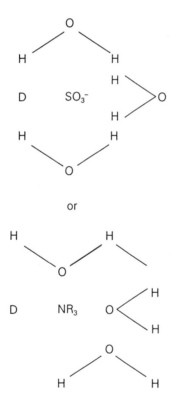

These so-called water **molecules of solvation** are attracted to other water molecules by hydrogen bonding and the net result is that the dye ions are kept apart. They are therefore prevented from coming together, which would tend to cause the dye to come out of solution. Essentially, the greater the number of solubilising groups on the dye molecule, the greater the number of molecules of solvation and the greater the dye's solubility.

> Depending upon their ionic character, dyes can be classed as being either anionic or cationic in type – forming dye anions or cations in solution. There are, however, a number of dyes which possess no ionising groups on their structure and which are unable to form dye anions or cations within the dyebath. These are known as **nonionic** dyes.

These nonionic dyes include the type of dyes called **disperse dyes** and as the name suggests, these form dispersions within the dyebath rather than solutions. Although such dyes have no ionic solubilising groups, they do often have other groups on their molecular structure which aid solubility. Consequently, hydroxyl (–OH) and amino (–NH$_2$) groups which may be present can produce a limited but significant solubility of these nonionic dye molecules. The uptake of nonionic dyes by the fibre depends upon a small number of dye molecules coming out of dispersion and dissolving in the dyebath prior to being adsorbed (taken up) by the fibre. Once adsorbed, these are then replaced by further dye molecules passing into solution from their dispersed form and so dyeing progresses.

The groupings on the nonionic dye molecule which aid dissolution (liquification) do so by hydrogen bonding with the water molecules. However, the level of solubility conferred on the dye molecule is very much less than that given by ionic solubilising groups. It must also be remembered that a dye's solubility is not simply influenced by the number and type of solubilising groups but is a feature of the overall molecular structure of the dye. As the dye's molecular weight increases, for example by the inclusion of an increased number of benzene rings, its hydrophobic properties are enhanced and its solubility reduced unless the number of solubilising groups present also increases.

Chemical class

Dyes are organic chemicals which are able to absorb and reflect visible light.

> In order for an organic molecule to be a useful coloured molecule, or **chromogen**, its structure must possess both one or more groupings called chromophores and one or more groupings called auxochromes. Chromophores provide the colour; auxochromes intensify and deepen colour.

A molecule containing **auxochromic** groups only will not be highly coloured and the presence of **chromophoric** groups is essential for the compound to be coloured. The chromophoric structures found in the dye molecule provide a further basis for dye classification, as the following examples show.

THE AZO CHROMOPHORE

Azo dyes contain one or more azo groups (–N=N–); these are the chromophoric parts of the dye, and can be found in most of the different application classes. The shade range provided by these dyes covers the yellow, orange, red and scarlet colours, though colours in other parts of the spectrum can be manufactured from azo dyes. Examples of mono and disazo dyes, containing respectively one and two azo groups, can be found below in Figures 21.1 and 21.2.

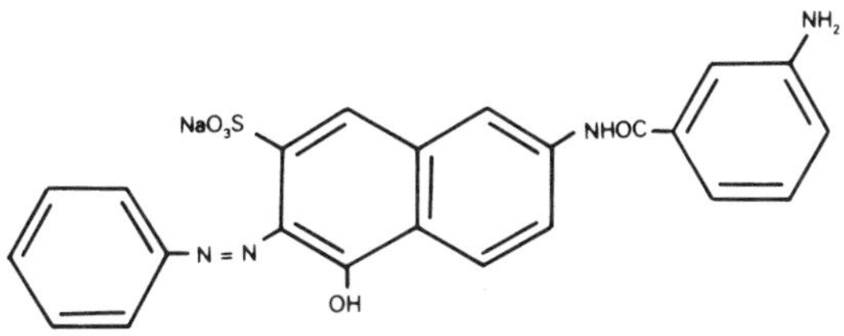

Figure 21.1   A mono-azo dye.

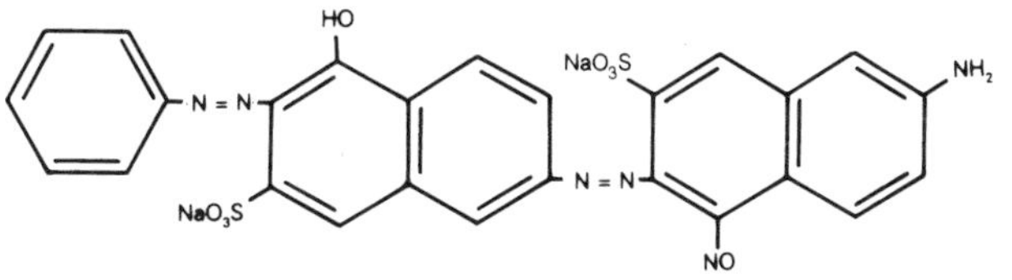

Figure 21.2   A disazo dye.

THE ANTHRAQUINONOID CHROMOPHORE

Despite not being a dye itself, anthraquinone (shown in Figure 21.3) is a useful basis for many dyes, one example of which is shown in Figure 21.4.

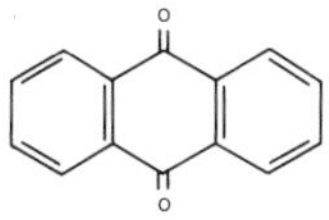

Figure 21.3   An anthraquinone.

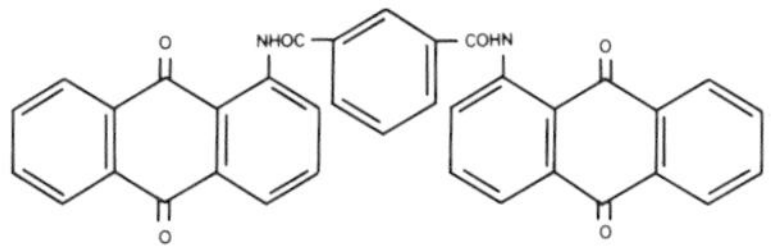

Figure 21.4   An anthraquinonoid dye.

Although not as numerous as azo dyes and more expensive to manufacture, anthraquinone dyes can still be found in most of the major application classes. They provide shades primarily in the blue/red, violet, blue and green parts of the spectrum, which are usually of good fastness to washing.

THE TRIARYLMETHANE CHROMOPHORE

Triarylmethanes are manufactured by substituting three of the hydrogen atoms on methane (CH_4) by other groups; one of the most common substituents being the phenyl group ($–C_6H_5$). So, triphenylmethane is a useful chromophore in a number of dyes, including that shown in Figure 21.5.

Dyes of this type are often extremely bright (sometimes fluorescent) and include red, blue and green shades. Unfortunately, their light fastness can be poor.

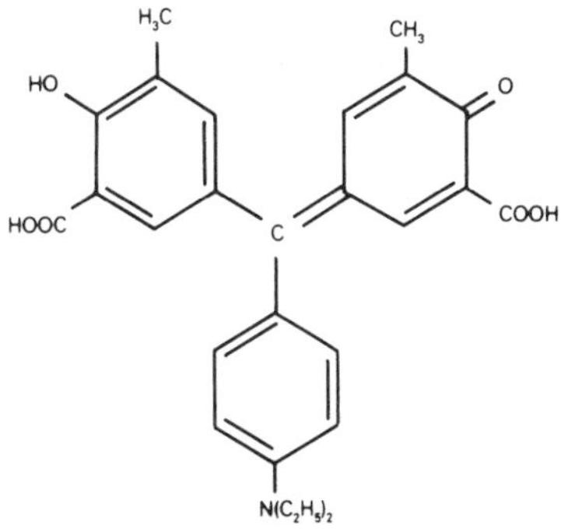

Figure 21.5   A triphenylmethane dye.

THE INDIGOID CHROMOPHORE

Indigo itself, shown in Figure 21.6, is a useful blue dye still employed in the dyeing of cotton yarn for denim fabrics.

Originally extracted from a plant, indigo is now manufactured synthetically and can form the source of a number of blue-based indigoid dye derivatives, such as that shown in Figure 21.7.

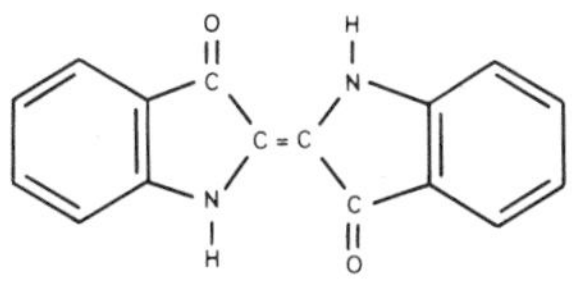

Figure 21.6   Indigo.

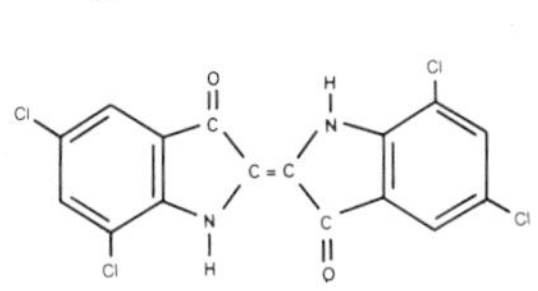

Figure 21.7   An indigo dye.

Many chromophoric types, other than the ones above, can be found in certain selected dyes. They are either used for the specific shades they can generate or their technical innovation over the existing products.

Application class

One important basis for categorising dyes, adopted by both manufacturer and user alike, is by their method of application. Dyes which form dispersions within the dyebath have already been referred to as disperse dyes and this is an important application class for use on synthetic fibres.

> An application class groups together dyes with similar application properties, though there can be some differences in precise application conditions between dyes of any one particular group.

The name of the application class is often an important guide as to their method of use, for instance acid dyes are applied from acidic dyebaths, reactive dyes chemically bond to the fibre and basic dyes form basic cations in acidic conditions.

Dyeing

Dyeing can be carried out on the textile when it is in a number of different physical forms, including loose stock, tow, tops, yarn, piece and garment. Dyeing itself can be undertaken either as a **batch** (or **exhaust**) process or as a **continuous** technique.

> During batch dyeing a certain length or weight of textile is dyed in a relatively compact dyeing machine for a predetermined length of time, often several hours. The dye liquor is either pumped through the stationary textile or the textile is circulated through the dye liquor. Alternatively, the dye liquor and textile are circulated together.

When dyeing loose fibre or yarn it is often more convenient to pump the dye liquor through the stationary textile to prevent loss or entanglement of the substrate. In a loose stock dyeing machine the loose fibres are therefore contained in bags or cages which are lowered into the dyeing vessel. Similarly, hanks or packages of yarn are lowered into the dyebath which is then circulated through them.

One effective batch dyeing method for delicate fabric constructions, including knitted fabrics, is the **jet dyeing** machine, where the textile is circulated through the dyebath with the aid of a jet of the dye liquor itself. This provides a relatively tension-free dyeing process.

For garments, it is far more convenient to load these into perforated drums, very similar to those of the domestic washing machine and then to rotate the drums in the dye liquor. Before the textile is removed from any batch dyeing process, the rinsing and soaping stages are usually carried out. These are necessary to remove unfixed dye and so assure that the product's dye fastness is achieved. They also remove any residual dyeing chemicals from the textile. Usually, however, the textile is removed from the dyeing machine in order that subsequent drying can be completed.

Table 21.1 Application classes of dye and their respective fibre types

Application class	Fibre type					
	Cellulosic	Protein	Polyamide	Polyester	Acrylic	Acetate
Direct	*	+	—	—	—	—
Reactive	*	*	+	—	—	—
Vat	*	+	—	+	—	—
Sulphur	*	—	—	—	—	—
Azoic	*	—	+	+	—	+
Acid	—	*	*	—	—	—
Mordant	—	*	+	—	—	—
Basic	—	—	—	—	*	—
Disperse	—	—	—	*	+	*

* = Fibres for which the dye is usually employed.
+ = Fibres for which the dye has a possible application.

Continuous dyeing, as the name suggests, involves the continuous application and fixation of dye onto the textile.

> In continuous dyeing, the prepared textile is first impregnated (soaked) with a suitable amount of dye liquor and then passed into a fixation chamber (often a steam-filled chamber) where dye fixation takes place in just a few minutes. Wash-off to remove the unfixed dye follows immediately, with the textile usually being dried at the end of the continuous dye line.

Continuous dyeing is ideal when a large amount of textile must be dyed the same shade, particularly when this textile is in a conveniently transportable form. Woven cotton and polyester/cotton fabric are often continuously dyed, as is acrylic tow which may be dyed with basic dyes as part of the fibre manufacturing process. Sometimes the nature of the dyeing process itself is appropriate to continuous techniques and this applies when dyeing cotton warp yarns with indigo dye for use in denims, where multiple impregnation and fixation steps are needed to generate a full-depth shade.

The stages of dyeing

Any dyeing process can be considered in terms of the simple model shown in Figure 21.8.

The dyeing medium, usually water, initially contains hundreds of thousands of dye molecules, one of which is shown as D. As dyeing progresses, there are three distinct stages which each dye molecule must pass through, numbered 1 to 3 in Figure 21.8.

During stage 1 the dye must be attracted to the fibre surface and the nature of this attractive force depends on the type of dye and fibre. For example, acid dyes form negative dye anions in the dyebath and wool and nylon fibres both have positively charged cationic sites when the dyebath is acidic. The force of attraction between acid dyes and wool or nylon is, therefore, partly an electrostatic one. Similarly, cationic basic dyes are attracted to anionic dye sites in acrylic fibres. However, there are other forces of attraction which can be quite significant and these include hydrophobic attractions, where the dye molecules prefer to be associated with the fibre surface rather than remain in the aqueous dyebath.

Once they have reached the fibre surface, the high level of attraction of the dye molecules for the substrate and the fibre's receptivity for the dye result in the dye molecules being rapidly adsorbed at the fibre/dyebath interface (stage 2 in Figure 21.8). Consequently, a high surface concentration of dye within the fibre is developed. The dye will now diffuse through the fibre during the final stage of the process (stage 3).

The way in which dyes diffuse through fibres depends on the nature of the fibre itself. Hydrophilic fibres (such as cotton, wool, silk and viscose) possess an internal network of water-filled pores and so the dye molecules or ions diffuse through these channels into the fibre. Conversely, hydrophobic fibres (polyester, polyamide, acrylic) have a low water adsorption and free space must be created within such substrates for dye diffusion to occur. For example, polyester fibres have polymer molecules which, when heated up to high temperatures, create free space by segments of the molecular chain twisting. The hole created by this allows the disperse dye molecules used to dye polyester fibres to enter the fibre; diffusion through the fibre then occurs as more holes or free volume are created. Consequently, high temperatures well above the boil are frequently used in the disperse dyeing of polyester substrates.

As the dye diffuses through the fibre, it attaches to the dye sites created and bonding occurs by a variety of physical and chemical mechanisms. Since dye diffusion into the fibre is the slowest part of the overall dyeing process it is often called the **rate-determining step** – in other words this stage determines how long it will take to dye the substrate. In the case of some dyes a supplementary fourth step is required in the dyeing process. For example, in the case of reactive dyes applied to cellulosic substrates, once the dye has diffused through and is evenly distributed within the fibre, the pH of the dyebath is increased. This encourages the dye to chemically bond to the fibre polymer molecules and the strong covalent bond produced accounts for the dye's high wet-fastness properties. This final bonding of dye to fibre is termed a **fixation** step.

> Dyes which have a high attraction for a particular fibre and which will generate a full-depth shade within it are termed **highly substantive** on that fibre.

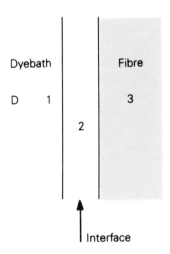

Figure 21.8 **The dyeing model.**

Dyers need to have an awareness of the dye's level of substantivity on the substrate and the measure of this is called affinity. Tests can be carried out by either the dye manufacturer or dye user to determine the affinity of a dye for a fibre.

THE EQUILIBRIUM PROCESS

The above description might imply that, during the dyeing process, dye is only ever adsorbed (taken up) by fibre. This would lead to an uneven dyeing with dye striking the fibre and bonding within it at the points of contact only. It is very important that during the dyeing process dye is also desorbed (released) by the fibre.

> Dye is constantly entering and leaving the fibre during the dyeing process and this promotes a level dyed effect. Dyeing can therefore be perceived as a two-way process or equilibrium reaction, in which dye (D) and fibre (F) are in equilibrium with dyed-fibre DF: D + F = DF.

As dyeing continues, more dye is taken up by the fibre than is lost from it back into the bath and there is a net increase of dye on the fibre. Eventually the dyeing reaches the **equilibrium point**, where there is no further increase in dye on the fibre. However, this does not mean that dye movement has now stopped. At the equilibrium point, dye can still enter and leave the fibre but it does so at the same rate. **Levelling** can still take place at the so-called end of dyeing and to create

uniformity in the dyed textile, it may be useful to encourage this for a set period of time.

A measure of efficiency in dyeing is given by determining both the rate of dye uptake to the equilibrium point and the amount of dye taken up at equilibrium. This last amount is called the **equilibrium exhaustion** of the dye and is a measure of how much of the dye originally present in the bath has exhausted onto the textile at equilibrium. Simple experiments can be designed to measure the percentage exhaustion of dye on to the textile at various stages of the dyeing process. **Rate of dyeing curves** can then be constructed similar to that shown in Figure 21.10, by plotting percentage exhaustion against time of dyeing. These are very useful indicators of dyeing efficiency. Ideally, dyes to be combined together for use in mixture shades should have similar rate of dyeing profiles.

Dyeing efficiency

The nature of the dye within the dyebath, the fibre's receptivity for the dye and the dye's substantivity on the fibre will all influence the successful outcome of the dyeing process. Process conditions such as the temperature and time of dyeing, as well as the role played by auxiliary chemicals in the dyebath, also contribute considerably to the dyeing efficiency.

Basic thermodynamic principles imply that, because dyeing is exothermic, maximum dye uptake is achieved by dyeing close to ambient temperatures. However, most dyeings are carried out at high temperatures often close to or even above the boil. Although there is then a slight reduction in the maximum amount of dye taken up by the

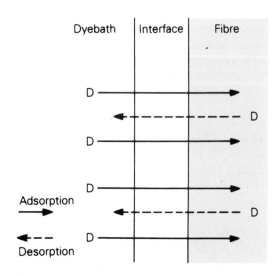

Figure 21.9 Levelling during dyeing.

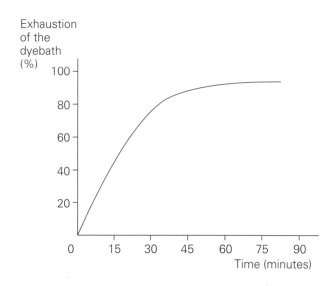

Figure 21.10 A typical rate of dyeing curve.

fibre, the overall rate of dyeing is greatly increased and this is demonstrated in Figure 21.11. Equilibrium is therefore reached in commercially-acceptable times by dyeing at high temperatures.

Most dyeing processes also require the addition of chemical auxiliaries to the dyebath. These auxiliaries perform one or more of the following functions.

1. They keep the dye in a stable physical form, for example dispersing agents are included along with disperse dyes to promote the formation of stable dispersions of these highly insoluble dyes.
2. They change the chemical nature of the dye, for example vat dyes are chemically reduced under alkaline conditions to promote their solubility and substantivity for cellulosic substrates.
3. They help to produce uniform dyeings, for example levelling agents are included when dyeing acrylic fibres with basic dyes; they slow down the rate of dyeing by competing with the dye molecules for sites within the fibre.
4. They adjust the dyebath pH to promote dye substantivity, for example acid dyes of low molecular weight are highly substantive on woollen textiles at low pH levels (pH 2–3).
5. They allow dye-fibre bonding to occur, for example reactive dyes covalently bond to cellulosic substrates when the dyebath is made alkaline.
6. They promote dye uptake during dyeing, for example anionic dyes are made to exhaust onto cellulosic substrates by the addition of sodium chloride (NaCl) or sodium sulphate (Na_2SO_4) into the bath.
7. They promote fibre receptivity to dye, for example auxiliary chemicals known as carriers are included during

the dyeing of polyester textiles to open the fibre up so that molecules of disperse dye can more easily enter.

Choice of colorants

When selecting colorants to use in dyeing there are several factors to consider. These include the influence of substrate type and form, the type of dyeing machinery available and the specification of the final product as stated by the customer.

Although each of these areas is discussed separately below, they all impinge on one another and must be counter-balanced in the selection of colorant.

THE SUBSTRATE

Table 21.1 indicates that there is no one single application class of dye that can be used on all the different fibre types. The dyer must choose those colorants which have the appropriate level of substantivity for the substrate being dyed. If this is a textile composed of a blend of fibres, different colorant types for each component of the blend may have to be chosen and a number of separate dyeing processes or a combined process carried out.

The dyer must also be conscious of the substrate's physical form, for example loose fibre, spun yarns, woven or knitted fabrics or final garments. A dye which may be difficult to apply in a uniform manner and which may tend to create unlevel dyeings would not be a good choice for dyeing fabric. Fabric must be dyed evenly or these variations in shade depth or hue are very obvious. On the other hand, loose fibre dyed prior to being spun into a yarn tends not to highlight such differences in the final product because the spinning of the yarn enables some of the colour differences present in the fibre to average out to an overall apparently uniform colour.

THE DYEING PROCESS

In order to create a dyed textile of appropriate quality, the dyer must be fully aware of the type of dyeing process to be used and the limitations imposed. For example, if fabric is being dyed in the open width it may be far easier to obtain a level dyeing than if the textile is processed in rope form. If the dyer is attempting to dye multiple batches of fabric all to the same shade, it may be better to do this by a continuous rather than a batch dyeing technique.

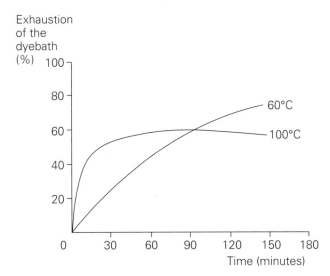

Figure 21.11 Influence of temperature on the rate and extent of dye uptake.

The liquor ratio of an exhaust dyeing process (the ratio of the volume of the dyebath to the substrate weight) can greatly influence the rate and overall amount of dye taken up. Package-dyeing machinery for yarn, and certain types of jet-dyeing machine for fabric, dye at low liquor ratios. This can improve the speed of dye uptake and the overall exhaustion levels achieved, though the reduced volume of water present means that dyes of good solubility or dispersion stability have to be used. Alternatively, certain types of winch-dyeing machine for fabric use high liquor ratios and only dyes of both good substantivity and levelling ability can be used, especially when mixed together within the same dyebath.

CUSTOMER SPECIFICATION

The customer will dictate a specification for the product that is to be dyed. This will detail the length or weight of textile needed and the shade or shades required, along with an end-product performance standard. This standard would include details of the fastness requirements for each shade.

> Dye fastness is defined as the ability of the shade to withstand external agencies without loss of or change in colour. Such external agencies would include washing, dry cleaning, rubbing, perspiration, heat and light.

Dye fastness testing is discussed in more detail later in the chapter.

A dyer needs to know the customer's tolerance for error when matching shades. Some customers permit very little variation in colour from that specified, while others might be more lenient. The dyer must also ensure that the shade range of dyes chosen will meet the customer's requirements. For example, it is often difficult to achieve bright shades on cotton (particularly turquoise blues and greens) with vat dyes.

If the customer requires a large amount of textile dyed to one shade, the dyer will have to produce several batches all the same colour when using exhaust dyeing equipment. The choice of dye is then crucial and only those dyes giving a high level of reproducibility in terms of the uniformity of the shade produced would be used.

The fastness specification of the end-product is determined by its end-use and quality. For example, inexpensive and lower quality curtaining fabric must be fast to light and to the loss or change of colour in home laundering; an expensive high-quality curtaining also needs to be dry-clean fast as this is the preferred method of cleaning used. Pigment colours or direct dyes may be adequate for the former product, but vat dyes must be employed for the latter. Even within one class of colorant there can be quite large variations in the fastness that can be achieved and so the dyer must choose colorants carefully.

In choosing dyes of adequate fastness, the dyer must also be aware of the effect of subsequent processes which may influence the colour of the product. Certain finishing processes can have advantageous effects on dye fastness, for example easy-care finishes can improve the wet fastness of many direct dyes on cellulosic fabrics. However, finishes can also have a detrimental effect; the same process may change the shade or lower the light fastness of the direct dye used. Many disperse dyes are sensitive to high temperatures and will evaporate off the textile; such dyes must be carefully selected for products to be heat-set after dyeing. Pre-dyed yarn can be woven along with undyed yarn to create colour-woven effects but the dyes chosen must withstand subsequent fabric preparatory processes carried out to deal with the previously unpurified yarn.

Provided the dyer is aware of any adverse changes on the shade or fastness of the colorants used which might arise during subsequent processing, he can compensate for this and make his choice accordingly.

Dye types and properties

Table 21.2 summarises the scope for use and properties of some of the major application classes of dye.

Printing

> Printing can be defined as the localised application of dye or pigment in a thickened form to a substrate, to generate a pattern or design.

Printed patterns may vary from simple geometric designs (stripes, spots) in a single colour, to very complex designs in up to 20 or more colours. Thickened pastes are used in printing to ensure the colour adheres precisely to the spot it has been applied to and does not spread over the textile to destroy the definition of the printed object.

Textile materials can be printed in any of the following states: slubbing (vigoureux printing); yarn (warp printing); piece goods (roller, screen and transfer printing); garments (screen and transfer printing); carpets (roller, screen, transfer and jet printing).

Most textiles are printed in the fabric form (piece goods) and this chapter will discuss these techniques.

Table 21.2 Summary of major dye types

Dye type	(Solubility/ionic character)	Fibre affinity	Dyebath auxiliaries	Fastness properties	End-uses	Comments
Direct	Water soluble (anionic)	Cellulosics (cotton, viscose)	Natural dyebath + salt	Light – poor/good Washing – poor	Low quality apparel Fabrics/linings/curtains	Cheap. After-treatment can improve fastness.
Acid levelling	Water soluble (anionic)	Protein fibres (wool, silk)	Acid + glaubers dyebath salt	Light – good/moderate Washing – poor	Carpet yarns, dress goods. Suitings, overcoats, knitting yarns.	The differences between the two types of acid are less evident on nylon compared to wool. Acid dyes have a higher affinity for nylon and better fastness.
Acid milling		Polyamide fibres (nylon)	Neutral/weakly acidic dyebath + levelling agent	Light – good Washing – good		
Vat	Insoluble in water (nonionic)	Cellulosics (cotton, viscose)	Alkali + reducing agent – to produce the anionic LEUCO solubilised form	Light – excellent Washing – excellent	High quality curtains, furnishing, shirts, towels, sewing threads.	Expensive. Bright colours often difficult to achieve.
Reactive	Water soluble (anionic)	Cellulosics (also protein and polyamide fibres)	Applied to cellulosics from a dyebath subsequently made alkaline	Light – good/excellent Washing – excellent	Curtains, furnishings, apparel fabrics, towelling, sewing threads.	Excellent shade range. High fastness due to covalent dye/fibre bond.
Basic	Water soluble (cationic)	Acrylics (also occasionally protein fibres)	Weakly acidic dyebath + levelling agent	Light – good/moderate Washing - good	Furnishings, apparel fabrics.	Bright shades, excellent tinctorial strength.
Disperse	Insoluble in water (nonionic)	All synthetics	Weakly acidic dyebath	Light – good/moderate Washing – good	Apparel fabrics, bed sheets, carpets.	Best fastness on polyester; though this substrate is also the most difficult to dye. Good levelling properties

Fabric printing methods

ENGRAVED ROLLER PRINTING

The printing colour is transferred continuously on to the fabric by engraved rollers, the repeat of the design being governed by the roller circumference (average 16 inches circumference, 42 inches long). Each roller applies only one colour in the design, while the thickened dye paste is held in the engraved printing area on the roller.

Engraved rollers are hollow steel cylinders, electroplated with a layer of copper into which the engravings are etched. The engravings are really a series of parallel channels, approximately 7/1000 to 8/1000 of an inch deep and there are between 35 to 50 of these channels to the inch (known as the scale of the roller). Finally, the roller is chromium plated to prevent damage by scratching and to prolong its printing life.

The most common type of roller machine consists of a large hollow metal pressure cylinder, around which the printing rollers are arranged. Each printing roller is individually driven, can be adjusted vertically and laterally to ensure correct register (placing relative to the other rollers) of the pattern, and is pressed into the pressure bowl. The printing roller is fed with colour from a colour box by a second brush-like roller. A sharp stainless steel blade (called a doctor blade) scrapes the roller surface immediately before printing, leaving the colour only in the engraved areas from where it can be transferred to the fabric as roller and fabric pass in contact with each other.

The fabric to be printed is fed on to the pressure cylinder on top of an endless rubber printing blanket to which it is stuck, so preventing any sideways movement and loss of register in printing. In its passage around the cylinder the fabric is printed by every roller in turn, each applying its colour and part of the design. Finally, after leaving the cylinder the cloth is dried, often by passage through a hot-air dryer and then over steam-heated cylinders.

Engraved roller printing can produce prints of extremely intricate detail, giving high production rates (40–60 metres per minute average). However, a major disadvantage is the long delay when changing patterns or colourways and also the reduced colour yield, due to the high printing pressures employed.

Figures 21.12 and 21.13 are line diagrams of single and multi-colour roller printing machines, showing the component parts identified above.

SCREEN PRINTING

Screen printing is basically a form of stencil printing. The screen consists of a synthetic fibre or metal gauze stretched taut over a frame. Parts of the gauze have the holes blocked off (non-printing area) and the printing paste is forced through the open printing areas by a rubber or metal blade, called a squeegee, and on to the fabric beneath.

In roller printing one roller is required for each colour in the design, but in screen printing, one screen is required for each colour.

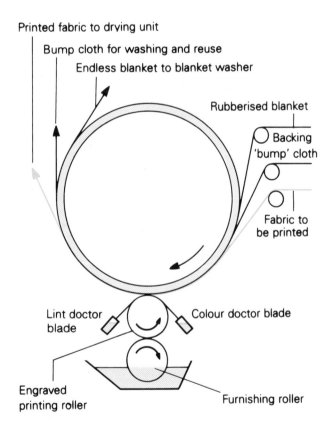

Figure 21.12 Single colour roller printing.

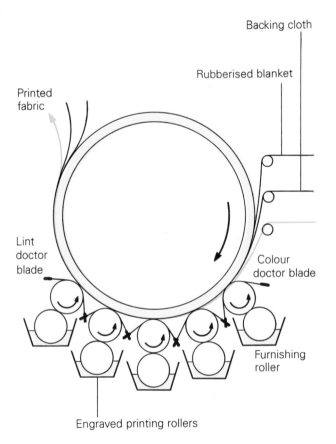

Figure 21.13 Multicolour roller printing.

In hand screen printing the fabric is stuck to the printing table, which is covered with a resilient felt, wax cloth or rubber material. Each screen is placed on the fabric in turn, the paste applied to one end of the screen and the squeegee drawn by hand through the paste and across the screen, forcing it through the open mesh areas on to the fabric beneath. Guide rails along the edges of the table ensure each screen is applied in register.

Although the highly skilled printer can produce good quality prints by a hand screen technique, the production rates are extremely slow and so automatic screen printing machines have been developed, of which there are two main types: flat-bed screen printing and rotary screen printing.

Flat-bed screen printing

The fabric is now in a continuous length, the immobile hand printing table being replaced by an endless conveyor belt. All the screens making up the pattern are arranged side by side above this belt and the belt is automatically set to move forward by one or several pattern repeats at a time. When the belt is stationary the screens are lowered, the colours are applied to the fabric and the screens are lifted for the belt to move the fabric on to the next repeat. Colour is pumped or hand-fed on to each screen and the squeegee movement is mechanised. Figure 21.15 shows the arrangement of the component parts of the **flat-bed printing** machine.

Two main types of squeegee system are used in the flat-bed machine. Either a conventional squeegee blade is driven forwards and backwards across the screen by a motor, or the squeegee is a small-diameter roller bar which is attracted to and rolled over the screen by a powerful electromagnet moving beneath the printing blanket. These two methods of colour application are shown in Figure 21.16.

Rotary screen printing

Flat-bed screen printing is an intermittent printing method and so cannot compete with roller printing in terms of its productivity. **Rotary screen printing** has been developed as a fully continuous screen-printing technique to rival engraved roller printing. Rotary screen printing uses seamless cylindrical screens which are composed of a nickel mesh with end-rings soldered or stuck on to tension the

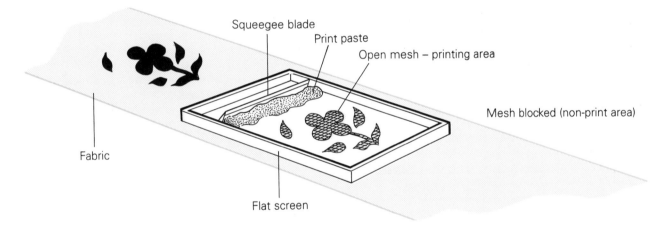

Figure 21.14 Hand screen printing.

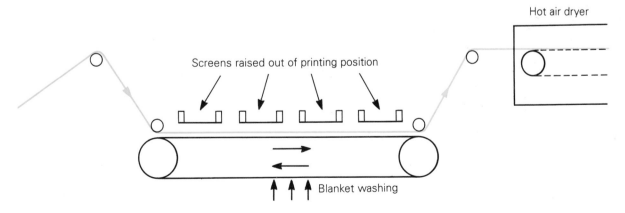

Figure 21.15 Flat screen printing.

cylinder and prevent collapse. Each rotary screen is positioned across the fabric and is independently driven at one end. As the screen rotates, it is fed internally with print paste which is forced through the open mesh areas by a stationary squeegee at the base of the screen and on to the fabric being carried beneath by the continuously moving conveyor. The squeegee may be either a conventional rubber, metal or polymeric blade, or again a metal bar held against the base of the screen by a stationary electromagnet beneath the printing blanket.

On most modern screen-printing machines, fabric is dried by a conveyor passage through a hot-air dryer. On both the flat-bed and rotary screen machines, the positioning of each screen can be very precisely controlled to ensure correct registration of the pattern. Recent innovations in screen design, particularly of rotary screens, have permitted intricate patterns to be printed by screen techniques which were only previously possible by engraved roller printing. This factor, along with the considerably reduced machine down-time associated with screen printing, are two of the reasons why engraved roller printing is experiencing a decline.

The layout of the machine and the methods of applying paste in rotary screen printing are shown in Figures 21.17 and 21.18 respectively.

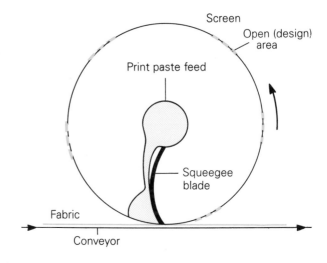

Figure 21.18 **Print paste application in rotary screen printing.**

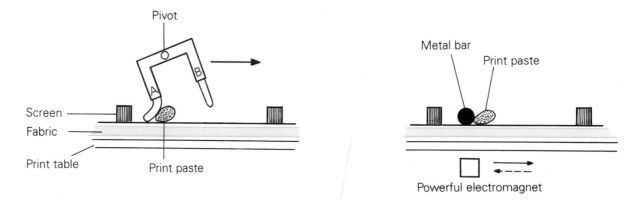

Figure 21.16 **Print paste application in flat screen printing.**

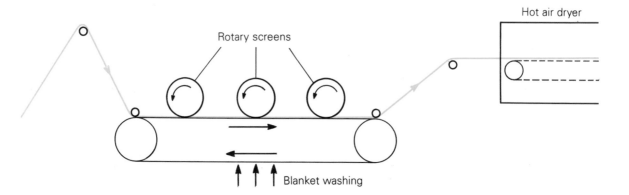

Figure 21.17 **Rotary screen printing.**

TRANSFER PRINTING

This third method of printing fabrics was originally designed for synthetic fibre fabrics, particularly polyester substrates. The special dyes used (selected disperse dyes) are first printed on to a cellulosic paper by conventional paper printing techniques or, nowadays, even by rotary screen type machines. The fabric to be printed and this printed paper are then passed into a transfer calender. In a typical transfer machine (Figure 21.19), the fabric/printed paper sandwich is held by the pressure exerted by an endless belt against a hot metal cylinder as it passes through the machine. This cylinder is usually heated internally by hot oil, reaching temperatures approaching 180°C. Under these conditions of controlled temperature, pressure and time, the dye becomes gaseous by a process of sublimation (change of state from a solid to a gas without becoming a liquid), transfers to the fabric and then diffuses into the fibres. After leaving this calender, the dye is usually adequately fixed for most end-uses, requiring no further fixation or wash-off processes.

The **vapour phase transfer** technique is limited only to synthetic fibres and although transfer methods for printing natural fibres are now available, they are not based on transfer via the vapour phase. This limitation in substrate type has severely restricted the use of the vapour phase transfer method in the bulk printing of fabrics, even though the ease of printing makes it attractive to the non-specialist printer.

Table 21.3 compares all the fabric printing techniques discussed in this section in terms of their productivity, costs and versatility.

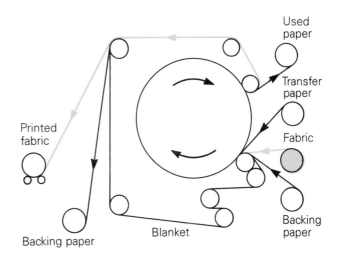

Figure 21.19 Vapour phase transfer printing.

Table 21.3 Comparison of fabric printing techniques

Parameter	Printing method				
	Engraved roller	Hand screen	Flat-bed screen	Rotary screen	Vapour phase transfer
1. Productivity	High	Very low	Low/moderate	Very high	Low/moderate
2. Machine 'down time'	High	Low	Low	Low	Very low
3. Capital cost	Very high	Very low	Very high	High	Low
4. Space requirement	Low	Low/moderate	Very high	Low/moderate	Very low
5. Operative skill level	Highly skilled	Low/highly skilled	Semi-skilled	Semi-skilled	Unskilled
6. Design element					
cost	High	Low	Low	Moderate/high	High (for long printing runs)
durability	High	Low	Low	Moderate	Paper unable to be reused
7. Design limitations complexity			Tone effects difficult		
	Very good – fine detail, tone effects	Can be very good but dependent upon parameter 5.	Good Very good	Very good	
pattern repeat size	Limited (max. 41 cm)	High	High	Moderate (max. 100 cm)	Dependent upon paper printing method
8. Fabric limitations	Width limitations; difficult to print delicate constructions	Width limitations	Wide widths possible	Wide widths possible	Confined to synthetics, particularly polyester
9. Efficiency of dye utilisation	Duller prints – 'crush' effects	Bright prints	Bright prints	Bright prints	100% transfer not achieved

Roller printing has declined in its use, vapour phase transfer printing has limited applications, flat-screen printing is appropriate for certain designs with very large pattern repeats and rotary screen printing has emerged as the single most important method for the bulk printing of fabric.

Post-print processes

After printing and drying, with the exception of vapour phase transfer printing, the dye has only been applied to the surface of the fibres in the printed area and, consequently, very little fibre penetration and bonding have taken place.

Most dyeing processes require heat and time to ensure adequate fastness and depth of shade, and so roller and screen printing operations are usually followed by a fixation process.

Fixation is usually performed by passing the printed fabric through a steam-filled chamber. The length of time required in the steam depends upon the particular dye, the fibre type and the temperature of the steam itself. For example, a reactive dye on a plain cotton fabric would require between 5 to 15 minutes in steam at 100°C (reduced to one to three minutes if the steam were superheated to 150°C). Most steaming processes are continuous, the cloth passing over a series of rollers or being carried in large loops through the steamer to provide the required fixation time.

During steaming, the steam condenses on the cold fabric to produce a localised dyebath, resulting in the dye and other chemicals in the print paste dissolving or dispersing and then diffusing into the fibres and fixing. Chemicals are often added to the print paste to aid this condensation process (for example, urea); although, of course, the definition of the printed object must be maintained and too much moisture on the fabric is to be avoided.

Following fixation, the printed fabric will usually require a washing process to remove any unfixed dye and thickening still present in the printed areas. Again, the conditions used depend upon the dye, fibre and wash-off equipment used, but a series of hot or cold rinses and a hot detergent treatment are usually required. The process is normally continuous, either in open width or rope form. After washing, the printed fabric is far less stiff and should possess the required dye fastness as detailed in the customer specification.

The effect of each of the post-print processes on the dye applied during printing is shown diagrammatically in Figure 21.20.

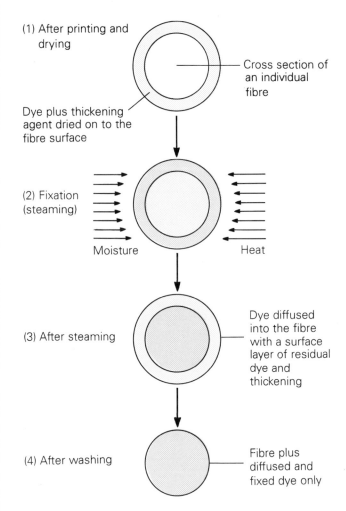

Figure 21.20 Effect of post-print processes.

Colorant selection for printing

The nature of the dye-fibre interaction and the bonding processes is just the same in printing as in dyeing techniques, only the method of dye application differs. Dye printing is simply a surface coating process which must be followed by fixation and wash-off to make the dye diffuse into the fibres and remove unfixed dye. Printers, therefore, tend to use the same specific dyes as dyers do for given fibres, for example reactive and vat dyes on cellulosics, acid dyes on wool and nylon, disperse dyes on synthetics.

There is a range of colorants which is used far more extensively by the printer than the dyer and these are pigment colours. Pigments are insoluble colorants with very little attraction (or affinity) for textile fibres. In printing, dispersions of these pigments are applied to the fabric along with a polymeric resin or binder. Under the appropriate conditions of acidity and heat, the resin gels to form a continuous crosslinked binder film over the yarns which locks the pigment in place on the surface of the fibres in the printed area. An acid catalyst is included in the print paste itself and printing is followed by a continuous baking process to encourage binder film formation and chemical crosslinking of molecules within this film to make it more durable.

Pigment printing is a technique used by many printers because the pigment can be bonded to any fibre type and so it is a simple system to use when printing blends, such as polyester/cotton. Provided there is enough binder present, no wash-off process is needed and this reduces processing costs, time and the amount of effluent produced. One problem which does arise is that the thickener remains in the printed area, trapped in the binder film and, even though special binder types and low solids thickeners are adopted, this can lead to a deterioration in the fabric's handle.

Traditionally, pigment prints could not achieve the fastness required. However, modern binder types have improved the durability of pigments and these tend to be extensively used in the textile printing of cotton and polyester/cotton fabrics.

Printing styles

DIRECT PRINTING

In the direct print style, every component part of the design is 'saved for', that is colours do not overlap and each has its own specific place on the fabric. In other words, each colour has a place saved for it on the fabric and the printing operation will ensure that the right colours are placed in the right saved-for locations.

If two colours are meant to touch, they should do just that and should not overlap to create a third, unwanted colour, as shown in Figure 21.21.

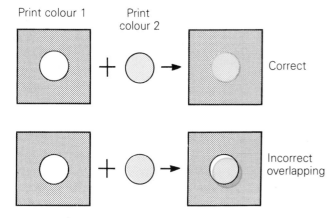

Figure 21.21 Direct printing.

The open circle in the square is the saved-for position for Colour 2. Successful printing is therefore dependent both on the skill of the printer and the viscosity/flow properties of the print pastes used.

OVERPRINTING

This is the term used to describe designs in which one or more colours are made to print wet-on-wet on top of colours just printed to create **fall-on effects**, as shown in Figure 21.22.

Very careful control must be maintained over paste viscosities and flow properties or the overprinted objects will spread into the background colour, producing a loss of print definition. Also the colourist must be aware of the effect of the colour beneath on the overprinted shade and compensate appropriately. However, overprinting can produce certain special colour and design effects. For example by allowing a printed dye to partially fall on to a previously printed pigment white colour, a tone effect can be obtained, that is two apparent depths of the same shade.

Colour 1

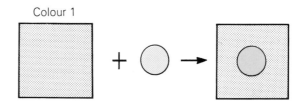

Figure 21.22 Fall-on effect.

DISCHARGE AND RESIST PRINTING

These two terms describe a clever combination of printing and dyeing techniques.

In true **discharge printing**, the fabric is first predyed. The dry fabric is then overprinted with print pastes containing a chemical which will destroy (or discharge) the colour of the dyed ground shade within the printed areas, but which at the same time will not affect the fixation or shade of the overprinted pastes (the head colours).

In **resist printing**, the printing process takes place first and the ground shade is either pad-dyed afterwards or is overprinted by the final screen on the printing machine itself. Again, the printed head colours contain a chemical which does not stop their fixation but which will resist the ground colour from fixing in the printed areas.

In one style of resist printing – **batik printing** – wax is first printed on to the fabric and then physically prevents any dyes subsequently applied by dyeing or printing techniques from fixing in the wax-printed areas.

The chemical used to discharge or resist the ground colour could be a reducing agent or even an alkali, depending upon the dyes being used. Importantly, however, the dye destruction does not take place in printing itself but in the subsequent steam fixation process, shown in Figure 21.23.

On certain fibres which are difficult to dye, such as polyester, a so-called discharge/resist technique is used in which the dyed ground is left unfixed by simply dyeing the fabric so that the dye remains only on the yarn surfaces. It is now far more easily destroyed by the discharge or resist chemical applied in printing. During fixation, the dyed ground is fixed in the non-printed areas but destroyed in the printed areas where the **head colours** are also fixed.

Discharge or resist printing techniques are technically difficult processes to carry out. The printer is printing 'blind' because a dark head colour applied on top of a dark dyed ground shade will be difficult to see and fit at the point of printing. The formulation of each print paste has to be accurately controlled. Too little of the discharge or resist chemical will mean that the ground shade is not fully removed or resisted. Such **undercutting**, shown in Figure 21.24, results in the ground colour contaminating the head shades. On the other hand, too much of the discharge or resist chemical can result in either the head colour itself being affected by the chemical or in a **haloing** effect. Haloing, as seen in Figure 21.24, is where the excess chemical

agent spreads beyond the printed area, destroying the ground colour around each printed object to produce a white halo effect.

Precise process control is also needed, particularly during drying and fixation stages. Although discharge/resist printing requires considerable expertise, customers are willing to pay a premium for the effects it can produce. Very pale, bright or even white print colours can be achieved on the darkest of backgrounds without problems of soiling or miss-fitting. In fact, for very busy or tight-fitting patterns, problems of fit can be reduced by the fact that the blotch or background colour has been predyed and so does not require fitting. Many customers like the two-sided effect which discharge printing can achieve on the lighter weight fabrics.

Effectiveness of coloration processes

Terminology

Coloured fabric is required to maintain its colour, that is to possess an acceptable amount of **colour fastness**. There are various treatments that the fabric may be subjected to during further processing and use, which may affect the colour fastness. These treatments are known as agencies. Examples of agencies are: rubbing, washing, water, perspiration, light and chlorinated water.

> There are two aspects to colour fastness: change (this is alteration in the depth of shade of the colour in the fabric); and staining (this is transfer of colour from the dyed fabric on to another fabric).

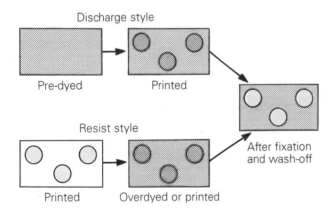

Figure 21.23 Discharge and resist style printing.

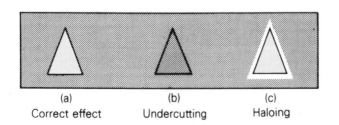

Figure 21.24 Discharge and resist possible effects.

Procedures

The number of agencies and the complexity of the tests means that this chapter can only discuss the basic principles of a few examples.

RUBBING

This is the simplest of all the fastness tests. A piece of white cotton fabric is placed over a peg which is rubbed against a specimen of the fabric to be tested a specified number of times under specified pressure. The white fabric is then removed and assessed for staining. This test can be carried out with the white fabric in the dry or wet states, as required. It is sometimes referred to as fastness to 'crocking' and the apparatus designed for the test as a **crockmeter**.

WET TESTS

A small rectangular specimen of the fabric to be tested is sewn between two specimens of undyed fabric, one made from the same fibre as the test fabric and the other made from a different fibre. This composite specimen is then treated with the appropriate agency. For example, perspiration – the specimen is treated with an artificial perspiration solution at 37°C for a specified time; or washing – the specimen is given a simulated domestic washing treatment under standard conditions in small metal pots using pure soap solution as the detergent. There are a number of different standard conditions varying in time and temperature to simulate different types of washing treatment.

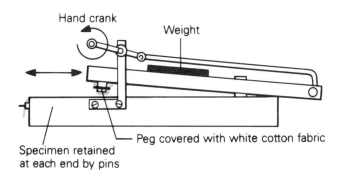

Figure 21.25   A crockmeter.

After the treatment, the composite sample is opened out and dried. The coloured specimen is assessed for change in shade and the adjacent undyed fabrics for staining.

LIGHT

This test is to assess the effect of sunlight. However, if the fabric is exposed under natural conditions, the test will take too long. Simulated sunlight is therefore used. Specimens are exposed to light from a lamp with the same characteristics as sunlight but with a much higher intensity. The specimens are exposed alongside eight samples of standard dyed fabrics with different light fastness (blue standards), and each test specimen and standard sample is partly covered during the exposure. The change between the exposed and covered parts of the test specimen is compared with the changes between the covered and exposed areas of the standard samples. The number of the standard showing the same change as the test specimen is the light fastness grade of the fabric. Staining does not apply to light fastness.

Assessment

The changes in shade and staining are assessed using **grey scales**, of which there are two types.

GREY SCALE FOR ASSESSING CHANGE

This consists of a series of squares, each divided into two parts. One half of each is the same neutral grey while the

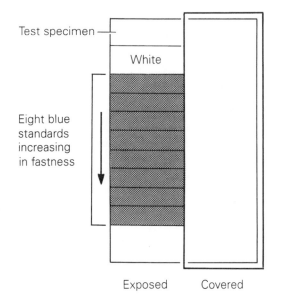

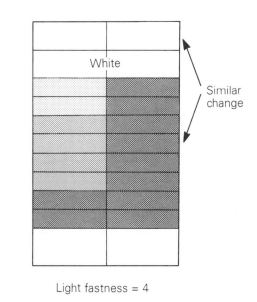

Figure 21.26   Light fastness.

other halves are progressively lighter grey. The difference between the two halves of the first square is zero. The difference between the two halves of the second square is a standard value. The difference between the two halves of the next three squares is twice that between the previous pair.

GREY SCALE FOR ASSESSING STAINING

This is similar to the grey scale for assessing change except that half of each square is white. The two halves of the first square are both white and the other halves are progressively darker grey.

USE OF THE GREY SCALES

The grey scale is placed in a sleeve with a window in it so that only one square can be seen at a time. Specimens of fabric before and after treatment with an agency are placed side by side under standard lighting conditions. The difference between the treated and untreated specimens is compared with the grey scale and the fabric colour fastness grade is the number of the grey scale square with the same difference. The fastness grade of the test sample is the number of the grey scale square whose two halves show the same degree of difference as the tested sample and the sample in its untested state (5 = best; 1 = worst).

CHECK YOUR UNDERSTANDING

● Textile substrates can be dyed or printed to add colour.
● Pigments are not water soluble and usually stick to the outside of the fibre.
● Dyes are water soluble and are usually adsorbed into the fibre.
● Dyes can be classed by ionic, chemical or application class.
● Cationic dyes are positively charged; anionic dyes are negatively charged. Nonionic dyes have no charge.
● Dyes are organic chemicals containing chromophores and auxochromes. Chromophores provide the colour, while auxochromes intensify and deepen the colour.
● The method of dye application can be used to class dyes as direct, reactive, vat, sulphur, azoic, mordant, ionic or disperse.
● Dyeing can be carried out on loose stock, yarn, piece or garment in a batch or continuous process.
● A model for dyeing involves three stages: attraction of the dye to the fibre; adsorption into the fibre; and diffusion through the fibre. Sometimes a fourth fixation stage is necessary.

● To produce a level dyeing, an equilibrium stage must be reached where dye is constantly leaving and entering the fibre with no further increase of dye on the fibre. This stage is often left for a set time to enable levelling to take place.
● Dyeing efficiency is influenced by temperature, time, the dye, the substrate and auxiliary chemicals.
● Auxiliary chemicals are used to: keep the dye in a stable physical form; change the chemical nature of the dye; produce uniform dyeings; adjust the dyebath pH; allow dye–fibre bonding; promote dye uptake; and promote fibre receptivity to the dye.
● Choice of colorant depends on: substrate type and form; dyeing machinery to be used; and customer specification.
● In printing, dye or pigment is mixed to form a thickened paste which is applied to precise places. Alternatively, dyes are printed on to paper then transferred to fabric by heat and pressure.
● Devices used to apply print paste are: engraved rollers; hand screens; flat-bed screens; and rotary screens. Transfer printing uses a heated cylinder and pressure to encourage the dye to transfer to the fabric.
● Fixation processes are used to ensure dye fastness and are usually carried out in a steam chamber. The time required to fix the print depends upon the dye and fibre type.

REVISION EXERCISES AND QUESTIONS

1 What is the disadvantage of a dye that contains no chromophore groups?
2 What is a chromogen?
3 Give an alternative name for an exhaust dyeing process.
4 How is dye adsorbed into hydrophobic fibres such as polyester?
5 What does 'highly substantive' mean?
6 If the laws of thermodynamics suggest that optimum dye uptake would be achieved at lower temperatures, why are most dyeings carried out at approximately 100°C?
7 Why is it not as important to have a level dyeing on loose stock as it is on fabric if both are destined for the same end-product?
8 How can finishes applied after coloration affect the choice of dye?
9 Why do pigments and dyes used in printing need to be thickened?
10 Why is rotary screen printing the most widely used method?
11 How are pigments applied to substrates?
12 Why are customers willing to pay a premium for discharge/resist printing?

Finishing processes

Introduction

Textile finishing covers an extremely wide range of activities which are performed on textiles before they reach the final customer. They may be temporary, for example the way socks are pressed before packing, or they may be permanent, as in the case of a permanently pleated skirt. However, what can be said is that all finishing processes are designed to increase the attractiveness or serviceability of the end-product. This could involve such techniques as putting a glaze on an upholstery fabric which gives it a more attractive appearance, or the production of easy-care finishes on dress fabrics which improve the performance of dresswear. A further aim of textile finishing may be described as improving customer satisfaction.

2. **raising** – plucking the fibres from a woven or knitted fabric to give a nap effect on the surface;
3. **cropping** – cutting the surface hairs from the fabric to give a smooth appearance, often used on woollen goods where the removal of surface hair by a singeing process is not possible.

Chemical processes may be described as those processes which involve the application of chemicals to the fabric. The chemicals may perform various functions such as **water repellency** or **flame retardancy**, or may be used to modify the handle of a fabric. Chemical finishes are normally applied in the form of an aqueous solution or emulsion and may be applied via a variety of techniques, the main one being the pad mangle, which is illustrated in Figure 22.1.

Finishing processes

> The finishing processes available to us can be divided into four main groups, which are: mechanical processes, chemical processes, heat setting and surface coating.

Mechanical processes involve the passage of the material through machines whose mechanical action achieves the desired effects. This is frequently accompanied by a heating process, usually to enhance the desired effects. The mechanical finishes, which will be discussed later in this section, may be listed as:

1. **calendering** – compression of the fabric between two heavy rolls to give a flattened, smooth appearance to the surface of a fabric;

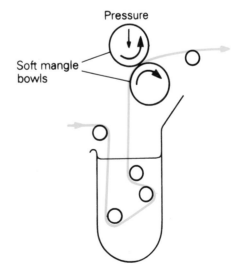

Figure 22.1 A pad mangle.

269

The pad-mangle system shows the fabric passing through a trough of chemical finish. It is then squeezed by a pair of nip rolls to ensure the even application of a fixed amount of the finish onto the fabric.

After the padding or application stage of the process the fabric is usually dried to remove the water from the fabric and some form of fixation of the finish is then performed. This commonly takes the form of a baking process in which the fabric is subjected to a high temperature for a short period. This enables the applied chemicals to form a more durable finish on the fabric.

Chemical finishes

> Chemical finishes involve the use of chemicals to modify the fabric in such a way that the serviceability of the fabric is improved and only rarely is the attractiveness improved.

From such diverse fields as **antistatic treatments** to flame retardant treatments, the chemical finishes which may be applied to fabrics are highly varied.

The chemical finishes that will be discussed in this section are as follows: handle modification; water repellency; mothproof, **antibacterial** and **antifungal** treatments; antishrink and **crease-resistant finishes**; flame-retardant finishes; and antistatic finishes.

Handle modification

> The use of starch as a stiffening agent for cotton articles has been used for hundreds of years. Once the starch granules have been swollen in boiling water they have excellent film-forming properties and are also excellent adhesives for cellulosic materials. When a dilute solution of boiled starch is applied to a woven piece of cotton and the fabric dried, the dried starch film will stick the warp and weft threads firmly together to give a stiff product.

One of the advantages of using starch is its hydrophilic character, which means that on contact with the skin it will adsorb moisture and soften. This explains to some extent why starch was once popular as a stiffening agent for shirt collars. Starch is still used, along with the soluble and modified starches developed for convenience, where a crisp, smooth finish is required on cotton goods.

The opposite of stiffening is, of course, softening and this is the most common handle modifier used today.

> Softeners work in exactly the opposite way to the stiffeners in that they lubricate the warp and weft of woven fabrics so that they slip more easily over each other. This results in a decrease in flexural modulus and hence the fabric bends more easily in the hand and consequently feels softer.

However, there is an additional factor in softening and this is the decrease which softeners bring to the coefficient of friction between the fingers and the fabric. This slippery feel that softeners give to the fabric is interpreted by the hand and brain as a smoother feel and this, combined with the decrease in flexural modulus, makes the fabric seem softer.

TYPES OF SOFTENER

Softeners range from the nonionic mineral oils, which may be used as assistants in the raising process, to the chemically sophisticated cationic softeners, which are substantive (have a great attraction) to some substrates such as cotton and acrylics and have a degree of permanence.

Water repellent finishes

Water is a substance with a very high surface tension which may be looked upon as the attractive force between the molecules of water that enable it to form drops when it is forced through a fine hole. When water is placed on a solid, if the attractive force between the water molecules and the molecules of the solid surface is greater than the attractive forces between the water molecules themselves, the water will spread over the surface of the solid. On the other hand, if the attractive force between the water molecules and the surface molecules is less than that between the water molecules themselves, water will not spread on that surface. Unfortunately for the textile finisher, the surface energy of most fibres is less than that of water and so pure water will only wet the cellulose-based fibres and then only when the fibre's protective wax coating has been removed.

A good rule of thumb is that liquids will only spread on surfaces with a higher surface tension than themselves. So, by examining the surface tension of solids, we should be able to see which surfaces are wettable by which liquids. Table 22.1 shows the surface tensions of some common liquids and solids, though it is more usual to speak of surface energy

Table 22.1 Surface tension of some common materials

Material	Surface tension Newtons per metre $(\text{Nm}^{-1} \times 10^{-3})$
Water	72.8
Glycerol	63.4
Peanut oil	32.6
Olive oil	32.4
Paraffin	30.2
Toluene	28.5
Acetone	23.7
Ethanol	22.8
PTFE	22.0
Polythene	31.0
Polystyrene	33.0
Polyester	43.0
Nylon 66	46.0
Cellulose	100–120

when referring to solids. If we then apply our rule on relative surface tensions, it can be seen that in general organic materials (those substances composed mainly of carbon and hydrogen) have a much lower surface tension than water and so will spread when a single drop is placed on a water surface. It is a common experience to see oil droplets from a car spread on a wet road surface, giving the familiar red-blue tint to the road. Water, however, will not spread on oil or an oily surface.

Early water repellent finishes were all based on the application of a mixture of waxes which were pliable at normal temperatures. These were, of course, well suited to protective clothing, but problems were encountered when the garments were cleaned. The search was on for water repellent treatments which were simple to apply but would also allow the treated garments to be cleaned.

It was noted that heavy metal soaps had water repellent properties and so the first attempt at the production of a durable treatment was to use the chromium salt of a fatty acid which was applied to cotton and then baked. This gave a certain durability to the treated fabric.

Some of the later treatments involved the use of other fatty acid derivatives and the most recent treatments involve the use of the fluorocarbons which are basically esters of polyacrylic acid and a perfluorinated hexanol.

Oil and soil repellency

If the contact angle between a liquid and a solid is less than 90°, the liquid will wet the solid. If, on the other hand, the contact angle is greater than 90°, the liquid will not wet the solid and the surface is termed non-wetting or repellent.

This is illustrated in Figure 22.2 where the angle between the tangent to the liquid at the point of contact to the surface of the solid is the contact angle.

OIL REPELLENCY

When a fluorocarbon is applied to a textile, the $-\text{CF}_2-$ groups will give the textile a very low surface energy which is not easily wet by oil. The majority of soil on textiles has oil associated with it and hence such surfaces will have an oil repellent property. Most natural oils and mineral oil have surface tensions of about 30 $\text{Nm}^{-1} \times 10^{-3}$ and all of these will fail to wet a textile surface which has been treated with a fluorocarbon. However, even with fluorocarbons applied to textiles under ideal conditions, it is rare to find a textile which will give resistance to oils of surface tension of less than 22 $\text{Nm}^{-1} \times 10^{-3}$. So n-heptane, with a surface tension of 20 $\text{Nm}^{-1} \times 10^{-3}$, will wet these surfaces completely. This property can therefore be used to assess the relative stain

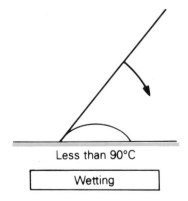

Less than 90°C

Wetting

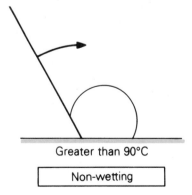

Greater than 90°C

Non-wetting

Figure 22.2 Contact angle of liquid on solid.

resistance of a treated textile surface, if a way can be found of gradually increasing the surface tension of the n-heptane. This can be done by adding small amounts of mineral oil to the n-heptane which forms the basis of the **Oil Repellency Rating Test** developed by the 3M Corporation.

OIL REPELLENCY RATING

To assess the ability of a textile to resist staining, a test was devised which correlated well with the ability of a textile to resist soiling in wear conditions. The test itself consists of a series of liquids of decreasing surface tension, which are then applied to the textile surface. The liquid from this series, which will just wet the textile, is then given a number which is known as the oil repellency rating. The liquids themselves were made by mixing various per centages of n-heptane with a mineral oil and these are shown on Table 22.2.

Table 22.2 n-heptane/mineral oil mixtures for the determination of oil repellency rating

Oil repellency rating	% mineral oil in n-heptane
150	0
140	10
130	20
120	30
110	40
100	50
90	60
80	70
70	80
60	90
50	100

The oil repellency ratings are now extensively used in the specification of stain resistant finishing and the ratings can be interpreted as follows:

1. Oil repellency ratings of 50–70 show only fair resistance to staining.
2. Oil repellency ratings of 80–90 show good resistance to staining.
3. Oil repellency ratings of 100 and above will give excellent resistance to staining.

SOIL RELEASE

This type of finish may be described as the ability of a treated textile to shed soil during the washing process. One of the problems in the laundering of textiles is the ability of the fabric to be wetted by the cleaning solution. Any treatments which encourage the wetting of the textile surface will act as soil release agents. The early types of soil release agents were polymers, containing hydrophilic groups which were deposited on the surface of the fibre. For example, polymers containing acrylic acid groups would be readily wetted by water. This can be illustrated in Figure 22.3.

Recently, there has been a tendency to use block co-polymers containing a hydrophilic and a hydrophobic component, particularly where polyester fabrics are concerned. The structure of these is as follows:

Block copolymer molecule
—polyethylene glycol—polyester—polyethylene glycol—
block   block   block

These materials act in the following manner. The hydrophobic part of the molecule – the polyester portion – can be adsorbed on the polyester fibre surface, leaving the hydrophilic portions of the molecule clear of the surface.

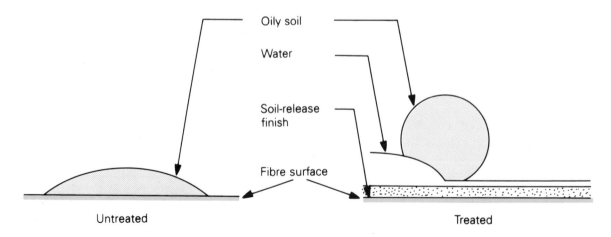

Figure 22.3 Action of a hydrophilic soil release agent.

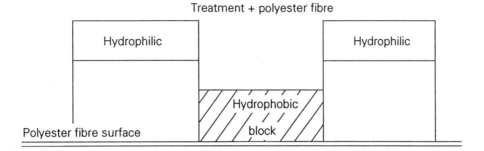

Figure 22.4 Treated polyester.

This leaves a readily wettable pathway for the washing water to move underneath an oily dirt particle and remove it. The treated polyester fibre consists of the components shown in Figure 22.4.

Mothproofing and insect damage

Billions of woollen goods are destroyed by various pests every year. It is not only the Clothes Moth which causes damage but also the Carpet Beetle and the Black Carpet Beetle.

It is only the larvae of these insects that destroy keratin (the wool protein), the adult Clothes Moth does not take in any food at all, while the adult beetle lives on other substances than keratin. In the face of the widespread occurrence of the keratin-eating pests, there is a very great need for the application of agents which would effectively stop the destruction of the wool fibres. The first of these was a dye called Martius Yellow which was used particularly on the army greatcoats in the First World War. It was found that when the wool greatcoats were dyed with this dye, they were left untouched by the moth grubs because they could not digest it. Many subsequent years were spent on the synthesis of dyestuffs having similar properties. However, it was realised that a certain minimum concentration was required for the insecticidal action and this was rarely compatible with the shade required by the dyer, so it was eventually abandoned.

> The older method of producing a mothproof finish by treating the wool with an insecticide was very popular. However, in view of the mounting environmental evidence against this type of compound, it has now been replaced by more acceptable materials, the main ones being the synthetic pyretheroids which were chosen because of their low animal toxicity.

Insecticides create significant problems, particularly when the effluent from the treatment plant is discharged into a river. Pyretheroids are toxic to fish and can cause severe problems.

Microbiocidal finishes

> Problems of hygiene are becoming more important to textile finishing and it is now generally realised that a **microbicidal** finish (anti-bacterial/anti-fungal) is valuable for certain textiles, as a precautionary measure to avoid reinfection and as a deodorant.

Perhaps at this stage it might be useful to define some of the terms we will be using:
Bacteriostatic:
A chemical which inhibits the growth of bacteria. The fabric which has been impregnated with a bacteriostat will stop the growth of germs, which will eventually die with time.
Fungistatic:
A chemical which inhibits the growth of fungi.

The words bactericidal, fungicidal and microbiocidal all mean that the chemical will kill micro-organisms. Here are just a few of the many micro-organisms with the infections they cause:
Staphylococcus aureus:
Found in mucus membranes, causing boils and abscesses.
Trichophylon menagrophytes:
Pus bacillus causes spots and boils.
Candida albicans:
Yeast-like mould which is the main cause of thrush and athlete's foot.

AREAS OF USE

The main use of microbiocidal finishes is for textiles which are being handled continuously by a large number of people. These include hotels, hospitals, institutional homes and student hostels, where mattress ticking, blankets and pillows, carpets and upholstery all come into contact with a large number of different individuals.

The normal amount applied depends on the efficiency of the particular product, but add-on weights of one to four per cent are commonly quoted.

RESIN FINISHING

> **Resin finishing** was originally developed in the mid 1920s to improve the crease recovery problems associated with cellulosic materials and to give them a recovery from creasing similar to that of wool. It was found that urea and formaldehyde would react with the hydroxyl groups in cellulose to form a bond which gave the product both good recovery from creasing and improved dimensional stability.

The cellulose molecules are crosslinked by resin. The resin plus a catylist, softener and wetting agent would be padded onto a cotton substrate at a pick-up of about eighty per cent; it would be padded on to the fabric at six to eight per cent, dried at 120°C to a residual moisture of eight per cent, cured at 160°C for three minutes, washed to remove any catalyst and unreacted resin and finally heat set to width and dried.

The resulting fabric from such a process would have an improved crease recovery. However, in addition to improving the crease recovery, it was also found that resin finishing improved the dimensional stability of the fabric to washing. So a fabric that in the untreated state would have a wash shrinkage of eight per cent would have a wash shrinkage of less than three per cent after resin finishing.

The shrinkage of fabrics during washing can have many causes, but when we are dealing with cotton goods there are two main causes. The first of these – relaxation shrinkage – was dealt with in the section on compressive shrinkage. The second is due to the swelling of the yarn by water adsorption. This can be illustrated below in Figure 22.5.

Figure 22.5 shows the effect of water adsorption. The fibre swells and the only way the yarn can accommodate the greater path length is by shrinking in length.

If the swelling of cotton can be prevented, so can swelling shrinkage. Resins can crosslink the cellulose chains and in so doing they also prevent swelling.

CREASE RECOVERY

The resins crosslink cellulose chains and they do so in the amorphous regions of the structure where the spacing between fibre molecules is relatively open. The effect of this

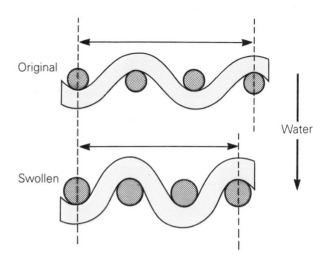

Figure 22.5 Swelling shrinkage.

is to give a more crystalline character to the fibre, so that if the fibre is distorted it will have a greater tendency to spring back to its original position. If the fabric is cured with a resin in a flat configuration it will have a tendency to recover to the original flat position. This pseudocrystalline character that the resin treatment gives the fabric also has the effect of making the fabric stiffer (increases the flexural modulus of the fabric). This in turn causes a decrease in both the **abrasion resistance** and the **tear strength** of the fabric. No one treatment can maximise all fibre properties; it is a case of prioritising according to the requirements of the end-product. A summary of the possible effects of resin treatment on cotton fabric is given in Table 22.3.

All the changes in physical properties can be accounted for by the fact that a crease-resistant finish will increase the flexural modulus (stiffness) of the cotton fibre or will crosslink the amorphous regions of the fibre. The decreased tear strength of the treated fabric may be explained by the fact that the more stiff a fabric becomes, the easier it is to tear it.

Table 22.3 Possible effects of resin treatment on cotton fabric

Property	Effect on resin treatment
Crease recovery	Improved
Wash shrinkage	Decreased
Stiffness	Increased
Abrasion resistance	Lowered
Tear strength	Lowered
Handle	Harsher
Effect on dyes	Tends to yellow
Environment	Formaldehyde
Bleach	Cl retention

Change in shade towards the yellow end of the spectrum occurs with all crease-resistant finishes.

The formaldehyde, which is liberated on the curing of these resins, can be retained by the fabric. In some countries, legislation exists to control the levels of formaldehyde which are permitted in certain garments, for example children's clothes. In such cases, zero formaldehyde resins have been developed.

Flame retardant finishes

One of the unfortunate characteristics of the vast majority of textile products is that they burn in air with a great deal of heat. Many fires in the home start with a textile material, so the inhibition of burning in textiles has been one of the most important tasks of the textile finisher over the last 20 years and has occupied an important place in textile research.

THE BURNING PROCESS

The mechanism of burning is a relatively simple process. For the combustion process to start there must first be an igniting source. This produces decomposition of the textile material which releases flammable gases and, in the presence of oxygen in the atmosphere, these ignite and form a flame. In this combustion process large amounts of heat are generated which in turn cause further decomposition of the textile, leading to more decomposition products and so spreading the combustion. This is a feedback process because once ignition has begun, the combustion will continue because

the heat generated by the burning decomposition products provides a feedback to the textile material causing further decomposition, until all the textile material is consumed. The process is illustrated in Figure 22.6.

When cellulose is heated, it decomposes into a series of flammable combustion products which, if a source of ignition is present, will ignite and continue to burn until all the textile is consumed or the flame is extinguished. The principle fuel produced during this decomposition is **levoglucosan**.

The levoglucosan is an excellent fuel which burns readily in the presence of air to give carbon dioxide and water. If cotton is treated with a strong dehydrating agent, this produces a black char and no flammable gases are evolved. It was found that all **Lewis acids** – those materials which have the ability to accept a pair of electrons – will act as dehydrating agents for cellulose at high temperature. Any material which does not affect the properties of cellulose at normal temperatures but which will decompose when heated to give a Lewis acid will act as a flame-retardant material. Cellulose starts to decompose at about 250°C, so for a flame retardant to work, the Lewis acid must be produced at temperatures below this figure. This is exactly what happens when ammonium phosphate is used as a flame retardant. At normal temperatures this salt is inert as far as the cotton is concerned, but as the temperature is raised it decomposes into ammonia which is given off as a gas and phosphoric acid. The phosphoric acid is a Lewis acid which catalyses the dehydration of the cellulose and suppresses the formation of flammable volatiles. In the early days of flame-retardant treatments, the soluble salts of phosphoric acid were used as finishing agents. However, these are soluble and the treatments were not therefore durable to washing.

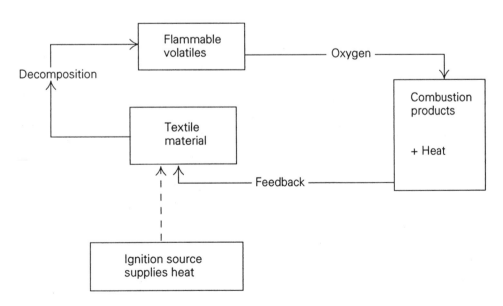

Figure 22.6 Initiation and propagation mechanism of combustion.

DURABLE FLAME-RETARDANT TREATMENTS

> There are two major flame-retardant treatments which are popular today: **Proban** (produced by Albright and Wilson) and **Pyrovatex** (produced by Ciba-Geigy).

The Proban process uses a phosphorus-containing material which is reacted with urea and the reaction product is padded on to cotton fabric and dried. The fabric is then reacted with ammonia and finally oxidised with hydrogen peroxide. The full reaction scheme is as follows: the fabric is padded with Proban CC, dried to a residual moisture content of 12 per cent, left to react with dry ammonia gas, is oxidised with hydrogen peroxide, washed off and dried again, and is finally softened.

There is no actual bonding to the surface of the cellulose but the insoluble Proban polymer is held by mechanical means in the cellulose yarns. Because of this, Proban-treated fabric has a rather harsh handle and some softening is usually required before the fabric is fit for sale.

Pyrovatex, on the other hand, is closely related to the crosslinked resins used in textile finishing and is in fact always applied with a crosslinked resin to form a chemical bond to the cellulose. The application scheme is as follows: pad the Pyrovatex and resin crosslinking agent plus catalyst, dry at 120°C, cure at 160°C for three minutes, wash in dilute sodium carbonate, then wash in water.

Since the reaction is with the cellulose, the flame retardant is chemically bound to the fibre and is therefore durable. Because the flame retardant has to be applied with a crosslink resin, the finished fabric has good dimensional stability and also excellent crease-recovery properties, making this finish the one preferred for curtains. Unfortunately, these desirable properties are not without disadvantages and the main one in the case of Pyrovatex is the loss in tear strength which occurs with this and all crosslinking systems.

These two materials represent the major flame-retardant treatments for cellulose.

FLAME RETARDANCY BY BACKCOATING

Regulations for furniture fire safety have been introduced in many countries and these often require that all upholstery materials should withstand certain tests. Backcoating is the main means by which many of these regulations are being met. The majority of backcoating formulations are based on the well known flame-retardant effect of the combination of antimony oxide and a halogen, usually bromine but chlorine is also used to a lesser degree. The mixture for this is one part of antimony oxide to two parts of a bromine containing organic compound. Softeners are often added to the basic formulation which modify the fabric handle. In addition, foaming agents may be included to enable the use of foam application techniques.

POLYESTER AND OTHER FIBRES

Flame-retardant treatments are now available for most of the synthetic fibres, the major one being polyester which is now sold in a non-burning form with the flame retardant built into the polymer molecule by the fibre maker. This has found many uses, particularly in the area of hospital bedding where the easy laundering characteristics of the polyester fibre make it an obvious choice. However, it does have one main drawback and that is the thermoplastic nature of the fibre itself, for when the flame-retardant polyester is subjected to a naked flame, it melts and forms molten drips which could, in the case of immobile patients, cause serious injury.

The alternative durably-treated cotton forms a hard protective char when subjected to the same treatment, which could protect the patient and act as a barrier to the flame.

Antistatic finishes

Static electricity is formed when two dissimilar materials are rubbed together; it cannot be formed if the materials are identical. When dissimilar materials are rubbed together, a separation of charges occurs and one of the materials becomes positively charged and the other negatively charged. The actual sign of the charge depends on the nature of the two materials which are taking part and this may be found from the triboelectric series, shown in Table 22.4. Materials at the top of the table will derive a positive charge when rubbed with any of the materials lower in the table.

Cotton has very good antistatic properties and few problems are encountered with this material. The basic reason for this is that the regain moisture content of cotton is high which provides the fibre with sufficient conductivity to dissipate any charge that might accumulate. In synthetic fibres, which have a low water content and are sufficiently non-conductive to hold a static charge on the surface, severe static problems can arise. Some synthetics, particularly polyesters, can sustain such a high charge density on the surface that they can actually ionise the air in the vicinity, giving rise to a spark which discharges the static that has been built up. In most cases, this results in a mild shock to the person experiencing this static discharge but where explosive gases might be present, it can result in disaster.

Table 22.4 The triboelectric series

Positive end
Polyurethane
Nylon
Wool
Silk
Rayon
Cotton
Acetate
Polypropylene
Polyester
Acrylic
PVC
PTFE
Negative end

> Antistatic treatments are based on the principle of making the fibre conductive so that high charge densities are dissipated before sparks can form.

This is done by the application of both anionic and cationic agents to the fibre. Typical structures for these materials are very similar to the softening agents used for cotton, which contain a long chain hydrocarbon with an ionic group at the end. One of the most interesting developments in the field of antistatic treatments has been the development of the Permolose finishes by ICI which consist of block co-polymers of ethylene oxide and a polyester. When polyester fibres are treated with this, the polyester portion of the co-polymer is adsorbed by the polyester fibre but the polyethylene oxide portion is incompatible with the polyester fibre and so remains on the surface, where it attracts water and forms a conductive surface on the polyester fibre.

Mechanical finishes

Calendering

> Calendering may be defined as the modification of the surface of a fabric by the action of heat and pressure.

The finish is obtained by passing the fabric between heated rotating rollers (or bowls) when both speed of rotation and pressure applied are variable. The surfaces of the rollers can be either smooth or engraved to provide the appropriate finish to the fabric, and the rollers may be made of various materials from hardened chromium-plated steel to elastic thermoplastic rollers.

Calendering is done for many purposes but the principal ones are: smoothing the surface of the fabric; flattening slubs; increasing the fabric lustre (silk-like to high gloss finishes obtainable); closing the threads of a woven fabric; increasing the fabric opacity; improving the handle of a fabric (softening); surface patterning by embossing; and consolidation of nonwoven fabrics.

The flattening of the fabric is illustrated in Figure 22.7, which shows the effect of the flattened yarn structure. This gives a greater light reflectance than the original rounded yarn structure in the first of the diagrams.

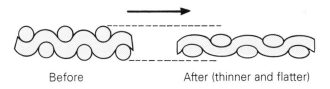

Before   After (thinner and flatter)

Figure 22.7 Effect of calendering on fabric.

TYPES OF CALENDER

In general, calenders have between two and seven rollers, with the most common being the three-bowl calender. Perhaps the most important factor in calender design is the composition of the rollers and their surface characteristics.

Textile calenders are made up from alternate hard steel and elastic bowls. The elastic bowls may be made from either compressed paper or compressed cotton on a steel core. However, a lot of modern calenders are made with a thick thermoplastic covering of nylon. These have the advantage that they are less liable to damage from knots, seams and creases than cotton and paper bowls, and this is important because such damage would mark off on to the calendered fabric. Nylon 6-covered rollers often enable the required effects to be achieved in a single nip, thus reducing the overall number of bowls.

In two-bowl calenders, it is normal to have the steel bowl on top so that any finish can be seen by the operator. This type of arrangement is often used with the nylon bottom bowl mentioned previously, especially where the calender is used for glazing or the embossed type of finishes.

The arrangement in which two steel-surfaced bowls are run in contact with each other only occurs in exceptional circumstances, for example for the compaction of non-woven fabrics. Here both bowls are usually oil heated so that some form of permanent heat setting of the fabric occurs.

An arrangement with two elastic bowls running in contact is not common but is sometimes used on cotton knit goods to obtain a soft handle.

The three-bowl calender was developed from the two bowl and with this type of calender it is normal to pass the fabric only through the top nip, with the bowls arranged steel-elastic-steel. The bottom bowl is used to keep the central elastic bowl smooth and so assist the finishing.

Pressure used in all of the above calenders can be varied between 10 and 40 tonnes, with running speeds up to 60 metres per minute. However, these are very much average figures. Pressure may be as low as six tonnes for a one metre wide calender to as high as 120 tonnes for a three metre wide calender. In addition, running speeds of 20 metres per minute are typical on an embossing calender, while on a glazing calender speeds of over 150 metres per minute have been quoted.

The temperatures to which the calender rollers are raised can vary from room temperature to 250°C, however it must be stressed that temperature control is of vital importance, with a tolerance of ±2°C being commonly quoted. Some generalisation can be made, for example for a 100 per cent cotton fabric: cold bowls give a soft handle without much lustre; warm bowls (40–80°C) give a slight lustre; hot bowls (150–250°C) give a greatly improved lustre, which can be further improved by the action of friction and waxes.

TYPES OF CALENDERED FINISH

1. *Swissing or normal gloss.* A cold calender produces a smooth, flat fabric. If the steel bowl of the calender is heated, the calender produces a lustrous surface in addition to smoothness. If a seven-bowl, multipurpose calender is used, a smooth fabric with surface gloss on both sides can be achieved.

2. *Chintz or glazing.* This gives the highly polished surface which is associated with glazed chintz. The effect is obtained by heating the top bowl on a three-bowl calender and rotating it at a greater speed than that of the fabric. The speed of this top bowl can vary between 0 and 300 per cent of that of the fabric. In certain cases, where a very high gloss is required, the fabric is often pre-impregnated with a wax emulsion which further enhances the polished effect. This type of calendering is often called friction calendering.

3. *Schreiner or silk finishing.* This is the name given to the silk-like finish on one side of the fabric. It is produced by embossing the surface of the fabric with a series of fine lines. These lines are usually at an angle of about 30° to the warp threads. The effect can be made permanent by the use of thermoplastic fabric or, in the case of cotton, by previous impregnation with a resin prior to drying and calendering. The effect becomes permanent and durable to washing when the resin is subsequently polymerised by baking.

4. *Delustering.* This is commonly achieved by passing the fabric through the bottom two bowls of a three-bowl calender, where these are both elastic. However, steel bowls with a special matt finish have been manufactured, which are very effective for this purpose.

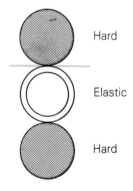

Hard steel bowl

Soft elastic bowl on a steel core

Figure 22.8 Two-bowl calender.

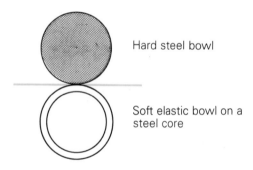

Hard

Elastic

Hard

Figure 22.9 Three-bowl calender.

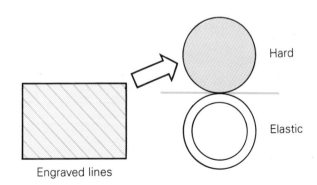

Engraved lines

Hard

Elastic

Figure 22.10 Schreiner finishing.

5. *Chasing.* The fabric is threaded through the calender in such a way as to press the fabric against itself several times. It is common to use a five- or seven-bowl calender, the fabric passing through each nip of the calender in two of three layers.

6. *Palmer finishing.* In this type of finish, the damp fabric is carried on the inside of a felt blanket round a steam-heated cylinder, often called a Palmer Drier. The face of the fabric, which is run on the surface of the heated cylinder, is lightly polished by it while the back of the fabric, which is in contact with the felt blanket, takes on a roughened effect. This finish is particularly popular for cotton drill fabric.

Raising

> Raising is the technique used to produce a brushed or napped appearance. It is achieved by teasing out the individual fibres from the yarns so that they stand proud of the surface.

The way this was done originally was to use the seed pod of the thistle which was known as a teasel. These teasels were nailed to a wooden board and the fabric was drawn over them. This produced a fabric with a hairy surface which had improved insulating properties. This method has been superseded by the use of rotating wire brushes, though teasels are still used where a very gentle raising action is required, such as in the case of mohair shawls.

MODERN RAISING MACHINES

All modern raising machines use a hooked or bent steel wire to tease the fibres from the surface of the fabric. The most important factor in the raising operation is the relationship between the point and the relative speed of the cloth.

The raising wires or card wires as they are called are mounted on a flexible base, which is then wrapped around a series of rollers, which are themselves mounted on a large cylindrical frame shown in Figure 22.11.

The raising action is brought about by the fabric passing over these rotating rollers and the wire points teasing out the individual fibres in the yarn. Since there are a large number of points acting on the fabric at any moment, the individual fibres must be sufficiently free to be raised from the fibre surface. This is influenced by a combination of the inter-fibre friction and the degree of twist in the raised yarns. For ideal raising the yarns should be of low twist and be lubricated.

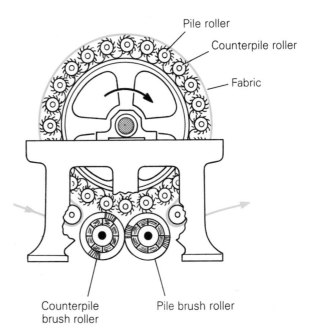

Figure 22.11 Raising machine.

Note that because the fabric runs in the warp direction over the machine, only the weft threads are at right angles to the rotating raising wires and so only the weft threads take part in the raising process.

RAISING ACTION

From Figure 22.11, it can be seen that both the card wire rollers and the cylinder to which these are attached may be rotated and it is the relative speed of these in relation to the fabric which determines the raising action. These actions are called the pile and the counter pile actions and are shown in Figure 22.12.

In the counter-pile action, the working roller rotates in the opposite direction to that of the cylinder, with the points of the wire moving in the direction of rotation. This action pulls individual fibre ends out from the surface.

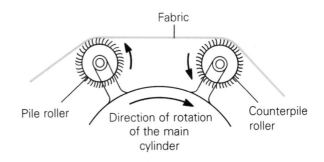

Figure 22.12 Pile and counterpile actions.

In the pile action, the points of the wire are pointing away from the direction of movement of the fabric and this results in an action where the raised fibres are subject to combing, which tends to tuck back the fibres into the body of the fabric. The most common raising action uses a combination of both these effects and produces an even raise over the whole of the fabric surface.

CROPPING OR SHEARING

This is a process by which the fibres which protrude from the surface of a fabric are cut to an even height. The principle used is that a spiral cutter rotates against a stationary blade and cuts off any material protruding from the fabric surface. Cropping has been described briefly in Chapter 20 where its role in wool fabric preparation processes was explored.

This principle is illustrated in Figure 22.13, which shows the fabric passing over the cutting bed and the protruding hairs on the surface being caught between the rotating head of the spiral cutter and the ledger blade. By raising and lowering the height of the cutting bed, the depth of cut may be varied. Obviously, the cutting action produces a great deal of cut pile and this must be removed by a strong suction, otherwise a large amount of fibre dust rapidly accumulates. To achieve an even cut and a smooth surface, several passes through the machine or a single pass through a multiple-head machine are required. Average speeds of about 15 metres per minute are commonly encountered.

One important use for this technique is the production of pile fabrics from a looped terry fabric. When this type of fabric is cropped, the top of the loops of the terry fabric are cut off and a velvet-like appearance is produced. Recently, knitted loop-pile fabrics have been produced and when these fabrics are sheared, a knitted velour is produced which has been widely exploited in the upholstery market.

Finally, in the production of high quality woollen suiting, cropping is often done as a final stage to remove surface hairs.

Sueding or emerising

This process is referred to as sueding or emerising or, in some instances, sanding because it involves the use of sandpaper or emery paper to abraid the surface of the fabric to produce a suede-like appearance. The abrasive material is wrapped around rotating rollers over which the fabric passes.

> The effect of emerising is to cut some of the fibres on the surface of the fabric and so to produce an abraided appearance on the fabric.

A line drawing of the process is shown in Figure 22.14.

The main difference between sueding and raising is that, in raising, the fibre ends are plucked out of the fabric whereas in sueding they are cut. This used to be a method by which imitation chamois leather was produced, but it is now used mainly in outerwear to produce the so-called 'peach skin' effect.

Compressive shrinkage

The shrinkage of fabrics on washing is a well-known phenomenon. It is caused in part by the production and processing stresses on the fabric.

Production stresses are introduced into the fabric by the tension placed on yarn during the weaving or knitting of the fabric and also by the torsional forces on fibres during production of the yarn. Processing stresses are introduced during the bleaching, dyeing and finishing of a fabric by pulling the fabric in the warp direction. This tends to remove the warp crimp from the fabric as illustrated in Figure 22.15.

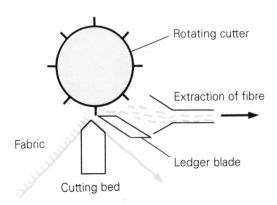

Figure 22.13 Cropping.

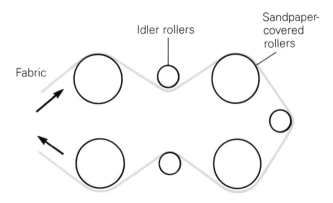

Figure 22.14 Sueding.

To replace the warp crimp and so minimise warp shrinkage, a process known as compressive shrinkage is carried out on the fabric to replace the crimp which has been pulled out in preparation and coloration processes. This may be illustrated in the following way: a strip of fabric is placed on a convex rubber surface and gripped at each end. As the rubber is allowed to straighten, the length of the fabric exceeds that of the rubber. However, if the fabric could be stuck to the surface of the rubber, the fabric would be subjected to compression and warp crimp would be introduced.

This principle is applied to the compressive shrinking machine, where the cloth is fed in a plastic state on to a thick rubber belt at point A in Figure 22.16. While the belt is in the convex position from A to B, the fabric merely lies on the surface, but at point B the belt starts to wrap its way round a large heated cylinder and so changes from a convex to a concave shape. This means that the surface of the rubber belt contracts and the fabric, which is held on to the surface of the rubber, is subject to a warp compression over the region C to D. The actual degree of shrinkage which takes place is controlled by the amount of fabric fed on to the rubber belt and the pressure between the heated metal cylinder and the belt (this increases or decreases the concave shape of the rubber belt).

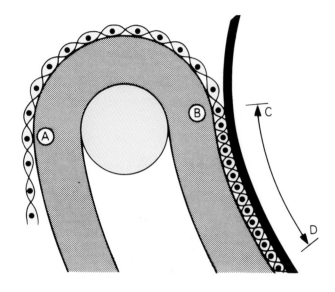

Figure 22.16   Compressive shrinkage.

Effectiveness of finishing treatments

Crease resistance

The resistance of a fabric to creasing can be assessed subjectively or objectively. The most popular objective method measures crease recovery angle.

A small rectangular specimen is folded double and placed between two glass plates under pressure so as to crease it. The creased specimen is then placed on a gauge and allowed to recover. The angle through which the folded specimen recovers is measured.

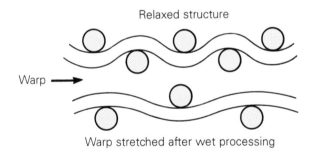

Figure 22.15   Warp tension in woven fabric.

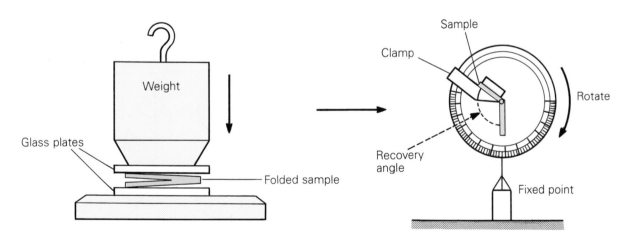

Figure 22.17   Crease recovery measurement.

Dimensional stability

> There are several processes and after-care agencies which can cause a change in the dimensions of a fabric, such as washing, dry cleaning, heat and steam.

A large square specimen of fabric is prepared and marked with a pattern of eight dots, a standard distance apart. This allows three-dimension measurements to be made in each direction. The fabric is then treated with the appropriate agency (washing, for example) under standard conditions. After drying under the appropriate standard conditions, the distances between the marks are remeasured giving three measurements in each direction. The average percentage change from the original dimensions is calculated.

$$\text{Dimensional change} = \frac{(\text{original dimension} - \text{final dimension})}{\text{original dimension}}$$

The **dimensional stability** in each direction is determined and quoted separately.

Flame retardancy

Flame retardancy is such a complex subject that the basic principles of evaluation will only be discussed.

A rectangular specimen is suspended vertically and a small gas flame applied under the bottom or near the bottom for a short period of time. Various observations and measurements may be made such as: the distance the flame travels; speed of flame travel; dimensions of any damage; or occurrence of smouldering.

The two directions of the fabric are tested separately and if the face and back are different they are also tested separately.

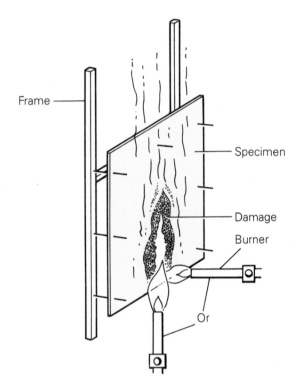

Figure 22.19   Flammability assessment.

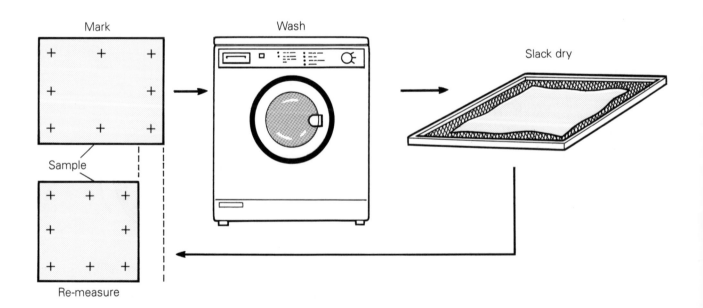

Figure 22.18   Dimensional stability measurement.

Water repellency

There are various methods of evaluating the water repellency properties of a fabric. One of the most realistic principles is to subject a specimen of fabric to an artificial shower of rain for a short period of time. The repellency properties of the tested specimen can be assessed subjectively or objectively in various ways: by subjective assessment of wetting on appearance; by measuring the per centage absorption calculated from the difference in original and final masses; by measuring the amount of water which penetrates; or by measuring the speed at which water penetrates.

It is also possible to measure the pressure required to force water through the fabric.

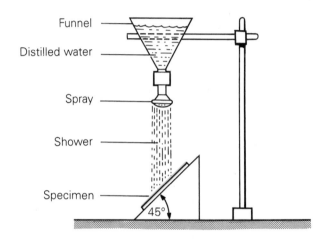

Figure 22.20 Assessment of water repellency.

Mechanical properties

The reasons for testing fabric mechanical properties depend on the intended end-use of the fabric. If the fabric is to be used for industrial purposes; it must be ensured that it is strong enough to perform effectively. If it is to be used for apparel then the main reason for measuring the mechanical properties is to ensure that it has not suffered any chemical damage during wet processing. Measurement of mechanical properties is much quicker than carrying out chemical tests.

BREAKING LOAD AND EXTENSION

There are several ways of preparing fabric specimens for the test.

1. *Frayed strip method.* This is used with certain types of woven fabric. Rectangular specimens are cut wider than required. Threads are removed from each side until the specimen is

reduced to a standard width. This method ensures that all the longitudinal threads extend the full length of the specimen and that none have been severed during specimen preparation.

2. *Cut strip method.* With some types of woven construction and with felted fabrics, it is impracticable to remove threads from the sides of the specimens. The specimens are therefore cut to the exact width required.

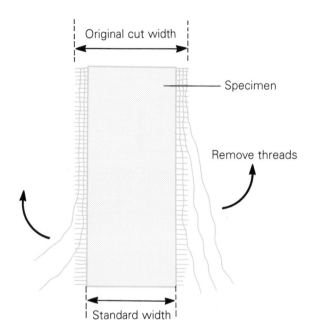

Figure 22.21 Specimen preparation – frayed strip.

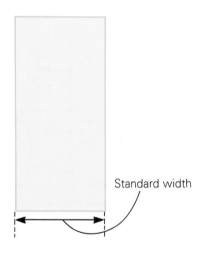

Figure 22.22 Cut strip method.

3. *Grab method.* Specimens of knitted fabric distort when stretched during the test if prepared as above. To overcome this problem the specimen is cut wider than the standard width but only the middle portion is gripped and stressed during the test.

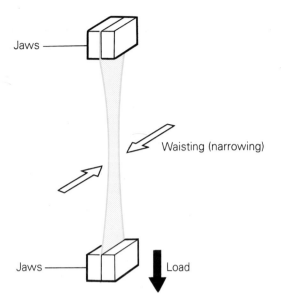

Figure 22.23 Fabric waisting during tensile testing.

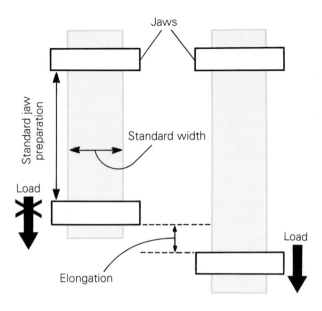

Figure 22.25 Fabric tensile testing.

The tear strength of a fabric is defined as the force required to continue a tear which has already started. There are several methods of specimen preparation. Some produce one tear and some produce two, so the results obtained are not comparable.

1. *Double rip method.* Rectangular specimens are prepared and two slits cut in the middle in the direction of the long axis.

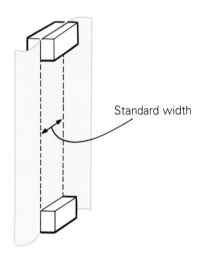

Figure 22.24 Grab method.

Specimens are prepared in the two directions. A specimen is gripped in the jaws of a tensile tester using a standard jaw separation. The specimen is elongated at a standard rate until it breaks.

The breaking load and breaking elongation are measured. The breaking elongation is converted to a percentage of the original jaw separation to give breaking extension.

$$\text{Breaking extension} = \frac{\text{breaking elongation}}{\text{original jaw separation}} \times 100\%$$

Measurements are made and quoted in the two directions separately.

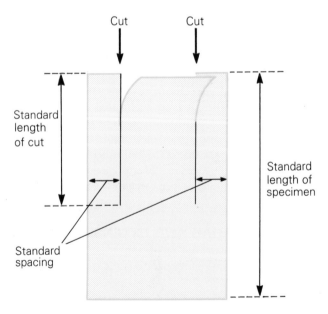

Figure 22.26 Specimen preparation for tear testing – double rip method.

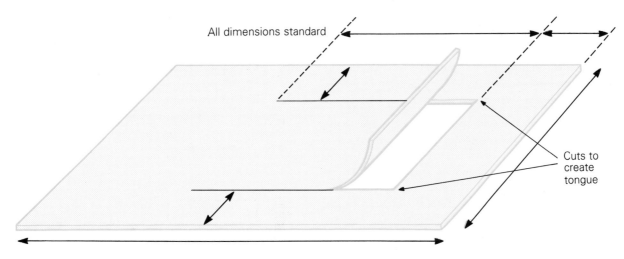

Figure 22.27   Tongue tear method.

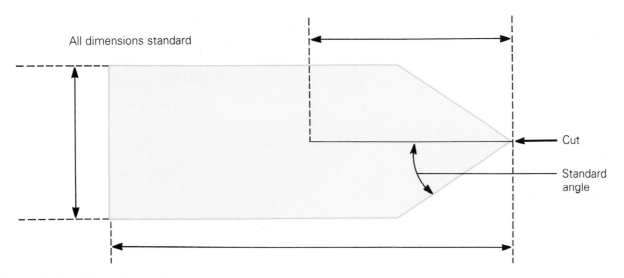

Figure 22.28   Wing rip method.

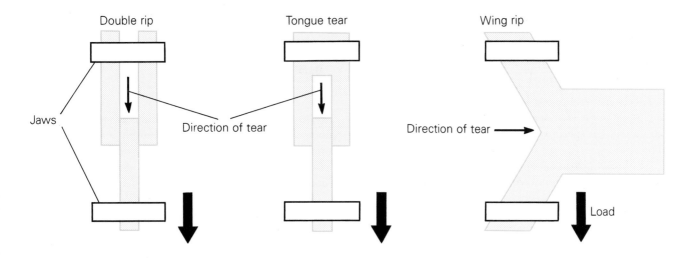

Figure 22.29   Fabric tear strength testing.

2. *Tongue tear method.* This is a similar method to the above but the cuts do not extend to the end of the specimen. They are cut so as to form a 'tongue'.
3. *Wing rip method.* The specimen shape and position of the cut are such that the specimen can be opened out to form a wing shape during the test.

Specimens are prepared with their long axes parallel to the two fabric directions. One part of the specimen is clamped in the top jaw of the tensile tester and the other part in the bottom jaw so that when the jaws are separated, the tear is propagated a specified distance.

From the graph of load against distance produced by the instrument, the median tearing force is determined. Separate determinations are carried out in each fabric direction. A tear in the weft direction ruptures the warp threads and vice versa. The graph produced is complex due to the fact that the threads are ruptured successively, making it difficult to analyse the results.

BALLISTIC TEAR STRENGTH

This method of determining fabric tear strength is used because it overcomes the problems of result analysis in the methods described above. In this method, the fabric is torn very rapidly by a falling pendulum and the mean tearing force determined.

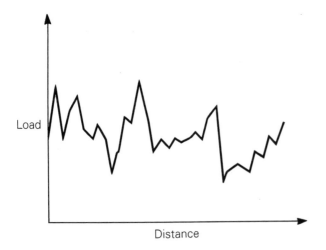

Figure 22.30 Fabric tear strength results.

The pendulum is initially in the horizontal position. The fabric is clamped between the pendulum and the fixed frame of the instrument. When the pendulum is released, the fabric is torn, absorbing some of the potential energy stored in the pendulum. The pendulum continues its swing rising up the other side and moving a pointer over a scale. The final height is lower than the initial height due to the absorption of energy.

Energy absorbed

$$= \text{initial potential energy} - \text{final potential energy}$$
$$= mgh_1 - mgh_2$$
$$= mg(h_1 - h_2)$$

since,

$$\text{energy} = \text{force} \times \text{distance}$$
$$\text{force} = \frac{\text{energy}}{\text{distance}}$$

The distance in this case is the distance moved by the pendulum during tearing of the specimen.

$$\text{distance} = 2 \times \text{length of tear}$$

Therefore,

$$\text{tearing force} = \frac{mg(h_1 - h_2)}{2 \times \text{length of tear}}$$

For a given instrument, m, g, h_1 and length of tear are constant, so the difference in heights is proportional to tearing force. The scale on the instrument measures this difference and is calibrated in force units.

The most popular instrument using the ballistic principle is the Elmendorf tear tester, originally developed for testing paper. With this instrument, the result indicated on the scale has to be multiplied by a factor (16, 32 or 64) depending on the mass of the pendulum. The pendulums are interchangeable.

BURSTING STRENGTH

The **bursting strength** of a fabric is the pressure required to rupture the fabric. Bursting strength measurement is commonly used with knitted and non-woven fabrics rather than breaking load and extension, as it does not suffer from some of the disadvantages of the latter method.

The fabric specimen is clamped by an anular clamp over a rubber diaphragm which is then inflated by pneumatic or hydraulic pressure until the fabric ruptures. The pressure inflating the diaphragm at this point is measured. The pressure measured is that required to rupture the fabric plus that required to inflate the diaphragm.

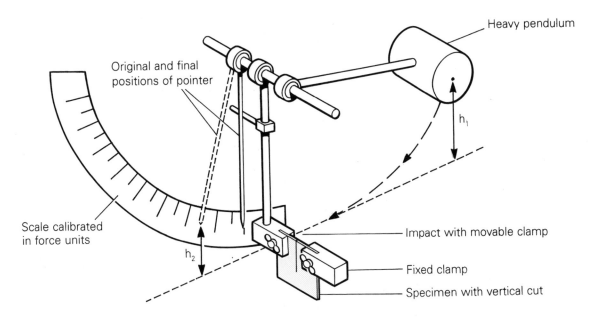

Figure 22.31 **Ballistic tear strength measurement.**

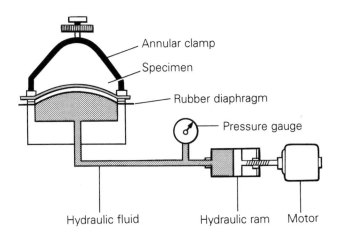

Figure 22.32 **Bursting strength.**

Fabric bursting strength
= pressure at time of rupture
− diaphragm inflation pressure

As the fabric is extended in all directions at the same time, measurements cannot be made in each direction as with most other fabric strength tests.

CHECK YOUR UNDERSTANDING

● Chemical finishing processes include: water repellency, oil and soil repellency, flame retardancy, handle modification (softening and stiffening), mothproofing, microbicidal finishes, resin finishes (crease resistance), and antistatic finishes.

● Mechanical finishing processes include calendering, raising, and cropping.

● Usually, chemical finishes are used purely to improve the performance of the end-product rather than its appearance. Finishes are usually applied as a solution or emulsion.

● Handle modification can mean softening or stiffening; starch has been used to stiffen cotton for hundreds of years while nonionic mineral oils or complicated cationic softeners lubricate the fabric, giving it a softer handle.

● Original water-repellent treatments would not endure cleaning. Modern repellents use fluorocarbons which gives the finish some durability. This method is also used for oil repellency.

● Soil release finishes contain hydrophilic polymers which create a wettable surface to the substrate, so that the washing water can move underneath dirt particles to remove them.

● Certain insects eat wool textiles. Some finishes can be applied which are indigestible to the insect or which are repellent.

● Microbicidal finishes, which prevent growth of germs and fungi, are used in hospitals, hostels, hotels or any other place where large numbers of different people come into contact with the textile.

● Resin finishes were originally used to give cotton crease recovery properties. Resins crosslink the cellulose molecules within the fibre producing a more resilient product.

● With new regulations being introduced by many countries, flame-retardant finishes are becoming more necessary. The two major flame retardant finishes for cotton are Proban and Pyrovatex.

● Calendering is modification of the fabric surface by use of heat and pressure. Possible benefits are: smoothing the surface of the fabric; increasing the fabric lustre; closing the threads of a woven fabric; improving the handle of a fabric; surface patterning by embossing; and consolidation of non-woven fabrics.

● Raising produces a brushed appearance to the fabric and is carried out by a machine which is similar to a woollen or worsted spinning carding machine – cylinders covered in fine wire, which tease the fibres from the fabric surface.

● Cropping cuts the fibres protruding from the fabric surface. It can be set to remove all the fibre or a specified pile height. It is used to cut terry towelling loops to give a velvet-like appearance, knitted loop pile to form a velour fabric and, as mentioned in Chapter 20, for surface hair removal from woollen goods.

● Sueding uses sandpaper to abrade the fabric surface to give a suede-like appearance.

● Compressive shrinkage is used to replace warp crimp which is removed by stresses in weaving and wet processing.

● There are various tests available to evaluate the effectiveness of the various finishing treatments. Crease resistance, dimensional stability and water repellency can all be measured. Flame retardancy is more complicated and there are many tests available.

● Mechanical properties of finished cloth are measured to ensure that there has been no chemical damage caused by wet processing. These tests include bursting strength, tear strength, breaking load and extension.

REVISION EXERCISES AND QUESTIONS

1 Why is a baking process commonly used after the fabric finishing stage?

2 In years past, fabric stiffening was the only method of handle modification. Can you guess why fabric softening is now much more popular?

3 What treatment was originally used for water repellency?

4 The original moth repellent for wool was a dye called Martius Yellow. Why was the idea of using certain dyes as insecticides abandoned?

5 What are the two reasons given for the use of microbicidal finishes?

6 Resin finishes improve crease recovery and dimensional stability. What are the disadvantages of this finish?

7 Why are antistatic finishes necessary?

8 How do calendar rollers produce a more lustrous fabric?

9 What yarn characteristics influence raising?

10 What after-care agencies can cause a change in dimensional stability?

11 Why are mechanical tests such as fabric breaking load measured after finishing?

Answers to questions and answering hints

Introduction

This section provides you with all the answers to the variety of questions and exercises given in the book. Always try a question or exercise yourself before you look at the answer. This will increase your understanding of the topic and give you practice in answering questions. If you are not sure of a particular answer, re-read the relevant section or chapter in the book to revise the work. You need to understand why a question has a particular answer, so that you can apply your understanding to similar types of question or exercise in your examinations and course assignments.

The book contains a variety of types of question and exercise. Find out the types of question that you will be expected to answer and their pattern. If possible, obtain past papers to support your work and revision. Some of the questions in the book require longer answers. We have provided hints on how to tackle these questions, and on the range of topics that you should include. Practise giving full answers to these questions and then check the answering hints to see that your have included all the relevant topics.

To revise a topic quickly you can also refer to the Check Your Understanding sections given at the end of each chapter, and the list of key words with definitions given at the end of the book.

Hints to answering questions in examinations and course work

☐ Read all the questions carefully before you try anything. Make sure that you understand what each question is asking you to do.

☐ Plan the time that you will spend on each question. Use the marks as a guide: the more marks a question is worth, the more time it is worth spending on it.

☐ If you have a choice of questions, try to make your choice and stick to it. Don't change your mind halfway through the examination.

☐ Make sure that you earn all the easy marks. Do not spend too long on a question you find difficult. Leave it; if you have time, you can try it again later when you have finished all the other questions.

☐ Keep an eye on the time. Make sure that you try all the questions you are required to answer.

☐ Always present your work as clearly as you can, whether you are writing or drawing. Make your work easy to follow for the examiner or assessor.

☐ Allow time at the end to check and improve your answers.

☐ In practical work, make sure that you understand what you are being asked to do by re-reading the question before you start. Follow all instructions carefully.

Chapter 1

1 Staple fibres are of a definite length, while continuous filaments are of indefinite length – as long as the package that they are wound on to.

2 Silk is the only natural filament.

3 If fibres can be dyed at the last stages of product processing the manufacturer can respond quickly to a customer's requirements for the latest shades, or the most popular shades.

4 The major subdivisions of natural fibres are protein, cellulosic and mineral.

5 The major subdivisions of man-made fibres are regenerated, modified regenerated, synthetic and mineral.

6 Whether it is made from staple fibres or continuous filaments; whether it is textured or not; yarn construction; and fabric construction.

7 Absorbency, softness, resilience, elasticity, warmth or coolness.

8 The flame retardancy of polyester is reduced by mixing with cotton.

9 Cotton.

10 Polyester.

Chapter 2

1 Wool and hair fibres (scales in the longitudinal section); cotton (convolutions in the longitudinal section); flax and other natural cellulosics (irregular longitudinal section and angular cross section).

2 There is a greater surface area for reflection for the same mass of fibre than there would be if coarser fibres were used.

3 It swells the fibre so that the cross section is near circular rather than bean shaped. Circular cross sections appear to be more lustrous.

4 The addition of delustrant particles makes the fibre appear to be less lustrous; the more particles added, the more matt the fibre will appear.

5 When looked at from a different angle, the textile will appear to have different coloured sheen. This is most noticeable if a bright fibre is dyed to a dark shade.

6
$$\text{Decitex} = \frac{\text{mass (g)}}{\text{length (m)}} \times 10\,000$$
$$= \frac{0.035}{100} \times 10\,000$$
$$= 3.5$$

7 In tensile testing the fibre is stressed in the direction of the main axis (along the fibre length). Tensile stress results in tensile strain.

8 If fibres are to be blended together they should ideally have very similar initial moduli. If they have vastly different moduli, one of the fibre types will contribute very little to the load-bearing initially.

9 The handle and drape of fabrics is largely dependent on the flexural and torsional rigidities of the component fibres.

10 Fibres will hold different levels of moisture at different temperatures and humidities. This will affect the mass of the fibre, and so any linear density measurements.

11
$$\text{weight of moisture} = \text{sample weight} - \text{dry sample weight}$$
$$= 5.55 - 5.0 = 0.55$$
$$\text{regain} = \frac{\text{moisture}}{\text{dry weight}} \times 100$$
$$\text{regain} = \frac{0.55}{5.0} \times 100$$
$$= 11\%$$
$$\text{content} = \frac{\text{moisture}}{\text{sample weight}} \times 100$$
$$= \frac{0.55}{5.55} \times 100$$
$$= 9.9\%$$

The sample is silk.

12 The fibres swell, causing yarns and so fabrics to shrink in length.

Chapter 3

1 Linear density is difficult and time consuming to determine for staple fibres.

2
$$\text{tex} = \frac{\text{mass (g)}}{\text{number of fibres} \times \text{cut length (mm)}} \times 1000 \times 1000$$
$$= \frac{0.00017}{100 \times 10} \times 1000 \times 1000$$
$$= 0.17$$
0.17 tex = 1.7 decitex

3
$$\text{Fibre diameter}(\mu m) = 2 \times \text{image width (mm)}$$
$$= 2 \times 11$$
$$= 22\,\mu m$$

4 The resonant frequency of vibration which depends on: sample length, tension (both of which can be made constant) and linear density.

5 a) Hand stapling is a purely visual subjective assessment, in other words it is a personal opinion.
b) The oiled plate method is slow, as it deals with single fibres. Many fibres would have to be measured to give a statistically significant result.

6 It is a more realistic measure, as fibres are never completely straight during processing.

7 Constant rate of elongation (CRE), because it is easy to achieve.

8 The balance principle. It uses unconventional units, gives no breaking elongation and no measure of the variation between fibres, only the average properties.

9 It is a slow process.

10 It tells us if the fibre is thermoplastic or not. If it shrinks away from the flame and melts into a bead, it is thermoplastic.

11 If it is cellulose it will smell like burning paper; if it is protein it will smell like burning hair.

12 Some fibres will dissolve in more than one solvent.

Chapter 4

1 Polythene has polymer chains that branch and so are unable to pack together efficiently.

2 The number of carbon atoms in the repeat unit. Nylon 6.6 is made from two monomers, each containing six carbon atoms, while Nylon 6 is made from one monomer containing six carbon atoms.

3 Glucose.

4 Some amorphous regions are necessary to give the fibre flexibility and reactivity to moisture and chemicals such as dyes.

5 Close packing of molecules means that efficient intermolecular forces can exist, binding the molecules together.

6 a) This develops as the fibre grows.
b) This can be altered by drawing.

Chapter 5

1 Not all polymers meet the requirements to melt without decomposition and be stable at least 30° above the melting point.

2 If the polymer is unsuitable for melt extrusion and will not dissolve in a volatile solvent, the final option is wet extrusion.

3 It orientates the molecules, aligning them to the main fibre axis.

4 Melt extrusion – polyamide, polypropylene, polyester. Solvent-dry extrusion – triacetate, diacetate, some polyacrylics. Wet extrusion – some polyacrylics, viscose.

5 Industrialised countries have high labour costs, so hand picking would be too expensive.

6 Cooking oil, cattle food.

7 They form neps, they dye to a lighter shade than mature fibre and they break easily.

8 Trash content, micronaire value, colour, length and strength.

9 Wool availability is dependent on: the number of sheep that can live on an area of land; the expense of producing the fibre; and man-made fibre substitutes.

10 Breed of sheep, climate and health of the individual animal.

11 By retting, the controlled decomposition of the plant by micro-organisms.

12 Trilobal fibres do not show soiling to the same extent as circular fibres.

13 One type of acrylic co-polymer will give affinity to acid or basic dyes.

Chapter 6

1 Silk.

2 Continuous filament yarns have filaments that are as long as the yarn itself; they do not need twist to impart strength, only to hold the filaments together during subsequent processing.

3 $T = \dfrac{\text{mass (g)}}{\text{length (m)}} \times 1000$

$= \dfrac{4.2}{100} \times 1000$

$= \mathbf{42}$

4 $\text{Cotton count} = \dfrac{\text{length (yd)}}{\text{grains}} \times \dfrac{7000}{840}$

$= \dfrac{120}{60} \times \dfrac{7000}{840}$

$= \mathbf{16.7}$

5 $\text{Cotton count} = \dfrac{590.5}{T}$

$= \dfrac{590.5}{42}$

$= \mathbf{14.1}$

6 $T = \dfrac{590.5}{\text{cotton count}}$

$= \dfrac{590.5}{16.7}$

$= \mathbf{35.4}$

7 $\text{Twist factor} = \text{turns per metre} \times \sqrt{T}$

$= 700 \times \sqrt{30}$

$= \mathbf{3834.1}$

8 This yarn could be used as a warp yarn.

9 The broad classification of end-products could be apparel, household and industrial/medical.

Chapter 7

1 Cleaning, reduction in mass per unit length, blending and production of a continuous rope of fibres.

2 Combing removes short fibres, impurities and improves fibre alignment.

3 By drafting (pulling the fibres past one another).

4 The draft from sliver to yarn would be too great for one machine to handle.

5 $\text{Draft} = \dfrac{\text{input } T}{\text{output } T}$

$= \dfrac{6 \times 4}{3.6}$

$= \mathbf{6.7}$

6 Fibres of equal length, free to move independently and presented to the drafting system in an orderly way.

7 Doubling improves the blend and uniformity of the product.

8 The twist angle remains constant, giving higher levels of twist in thin places and lower levels of twist in thick places.

Chapter 8

1 $\dfrac{5.2 - 1.8}{5.2} \times 100 = \mathbf{65.4\%}$

2 Long term:
- variation in moisture content of the fibre during weighing;
- change of fibre supplier; and
- using dyed fibres from a different dye lot.

Short term:
- inadequate fibre separation;
- inadequate number of doublings; and
- too few fibres in the yarn cross section.

3 Change the sliver from tex to kilotex: $\dfrac{3500}{1000} = 3.5$ kilotex

$\text{Actual draft} = \dfrac{\text{input weight}}{\text{output weight}} = \dfrac{400}{3.5} = \mathbf{114.3}$

4 $3.9 \times 2 = 7.8$ kilotex polyester
            $4.0 \times 4 = 16.0$ kilotex cotton
total weight $= 7.8 + 16.0 = 23.8$ kilotex

$$\% \text{ polyester} = \frac{7.8}{23.8} \times 100 = \textbf{32.8\%}$$

$$\% \text{ cotton} = \frac{16}{23.8} \times 100 = \textbf{67.2\%}$$

5 This can be used to upgrade a cheaper raw material. It has recently been used to improve rotor spun yarns.

6 If too little twist is inserted, the roving will stretch during processing, causing variations in yarn thickness. If too much twist is inserted, there will be difficulty in drafting the roving at the ringframe.

7 Turns per metre $= \dfrac{\text{spindle revs } /\text{min}^{-1}}{\text{front roller delivery rate m/min}^{-1}}$

$$= \frac{15\,000}{16} = \textbf{937.5}$$

Chapter 9

1 The appearance is closer to that of staple-spun yarns. Different filaments can be mixed at the air jet, giving a wide range of blending possibilities. Non-thermoplastic filaments such as viscose can be textured.

2 a) Stretch-type yarns.
   b) Bulk yarns.

3 i) Sequential draw texturing; and
   ii) simultaneous draw texturing.
   In i), the two processes of drawing and texturing are separate from each other – there are two separate zones, drawing first, followed by texturing. In ii), undrawn yarn is fed to the texturing zone where it is simultaneously drawn and textured.

4 Crimping of man-made staple fibres.

5 Air-jet textured yarns are closer in appearance to staple-spun yarns. Other texturing methods have the higher speeds that would be required to link texturing directly to filament extrusion.

6 The worsted processing system.

7 Lower production costs due to a reduced number of processes; a saving in floor space; faster changeover times from one production run to another; improved evenness, cleanliness and fibre alignment leading to the possibility of spinning finer yarns; and possibility of producing high bulk yarns.

8 The system cannot cope with filaments of less than 1.2 decitex, and has a required fibre length of less then seven centimetres.

9 A relaxing process, using an autoclave, is needed because fibre characteristics have been altered by the stretch-break conversion method.

Chapter 10

1 This usually refers to the thickness of hand knitting yarns. Two-ply has two single strands plied together, three-ply has three single strands etc.

2 Embroidery – lustre.
   Poplins/voiles – regularity.
   Webbing – tenacity.
   Sewing threads – balance and tenacity.
   Hosiery – balance and regularity.

3 If a knitting yarn is not balanced, the resulting snarls will cause broken needles and/or holes in the fabric.

4 a) The tex system units were used, so either: 12 tex Z 700 × S 400; R 35 tex, or: R 35 tex S 400/3 Z 700; 12 tex.
   b) 2/20s. The rough count would be 10s woollen count.

5 The high capital outlay cost is the major disadvantage of the two-for-one twister.

6 Fancy yarns are not very hard wearing and will either be unable to withstand the stresses involved in fabric manufacture or will not perform adequately for the end-use.

7 The linear density only relates to the average yarn diameter. Some fancy yarns have very large effects, which means that the diameter might increase by 100 per cent, 200 per cent or more in certain places along the length of the yarn.

Chapter 11

1 a) $\text{tex} = \dfrac{\text{weight (g)}}{\text{length (m)}} \times 1000$

$$\text{tex} = \frac{5.8}{100} \times 1000 = \textbf{58}$$

   b) $\text{cc} = \dfrac{\text{length (yd)}}{\text{weight (grains)}} \times \dfrac{7000}{840}$

$$= \frac{120}{17} \times \frac{7000}{840} = \textbf{58.8}$$

c) The yarn in b) is the finest. The higher the number the finer the yarn with an indirect system, the higher the number the coarser the yarn with a direct system.

2 Change the units if necessary (25 mm = 2.5 cm).

$$\text{Strain \%} = \frac{\text{elongation}}{\text{initial length}} \times 100$$

$$= \frac{2.5}{50} \times 100 = \textbf{5\%}$$

$$\text{Load in N} = \text{mass (kg)} \times \text{acceleration } (\text{ms}^{-2})$$

$$\frac{160}{1000} \times 9.81 = 1.57$$

$$\text{Stress} = \frac{\text{load}}{\text{linear density}} = \frac{1.57}{9} = \textbf{0.17 N/tex}$$

3 The two factors causing yarn unevenness are variations in the fibre diameter, and variations in the number of fibres in the yarn cross section.

4 a)
$$\text{Actual } CV\% = \frac{sd}{X} \times 100$$
$$= \frac{2.5}{30} \times 100 = 8.33\%$$
$$\text{Limit } CV\% = \frac{k}{\sqrt{n}}$$
$$= \frac{106}{\sqrt{200}} = 7.49\%$$
$$\text{Index of irregularity} = \frac{\text{actual } CV}{\text{limit } CV}$$
$$= \frac{8.33}{7.49} = 1.1$$

b) The closer to 1 the index is, the more regular the yarn. This is a very regular yarn.

Chapter 12

1 Weaving, warp knitting and stitch bonded non-wovens.

2 Some processes require minimum friction during unwinding, such as weft knitting, in which case a larger angle taper is needed. Other processes are not as critical, so a shallower angle is used because this provides a compromise between maximum yarn on the package and suitable unwinding properties.

3 Some yarns cannot withstand the friction from drum-driven winders. Delicate staple yarns and continuous filament yarns are wound on spindle winders, eliminating the need for friction contact with the yarn package.

4 Precision winders can be set for close winding and this close packing puts as much yarn on the package as possible. Sewing threads are a typical example (the longest length of yarn possible is required from a small package).

5 Patterning can cause unlevel dyeing due to varying densities within the package. Sloughing-off, where more than one coil of yarn is removed from the package at once is common with patterning, causing end-breaks.

6 What is acceptable in the particular end-product determines how critically the clearer must be set.

7 If the unwinding tension varies it can cause end-breaks, barre fabric with filament yarns and 'repping' or lines in the fabric width.

8 Creeling systems such as magazine creeling or duplicate creels enable creeling to be carried out at the same time as warping.

9 The centre of the beam is now driven directly by motor. If the beam speed remained constant, the yarn speed and so the yarn tension would increase as the beam diameter increased, causing uneven density and crushing the yarn on the inner layers of the beam.

10 Both can be used, but section warping is preferred for complicated patterned warps.

11 Several warper's beams are passed through a size box which immerses the ends in the size liquor. Excess size is squeezed off before drying. The headstock of the sizing machine builds up a weaver's beam from the sheets off the warpers beams.

12 Sometimes the new warp is not made to the same specification as the old warp. The drop wires, healds and reed need to be cleaned and replaced occasionally. The widest looms cannot be knotted.

Chapter 13

1 In weft knitting loops are formed across the width of the fabric, with yarn fed at right angles to the fabric. In warp knitting, loops are formed down the fabric, with yarn fed in line with the fabric. In warp knitting, each needle must have at least one yarn to feed it. In weft knitting, as little as one yarn per machine can be used.

2 Plain single jersey fabric.

3 Courses per centimetre multiplied by wales per centimetre.

4 This is the front of the fabric on the machine, rather than the 'right' side of the fabric from the user's point of view.

5 Rib and interlock.

6 Tuck stitches hold the old loop of yarn, take more yarn, but do not knock-over the old loop, leaving both loops in the needle hook. Miss-stitches hold the old loop of yarn, but do not take more yarn and do not knock-over the old loop, leaving the old loop only in the hook of the needle.

7 A purl machine. The double-headed needle is pushed from one bed to the other, knitting first on one head of the needle, then on the other.

8 On rib machines the two sets of needles are positioned alternately one from each bed. On interlock machines the needles from each bed oppose each other.

9 The course length is equal to the total number of loop lengths produced by the machine in one complete cycle. The number of needles knitting in one course × loop length = course length.

10 Yarn feed rate effectively controls the loop length. Variations in yarn tension lead to variations in feed rate and so loop length variations.

Chapter 14

1 a) A drop in sales of shirting and sheeting due to the lack of comfort.

b) Competition from new textured weft knitted fabrics.

c) Inability to warp knit staple fibre yarns, and so an inability to compete with woven polyester/cotton fabrics.

2 a) Development of needles and yarns to enable commercial staple fibre warp knitted fabrics to be produced.

b) Diversification into geotextiles, technical fabrics and lace.

3 Each needle in the knitted width must receive at least one yarn per course.

4 Front guide bar 1-0/1-2; back guide bar 2-3/1-0. Reverse locknit.

5 Queenscord.

6 Locknit, used for underwear/lingerie.

7 Laying-in is used to create pattern effects, for example, a coarse or fancy yarn is often in-laid in a light weight curtain fabric. Self coloured coarse or lustrous yarns are in-laid in lace fabrics.

Chapter 15

1 Using a staple-spun yarn rather than a filament yarn will give a hairy, more irregular appearance to the fabric. A highly twisted yarn could produce a voile or crepe fabric with surface texture, while a plain weave fabric composed of continuous filament yarn would have a lustrous, very smooth appearance with minimal friction.

2 Length of warp: $(c + 1) = \dfrac{L_y}{L_f}$

$$L_y = (c + 1)L_f$$

$$L_y = \left[\frac{(6.5)}{100} + 1\right]500$$

$$= 1.065 \times 500$$

$$= \mathbf{532.5\ m}$$

Width of fabric: $(c + 1) = \dfrac{L_y}{L_f}$

$$L_f = \frac{L_y}{(c + 1)}$$

$$= \frac{1.5}{[(5.5/100) + 1]}$$

$$= \frac{1.5}{1.055}$$

$$= \mathbf{1.42\ m}$$

3 Warp weight = $20 \times 100 \times [1 + (4.5/100)] \times 30/1000 = 62.7$
Weft weight = $15 \times 100 \times [1 + (6/100)] \times 40/1000 = 63.6$
Fabric weight = $62.7 + 63.6 = 126.3$ grams per square metre.

$$K_1 = \frac{20 \times \sqrt{30}}{10}$$

$$= 10.95$$

$$K_2 = \frac{15 \times \sqrt{40}}{10}$$

$$= 9.49$$

$$K_c = 10.95 + 9.49 = \mathbf{20.44}$$

4 Weft-faced fabrics require more picks per centimetre. They take longer to weave than the warp-faced equivalent.

5

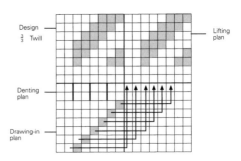

Chapter 16

1 The two layers of warp sheet forming a triangle in front of the reed.

2 The place where the warp ends and weft picks interlace to form the fabric.

3 The weft patterning mechanism.

4 Yarn type; width of fabric; method of weft insertion (dependent on yarn, fabric structures, patterning requirements, selvedge required); shedding system (dependent on desired range of weaves); special features, such as pile fabric requirements; and speed.

5 Shuttle.

6 Altering the height of the backrest can put greater tension on one warp sheet, improving the end spacing. The timing of shedding and weft insertion can minimise end grouping.

7 When there are more ends per centimetre than heald eyes available. The ends need to be split over two or more heald shafts, which will move in unison.

8 In a closed shed the healds must move to a level position after every pick, which could be wasted movement if the end is to remain in the same position for consecutive picks. In a fully open shed, the heald only moves when required, giving a speed advantage.

9 This is necessary to keep the shed angle at the feel (and so the shed size) constant.

10 A shuttle is the slowest method of weft insertion.

11 Weft patterning is achievable without reducing machine speed on a rapier loom.

12 If a hydrophilic yarn was used, it would retain too much water, take too long to dry, or cost too much to dry, and it might encourage fungal growth such as mildew.

13 When weft insertion speeds are high, this leads to high weft end-breaks. A weft accumulator lets the yarn supply be withdrawn under virtually no tension, reducing stress on the yarn.

14 To give more time for weft insertion.

15 The fabric width, when removed from the loom, should be correct. If it is, the warp tension should be correct.

16 To hold the cloth to the correct width, as it will try to contract and in so doing could damage the reed.

17 None, the warp ends can be arranged in any sequence.

18 A broken pattern.
19 Shuttle and projectile looms.
20 The tuck selvedge.

Chapter 17

1 They contain yarns and use a modified warp knitting machine, and some would class this as a form of knitting.
2 The carding action orientates fibres. To produce a randomly orientated web, the fibres must somehow be dispersed after separation by a carding cylinder.
3 Webs are superimposed by a cross-laying action which turns the individual card webs through roughly 90° to the machine direction.
4 Parallel-laid webs. Randomly orietated webs are the most expensive.
5 It has better draping properties, while maintaining a reasonable strength.
6 Hydroentangled fabrics are interlaced by water jets; needle-punched fabrics are interlaced by the action of barbed needles.
7 Self-bonded fabrics need only heat and pressure; the actual fibres melt and bond together. Other thermal bonding processes use other binding fibres, powders or bicomponent fibres, in addition to heat and pressure.

Chapter 18

1 $\text{tex} = \dfrac{\text{grams} \times 1000}{\text{number of threads} \times \text{length in metres}}$

$= \dfrac{0.5 \times 1000}{50 \times 0.235}$

$= \textbf{42.5 tex}$

2 $\text{crimp \%} = \dfrac{(\text{straightened length} - \text{crimped length})}{\text{crimped length}} \times 100$

$= \dfrac{(33.2 - 30)}{30} \times 100$

$= \textbf{10.67\%}$

3 $\text{Stitch length} = \dfrac{\text{course length}}{\text{number of stitches}}$

$= \dfrac{450}{900}$

$= \textbf{0.5 cm}$

4 Mass per square metre = weight in grams × 100 for 10 ×10 sample

$= 2.65 \times 100$

$= \textbf{265 g}$

Chapter 19

1 Handling of different forms of textile (loose stock, yarn, fabric, garments) requires specific machinery because one processor could not hope to possess and master all the necessary machinery.

2 If demand falls for the specific end-products that the company produces, the wet-processing department might have to do work for outside companies to avoid standing idle.
3 It is difficult to handle garments so that they can be processed continuously.
4 Knitted or woven patterns need different coloured yarns. Loose stock could be dyed before spinning, then yarn produced from this could be used.
5 Independent companies specialise in specific techniques and may be able to command higher prices.

Chapter 20

1 To enable following wet processes such as dyeing and printing to be carried out effectively.
2 They form a hard black residue on burning that is difficult to remove.
3 Quenching in water extinguishes any remaining sparks.
4 Sizing would hinder the knitting process and be of no benefit as the stresses involved in knitting are much lower than those involved in weaving.
5 If the recommended temperature for the particular enzyme is exceeded, the enzyme will be denatured, rendering it useless and this cannot be reversed.
6 Fats or oils are treated with a strong alkali. This produces a salt of the fat or oil (a soap). The insoluble impurity has now been broken down into a soluble one and the resulting soap helps break down other impurities.
7 If it falls to neutral, the sodium hypochlorite forms hypochlorous acid, degrading the cellulose and sometimes giving off chlorine gas which is toxic.
8 If the substrate is given a slack mercerisation, it will shrink and will not have increased lustre.
9 Mercerisation swells the immature fibres, increasing lustre and dye acceptability, and giving a deeper shade.
10 Cropping is a controlled removal of hair, enabling a defined pile height to be produced. This is not possible with singeing, which removes all the hair.
11 For successful yarn dyeing (for colour woven fabrics, for example) the yarn must first be scoured.
12 When it is unintentional, for example if a wool garment is not laundered under the correct conditions it will felt, shrink and became unwearable.
13 If the fabric distorts after scouring, it will have to be flattened before it can be successfully processed in open width form, such as for printing.
14 If the molecular weight has reduced it is chemical damage. Mechanical damage does not affect molecular mass.

Chapter 21

1 It will have no colour.
2 A coloured molecule.
3 Batch dyeing process.

4 Free space within the fibre must be created by high temperature which twists parts of the molecular chain, creating holes which allow the dye molecule to enter.

5 If a dye has a high attraction for a particular fibre and will produce a full-depth shade on it, the dye is termed highly substantive on that fibre.

6 The rate of dyeing is greatly increased at higher temperatures, even though there is a slight reduction in the dye uptake. This time factor is essential from a commercial point of view.

7 Blending during the spinning operation can even out any shade differences in the dyed loose stock.

8 Some finishes have an effect on dye fastness and not all are to the good. Heat setting can evaporate disperse dye from the textile.

9 This ensures that the definition of the print is not lost by colour running.

10 Rotary screen printing can produce intricate patterns and has a considerably reduced down-time in comparison to roller printing. Roller printing has a high machine down-time, transfer printing is limited to synthetic substrates, hand screen printing is very slow, and flat-bed screen printing is more expensive to set up and not as fast.

11 A resin or binder is used to form a film over the substrate which locks the pigment beneath on to the fibre surface.

12 Customers appreciate the effects of bright colours on dark backgrounds and the reversible effect, which are lacking in other print methods.

Chapter 22

1 To form a more durable finish on the fabric – fixing.

2 Fabric stiffening was carried out on cotton fabrics to give a smooth, crease-free appearance. With modern crease resistant finishes this is no longer necessary. Fabric softeners improve the comfort of the textile and so are often used.

3 Wax coating.

4 The dyes that could be used as insecticides were not the shades that were desirable.

5 To prevent reinfection and as a deodorant.

6 It reduces the abrasion resistance and tear strength of the fabric.

7 Hydrophobic fibres can build up a static charge due to their non-conductivity, causing sparks and mild shocks to people. This could be a fire hazard.

8 They flatten the fabric which gives a greater light reflectance. To give a higher gloss, the fabric could be waxed first.

9 Low twist, lubricated yarns are the best. Inter-fibre friction is also a factor; the higher the friction, the more difficult to raise.

10 Washing, dry-cleaning, heat, steam.

11 This is an indication of whether the fabric has been chemically damaged during wet processing.

Key words and definitions

Abrasion resistance   The ability of the textile to resist the affects of wear in use.

Adhesive bonding   *See* **Fabric forming**.

Air-jet   *See* **Texturing** and **Weft insertion**.

Amorphous regions   *See* **Molecular orientation**.

Anions   *See* **Dyeing**.

Antibacterial/fungal treatment   A chemical finish applied to fabric to prevent attack by fungus or bacteria.

Antistatic treatment   A chemical finish applied usually to loose stock (fibre) to prevent static problems during processing. The fibre is made conductive so that charges are dissipated before sparks can form.

Assembly winding   Arranging two or more yarns parallel to each other on a package. This is usually done as a stage in plying yarns, prior to the actual twisting operation.

Auxochrome   Intensifies and deepens colour.

Backwashing   Wool scouring after carding to remove surface dirt.

Bacteriostatic   *See* **Microbicidal finish**.

Bang-off   A term used to describe the action of the sley stopping suddenly.

Barrenness   Visible stripes in the weft direction on both woven and knitted fabrics, caused by either yarn faults or fabric manufacturing faults.

Bast fibre   A natural cellulosic fibre, taken from the stem of a plant. Examples include flax and jute. The fibre is removed by a process known as retting, which rots the plant stem.

Batch processing   The material is arranged in distinct lots for processing purposes, rather than being processed continuously.

Batik   A wax or gum resist is used to create designs on fabric. Cracks in the wax create the characteristic veined effect.

Beam   A multi-end package containing a large number of parallel threads, usually several thousand metres long. The *flanges* at both ends support the threads as they build up on the barrel. The *pike* is used to mount the beam in the machine and the *ruffle* is used to break the beam during unwinding.

Beaming   *See* **Warping**.

Bearded needle   *See* **Weft knitting**.

Beating-up   *See* **Weaving**.

Bicomponent fibre   A fibre manufactured from two different polymers.

Bleaching   A wet preparation process used primarily to improve the whiteness of the textile.

Blending   Mixing of component fibres to form a uniform blend of raw materials. *Direct continuous blending* can be done by one of the following systems: hopper blenders; automated bale openers; and in-line blending machinery. In *drawframe blending*, slivers composed of different fibre types are blended at the drawframe. This is a popular method of blending polyester fibres with cotton fibres and is also useful because of the vastly different cleaning requirements of the fibres. *Mixing* usually refers to the combining of fibres of the same type, for example mixing of different bales of cotton.

Blowing   A steam process carried out on fabric during wet processing to set the fabric dimensions (not permanent on wool or other non-thermoplastic fibres).

Bobbin and flyer twisting   *See* **Twisting**.

Boll   *See* **Cotton**.

Brocade   A heavy fabric using a combination of weaves.

Broken pattern   *See* **Pirn**.

Bulked staple yarn   This is a method of producing a bulky yarn by mechanical or chemical means. *See also* High bulk acrylic yarns.

Bursting strength   The multi-directional resistance to rupture of a circular fabric specimen.

Cabled yarn   A yarn consisting of two or more ply yarns twisted together. It takes at least two separate twisting operations to produce a cabled yarn.

Cake   A package of continuous filament yarn.

Calendering   Compression of a fabric between two heavy rollers to give a flattened smooth appearance to the fabric surface. *Chintz/glazing* is a high-gloss finish, caused by running one calender at a higher speed, and optional impregnation of the fabric by a wax emulsion for an enhanced effect. In *Palmer finishing*, the face of damp fabric is polished by a steam-heated cylinder and the back is given a rough effect by contact with a felt blanket. *Schreiner/silk finishing* embosses the fabric with fine lines on one side, usually at 30° to the warp. Chasing is a variation of this, where the fabric is superimposed on itself to create lines and so a softer sheen. In *swissing/normal gloss*, the heated calender produces a lustrous surface and both sides may be glossed.

Cams   These govern the vertical movement of the needles in a knitting machine. *See also* **Shedding** and **Yarn winding**.

Capacitance measuring instruments   *See* **Regularity**.

Capstan/coil friction   A friction assessed by comparison of the input and output tensions of yarn around a cylinder.

Carbonising   Removal of cellulosic impurities from wool by acid treatment, followed by neutralisation by alkali.

Carding   Separation of staple fibres into individual fibre state.

Cleaning and some fibre orientation can occur at this point. The main actions are carding and stripping. The *revolving flat card* is the carding machine used to process short staple fibres. The main carding actions are carried out by a series of metal strips, called flats, and a large cylinder. All surfaces covered in fine wire. The *roller and clearer card* is the machine used to process long staple and waste fibres. The main carding actions are carried out by pairs of rollers arranged around a large cylinder. All surfaces clothed in fine wire.

Cations   *See* **Dyeing.**

Cellulose acetate   A modified regenerated fibre.

Cellulosic fibre A fibre formed from cellulose. It can be natural (e.g. cotton and flax) or man made (e.g. viscose, which is a regenerated cellulose).

China grass   *See* **Ramie.**

Cheese   A single-end wound package with parallel sides and a taper angle of zero.

Chintz/glazing   *See* **Calendering.**

Chlorine test   Used to identify fibres. If chlorine is present and nitrogen is absent, the fibre is a chlorofibre; if chlorine is present but nitrogen is present, it is a modacrylic. If chlorine is not present, further tests are necessary. *See also* **Nitrogen test.**

Chromogen   A coloured molecule, which to be useful as a dye must possess chromophores and auxochromes. *See also* **Auxochrome** and **Chromophore.**

Chromophore   Provides the colour in a dye.

Classers   These are people who are trained to classify a batch of cotton according to the rules of the bodies who are buying or selling. The fibre length, colour and trash content are used, with standard samples, to give a subjective assessment of grade or class.

Clearing   *See* **Weft knitting.**

Closed lap   *See* **Guide bar.**

Cloth control   Used in weaving. The temple controls the cloth width at the fell and the pick density is controlled by the cloth take-up roller. *See also* **Weaving.**

Coagulating bath   A chemical bath used to solidify filaments extruded during wet extrusion.

Cobwebbing   A fault in yarn preparation. When the coil angle is too large, coils slip off the edges of the package causing this stitching pattern. It makes unwinding very difficult, if not impossible.

Cockling   A wrinkled appearance of the fabric caused by uneven shrinkage.

Coefficient of friction   A number used to indicate the relative friction; the higher the number, the greater the friction.

Coefficient of variation   *See* **Regularity.**

Coil angle   *See* **Yarn winding.**

Coloration   Application of colour to a textile, by dyeing (all over) or printing (discrete areas).

Colour fastness   This is the ability of the substrate to maintain its colour despite external agencies such as perspiration, rubbing or washing. There are two aspects to fastness: change (alteration in the depth of shade); staining (transfer of colour from the substrate onto another substrate). *See also* **Grey scales.**

Comberboard   A device used to control the position of the healds.

Combing   Removal of a predetermined per centage of short fibres prior to the spinning operation. *Semi-combing* is the removal of approximately 4–7 per cent of fibres. *Combing* is the removal of approximately 12–17 per cent of fibres. *Super combing* is the removal of approximately 17–20 per cent of fibres. *Double combing* is hardly ever carried out. It involves two combing operations; the removal of approximately 5 per cent in the first operation and up to 20 per cent in the second.

Compound needle   *See* **Weft knitting.**

Condenser cage   A cylindrical mesh used to collect fibre on its surface.

Condenser yarn   A staple yarn spun from waste fibres on a system very similar to the woollen system.

Cone   A single-end wound package, with one of a number of taper angles, e.g. 3° 30′; 4° 20′; 9° 15′.

Continuous filament   A fibre of continuous length.

Continuous filament yarn   *See* **Yarn.**

Continuous processing   The material to be processed is done so continuously, rather than being split up into distinct lots or batches.

Co-polymer   A polymer consisting of two different monomers.

Cop-end effect   This is a fault in yarn preparation. It can happen in pirn winding, when the tension increases from the tip to the base of the pirn, causing less weft crimp and so lines in the cloth known as repping.

Core yarn   *See* **Yarn.**

Cotton   A natural cellulosic fibre, formed on the coat of the seed of the bush. After flowering, a seed pod, or boll, is formed containing roughly 30 seeds, each covered with millions of cotton fibres. These fibres have a two-stage growth; first they grow fully in length, then they are thickened internally by layers of cellulose. When the boll is ripe it opens, allowing the sun to dry the fibres. *See also* **Classers**, **Ginning**, **HVI** and **Neps.**

Count of yarn   There are various systems used to express the length per unit mass or mass per unit length.

Indirect (length per unit mass)
- Cotton count. The number of hanks of 840 yards length that weigh one pound.
- Metric count. The number of kilometre lengths that weigh a kilogram.
- Woollen count (Yorkshire). The number of hanks of 256 yards length that weigh one pound.
- Worsted count. The number of hanks of 560 yards length that weigh one pound.

Direct (mass per unit length)
- Decitex. The weight in grams of 10 000 metres.
- Denier. The weight in grams of 9000 metres.
- Tex. The weight in grams of 1000 metres.

Course length   *See* **Weft knitting.**

Course   *See* **Weft knitting.**

Cover factor   *See* **Woven fabric parameters.**

Crabbing   Used on worsted fabric to give a smooth, flat wrinkle-free fabric for further wet processing.

Crank   *See* **Shedding.**

Crease resistant finish   A chemical finish, for example a resin finish applied to cotton fabric when flat will make the fabric tend to recover to its flat state.

Creel   Arrangement used to house supply packages. A *magazine creel* allows the tail of the yarn from the supply package to be attached to the leading end of yarn from the new package. This should allow automatic transfer from one package to the other. Using *duplicate creels*, either the headstock or creels move sideways so that one creel can be used while the other duplicate creel is being restocked. A *truck creel* contains a number of separate truck sections which can be moved as required; each creel requires several trucks. A *reversible creel* allows the position of the old and new packages to be reversed at the end of a run.

Crimp The waviness or distortion in a yarn caused by interlacing in fabric.

$$\text{Crimp \%} = \frac{(\text{straightened length} - \text{crimped length}) \times 100}{\text{crimped length}}$$

Crimp rigidity A measure of the effectiveness of the texturing process carried out on continuous filament yarns.

Crockmeter An instrument used to rub a fabric specimen in order to assess its wet or dry colour fastness to rubbing.

Cross tie A jacquard positioned over the sides of the loom. *See also* **Straight tie.**

Cropping A process used to control the height of surface hairs on fabric. Used on fabrics containing wool fibres, it is a more controlled method than singeing.

Crush cut A tow-to-top conversion method employing a cutting roller and anvil to cut the tow to the required staple lengths.

Crystalline regions *See* **Molecular orientation.**

Damask A fabric using a combination of different weaves in selected areas to create a pattern.

Dead cotton A term used by wet processors for immature cotton fibres.

Decitex *See* **Count of yarn.**

Dent *See* **Reed.**

Denting plans *See* **Weave repeat.**

Dernier *See* **Count of yarn.**

Desizing Removal of size applied at the weaving preparation stage.

Diamond barring A fabric fault caused when a regular or periodic yarn fault creates a diamond pattern.

Dimensional stability The ability of a fabric to retain its dimensions. These can be affected by such as washing, dry cleaning, heat and steam.

Direct printing *See* **Printing styles.**

Discharge printing *See* **Printing styles.**

Disperse dyes *See* **Dyeing.**

Dobby *See* **Shedding.**

Double jersey *See* **Weft knitting.**

Doubling *See* **Drawing.**

Drafting This is the attenuation or stretching out of a fibre assembly. Drafting aligns fibres. *Apron drafting* uses aprons to control short fibres in the main drafting zone. These aprons are like very wide rubber bands and are driven by the slower pair of rollers. *Drafting zones* are the areas between pairs of drafting rollers where drafting occurs. *Drafting waves* are thick places followed by thin places. They occur when there is insufficient control of the fibre mass during drafting. *Floating fibres* are those which are too short to be controlled properly during roller drafting. They are controlled by the surrounding fibres rather than by contact with the drafting rollers. *Hooked fibres*: the arrangement of fibres can be either straight, hooked at one end, or hooked at both ends. When fibres leave the carding operation, there are a majority with trailing hooks. This can present problems during drafting. *Pressure bar drafting* is used on drawframes to control fibres during drafting. *Roller drafting* is the most common method of drafting, where pairs of rollers moving successively faster to draw out the fibre mass passing between them.

Draw texturing A texturing process which is combined with the drawing stage of filament yarn manufacture.

Drawframe blending *See* **Blending.**

Drawing A process involving drafting of slivers accompanied by *doubling* which combines two or more intermediate products to make a final product, and improves blending and the regularity in terms of linear density. The whole drawing process improves fibre alignment, blending and regularity. Filaments must be drawn or stretched to align the molecules within, so developing optimum tensile properties. This is often carried out by pairs of rollers known as godets.

Drawing-in The action, in preparation for weaving, of threading a warp end through a drop wire or warp spin stop motion, heald eye and reed dent. The drawing-in plan is an indication of the order that the warp ends are drawn through the eyes of the healds.

Drawing-in plans *See* **Drawing-in** and **Weave repeat.**

Drop wire *See* **Drawing-in.**

Drum traverse *See* **Yarn Winding.**

D/S ratio The ratio of ply twist to single twist in a ply yarn. Different ratios will optimise different properties, such as maximum lustre or maximum strength.

Dummy selvedge Created to enable a severing action of the unsightly edge of a fringe selvedge.

Dye An organic chemical, able to absorb and reflect visible light. *Highly substantive dyes* have a high attraction for a particular fibre and give a full-depth shade. *See also* **Auxochrome, Chromogen** and **Chromophore.**

Dyeing Application and even distribution of colour to a substrate. *Anions* are negatively charged dye ions. *Cations* are positively charged dye ions. *Disperse dyes* are nonionic dyes which form dispersions within the dyebath rather than solutions. *Dyestuffs* are chemicals used to add colour to a substrate. *Equilibrium dyeing* is a two-way process in which dye and fibre are in equilibrium with dyed fibre. *Equilibrium exhaustion* is the amount of dye taken up at equilibrium. *Fixation* is the final bonding of the dye to the fibre, requiring a separate final stage at the end of dyeing in some cases. *Levelling* promotes an even distribution of dye throughout the substrate. *Nonionic dyes* possess no ionising groups on their structure. The *rate of dyeing curve* plots percentage exhaustion against time of dyeing, giving an indication of the dyeing efficiency.

Dyestuffs *See* **Dyeing.**

Elastane A man-made fibre which can extend reversibly to at least three times its original length.

Elastic recovery This is the immediate change in elongation after the load is removed.

Emulsion scouring Removal of grease from wool fibres by the action of hot water, detergent and agitation. The grease forms an emulsion in the scouring liquor.

Engraved roller printing *See* **Printing methods.**

Enzymatic desizing This method uses enzymes (specifically amylases) to convert the starch size to water-soluble sugars.

Equilibrium exhaustion *See* **Dyeing.**

Extrusion Manufacture of man-made fibres/filaments, sometimes called spinning. Polymer, in a liquid state, is forced through a spinneret (a plate-like a shower head) to form filaments. *Melt extrusion* is the simplest form of extrusion, where the polymer is heated, extruded then cooled. In *solvent-dry extrusion*, the polymer must be dissolved in a solvent before extrusion then drying. In *wet extrusion*, the polymer is dissolved in a solvent, then extruded into a chemical bath known as a coagulating bath to solidify the filaments.

Fabric analysis This involves the determination of: fabric construction; yarn linear density; yarn crimp; thread densities; course length and stitch length for knitted fabrics.

Fabric forming Several methods are available to bond webs so they form fabrics. *Adhesive bonding* occurs either by saturation in adhesive or spraying with adhesive, or foam impregnation or powder/film form (with thermal bonding). *Hydroentangling fibres* are interlaced by the action of high pressure water jets. *Needle punching fibres* are interlaced by the action of barbed needles. *Stitch bonding* is done by a modified warp knitting machine which forms knitted loops down the length of the web to form a fabric. *Thermal bonding* can be used to bond bicomponent fibres, bonding sheath to sheath; using adhesive powder or film.

Fabric weight   *See* **Woven fabric parameters**.

Fall-on effects   These are created during overprinting where colours are printed directly on top of colours just printed, wet on wet.

False-twist texturing   *See* **Texturing**.

Fancy yarn   A yarn with the deliberate addition of irregularities, such as slubs, to create a textured effect.

Fasciated yarn   *See* **Yarn**.

Feeding   *See* **Weft knitting**.

Felt   The original non-woven fabric. Wool or hair fibres are submitted to the action of moisture, heat and agitation, which causes them to entangle (a non-reversible action due to the surface scales on the fibre). Felt can also be formed from a woven or knitted fabric which is later felted (heat, moisture and agitation) to obscure the fabrics real construction.

Fibre   A flexible, fine substance with a high length to thickness ratio. *Fibre length*: straightened, extent, hand stapling, staple diagram.

Finishing   Processes carried out on a textile to make it more suitable for its intended use.

Fixation   *See* **Dyeing**.

Flame retardancy   This can be altered by a chemical finish applied to fabric. Flame retardants include the following. *Levoglucosan* is a fuel produced when cellulose is decomposing due to heat. It burns readily in the presence of air. *Proban* is an insoluble polymer which is held in cellulose yarns by mechanical means. This gives it a harsh handle. *Pyrovatex* is applied with a crosslinked resin and forms a chemical bond with the cellulose. It has a durable finish with good dimensional stability, but a reduced tear strength. *See also* **Lewis acids**.

Flanges   *See* **Beam**.

Fleece   *See* **Wool**.

Flexural rigidity   Resistance of a material to bending.

Floating fibres   *See* **Drafting**.

Fluorescent brightening agents   This finish increases the apparent reflectance of a material by converting ultraviolet radiation into visible light, so increasing the brightness.

Friction spinning   *See* **Twisting**.

Friction spun yarn   *See* **Yarn**.

Fully fashioned   Knitting which is shaped on the machine (straight bar) during knitting.

Fully orientated yarn (FOY)   *See* **Orientation**.

Fungistatic   *See* **Microbicidal finish**.

Gassed yarn   Passed rapidly over a flame to remove any surface hair.

Gear crimping   *See* **Texturing**.

Geotextile   A textile material used by civil engineers.

Gillbox   The worsted equivalent of a drawframe, used to align fibres in a sliver and improve regularity. Blending of slivers may be carried out at this stage.

Ginning   This is the removal of the cotton fibres from the seed.

Godets   Rollers used to draw man-made fibres after extrusion; sometimes heated for 'hot drawing' as opposed to 'cold drawing'. The *draw ratio* is the relative difference in the speed of the pairs of godets.

Grey scales   There are two types of grey scale: one for assessing change, the other for staining. Fabrics are compared against the scale, treated and untreated, and the grade given is the number of the grey scale with the same difference as the sample. A number is given between five and one, one being worst.

Guide bar   Used on knitting machines. Contains guide eyes that control the movement of feed yarns. An *overlap* is the lateral movement of the guide bar on the hook side of the needle, usually over one needle space. An *underlap* is the lateral movement of the guide bar on the side of the needle remote from the hook. This movement is limited by mechanical considerations only. *Open lap*: the underlap is made in the same direction as the preceding overlap. *Closed lap*: the underlap is made in the opposite direction to the preceding overlap. In *open pillar stitch* only the overlaps are made, while for *miss-lapping*, neither overlaps nor underlaps are made (used on the back guide bar). For laying-in, no overlaps are made, only underlaps (used on the back guide bar). *Pattern chains* give an accurately timed sideways *shog* which moves the guide bar. *Notation point paper* is used, where each dot represents a needle, each row of dots a course. Successive courses are read upwards from bottom to top and needle spaces are numbered right to left.

Haloing   During discharge or resist printing, if the chemical used to resist or discharge the ground colour spreads beyond the area printed by the head colour, a white halo effect is created around the printed area.

Handle   The feel or tactile properties of textiles.

Hard edges   This is a fault in yarn preparation. It occurs where the yarn reverses direction during traversing; producing a build up of yarn due to the momentary slowing down of the yarn. If this is too severe, it will cause problems in package dyeing due to the uneven density.

Head colours   These are colours overprinted on to predyed cloth during discharge printing, or they are pre-printed on to cloth yet to be dyed in resist printing.

Heald   This is a metal wire with an eye hole which controls the movement (up or down) of a warp end during weaving. Heald movement causes a split in the warp end during weaving. Heald movement causes a split in the warp sheet called a *shed*. *See also* **Weaving**.

Heat setting   Heating thermoplastic fibres to the correct temperature for the correct time to produce a permanent retention of the shape of the fibre at the time of setting.

High-bulk acrylic yarns   The majority of these yarns are now produced on the tow-to-top conversion system. Relaxed and unrelaxed fibres are blended prior to spinning. The resulting yarn or fabric is heat treated to relax the unrelaxed fibres, causing the pre-relaxed fibres to buckle, bulking up the yarn or fabric. *See also* **Bulked staple yarn**.

Homopolymer   A polymer consisting of one type of monomer.

Hooked fibres   *See* **Drafting**.

Hopsack   A balanced matt or basket weave where two or more yarns move together in plain weave interlacing.

Horizontal organisation   One in which each part in the process towards an end-product is carried out by a different company. *See also* **Vertical organisation**.

Hose   Weft knitted circular structure, e.g. tights. *Half hose*, e.g. socks.

HVI High-volume instrumentation is now being used to objectively assess every bale of cotton grown in the USA. This testing equipment is also used by some spinners to enable every bale to be tested before use.

Hydroentangling fibres *See* **Fabric forming**.

Hydrogen bonds *See* **Intermolecular forces**.

Initial modulus Given by the slope of the first part of the stress/strain curve. The effects are usually elastic in this area.

Interlock *See* **Weft knitting**.

Intermolecular forces Those forces which hold molecules together. There are three which are important to textile fibres: *hydrogen bonds* (the strongest bonds); *polar bonds*; and *Van der Wall's forces* (the weakest bonds).

Jacquard *See* **Shedding**.

Jet dyeing A dying machine using jets of fluid to circulate the fabric in rope form.

Keratin The protein that wool fibres are composed of.

Knit de knit *See* **Texturing**.

Knock-over *See* **Weft knitting**.

Lap A continuous sheet of staple fibres used to feed a card.

Latch needle *See* **Weft knitting**.

Laying-in *See* **Guide bar**.

Lea A length of 120 yards of yarn in hank (a continuous loop) form.

Let-off *See* **Weaving**.

Levelling *See* **Dyeing**.

Levoglucosan *See* **Flame retardancy**.

Lewis acids These materials have the ability to accept a pair of electrons. They act as dehydrating agents for cellulose at high temperatures, suppressing the formation of flammable volatiles. A material which decomposes when heated to form a lewis acid acts as flame-retardant material

Lifting plans *See* **Weave repeat**.

Linear density *See* **Count of yarn**.

Linen A yarn or fabric made from flax fibre which is a bast fibre.

Lint Good cotton fibres removed from the seed during the ginning process.

Locknit *See* **Two guide bar structures**.

Long-staple spinning Staple spinning of fibres which are more than 60 millimetres (2.5 inches) in length.

Looming This is a yarn preparation. It involves knotting or drawing ends through a drop wire eye, heald and dent.

Loose stock A term used by wet processors to describe a mass of fibre.

Lustre The degree to which a material reflects light – its shine.

Matt *See* **Plain weave**.

Melt blown *See* **Webs**.

Mercerised cotton Cotton fibres that have been treated with a concentrated solution of a caustic alkali. This increases strength and dye affinity. If carried out with the material under tension, it also increases lustre. *Slack mercerisation* is treated as above but without tension, resulting in all the benefits except the increase in lustre.

Merchant converters A company which does not carry out any processing, but arranges processing through other companies when they have a buyer for the end-product.

Metallised yarn *See* **Yarn**.

Microbicidal finish One that kills micro-organisms. A *bacteriostatic* is a chemical which inhibits the growth of bacteria. A *fungistatic* inhibits the growth of fungi.

Micronaire A combined measure of cotton fibre maturity and fineness using air permeability. A low value indicates either fine fibres and/or immature fibres.

Milling The deliberate action of felting a fabric (causing an irreversible entangling of the fibres). This can obscure the fabric construction, depending upon the fibre type.

Mineral fibre A fibre formed from minerals. There is only one naturally occurring mineral fibre: asbestos.

Miss-lapping *See* **Guide bar**.

Modified regenerated fibre A fibre of natural origin that has been both physically and chemically modified.

Moisture content The mass of the moisture in the material expressed as a percentage of the total mass of moisture and material.

Moisture regain The mass of moisture in the material expressed as a per centage of the oven-dry mass of the material.

Molecular orientation The arrangement of molecules within a fibre. *Crystalline regions* are areas of high molecular orientation, conferring properties such as tensile strength to fibres. *Amorphous regions/non-crystalline regions* are less ordered regions which confer properties such as flexibility and reactivity to fibres.

Monofilament A continuous filament yarn containing only one filament.

Monomer The repeat unit of a polymer.

Multifilament A continuous filament yarn containing more than one filament.

Needle punching fibres *See* **Fabric forming**.

Neps These are fibres which have rolled up into a ball, and appear as a white speck in fabric. Immature fibres will often form neps, though another cause can be poor ginning or poor carding. If immature fibres form these neps and are not removed by carding or scouring in fabric form, they become more obvious when dyed because immature fibres take up less dye, and appear as pale specks.

Nitrogen test Used to identify fibres. *See also* **Chlorine test**.

Non-wovens A manufactured web of directional or randomly orientated fibres, bonded by friction and/or cohesion and/or adhesion, excluding paper. *See also* **Fabric forming** and **Webs**.

Nonionic dyes *See* **Dyeing**.

Notation *See* **Guide bar**.

Oil repellency rating This is used to assess the stain resistance of a textile. A series of liquids with decreasing surface tension are applied to the textile and the one which just wets the textile determines the number or oil repellency rating that is given to the textile.

On-line monitoring The continuous monitoring of a machine or process from a production and/or quality point of view.

Open lap *See* **Guide bar**.

Open pillar stitch *See* **Guide bar**.

Opening and cleaning A mechanical process used in short-staple spinning to open out and reduce fibre tuft size, and to remove impurities. Methods use spiked surfaces, beaters or air currents.

Orientation Fibres are oriented by drawing (stretching), which aligns the molecules within the filament. *Fully orientated yarn* (FOY) has been fully drawn to achieve optimum tensile properties. *Partially oriented yarn* (POY) is a filament that has not been fully drawn.

Overlap *See* **Guide bar**.

Overprinting *See* **Printing styles**.

Palmer finishing *See* **Calendering**.

Parallel laid *See* **Webs**.

Partially oriented yarn (POY) *See* **Orientation**.

Pattern chains *See* **Guide bar**.

Patterning A fault in yarn preparation. This is a winding fault caused by coils on adjacent layers of the package being superimposed. It occurs when the wind per double traverse is equal to an integer. It has adverse effects on unwinding properties and package dyeing. It happens intermittently on random winders unless they are fitted with an anti-patterning device. Depending on the initial settings of the precision winder, patterning will happen continuously or never.

Periodic variations   *See* **Regularity**.

Pick cramming   *See* **Weft insertion**.

Pickfinding   Finding the correct shedding position and returning the cloth fell to the true weaving position after an interruption in weaving.

Piece dyeing   Dyeing of a length of fabric.

Piece glass   A small, low-magnification eyepiece with an attached scale.

Pigment   A substance used to add colour which is not water soluble and which usually adheres to the surface of the fibre.

Pike   *See* **Beam**.

Pilling   Entangling of fibres to form balls or pills which stand proud of the fabric surface. This happens through wearing and laundering.

Pirn   A single-end package designed to fit inside a shuttle to supply weft yarn. If the print runs out of yarn before being replaced, a fault known as a *broken pattern* occurs, where part of a pick is missing.

Plain single jersey   *See* **Weft knitting**.

Plain weave   The simplest of all the woven structures. It has the greatest stability and firmness. *Square sett plains* have similar production details for both warp and weft. *Warp-faced plains* have a greater amount of warp than weft. *Weft-faced plains* have a greater amount of weft than warp. *Rib and matt weaves* are developed from plain weave.

Ply yarn   Two or more single yarns are twisted together in one operation to form a two-ply or three-ply yarn etc. Also known as a folded or doubled yarn.

Polar bonds   *See* **Intermolecular forces**.

Polymer   A long chain molecule consisting of monomer units.

Polymerisation   Where monomer units join to form a long chain molecule known as a polymer. In *addition polymerisation*, all the atoms present in the monomer are also present in the polymer; the monomer units simply add to each other. In *condensation polymerisation*, small molecules (usually water) are eliminated during the reaction. The *degree of polymerisation* is the length of the long chain molecule, that is the number of monomers. *See also* **Co-polymer** and **Homopolymer**.

Poplin   A fabric with ribs in the weft direction.

Positive feed device   A mechanism on a weft knitting machine designed to ensure that the correct length of yarn is fed to each feeder on the machine per revolution to give an accurate and consistent stitch length.

Preparation   Processes carried out on a textile to prepare it for coloration and/or finishing.

Press-off   Where all the stitches on the knitting machine are accidentally cast off, leaving the machine bare.

Principles of load measurement   Mechanical principles include the following: balance principle; inclined plane principle; pendulum lever principle; Pressley fibre bundle strength; and the strain gauge principle. *See also* **Tensile testing**.

Printing   The production of a design by application of a dye or pigment in a thickened paste form. *See also* **Fall-on effects**, **Haloing**, **Head colours** and **Undercutting**.

Printing methods   There are several methods of printing on to fabric. In *engraved roller printing*, colour is transferred continuously on to the fabric by engraved rollers. Each roller applies one colour in the design. Each screen in *screen printing* is made from a synthetic mesh or metal gauze and part of the gauze is blocked off to create the non-printing area. Colour is transferred on to the fabric through the open printing areas by a rubber or metal blade. *Flat bed printing* is an intermittent method. All the screens needed to make the design (one per colour) are arranged side by side above a conveyor belt. The fabric is fixed to the belt, the screens are lowered, colour applied, and the screens are raised again. The belt advances the fabric one repeat length and the process starts again. In *rotary screen printing*, the mesh or gauze is in the form of a seamless cylindrical screen. Like engraved roller printing, colour is transferred continuously, with each screen applying one colour in the design. Dyes are printed on to paper for *vapour phase transfer printing*. The paper and the fabric are then pressed together under heat. In this process, the dye becomes gaseous, transfers on to the fabric and diffuses into the fibres.

Printing styles   There are various printing styles. In *direct printing*, every part of the design is saved for so that the colours do not overlap. In *overprinting*, one or more of the colours print wet on wet; one colour on top of one just printed. The fabric is dyed first for *discharge printing*. The dry dyed fabric is then overprinted with head colours and chemicals to destroy the ground shade. In *resist printing*, the printing takes place first and the ground shade is applied afterwards. The head colours contain a chemical to resist the ground shade in the pre-printed areas.

Proban   *See* **Flame retardancy**.

Producer package   A package containing continuous filament yarn, slightly twisted.

Projectile   *See* **Weft insertion**.

Propeller traverse   *See* **Yarn winding**.

Protein fibre   A fibre formed from protein. They are either natural (e.g. wool and silk) or regenerated protein fibres.

Purl   *See* **Weft knitting**.

Pyrovatex   *See* **Flame retardancy**.

Queenscord   *See* **Two guide bar structures**.

Raceboard   A support for the shuttle or rapier as it traverses the shed. Part of the sley, in the front of the reed.

Raising   Plucking fibres from fabric to give a nap effect on the surface.

Ramie   A bast fibre (from the stem of the plant) noted for its lustre. The ribbons of fibre obtained after retting are known as *china grass*.

Random winder   *See* **Yarn winding**.

Rapier   *See* **Weft insertion**.

Raschel machine   Complicated warp knitting machine. It has up to 78 guide bars, using continuous filament yarns or staple fibre yarns. *See also* **Guide bar** and **Tricot machine**.

Rate determining step   The stage at which dye diffuses into the fibre, which dictates the speed of dyeing.

Rate of dyeing curve   *See* **Dyeing**.

Reed   A metal device, like a comb but not closed at both ends, used to push the weft pick up into the fell of the cloth. The space between the reed wires is referred to as a *dent*.

Regenerated fibre   A fibre of natural origin that has been physically modified.

Regularity   The uniformity of a product. This usually refers to the uniformity in mass per unit length for a yarn, unless otherwise specified. *Capacitance measuring instruments* electronically measure the thickness of material passing between two capacitance plates. This information is used to give statistical values of regularity. *Coefficient of variation* is a statistical measure of the level of variation compared to the mean value. The higher the number, the more irregular the material (usually expressed as a per centage). The *index of irregularity* is how the actual yarn compares to the best possible yarn achievable (how it compares with the limit of irregularity). The *limit of irregularity* is the best possible regularity that can be achieved for that thickness of yarn spun from that particular fibre type. *Periodic variations* are those which regularly occur in the mass per unit length of a yarn or material prior to spinning:

- short-term variations occur from between one and ten times per fibre length;
- medium-term variations occur from between ten and one hundred times per fibre length; and
- long-term variations occur over one hundred times per fibre length

Relative humidity The ratio of the amount of water vapour in the air compared to the amount of water vapour at saturation level at the same temperature.

Repp A fabric with a pronounced weft-way rib.

Repping *See* **Cop-end effect.**

Resin finishing This was developed originally to improve crease recovery properties in cotton fabrics. It was also found to improve dimensional stability to washing, that is it produced less shrinkage. The disadvantages are that this finishing reduces the abrasion resistance and tear strength of the fabric. *See also* **Crease resistant finishing.**

Resist printing *See* **Printing styles.**

Reverse locknit *See* **Two guide bar structures.**

Rib *See* **Plain weave** and **Weft knitting.**

Ring-spun yarn *See* **Yarn.**

Ring twisting *See* **Twisting.**

Robbing back During knitting, yarn is taken from a previously knitted stitch to make the current stitch.

Roller nip The contact point between a pair of rollers.

Roller setting The distance between the nip point on successive pairs of rollers.

Rot steeping A desizing method using bacteria to degrade the starch size. It is difficult to control.

Rotor spinning *See* **Twisting.**

Rotor-spun yarn *See* **Yarn.**

Ruffle *See* **Beam.**

Satin *See* **Two guide bar structures.**

Satin/sateen A basic weave using long floats (lengths of yarn with no interlacings). Usually constructed using smooth lustrous yarns, a satin is warp faced while a sateen is weft faced. Binding points should not touch. *Irregular satin/sateens* are modifications of the weave.

Schreiner finishing *See* **Calendering.**

Scouring A wet, or chemical, cleaning process. It is carried out on raw wool fibre, or on fabric of various fibre types as part of the preparation processes. In *emulsion scouring*, raw wool fibre is separated from its impurities by use of hot water and detergents which form an emulsion of the grease.

Screen printing *See* **Printing methods.**

Scrim A lightweight basecloth.

Self-twist spinning *See* **Twisting.**

Self-twist yarn *See* **Yarn.**

Selvedges Prevent the cloth from fraying. They provide additional strength to withstand the strain of weaving and wet processing. Types of selvedge include tuck, leno, helical, hairpin.

Sett *See* **Woven fabric parameters.**

Sharkskin *See* **Two guide bar structures.**

Shed types In a *bottom closed* shed, all the heald shafts return to the bottom position after each pick; in a *centre closed* shed, all the heald shafts return to the centre after each pick; in a *fully open* shed, the healds remain where they are after each pick until they are selected to change. A *semi open* shed is similar to a fully open shed, but the healds at the top lower slightly after each pick.

Shedding A primary weaving motion. Types of shed are bottom closed, centre closed, fully open and semi open. The following are shedding systems. In *cam* shedding, the heald frames are moved by cams which can be positive or negative. This system is becoming more popular with modern high-speed machines. For *crank* shedding, heald frames are raised and lowered by a crank on a two-pick cycle, which means it is only suitable for plain weave. *Dobby* shedding can be either positive or negative, and modern systems are computer controlled. In *jacquard* shedding, ends are controlled by individual healds, not a heald frame. Modern systems are computer controlled. *See also* **Weaving.**

Shog *See* **Guide bar.**

Short-staple spinning Staple spinning of fibres of between 10 millimetres (0.5 inches) and 60 millimetres (2.5 inches)

Shuttle *See* **Weft insertion.**

Shuttle interference This is where the top warp sheet has to bend around the front wall of the shuttle as it leaves or enters the shed.

Silk The only natural continuous filament. It is a protein fibre formed by the larvae of a moth (known as a silk worm) to form its cocoon.

Singeing A process used to burn off surface hairs from a fabric.

Sinkers Used in knitting to aid knock-over and/or control the fabric.

Sizing This is a yarn preparation. A coating of starch-based adhesive is applied to the yarn to improve the weavability. A sizing machine consists of a creel, size box, drying zone and headstock.

Skip draft A draft other than a straight draft (where the next available heald shaft is selected) used where more than the minimum number of heald shafts is being used.

Slack mercerisation *See* **Mercerised cotton.**

Smash When the reed attempts to beat-up with the shuttle or other weft insertion medium still in the shed. This usually results in a large number of ends being broken, and sometimes in damage to the reed.

Snarling tendency The tendency of a yarn to untwist, snarling up on itself if not under tension. A balanced yarn has little or no tendency to untwist.

Soil release The ability of a textile to shed dirt during washing.

Solvent tests A series of tests used for fibre identification purposes.

Specification The technical description of a product, usually containing tolerance limits. For example, if a yarn is specified as 30 tex, plus or minus 2 tex, it must be between 28 and 32 tex.

Spin finish A chemical dressing applied to man-made fibres to aid processing. Spin finishes might contain antistatic agents, aids to fibre cohesion or fibre lubrication.

Spinneret *See* **Extrusion.**

Spun-laid webs *See* **Webs.**

Stage twisting A system of producing yarn which consists of two stages: low-level twist is inserted by ring twisting; higher-level twist is inserted by uptwisting.

Staple fibre   A fibre of definite length.

Staple-spun yarn   *See* **Yarn**.

Stentering   A process used to head set fabric to full width, often used to control fabric width.

Stitch bonding   *See* **Fabric forming**.

Stitch density   *See* **Weft knitting**.

Stitch length   *See* **Weft knitting**.

Straight bar   *See* **Fully fashioned**.

Straight tie   A jacquard positioned over the back or front of the loom. *See* also **Cross tie**.

Stretch break   A tow-to-top conversion method in which the filaments are stressed until they break.

Stuffer box texturing *See* **Texturing**.

Substantive   *See* **Dye**.

Substrate   A material to which dyes and chemicals may be added.

Swissing   *See* **Calendering**.

Synthetic fibre   A fibre made from chemicals.

Take-up *See* **Weaving**.

Tape/split film yarn   *See* **Yarn**.

Taper   *See* **Yarn winding**.

Taper line grating   A transparent plate with parallel lines which creates an interference pattern when placed on fabric. The threads per inch or centimetre of the fabric are indicated by this pattern.

Tear strength   The fabric's ability to resist tearing. The tests used start with a cut or cuts in the fabric which are placed in the jaws of the testing instrument and stressed.

Technical back   The back of the knitted fabric on the machine rather than the 'wrong' side from the user's point of view.

Technical face   The front of the knitted fabric on the machine, rather than the 'right' side from the user's point of view.

Temple   A fabric guide used to keep the fabric to full width during the waving process.

Tensile testing   Stressing the material along its main axis. This can be done using the following conditions: constant rate of extension (CRE); constant rate of loading (CRL); constant rate of traverse (CRT). *See also* **Principles of load measurement**.

Tex   *See* **Count of yarn**.

Texturing   Permanent deforming of continuous filament yarns to give properties and appearance similar to staple-spun yarns. There are three types of *textured yarn*:

- stretch yarn, in which the stretch characteristic of textured yarn is optimised;
- modified stretch yarn, where some of the stretch characteristic is traded for more bulk; and
- bulk yarn, in which the bulk characteristic is optimised.

Air-jet texturing produces yarns that most closely resemble staple-spun yarns. It produces bulk yarns. *False-twist texturing* was originally an intermittent process but is now continuous. It produces stretch yarns. Other texturing methods include: *stuffer box texturing*, which is now most commonly used for crimping man-made fibres before they are cut into staple lengths; *knit de knit*, in which the filaments are knitted, heat set, then unravelled; and *gear crimping*, where heated filaments are deformed by passing them between the teeth of spur gears. *See also* **Draw texturing**.

Thermal bonding   *See* **Fabric forming**.

Thermoplastic   A material that deforms in heat without changing chemically.

Thread density   The number of yarns per unit area.

Threading   This is a yarn preparation. Warp ends are threaded through guide bar eyes for warp knitting or stitch bonding.

Tightness factor   *See* **Weft knitting**.

Top   A slang term for a sliver, used in the worsted industry.

Torsion rod   The device used to propel the projectile through the shed during weft insertion.

Torsional rigidity   The level to which a material is resistant to twisting.

Tow   A 'rope' of continuous filaments.

Tow-to-top conversion The process of forming a sliver, or top, directly from a rope, or tow, of continuous filaments. *See also* **Crush cut** and **Stretch break**.

Trash   The term given to the impurities found in raw cotton.

Traverse mechanism   *See* **Yarn winding**.

Trick   A groove cut into the needle bed of a knitting machine to allow vertical movement of needles.

Tricot   *See* **Two guide bar structures**.

Tricot machine   The simplest warp knitting machine, using bearded or compound needles. There are usually two guide bars, using continuous filament yarn, but up to five guide bars are possible. High speed. *See also* **Guide bar** and **Raschel machine**.

Twill weave   All the ends lift alike, but each one starts its lift one pick higher or lower than the end adjacent to it. This forms diagonal lines in the fabric. If these run from bottom left to top right, it is a Z twill, while bottom right to top left is an S twill. *Pointed twill* is created by reversing the direction of the twill to give a neat point. *Herringbone twill* is a reversal of the twill direction and the lift is reversed. *Diamond twill* can be created in a number of ways to produce a diamond pattern. *Elongated twills* can be created by modifying the step of the twill.

Twist   In yarns, twist is designated S or Z twist, depending on whether the angle of the fibres within the yarn make the centre of a letter S or Z.

Twist factor   An indication of the twist characteristics, irrespective of the yarn linear density.

$$\text{Twist factor} = \sqrt{\text{tex}} \times \text{turns cm}^{-1}$$

$$\text{Twist factor} = \frac{\text{turns inch}^{-1}}{\sqrt{\text{cotton count}}}$$

Twist interference   This is a fault in yarn preparation. It can happen on a drum traverse winder if a delicate low-twist yarn is wound. The traverse motion can cause untwisting as it rolls the yarn, causing breakages.

Twisting   A method used to impart strength to a fibrous structure. Many methods are available: bobbin and flyer twisting; friction spinning; ring twisting; rotor spinning; self-twist spinning and wrap spinning.

Two-for-one twisting   A method of obtaining two turns of twist in a ply or cabled yarn for one turn of the twisting element

Two guide bar structures   Fabrics produced on a warp knitting machine using two sets of yarns, e.g. reverse locknit, locknit, tricot, queenscord, satin, sharkskin.

Undercutting   During discharge or resist printing, if the ground colour is not fully removed or resisted, it will contaminate the head colours, giving an undercutting effect.

Underlap   *See* **Guide bar**.

Van der Wall's forces   *See* **Intermolecular forces**.

Vapour phase transfer   *See* **Printing methods**.

Ventile fabric   Made from Egyptian cotton, with the D/S ratio set so that the singles twist is virtually zero after doubling. It is then woven into a very dense fabric.

Vernier take-up   An adjustable cam to vary the pick density.

Vertical organisation   One in which all stages in the production towards an end-product are carried out by the same company. *See also* **Horizontal organisation**.

Viscometer   Instrument used to measure viscosity.

Viscosity   A measure of how free flowing a liquid is. If a liquid is too viscous it will not flow easily enough.

Wale   *See* **Weft knitting**.

Warp control   A secondary weaving motion. The let-off motion can be positive or negative. The main purpose is control of the warp tension, this affects the crimp ratios in both warp and weft, and the end-breakage rate. *See also* **Weaving**.

Warp knitting   Loops are formed down the length of the fabric. The yarn is fed vertically to the machine with at least one thread per needle.

Warp protectors   Used during weaving along with free-flying weft insertion media (*See* **Shuttle** and **Projectile**) to protect the loom and warp sheet. If the shuttle or projectile has not traversed the loom, the protector motion will automatically stop the loom before beat-up.

Warp stop motion   A drop wire attached to each warp end which operates either an electronic or mechanical system to stop the loom if the end breaks.

Warping   A yarn preparation. This is also known as beaming; the production of a beam containing a large number of individual threads wound parallel to each other. *High-speed beaming* is the production of warper's beams, which contain a fraction of the number of ends required on the final weaver's beam, but many times the required length. It is also used to produce beams for warp knitting and stitch bonding. *Section warping* is when short runs or complicated patterns are processed. Sections of beam are wound separately and are then pulled off the drum all at once on to a beam. Also known as horizontal mill warping.

Water jet   *See* **Weft insertion**.

Water repellency   A chemical finish applied to fabric to resist absorption of water.

Waxing   *See* **Yarn lubrication**.

Weave   The order of interlacing of warp ends and weft picks; there are four basic weaves: plain, twill, satin and sateen. There are many other weaves in addition to the basic weaves. *Huckaback* is based on plain weave, with an introduction of long floats to give good moisture absorbency. *Mock leno* is a fabric produced with holes to imitate an open gauze or net. *Honeycomb* provides a cell-like texture to the surface of the fabric, and again floats give good moisture absorbency. *Brighton honeycomb* has one textured side, where *ordinary honeycomb* has a similar textured effect on both sides. *Crepe* weave gives a textured surface in a similar way to the plain weave fabric produced with crepe yarns. *Bedford cord* gives a fabric with raised longitudinal warp-way lines. *See also* **Plain weave**, **Twill weave** and **Satin/sateen**.

Weave repeat   The smallest number of threads required to show all the interlacings in the pattern. *Drawing-in plans* indicate the order in which the warp ends are drawn through the heald eyes. *Denting plans* show the arrangement of warp ends in the reed. *Lifting plans* show how each heald shaft is lifted on each pick in the design. *Combined weaves* are a combination of several different weaves in one fabric. *Colour and weave effects* are visual effects created when different coloured threads are woven in a precise order related to the weave, for instance crowsfoot, dogtooth, basket.

Weaving   Interlacing of warp and weft threads to form a fabric.

The *primary motions of weaving* are shedding, weft insertion and beating-up.

- Shedding controls the warp ends to form the shed.
- Weft insertion projects the weft pick through the shed.
- Beating-up is the reed action of pushing the weft pick into the fell of the cloth.

Secondary motions of weaving are let-off, take-up and weft selection.

- Let-off controls the tension in the warp sheet.
- Take-up controls the pick density.
- Weft selection is only necessary when the weft must be varied.

Ancillary motions of weaving are warp and weft stop motions, warp protectors, and weft replenishment.

Weaving shed   The building housing the weaving and associated machines.

Weaving without weft   Where a number of picks are missing from the cloth.

Webs   These can be made from staple fibres or continuous filaments. *Continuous filament webs* are spun-laid webs, formed when polymer is extruded into filaments then deposited on to a support before bonding. *Melt-blown webs* are formed in a similar way, but as the filaments are extruded, they are broken into staple lengths by air currents before being deposited. They are not true continuous filament webs. *Staple fibre webs* can be wet-laid (usually with random orientation), or dry-laid with parallel, cross or random orientation.

Weft accumulator   A device used to store weft yarn at a low, constant tension immediately prior to weft insertion.

Weft insertion   A primary weaving motion. Weft insertion is carried out by the following media: shuttle, projectile, rapier, air jet or water jet. The *shuttle* is a free-flying weft package carrier containing enough weft for several picks. It is the most versatile weft-insertion method, but has a severe mechanical speed limitation. The *projectile* is a free-flying metal object with jaws which grip the weft (enough for one pick only) and pull it through the shed. It is reasonably flexible, with high production rates. A *rapier* is a positively driven metal rod or ribbon which pulls the weft through the shed. It can be a single or double rapier, flexible or rigid and is popular for weaving with frequent pattern changes. It is slower than projectiles. In *air-jet insertion*, the weft is carried through the shed by a jet of air, and relay air jets, wide weaving widths are possible. This method has high production rates. Finally, in *water-jet insertion* a jet of water carries the weft through the shed. This method can only be used with hydrophobic yarn, but it does have a high production rate. *Pick cramming* is a deliberate retardation of the cloth take-up motion to insert more picks per centimetre in a given part of the weave repeat. *See also* **Weaving**.

Weft knitting   Loops are formed across the width of the fabric. The yarn is fed at right angles to the machine which can knit from one thread up to 192 threads. *Courses* are rows of loops across the width of the fabric. *Wales* are vertical columns of loops. *Stitch density* is the product of courses and wales per unit length, where the unit used is loops per square centimetre. *Stitch length* is the length of yarn in one knitted loop, where the unit used is the millimetre. The *course length* is controlled on modern machines by positive feed devices, and measured by a yarn length counter or yarn speed metre. The *tightness factor* is the ratio of the area covered by yarn in one loop to the area occupied by the loop. The following *fabric types* are produced by weft knitting:

- plain single jersey is formed using one set of needles;

- double jersey is formed using two sets of needles (it can be a rib or interlock structure); and
- purl is formed using a two-headed needle.

The following *stitch types* can be used in weft knitting:

- knit is the stitch produced when the needle clears the old loop, receives new yarn and knocks-over the old loop from the previous knitting cycle.
- tuck is the stitch produced when the needle takes a new loop without clearing the previously formed loop so that loops are accumulated on the needle; and
- a miss-stitch is produced when the needle holding the old loop is not raised so misses the new yarn.

The following *needles* are in common use for weft knitting:

- the latch needle a self-acting needle;
- the compound needle has two parts, the hook and tongue, which are controlled separately; and
- the bearded needle, which needs an additional element to close the beard (hook) during knitting.

Weft mixing   The practice of using more than one supply of weft yarn during weaving for successive picks. This attempts to avoid weft bars (visible stripes in the cloth) due to irregular yarn.

Weft replenishment   Replacement of the weft, either a new pirn on shuttle looms, or usually some form of magazine creeling on more modern non-shuttle looms.

Weft selection   *See* **Weaving.**

Weft stop motion   A device used to stop the loom if there is a weft break – a piezo electronic detector on modern machines, or weft forks on older shuttle looms.

Wet-laid webs   *See* **Webs.**

Wettability   The level of ease with which a substrate will absorb liquid.

Wool   A natural protein fibre forming a sheep's *fleece* (the whole of the sheep's coat removed during shearing). *Wool quality* can refer to the fineness of the fibre, in which case the higher the number, the finer the fibre. *Wool classing* is where the fleeces are subjectively assessed by people and graded or classed according to the rules of the body who are buying or selling. The fibre fineness, strength, lustre and length are all taken into account.

Woollen   This processing system was originally for wool fibres. There is no attempt made to align the fibres, giving a bulky, soft warm yarn.

Worsted   A processing system originally used for the best quality fine wool fibres. Fibres are aligned to give a compact, smooth, regular fine yarn, usually for weaving into fine suiting fabric.

Woven fabric parameters   There are several specific parameters, and they are listed here. *Sett* is the thread density, number of picks and ends per centimetre. *Fabric weight* is the weight of yarn per square metre. *Cover factor* is the area covered by yarn compared with the total area covered by the fabric. *Weave* is the order of interlacing of warp ends with weft picks. *Crimp* is the amount of bending as a thread interlaces with those in the opposite direction in the fabric.

Wrap spinning   *See* **Twisting.**

Wrap-spun yarn   *See* **Yarn.**

Yarn   Long, fine and flexible, made from staple fibres and/or continuous filaments, held together with or without twist. *Continuous filament yarn* is composed of continuous filaments which are as long as the yarn itself. A very small amount of twist is often used to prevent the filaments from separating during processing. *Core yarn* is usually a continuous filament core with staple fibres wrapped around as a sheath. *Fasciated yarn* is a staple-fibre yarn with a core of parallel fibres held together by a sheath of wrapper fibres. Air-jet spinning produces such a yarn. *Friction spun yarn* is a staple yarn where twist is imparted by means of a pair of friction rollers which roll the fibres in their nip. *Metallised yarn* can be composed of separate filaments or fibres of metal, or in a tape form. It is sometimes laminated. *Ring-spun yarn* is a traditional staple yarn produced on the ringframe. It can be short-staple or long-staple yarn. The action of the spindle, ring and traveller enable twisting and winding-on to happen simultaneously. *Rotor-spun yarn* is a staple yarn produced by the open-end rotor machine, almost exclusively for short-staple yarns. The flow of fibres from a sliver is interrupted by an opening roller. Fibres are then assembled in the groove of a rotor whose rotating action causes a seed yarn to twist, twisting fibres into its end, so producing new yarn continuously. *Self-twist yarn* is a ply yarn with alternating S twist and Z twist, with regions of no twist between in both singles and ply. *Staple-spun yarn* is a yarn composed of staple fibres, usually held together by twist. *Tape/split film yarn* is a yarn formed from a sheet of material cut into thin strips. *Wrap-spun yarn* is a parallel core, usually composed of staple fibres, held together by means of a thread wrapping around the outside. This type of yarn is almost exclusively for long-staple fibres, often using a continuous filament yarn for the wrapper thread.

Yarn clearing   A yarn preparation. This is fault removal, usually carried out by electronic sensors on modern winding machines. The yarn is continuously monitored, the clearer is set to cut the yarn if it has thick (and sometimes thin) places beyond the preset limits.

Yarn lubrication   A yarn preparation. It is used to modify the frictional characteristics of yarn, especially for weft knitting purposes, and usually a wax or oil is used.

Yarn preparation   Preparing yarn for the customer (weaver, knitter, wet processor). *See also* **Cobwebbing, Cop-end effect, Hard edges, Looming, Patterning, Sizing, Threading, Twist interference, Warping, Yarn clearing, Yarn lubrication** and **Yarn winding**

Yarn winding   A yarn preparation. *Single-end winders* only deal with one yarn at a time; *multi-end winders* deal with many yarns to form the required package. The *traverse length* is the distance across the package covered by yarn. The *taper* is the angle of the cone package centre (a cheese may be considered to be a cone with a taper angle of zero). *Wind per double traverse* is the number of times that the yarn passes completely around the package while it completes a double traverse. In *random winding*, the wind per double traverse decreases as the package diameter increases, while in *precision winding*, the wind per double traverse remains constant throughout the package build. The *coil angle* is the angle between the direction of the yarn on the package and the traverse direction (usually between 81° and 68°, though it is 80° and 70° for continuous filament yarns). *Drum winders* drive the yarn take-up package by surface contact with a driving drum. *Spindle winders* drive the yarn take-up package by the package spindle. The *traverse mechanism* gives the lateral motion to the yarn in order to cover the package. The yarn guide eye is given an oscillating motion by a *cam* drive which lays the yarn on the package in a helical pattern. The yarn is given its lateral motion by a groove cut into the surface of the driving *drum*. The yarn is guided in one lateral direction by one blade of the *propeller*, then returned by the opposing blade.

Yield The amount of good wool fibre gained from the scouring process compared to the total greasy wool. Usually expressed as a percentage.

Yield point The point at which the stress/strain curve bends down towards the strain axis. If a fibre is deformed beyond the yield point it will not return to its original dimensions.

Index